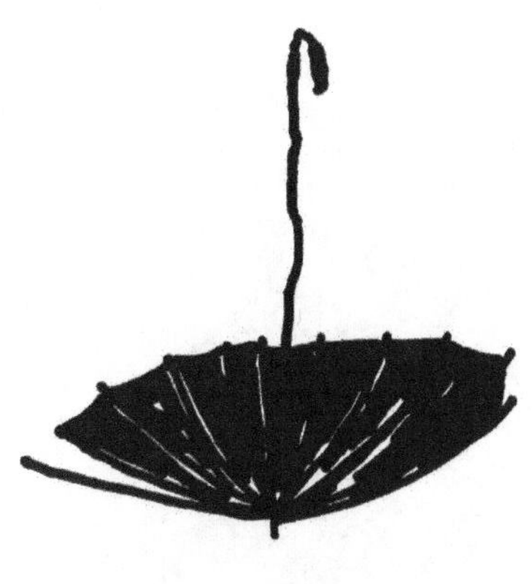

good deed rain

Pacific Northwest Artist Series

- *A Flutter of Birds Passing Through Heaven: A Tribute to Robert Sund* (2016)

- *In the Valley of Mystic Light: An Oral History of the Skagit Valley Arts Scene* (2017)

- *Go with the Flow: A Tribute to Clyde Sanborn* (2018)

- *Taking Her Sides on Immortality,* Robert Huff (2019)

- *The Robert Huck Museum* (2022)

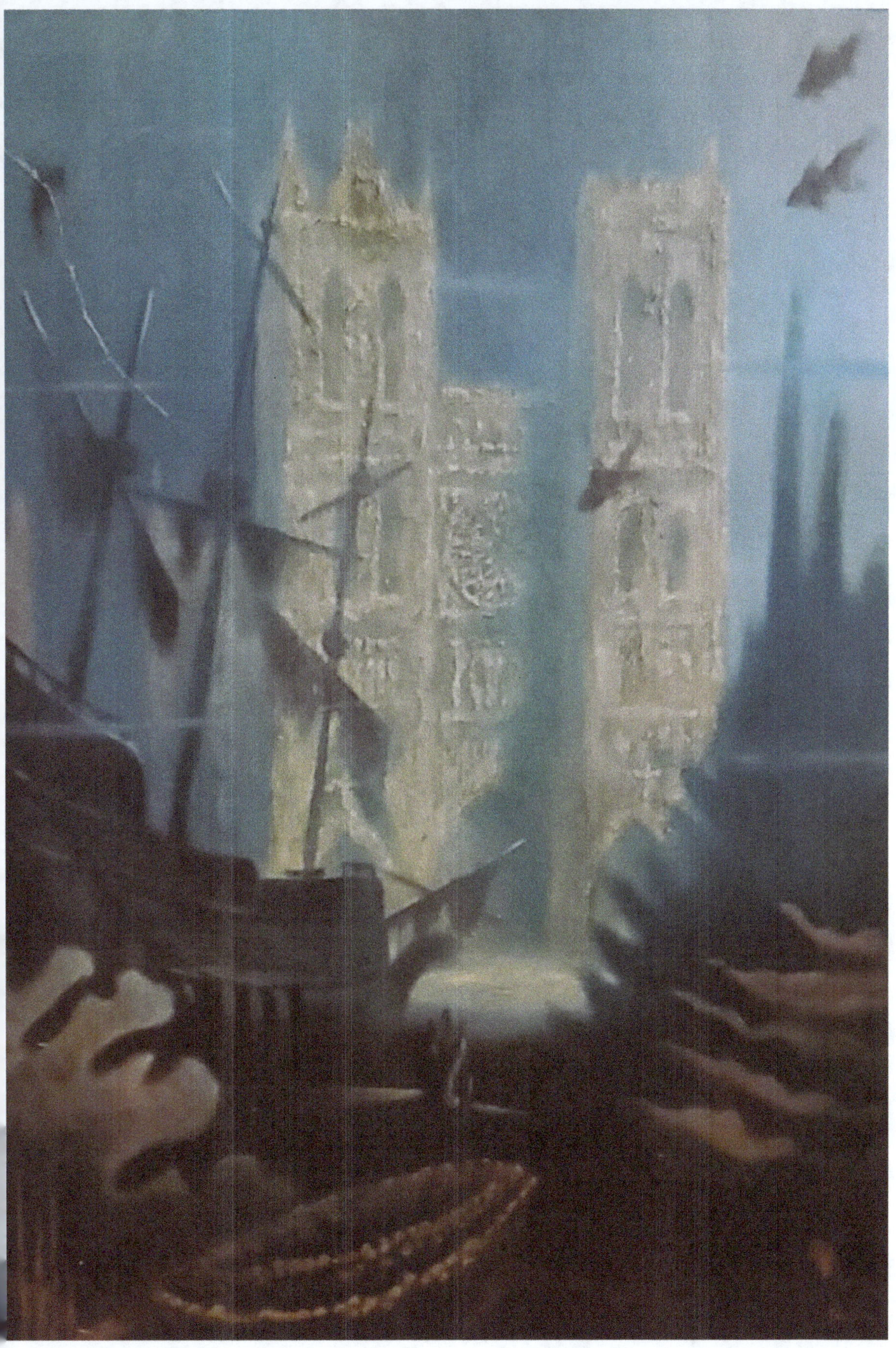

The Robert Huck Museum © 2022
Allen Frost, Good Deed Rain
Bellingham, Washington
ISBN: 978-1-0879-4493-7

Cover Production: Fred Sodt

Thank you to the Portland Art Museum for your generosity.

For Sarah & Clay

The
ROBERT HUCK MUSEUM

Edited by Allen Frost
with assistance from
Sarah Neugebauer & Clayton Huck Brown

Good Deed Rain ◊ Bellingham, Washington ◊ 2022

Outside of town next to a pond, there's a house with a museum in a room upstairs. Paintings lean in the eaves. Stacked conservation boxes are filled with prints, woodcuts and sketches, photographs, artifacts, notebooks. An exhibition poster leans against the leg of the table:

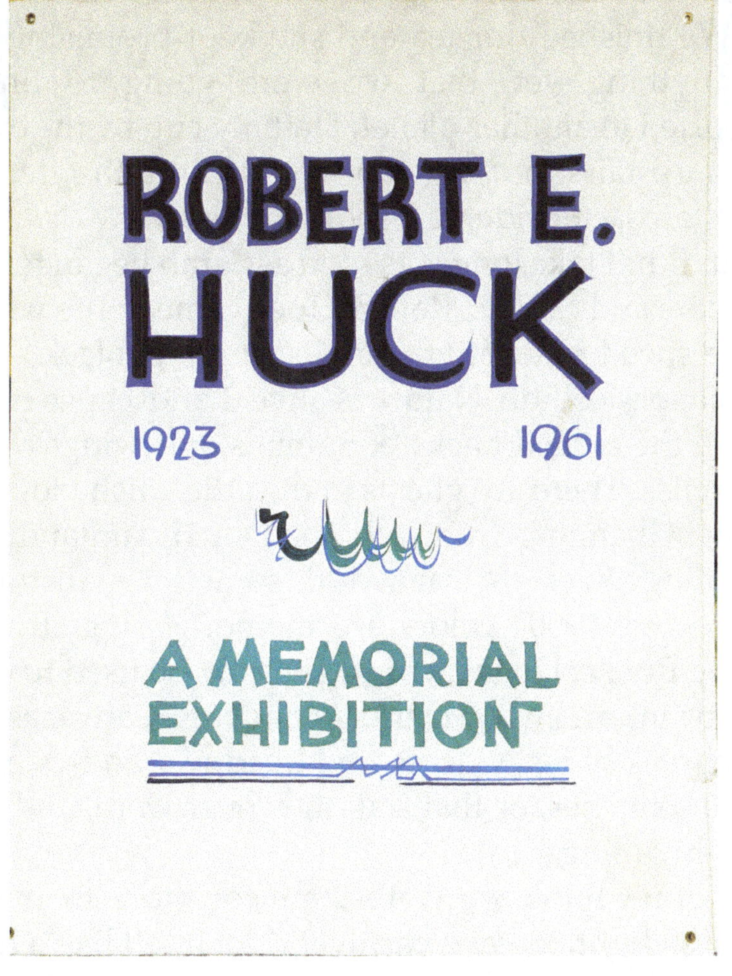

Sarah Neugebauer invited me and my father-in-law to visit. Robert Emerson Huck was Sarah's mother Dorothy's first husband. He died four years before Sarah was born. For more than twenty years, Sarah and her brother Clayton Huck Brown, Robert's son, have been the guardians of the Huck Museum.

Fixing tea for us in the kitchen, she showed us a few of her favorite artworks. A hawk, brushed like a Japanese master. A framed painting of aquarium science fiction. On the table beside us sits a carved owl Huck made. I didn't know much about him yet but I could feel the unseen wheels were in motion.

Sarah and I met a few years ago when I trapped a mouse under a cardboard box at work. Facilities Management sent her over to our office, to safely transport and release the mouse into the woods near parking Lot 10G. This strange beginning that led her to my job at the art department also gave her the chance to tell me about Bob Huck.

We finished our tea and she kept promising you haven't seen anything yet, that we were going to find ourselves transported to another planet. I left my cup by the owl and Sarah took us upstairs the way you would climb the steps of a rocket ship rollercoaster ride, to a room in the air.

It didn't take long — as soon as Sarah began to turn through the papers and canvas, Robert Huck came to life with a roar. We pick up speed fast until the ink is running, black streaks, bright paint, shapes collide. Nature is alive. Landscapes turn into owls, hills are the arched backs of animals and wings. People live in gaunt relics. There are ghosts in the attic…fish-clouds in the sky, a torment hanging from a branch. A dreamland takes shape. Sometimes a crystal-clear world, sometimes abstraction. Those kaleidoscope 1950s colors are memories, big drive-in screens showing Robert Huck movies. The way he used to see the world linked by ink and watermarks. Woodcuts. Canvases outstretched like animals hides. Curves and shadows and pools. Piers that become scratches, or that's all they ever were, and you're dizzy and seeing things.

I don't think we were there for more than an hour, but Sarah was right, it was a carnival ride. It felt like a haunted train thundering past. Black charcoal. All the lines are rushing and the windows are blurred and the wheels and rails are shaking the floor.

Robert Emerson Huck was just 38 years old when he died, but the work that fills this museum is the legacy of a visionary artist, from his schooldays to his sudden end.

We only went through half of the museum that first visit, but it stayed in my head as we drove home. I was seeing Mount Baker Highway the way he would. Steering through his dreamworld, shadows cut into view. Once I got back home, it was enough for me to know this book was meant to appear. It was already here, it has been waiting to be seen.

This won't be a book of too many words, I want to let the artist tell the story. In the Robert Huck Museum the walls are pages. I hope that when you go through, you experience this as I did on that first visit, overwhelmed.

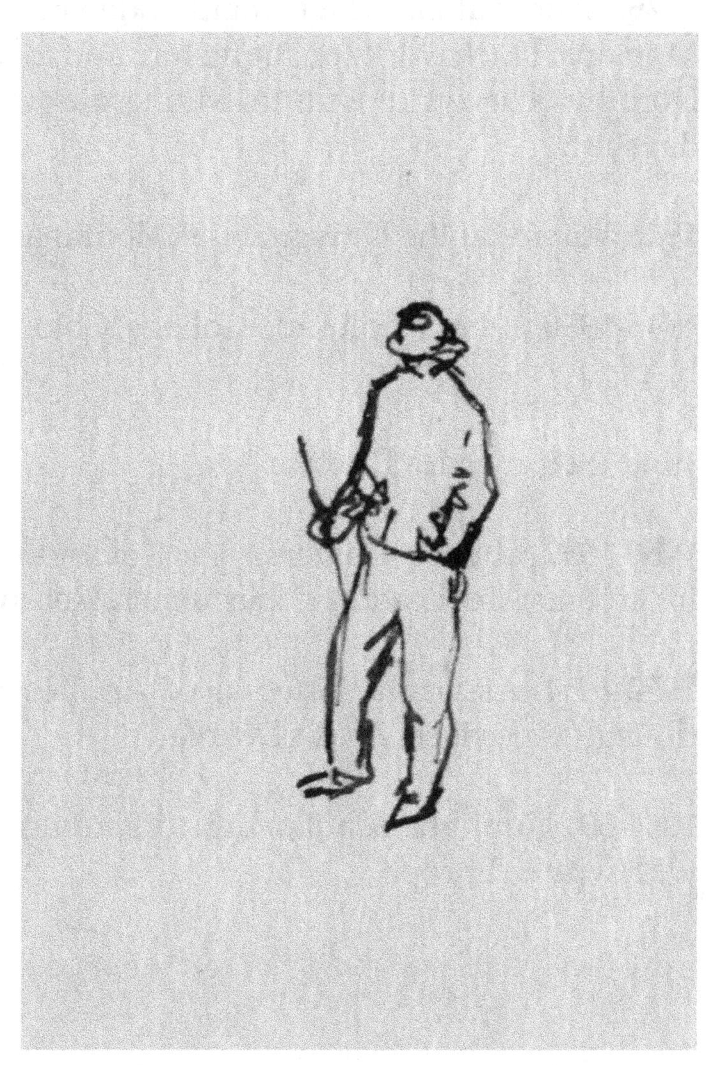

BIOGRAPHY

February 26, 1923, Robert Emerson Huck is born, the son of Ethel and Harry Milton Huck in Kalispell, Montana.

1939-1942, attends Flathead High School in Kalispell.

1942-1945, serves with the Signal Corps, United States Army. Stationed in Anchorage with the Alaska Communications System, and for Boeing in Seattle as a military draftsman.

1946, is hired at Lake McDonald Lodge in Glacier National Park, Montana. Huck works on nightshift, and in the morning he meets Dorothy Schroeer of Duluth, Minnesota who starts work on the dayshift.

1946, studies at the University of Montana.

1946-1950, attends Colorado College, Colorado Springs. Receives B.A.

June 1948, marries Dorothy.

1950-1952, attends University of Colorado. Part-time instructor in Art and Architecture departments. Receives M.F.A.

1952-1954, Assistant Professor of Art, Northern State Teachers College, Aberdeen, South Dakota.

1954-55, Fulbright Scholarship to study art in Italy. Traveling with wife in Europe.

September 1955, hired as Assistant Professor of Art at Oregon State College [Oregon State University], Corvallis, Oregon.

Befriends poet Robert Huff. Huff is an English instructor at Oregon State from 1955-1960 and is later hired in 1964 by Western Washington State College [Western Washington University] in Bellingham.

1958, birth of son, Clayton.

Summer 1960, completes the First National Bank mural in Kalispell, Montana.

March 13, 1961, dies in automobile accident north of Corvallis, Oregon.

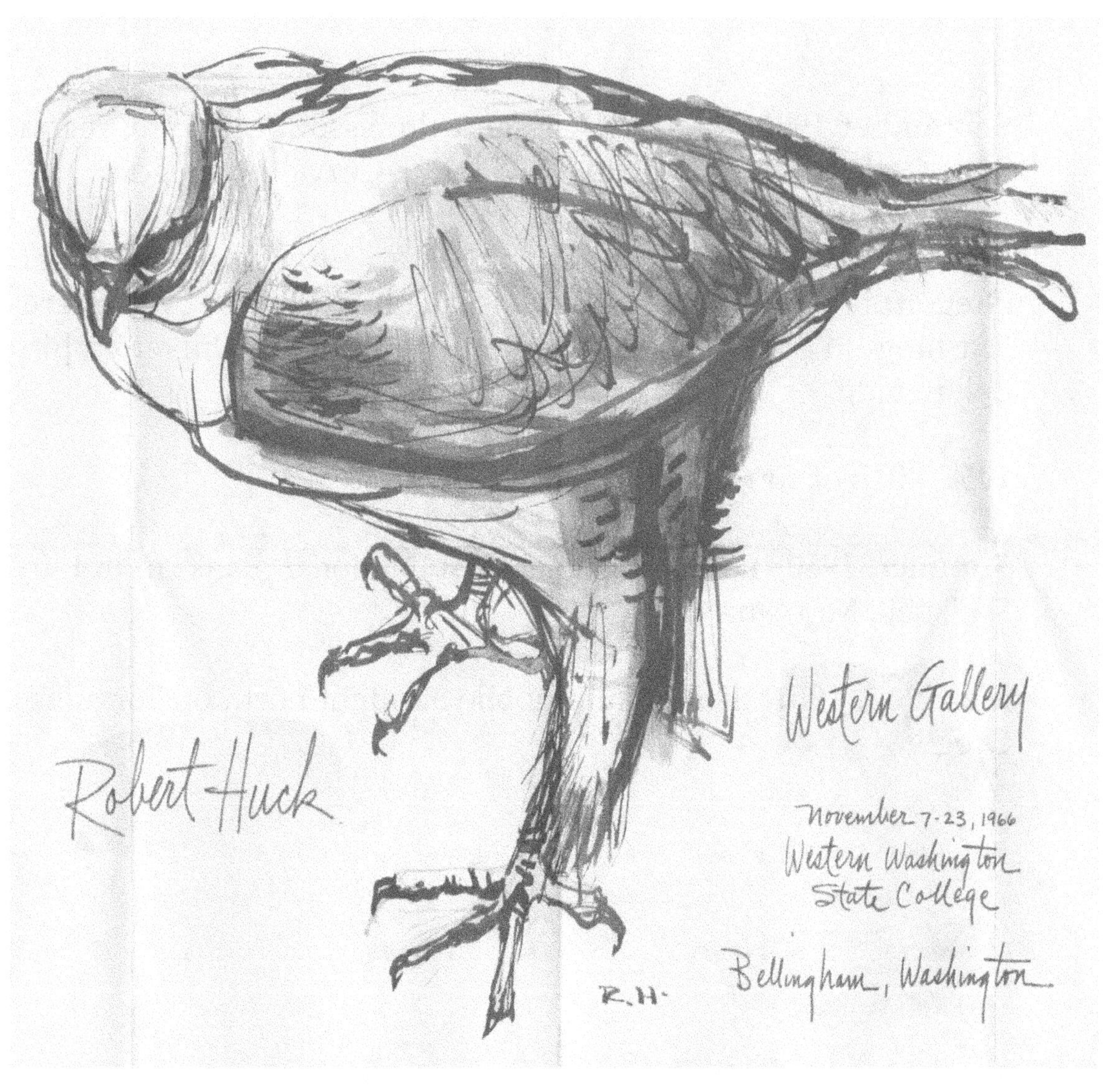

Robert Huck Memorial Exhibition, November 1966, Western Washington University. Facing page: poem by Robert Huff

12

A POSTHUMOUS EXHIBITION
OF THE ART OF ROBERT HUCK

Well, here we are, Bob.
Mountain, bird, bay, me . . . a gathering.
Black melancholy sun
Hanging beside a sea growth
In a rock. Light? Oh, light's
As glacial on the mountain,
On the falcon, on the ruins,
On the swan, as light can be.
It's in your tide pool—this one—where,
Uncoiling at the core,
It actually is growing
Now, is moving through the thing.
Earth people live to learn
About the deep. Dead center,
Bob, the seed that caught your eye,
Isn't it warm dead center?
Isn't that light inside?
The eagle and the hunters and the owl
Hang in the blizzard of our lives
With me, while there you are
All lit up, more at ease
Than when we talked of being
Here in heaven by the sea.

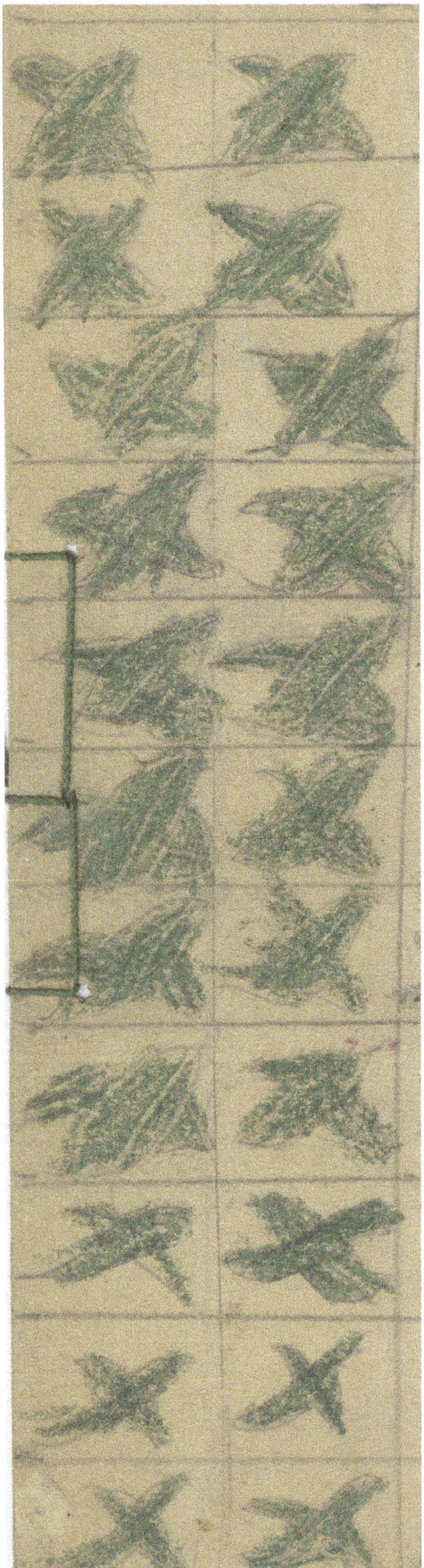

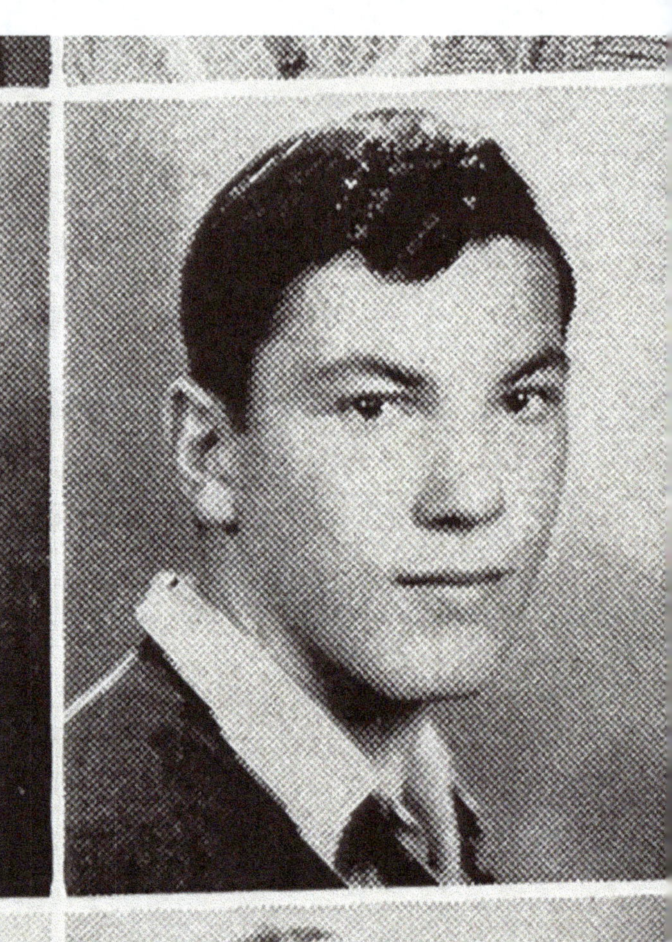
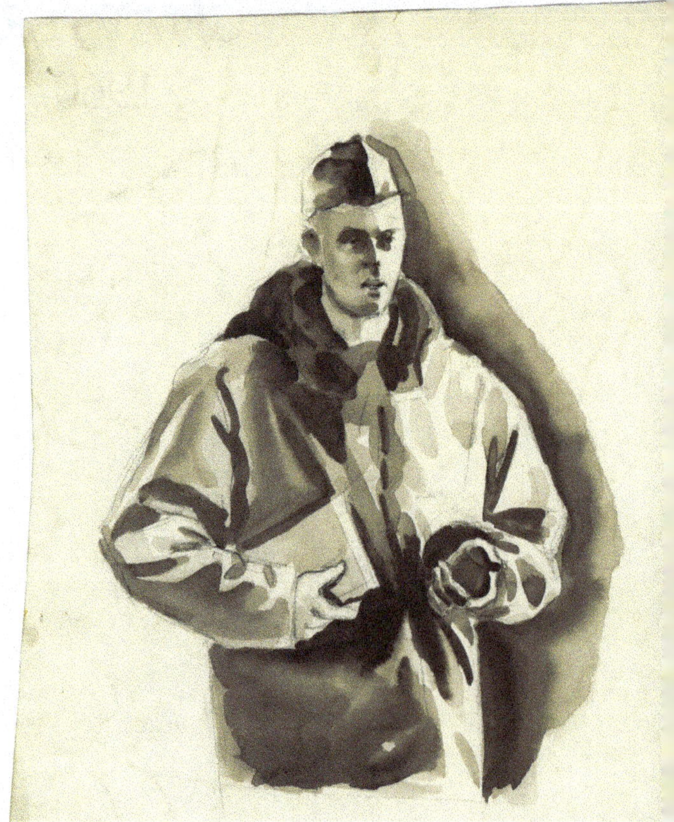

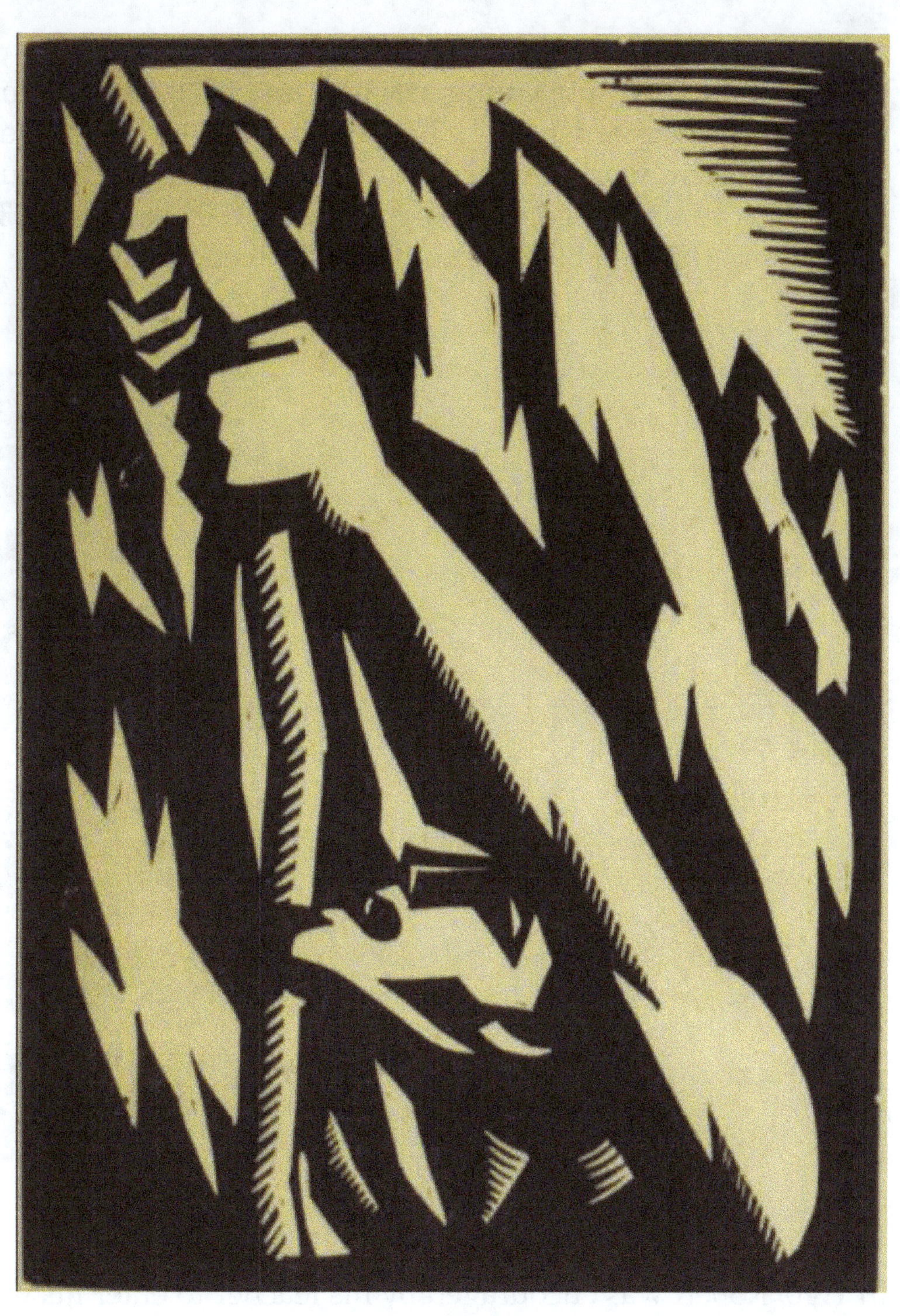

1923-1949

When Robert was quite young, teachers and friends told him he was a natural born artist, but he had to prove it to himself by years of hard, sincere work. Robert's career dates back to the fourth grade. He drew a formidable looking lion on the blackboard. The teacher and children liked it pretty well, he remembers. (1)

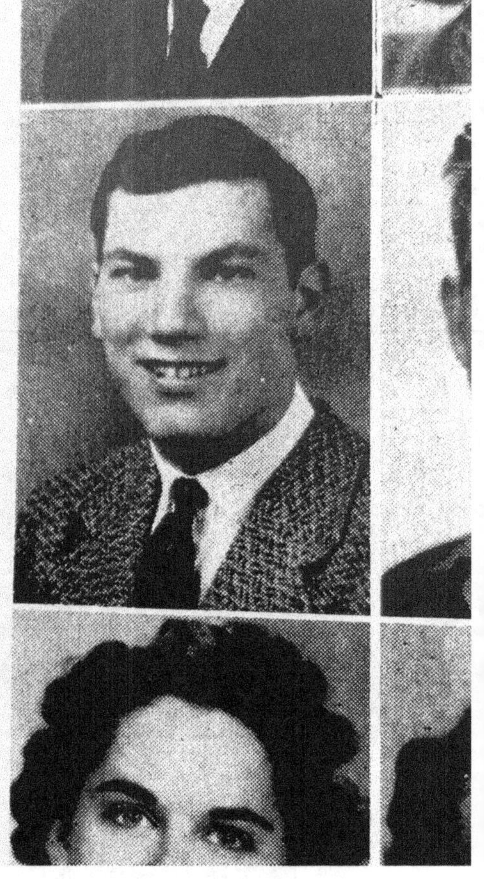

In 1940, Robert was encouraged by his teacher to enter his work in the Art Section of the *America Magazine Youth Forum*. He received a $10.00 cash award and a certificate signed by Norman Rockwell. In 1943 he was sent to Montana State College for high school week to take part in scholastic contests. He received a medal, a First in Art and a scholarship. (2)

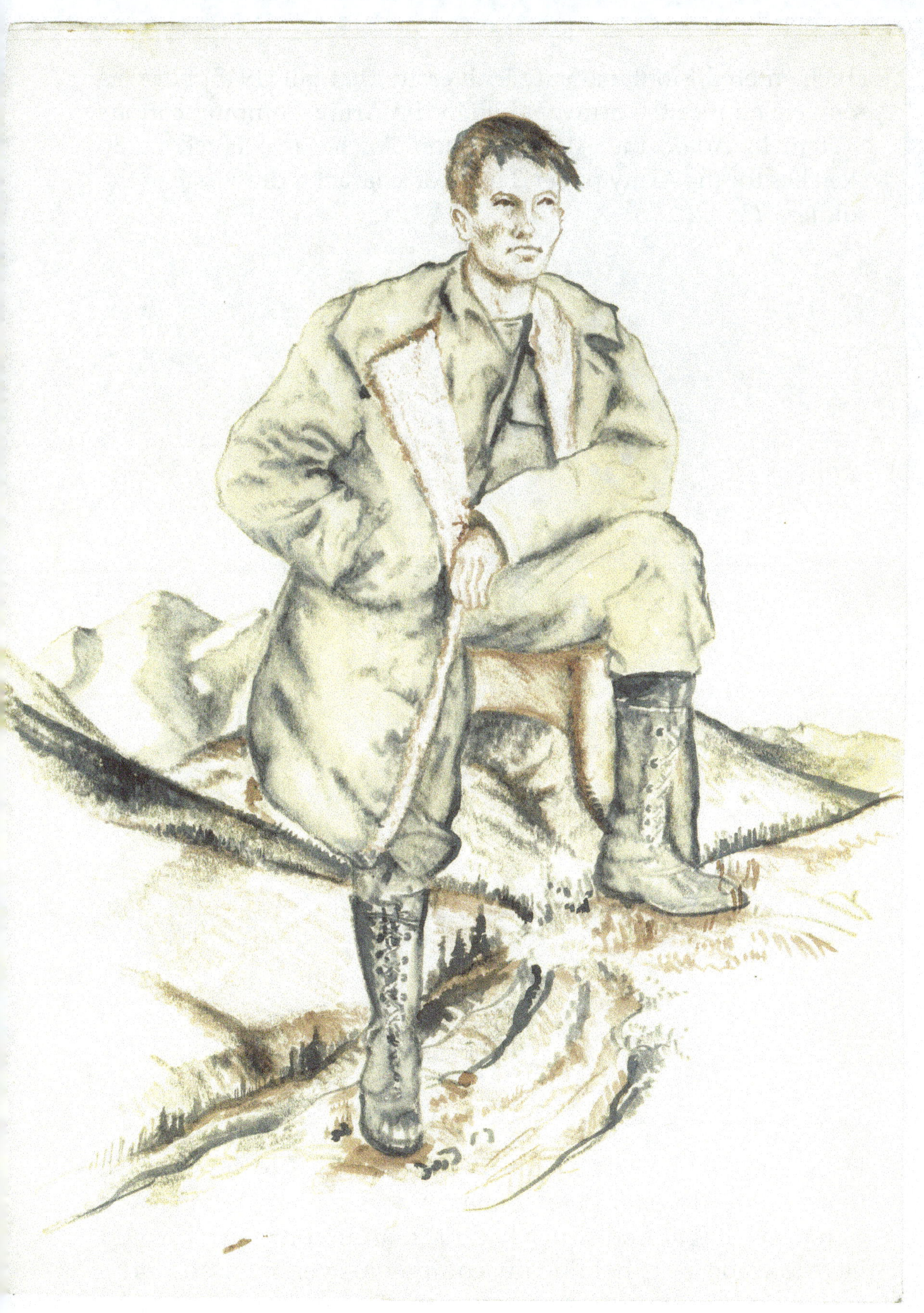

Huck entered Montana State University that fall [1943] but was soon called into the army. While in the Army Communications System in Adak, the Aleutians, and Anchorage, Huck made sketches for the Army paper. He made character drawings of the soldiers. (3)

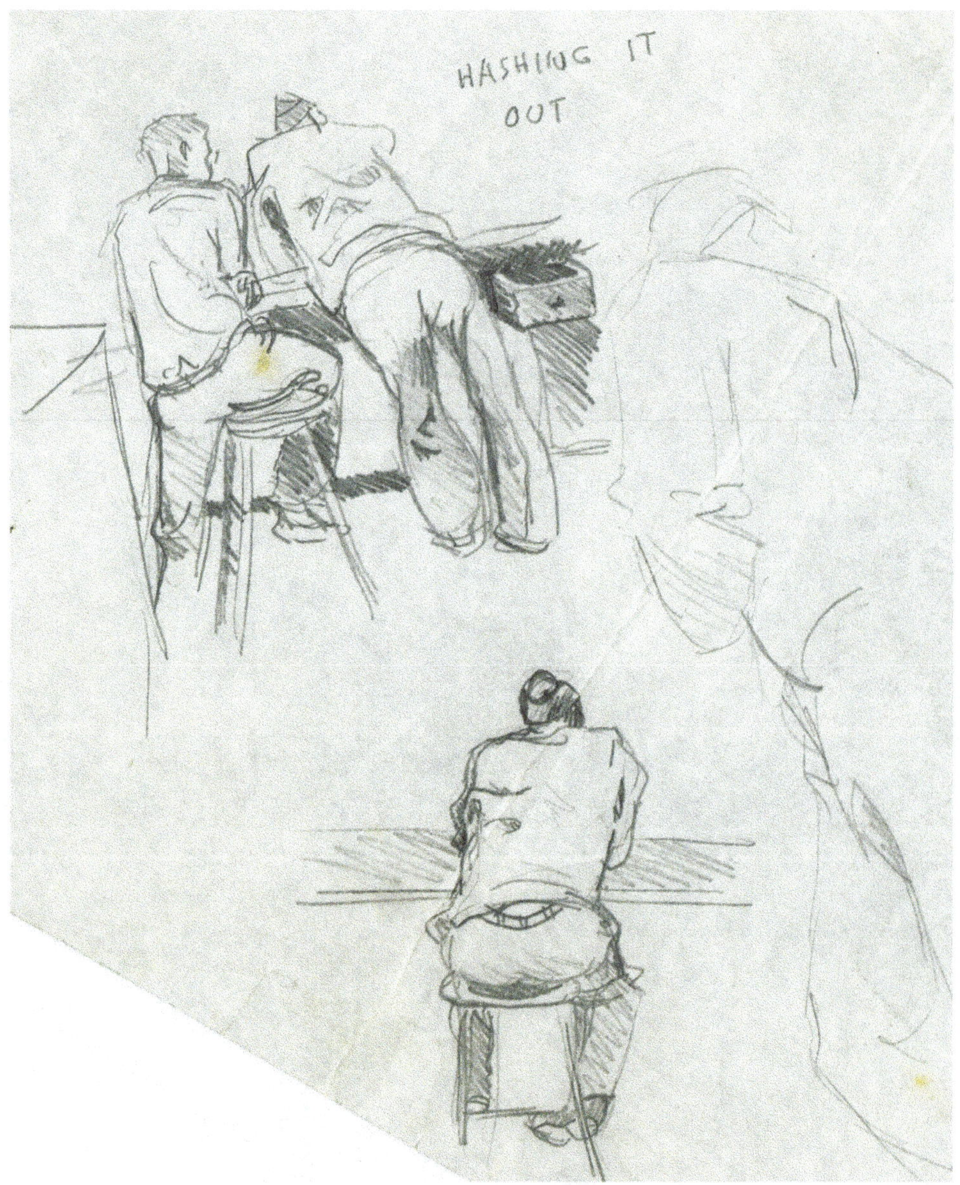

Huck said that he kept a sketch pad and pencil with him at all times. "I used to wade out into the marshes at times. When ready to return I might find water had risen around me and I would have to wade back, holding my equipment over my head." (4)

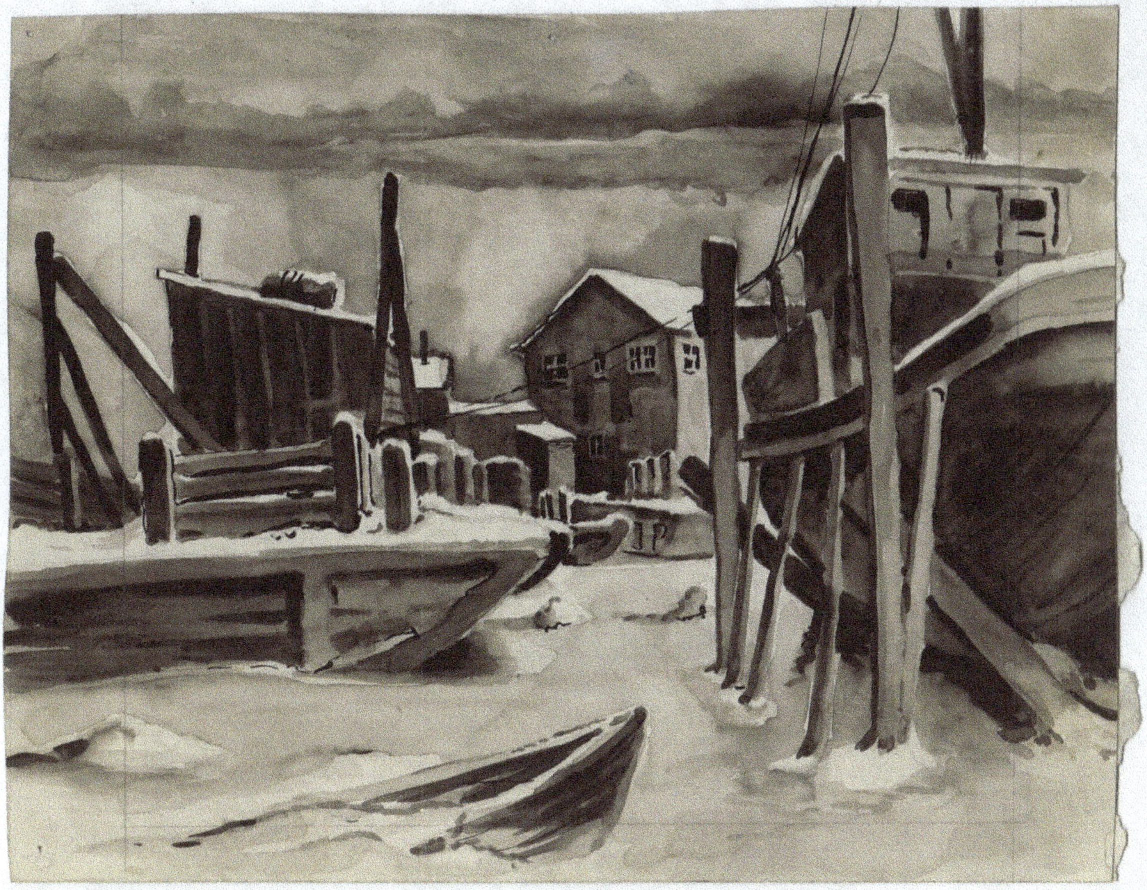

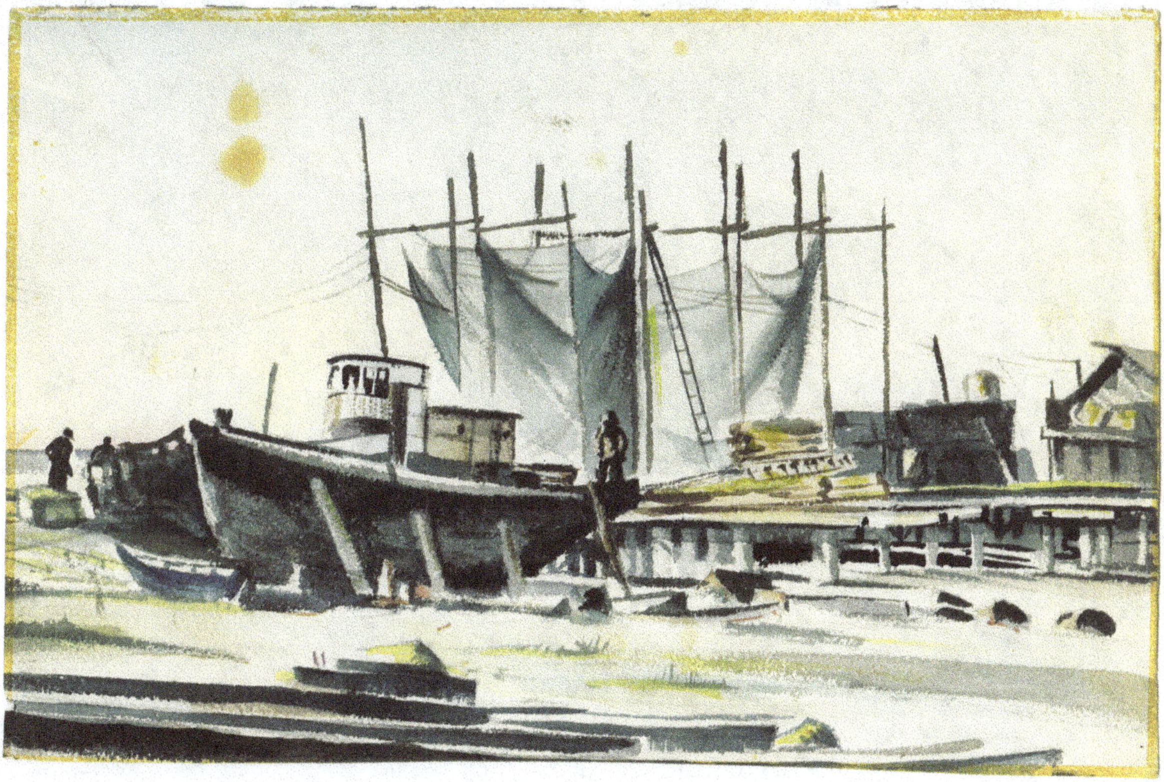

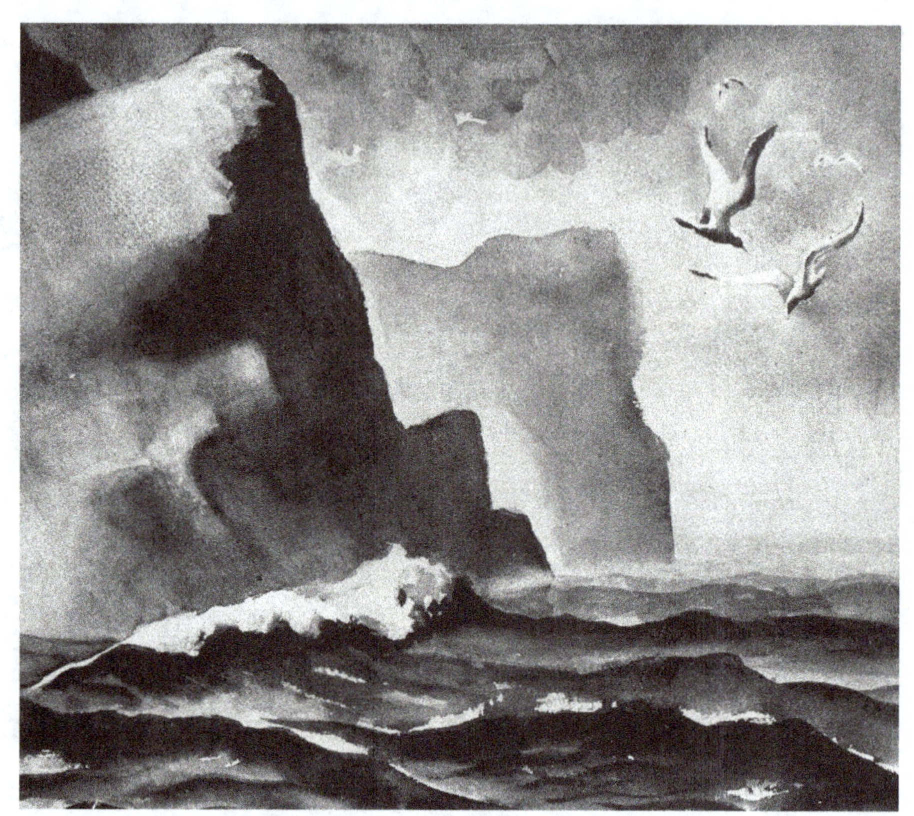

"Alaska Seascape"

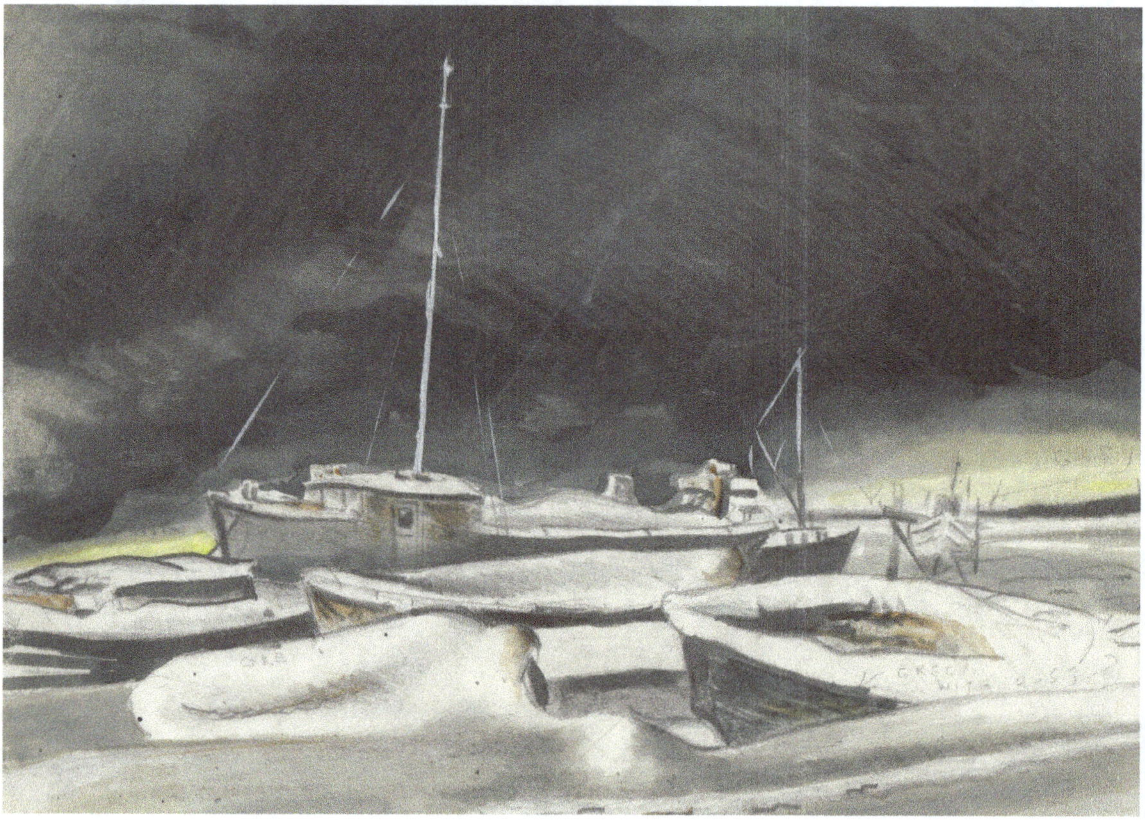

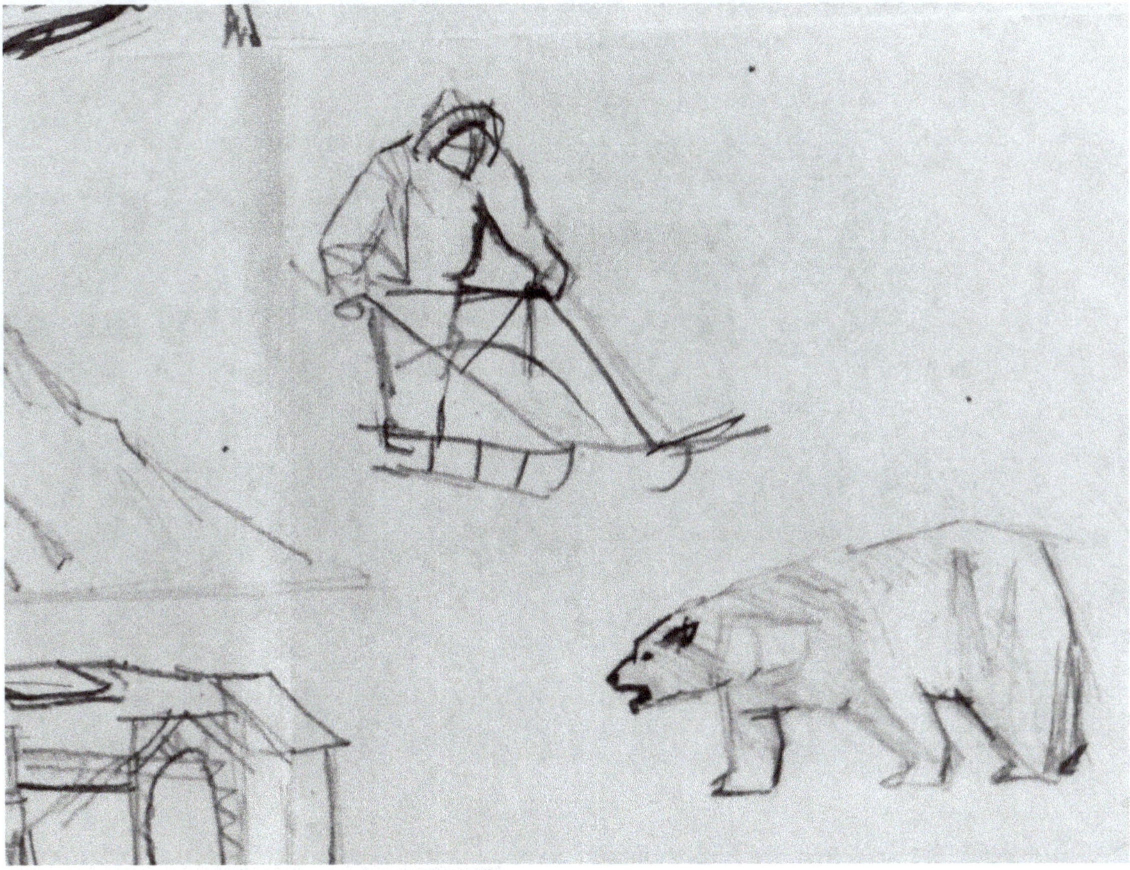

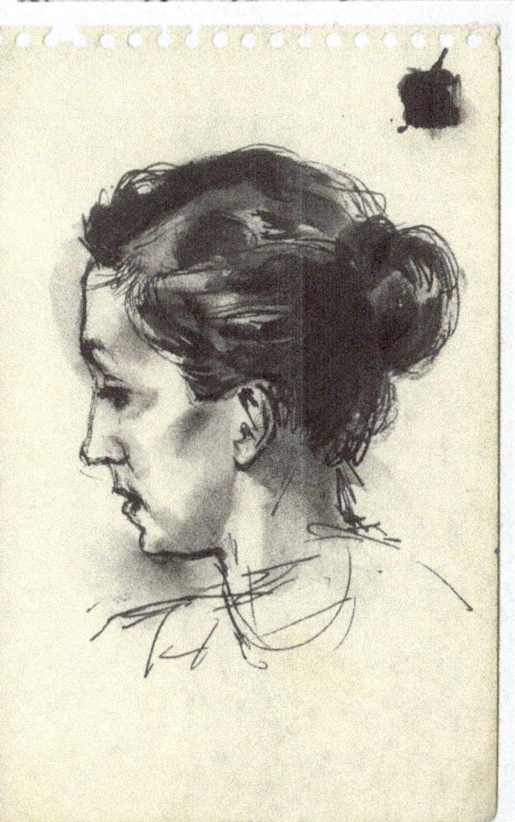

Alum's Art Work Will Be Displayed

Pfc. Robert E. Huck's pictures will be displayed in the Women's Art Club Building Sunday afternoon.

Huck has been in Alaska two years doing drafting work in the Alaska communications system at Anchorage.

He attended the university in 1942-43. Huck is the son of Mr. and Mrs. H. M. Huck of Kalispell.

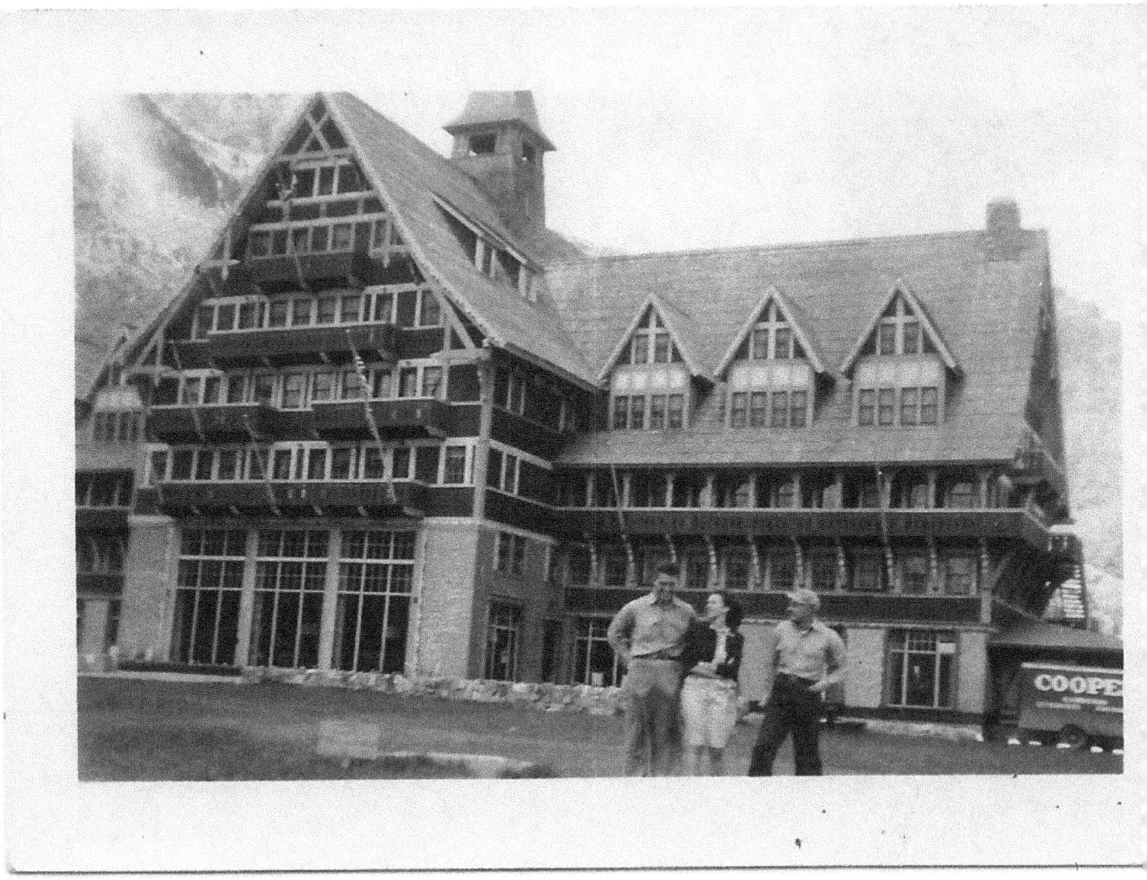

1946. Lake McDonald Lodge in Glacier National Park, Montana.

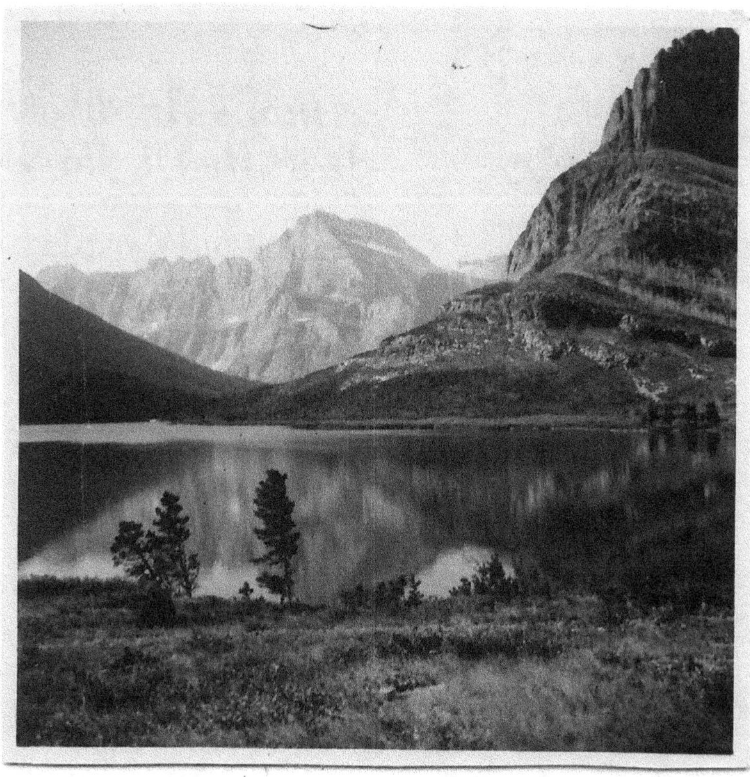

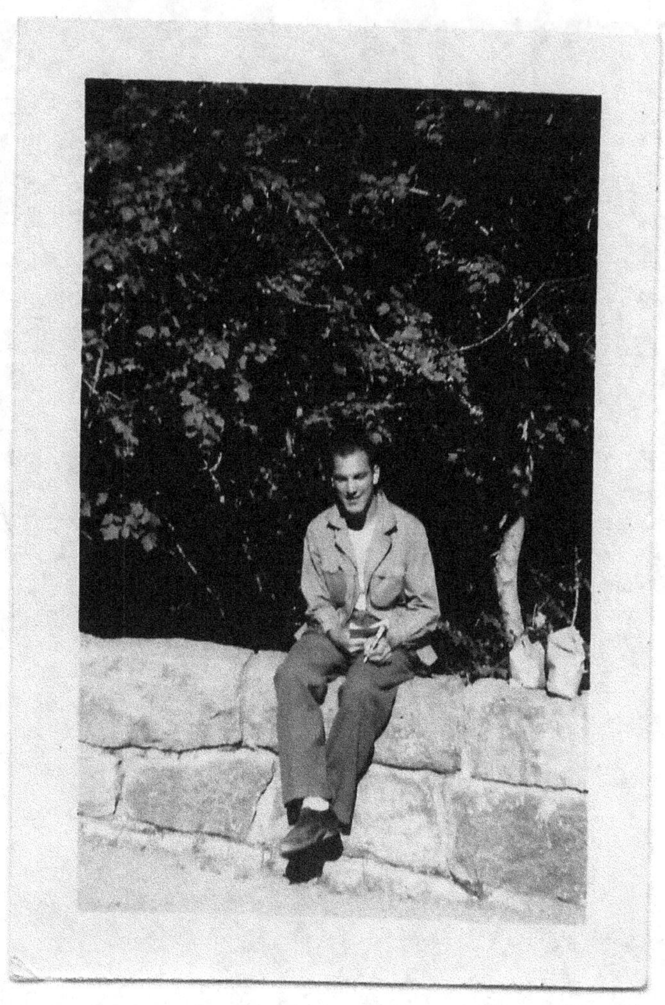

Huck with notebook above, and with Dorothy below.

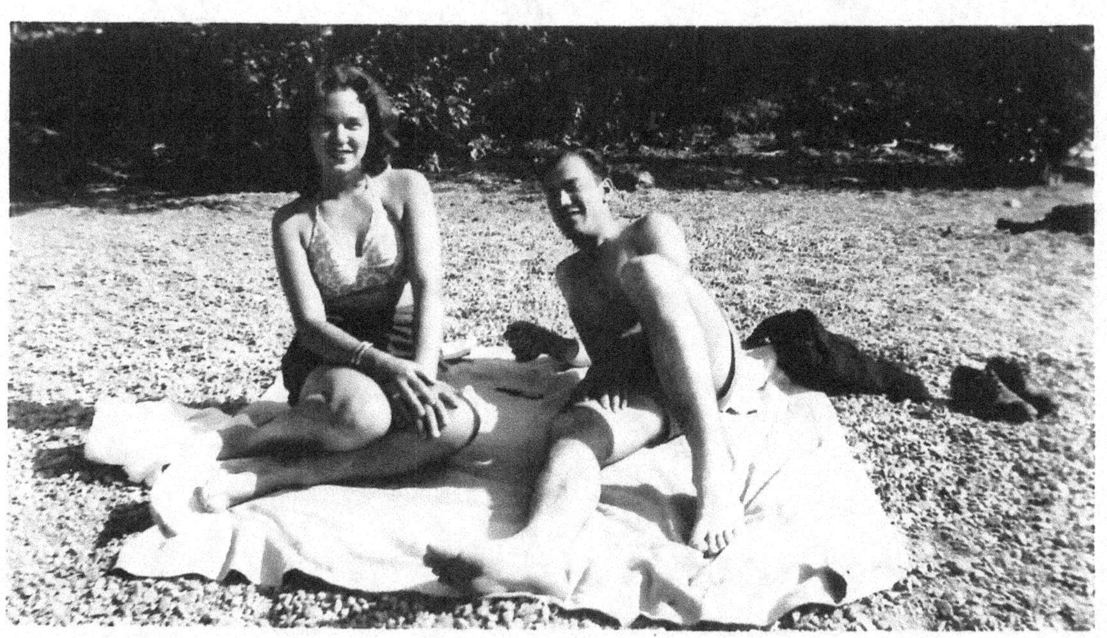

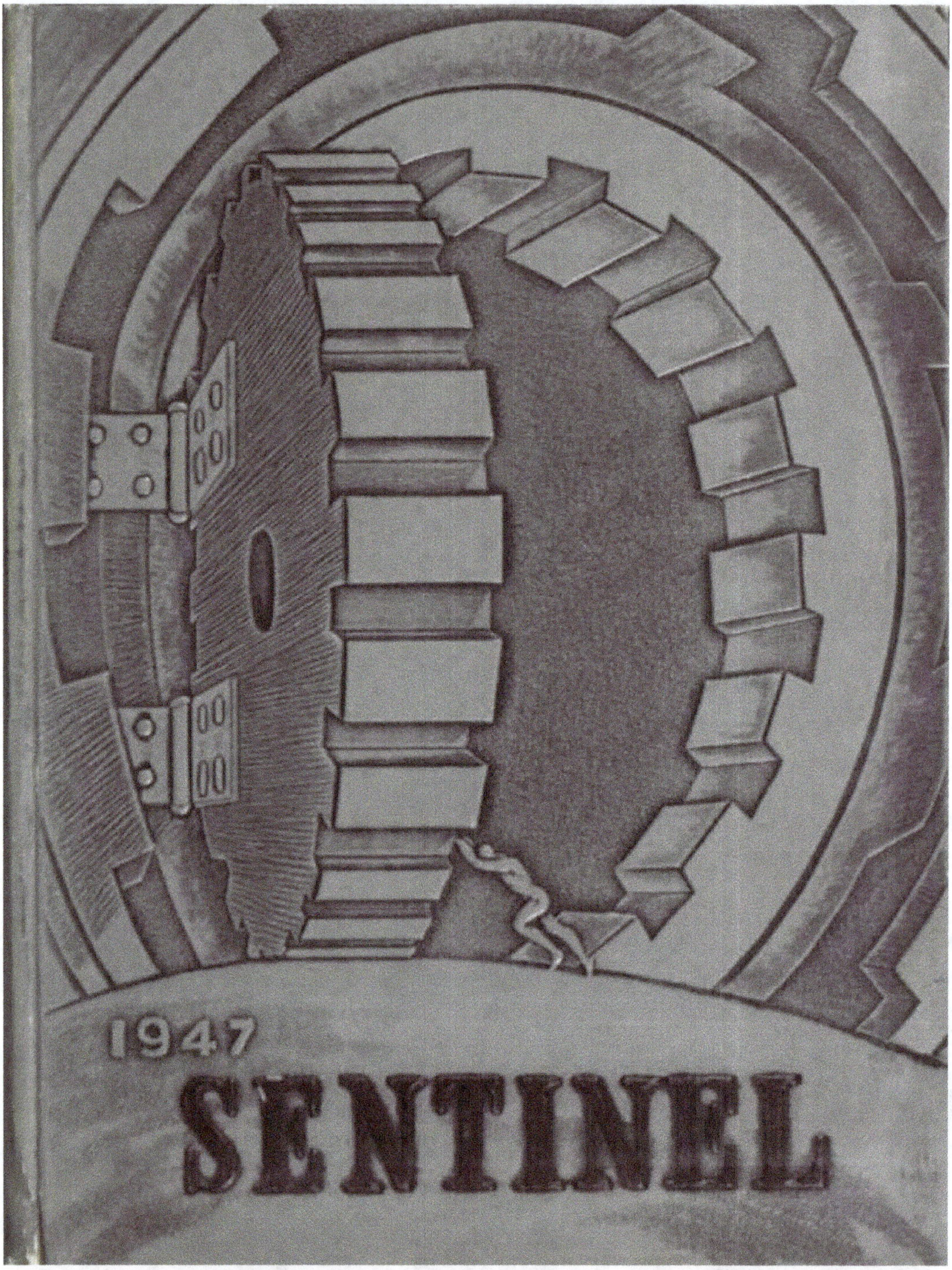

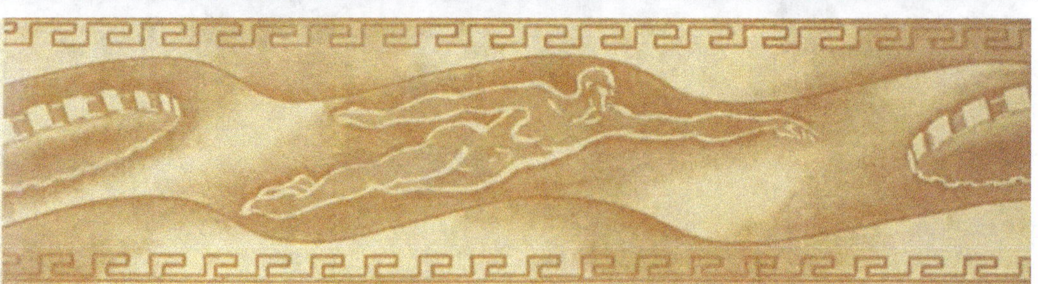

1947
SENTINEL

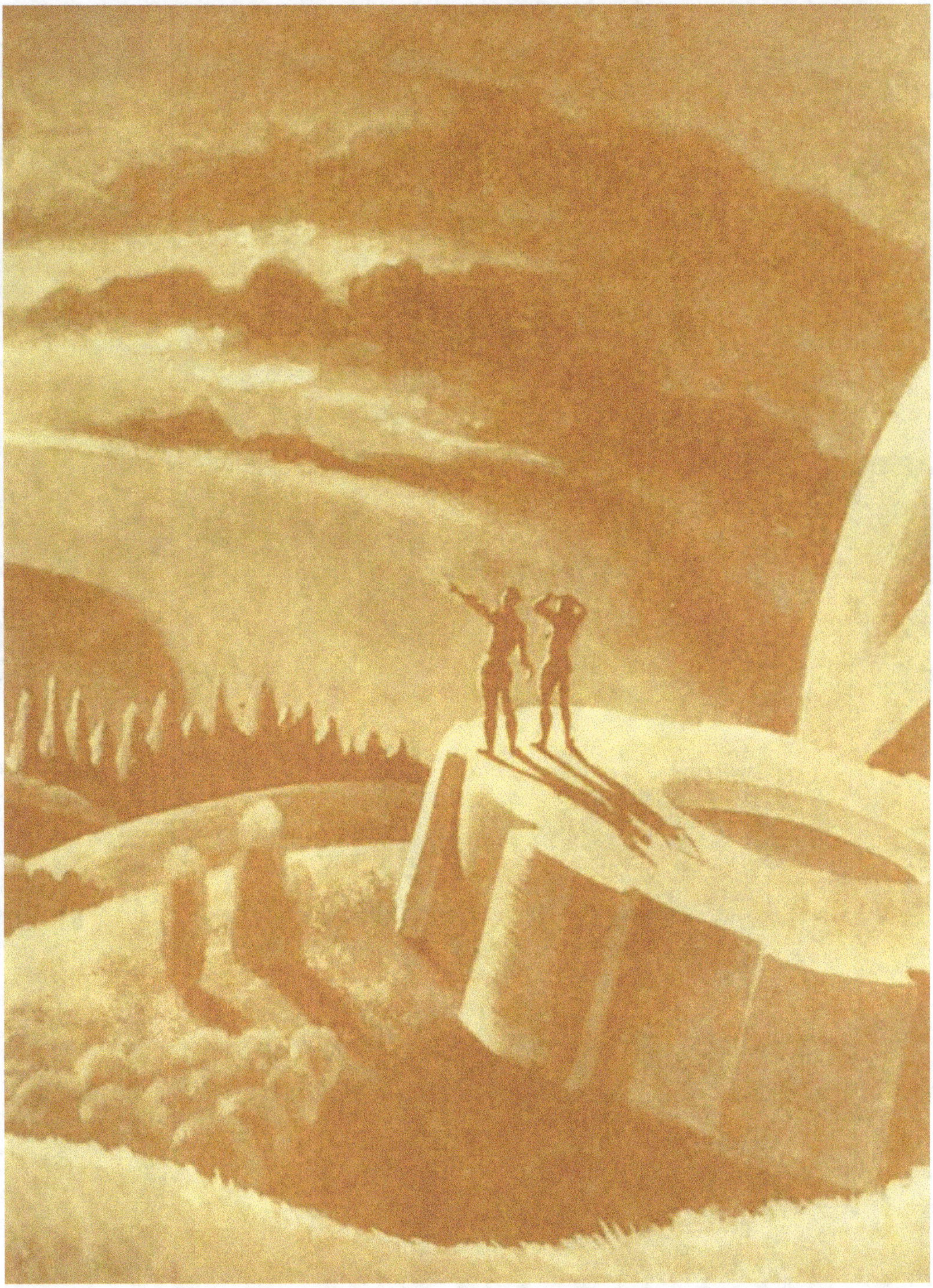

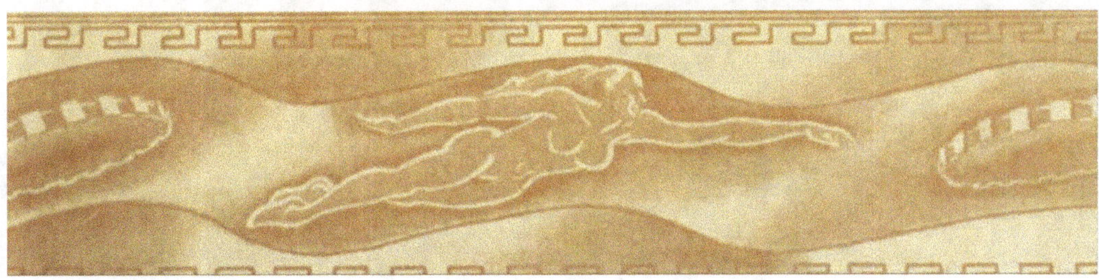

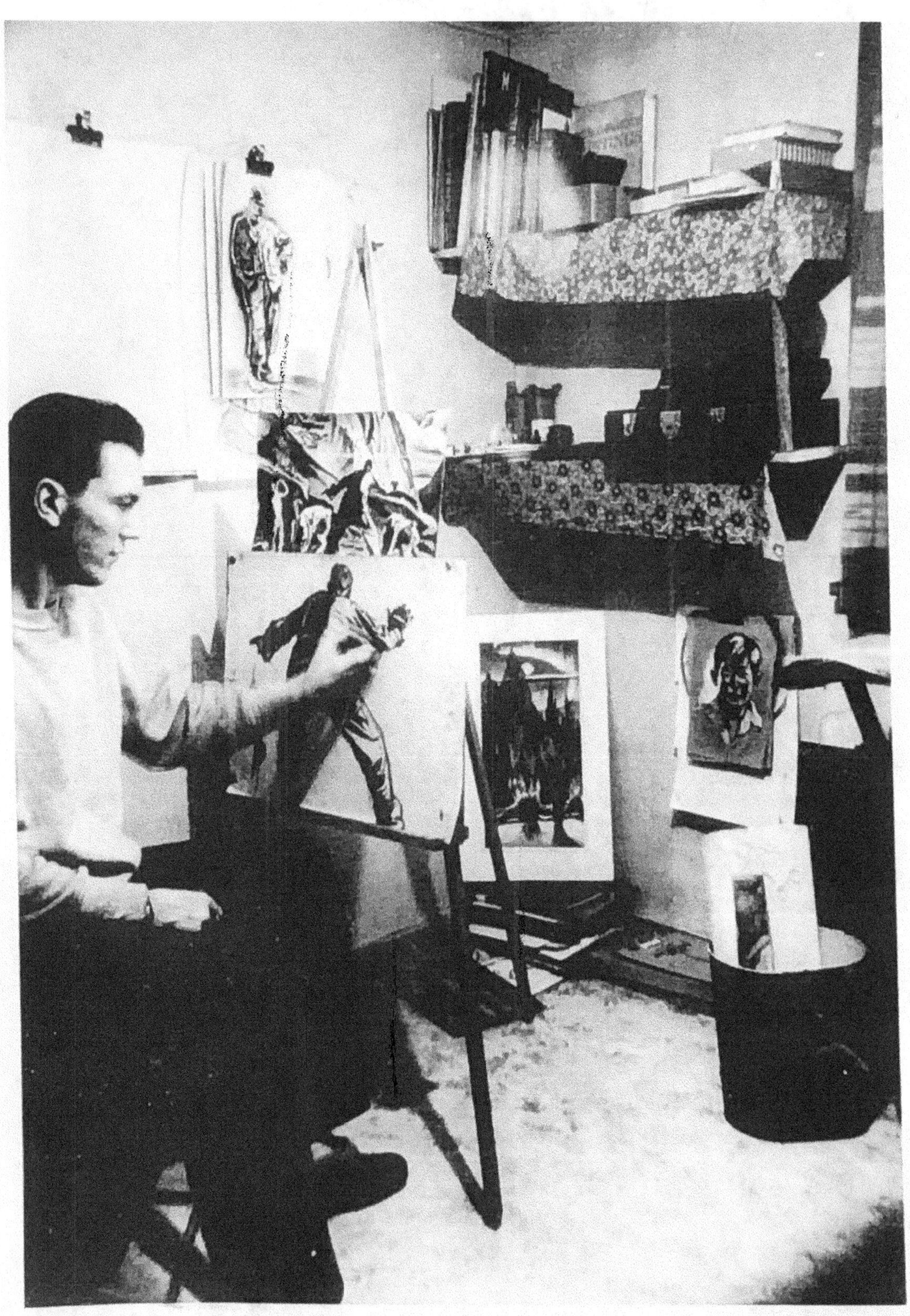

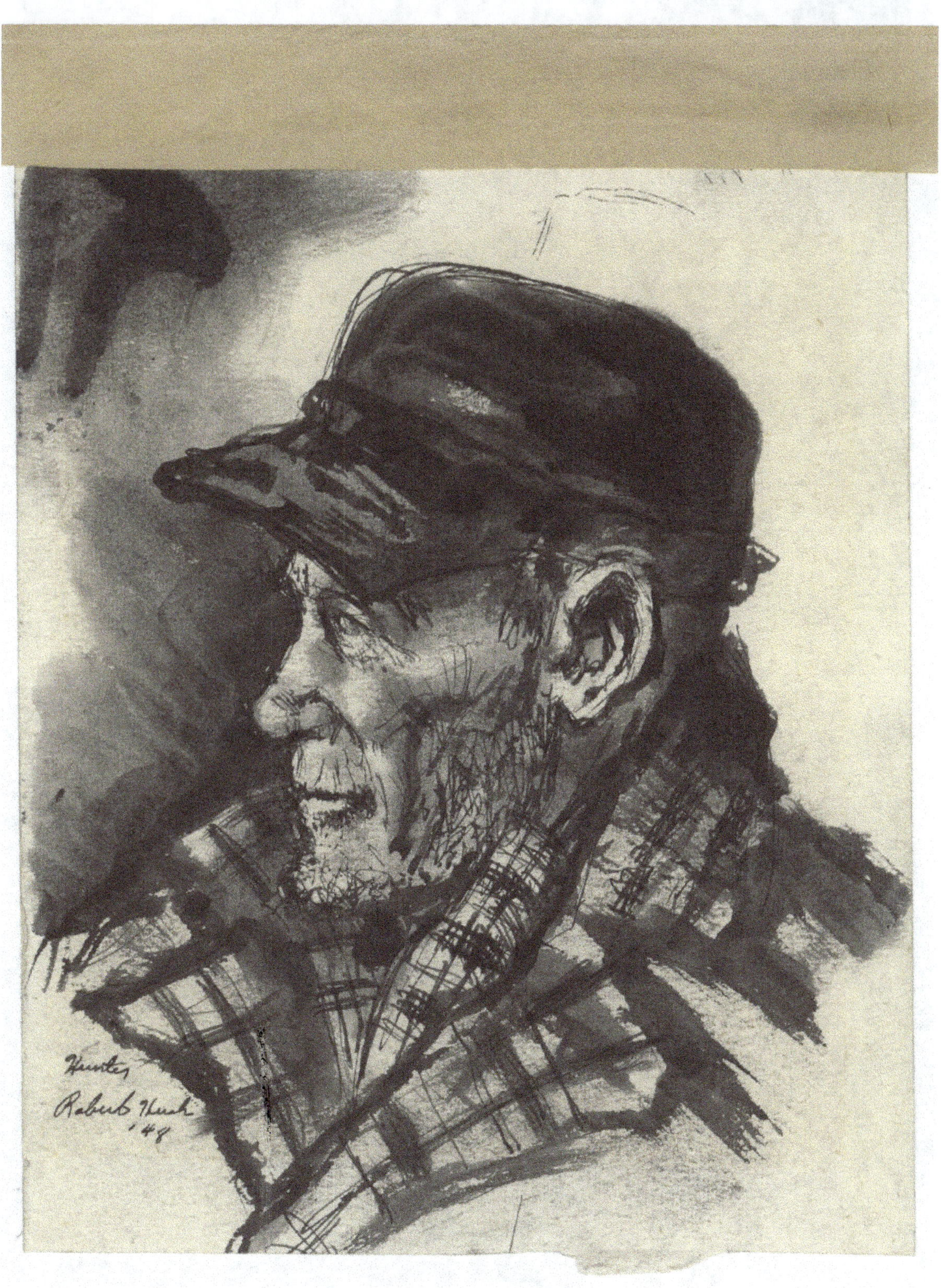

"Hunter" (1948)

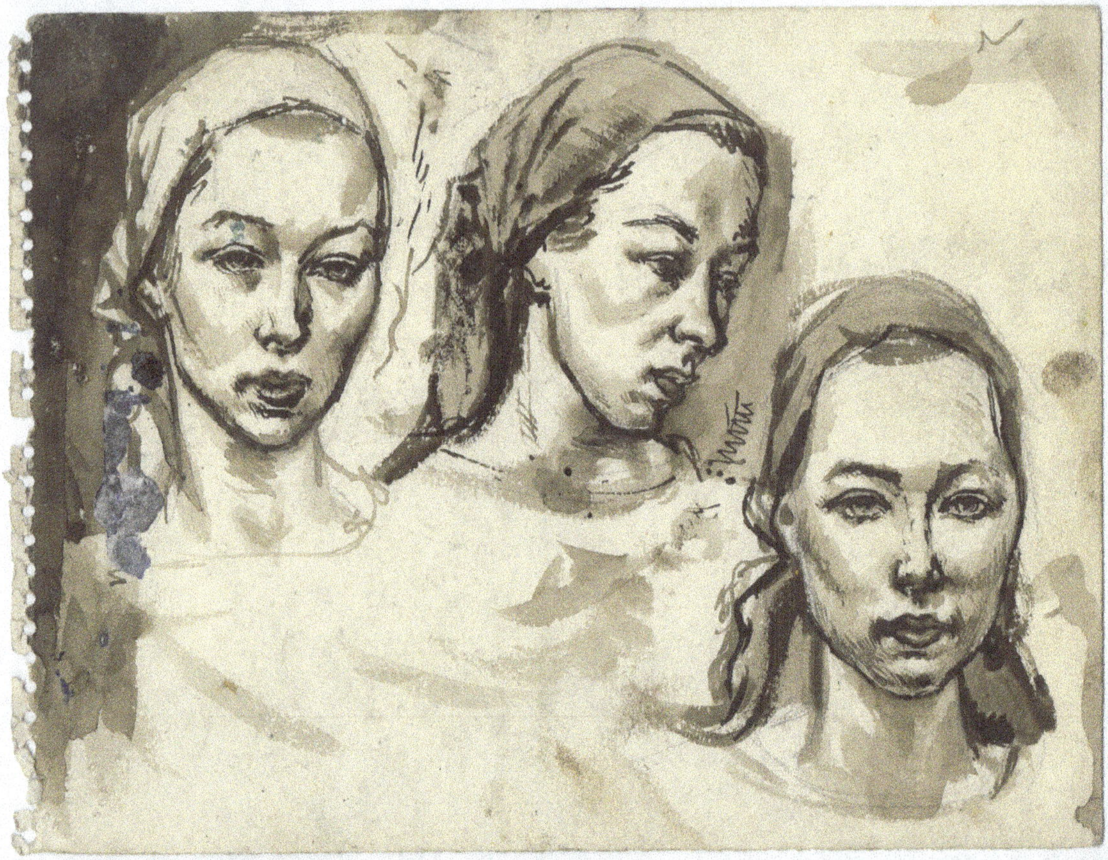

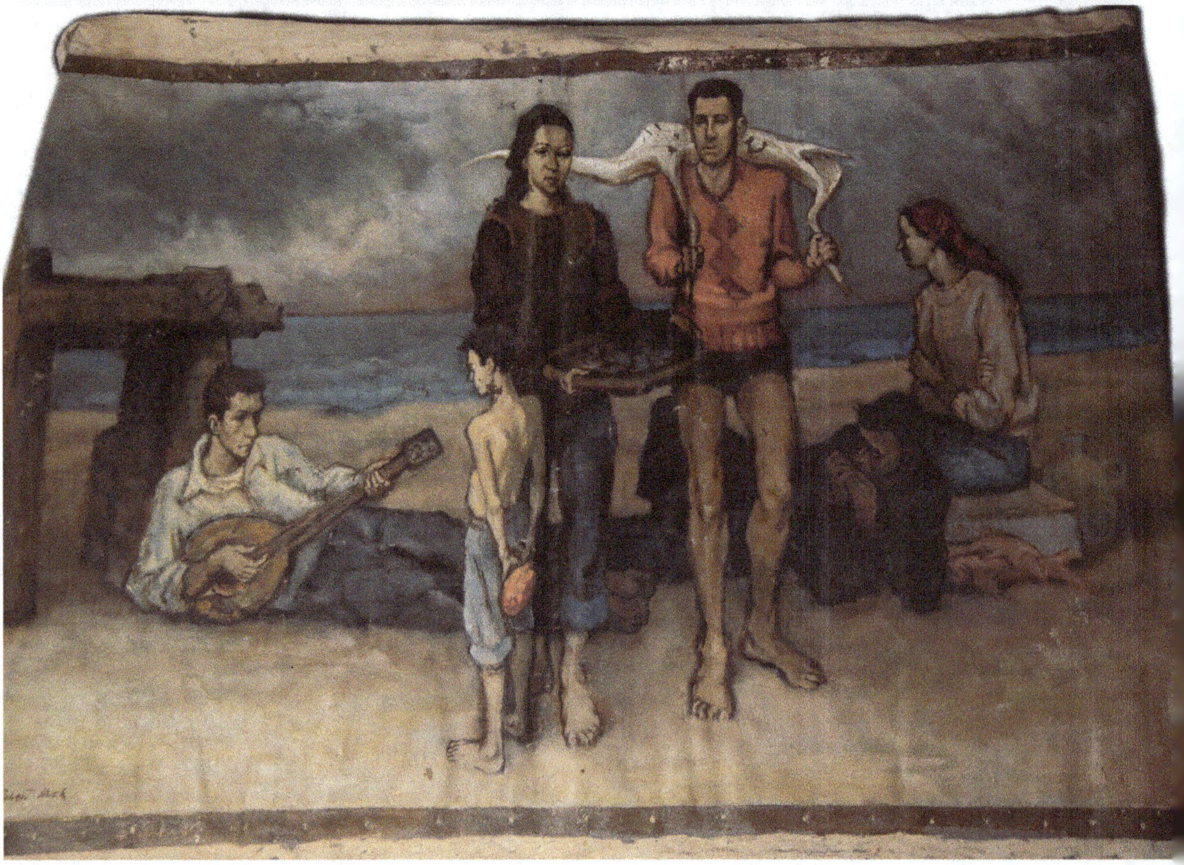

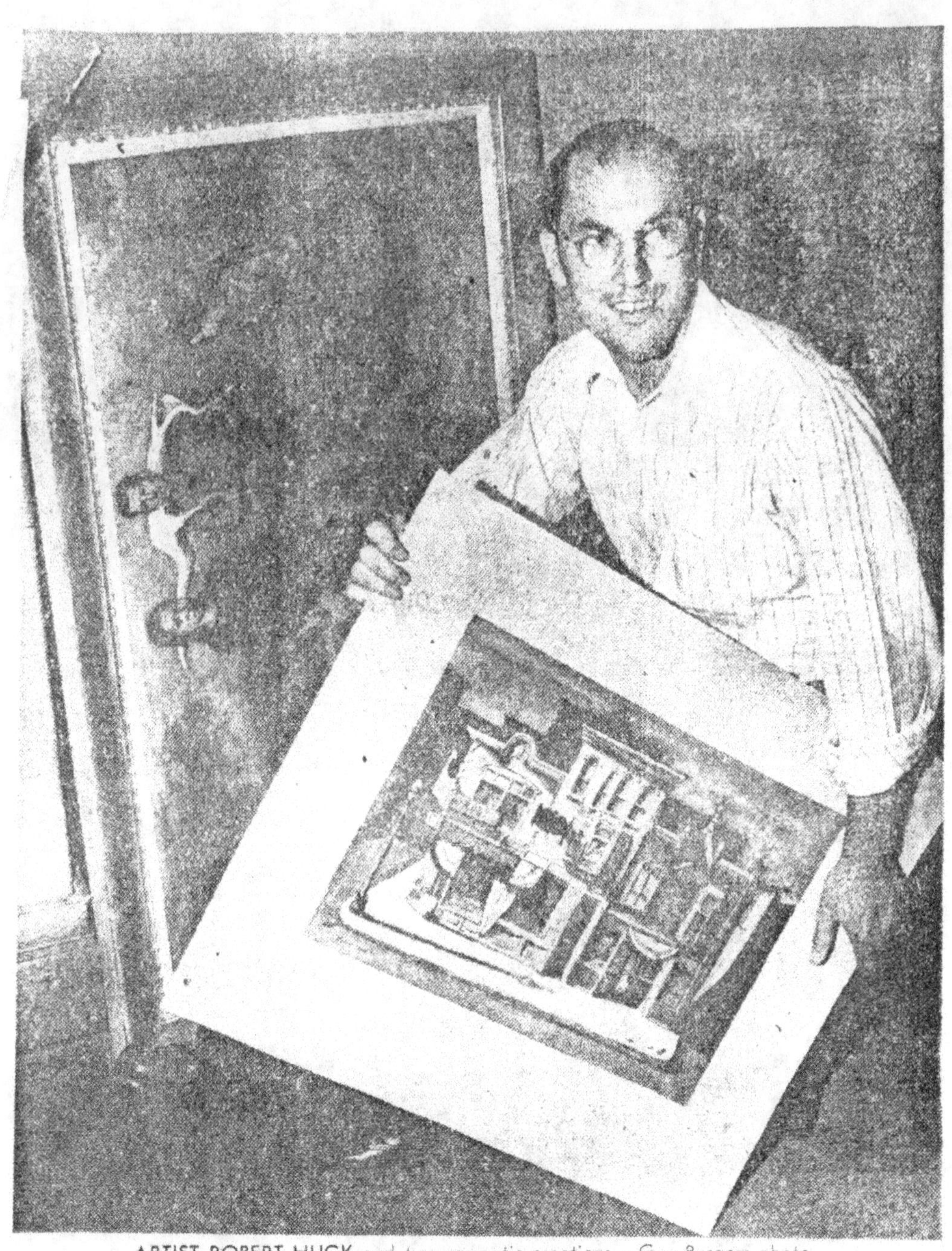

Robert Huck to Show Paintings
CITIES, SEA, MOUNTAINS HOLD HIS IMAGINATION

The first one-man showing of Huck's artwork takes place in Colorado Springs, Colorado College, August 1949.

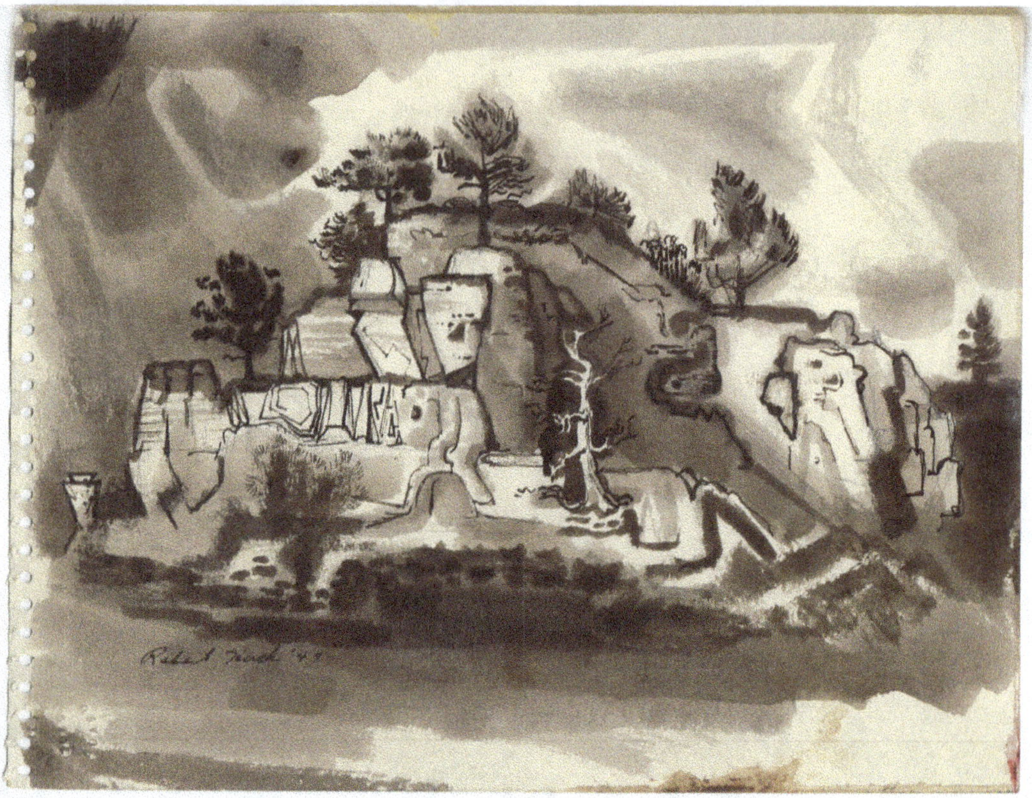

"By transforming nature into definite rhythms and patterns, I attempt to express my inner feelings." (5)

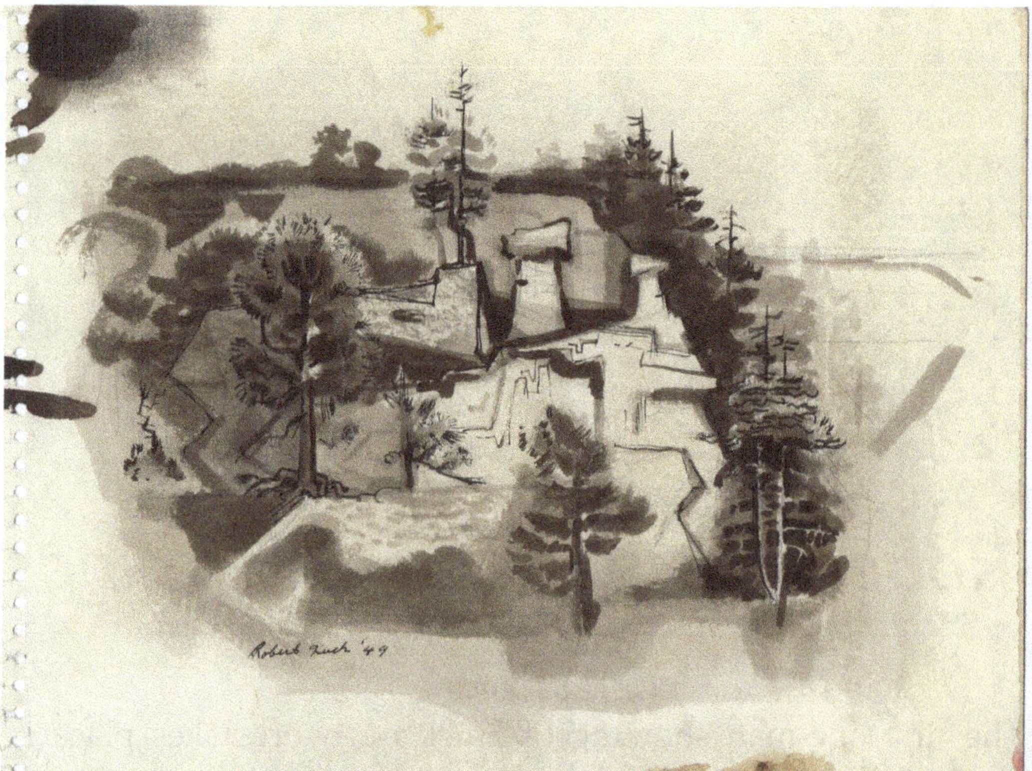

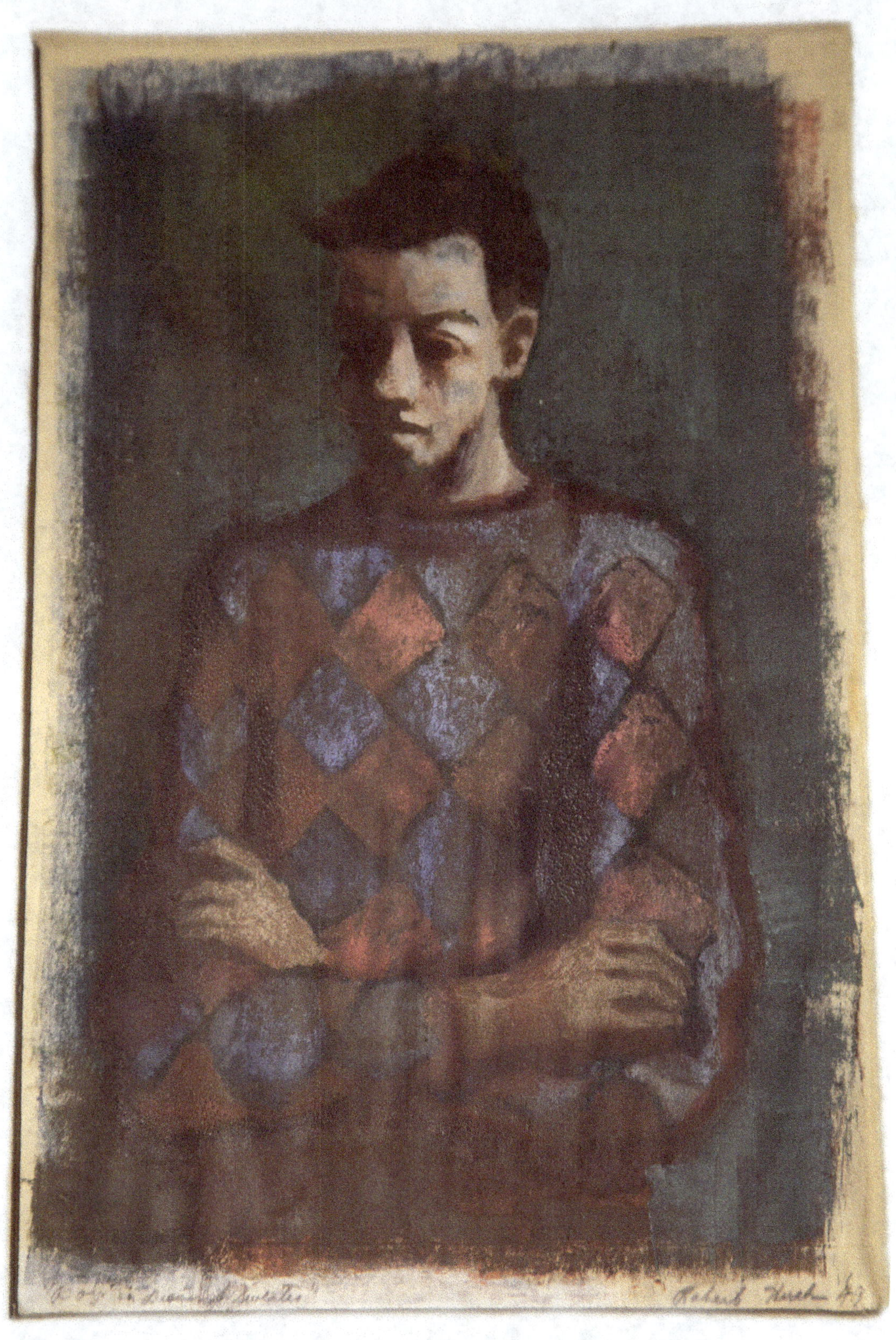

"Boy in Diamond Sweater" (1949)

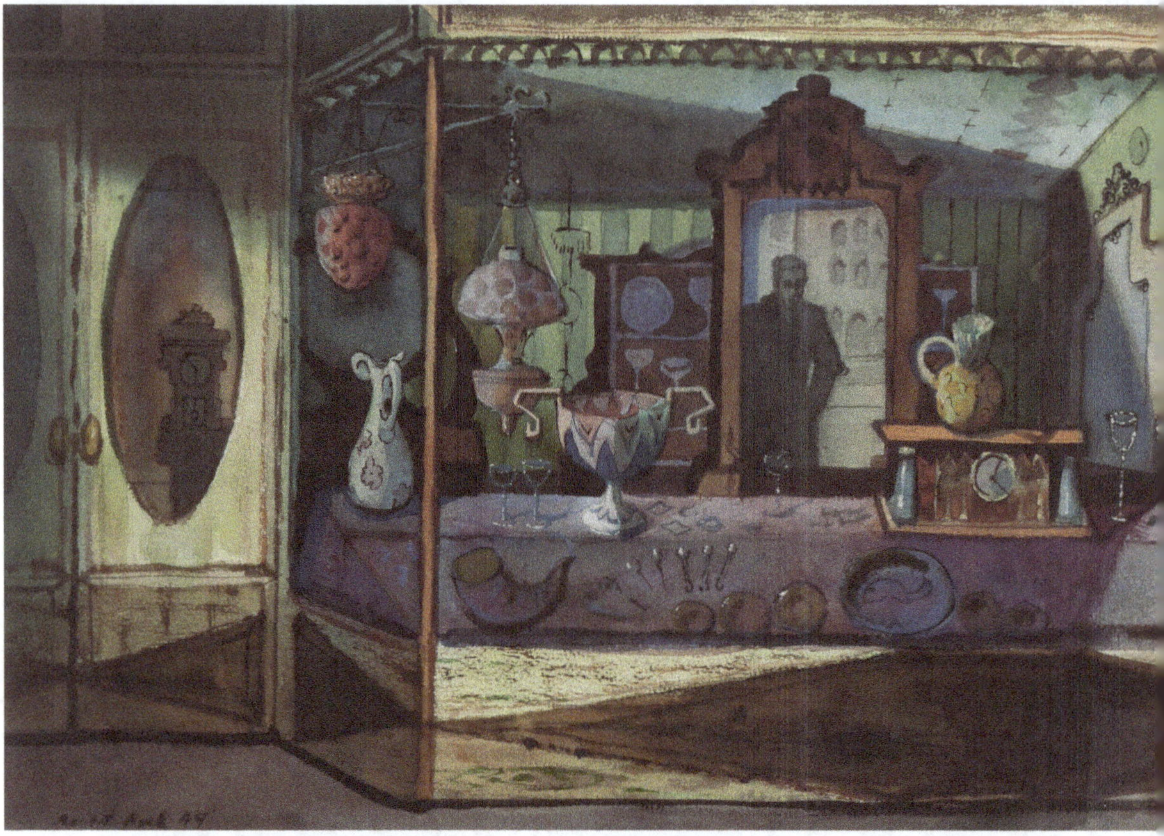

"Antique Store" (1949)

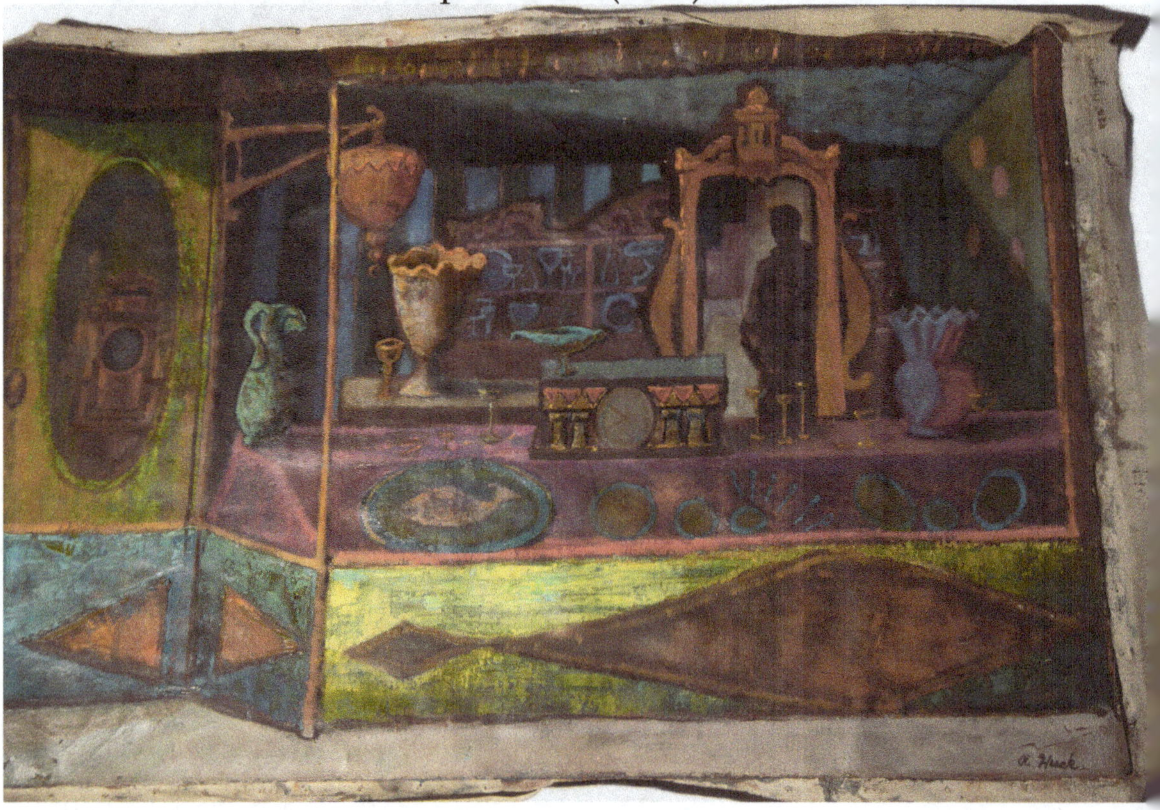

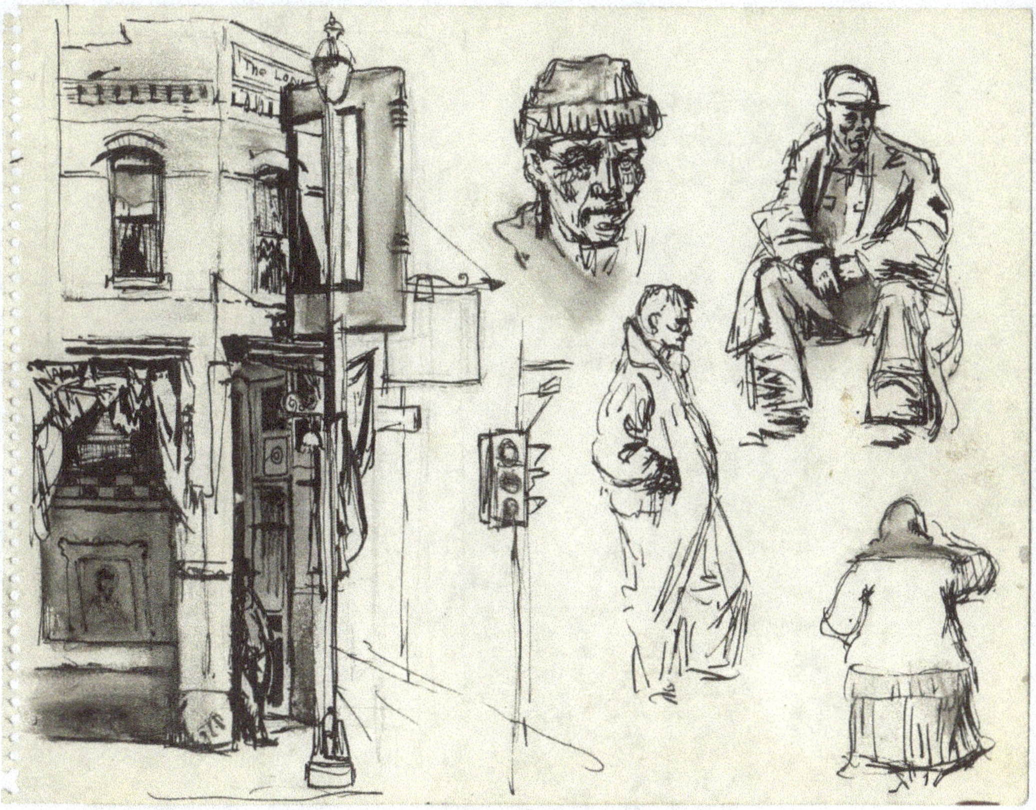

"I have used single human figues, such as beachcombers, mountaineers, and city dwellers to express by gesture, posture and color the mood which I have felt in their environment."

Colorado Springs Gazette Telegraph, 8/16/49

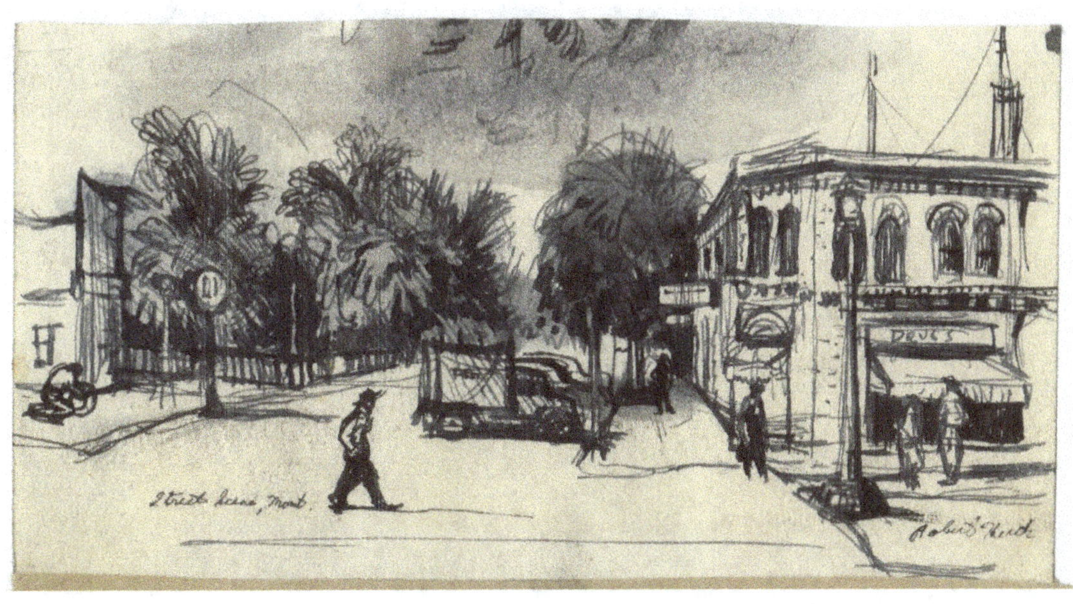

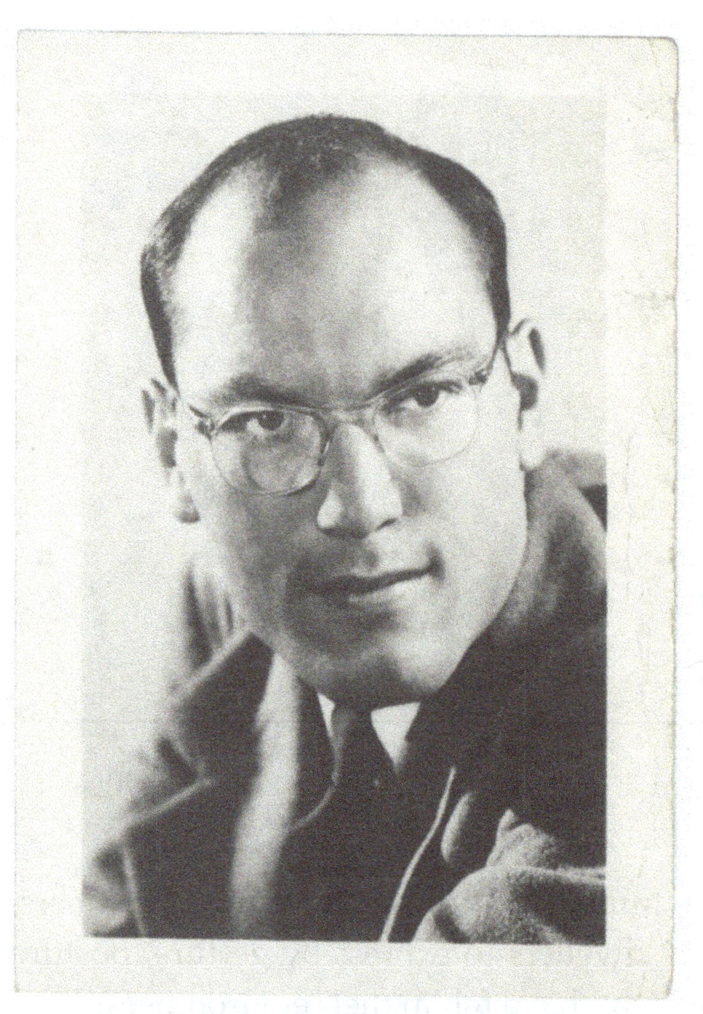
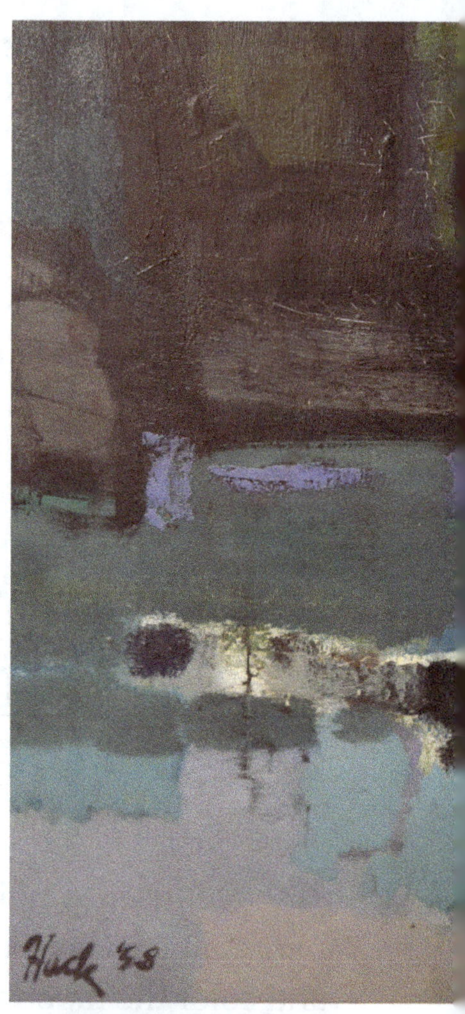
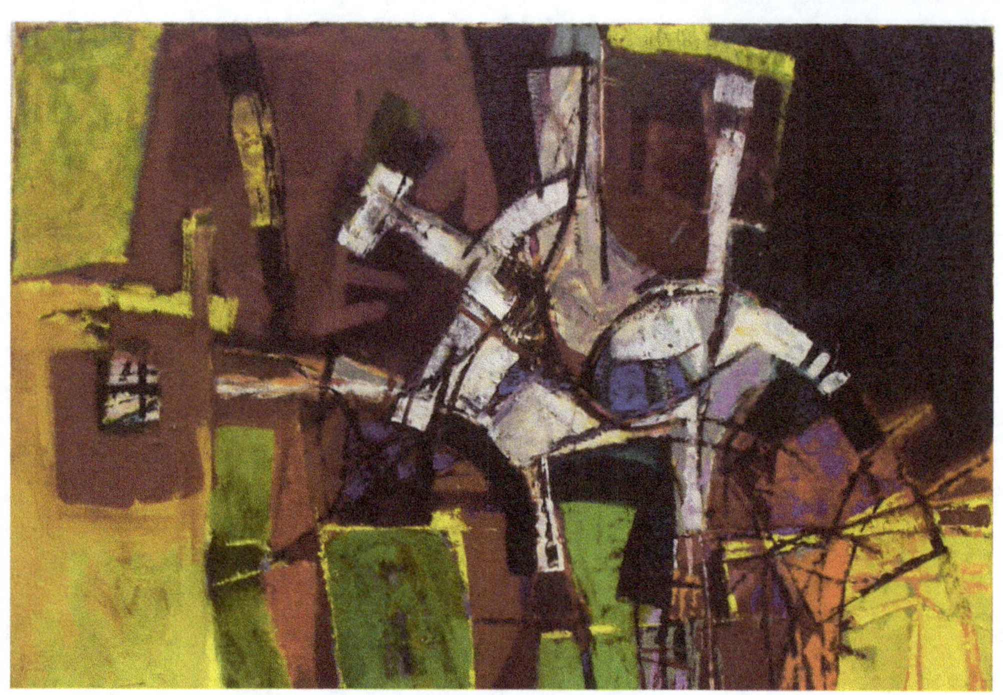

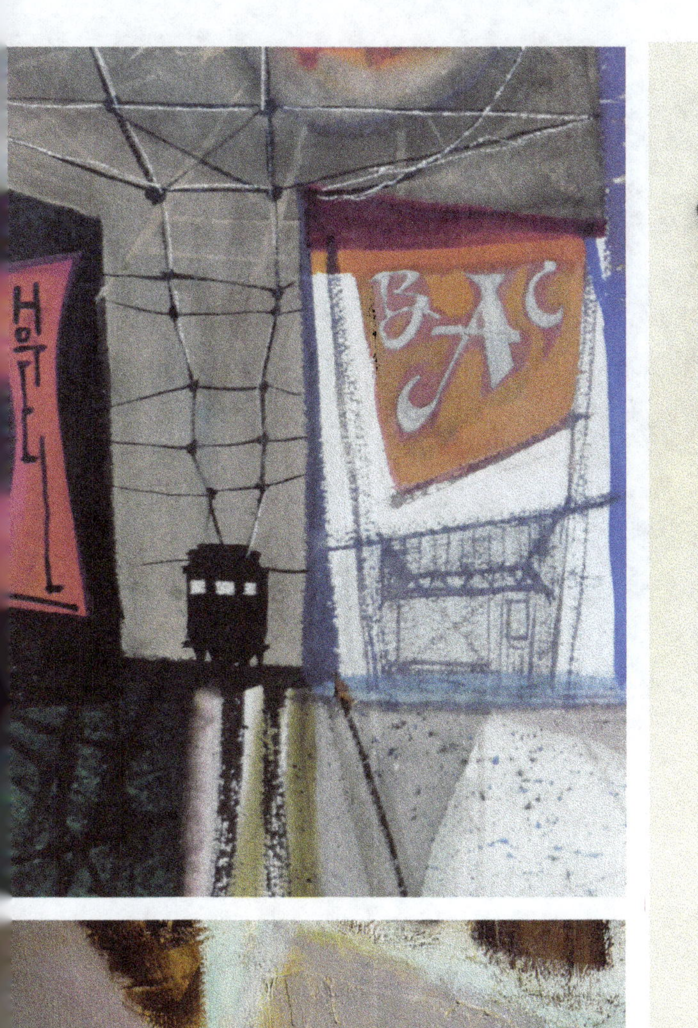

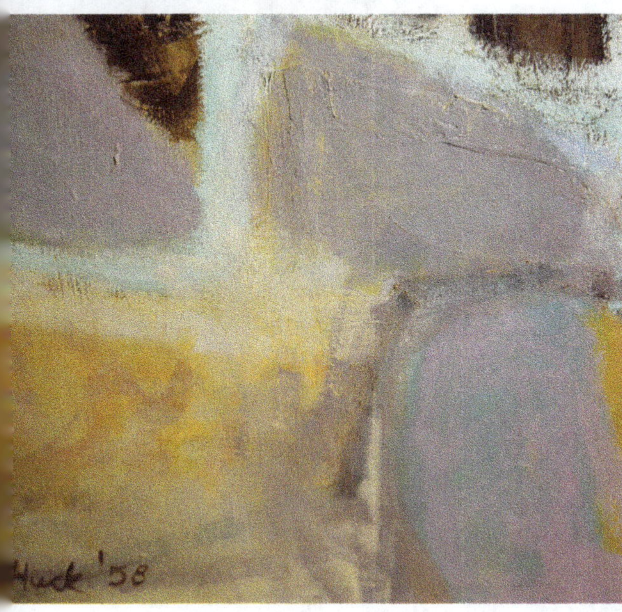

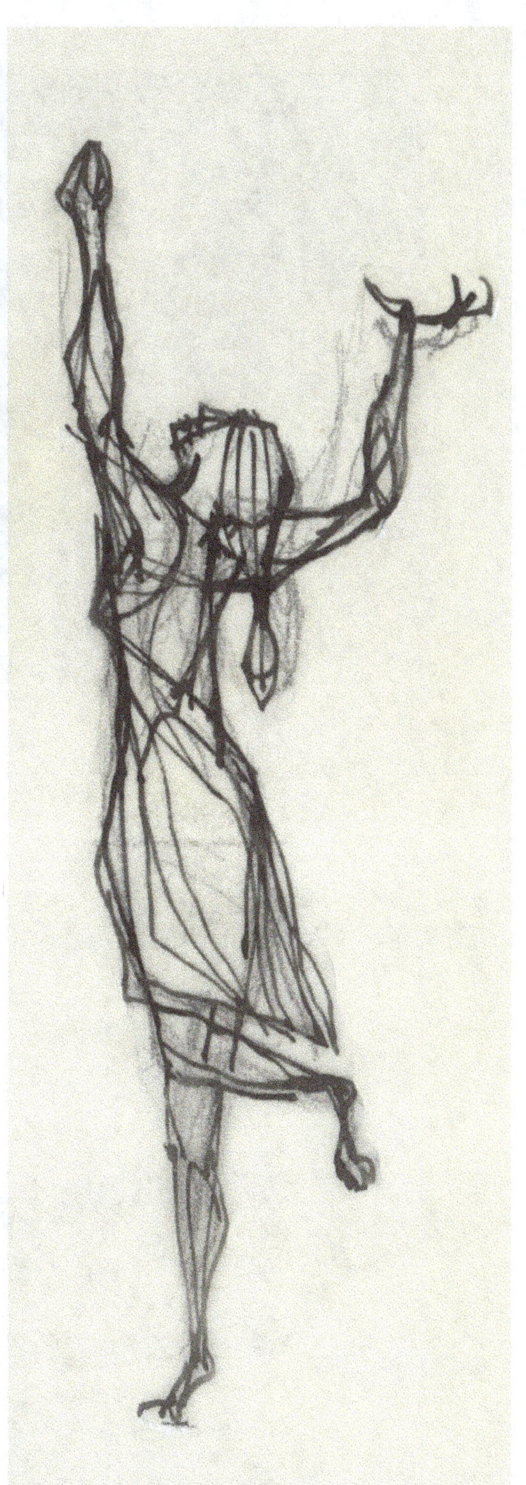

The 1950s

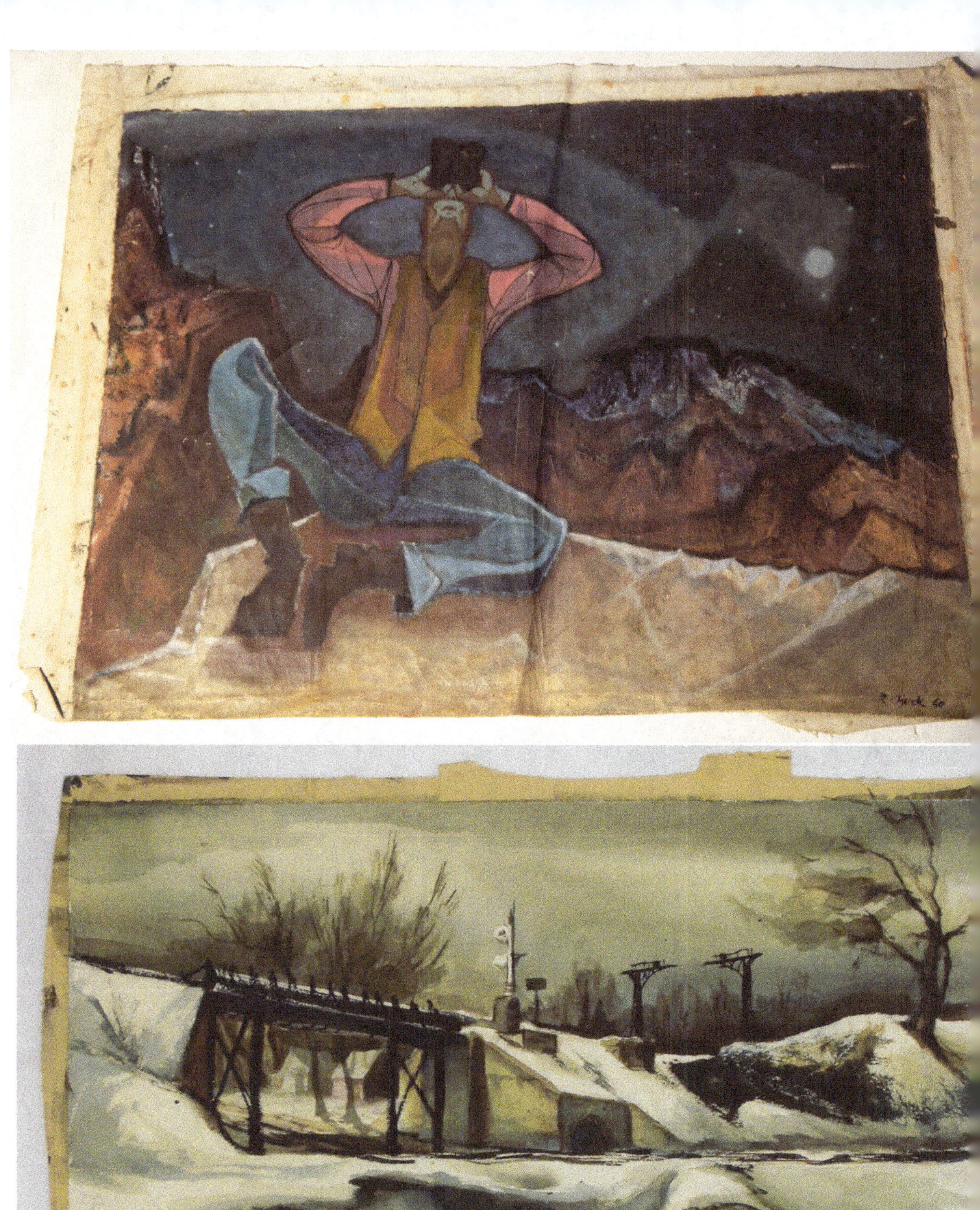

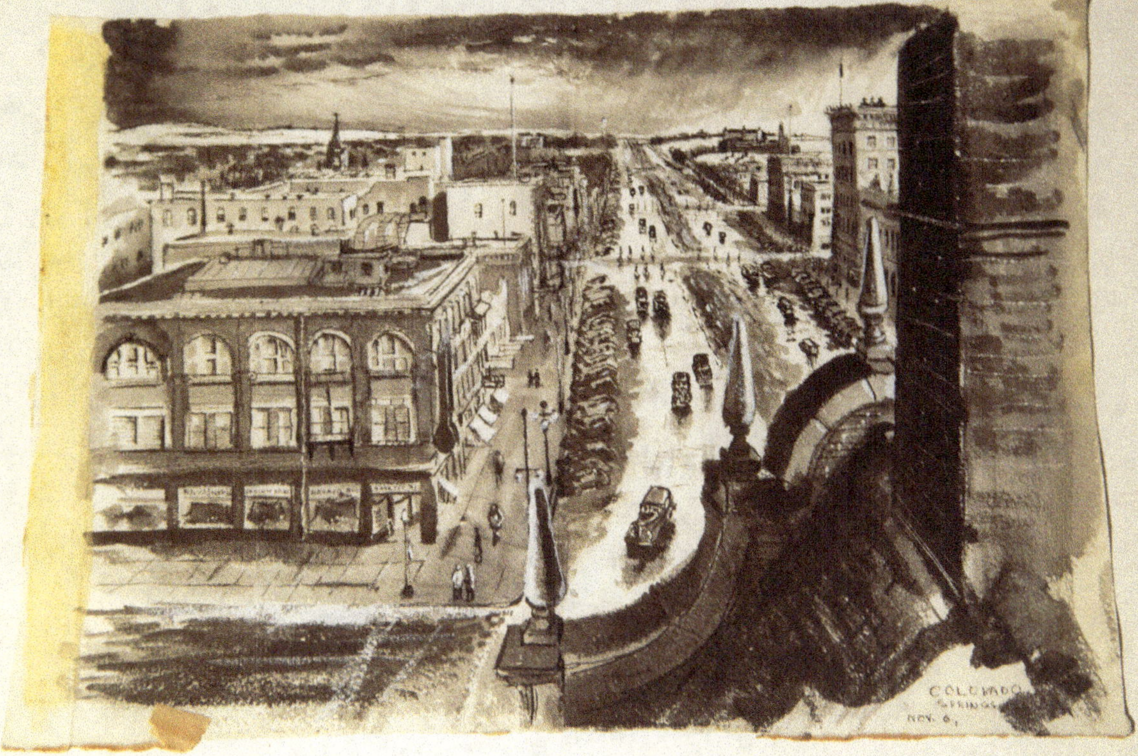

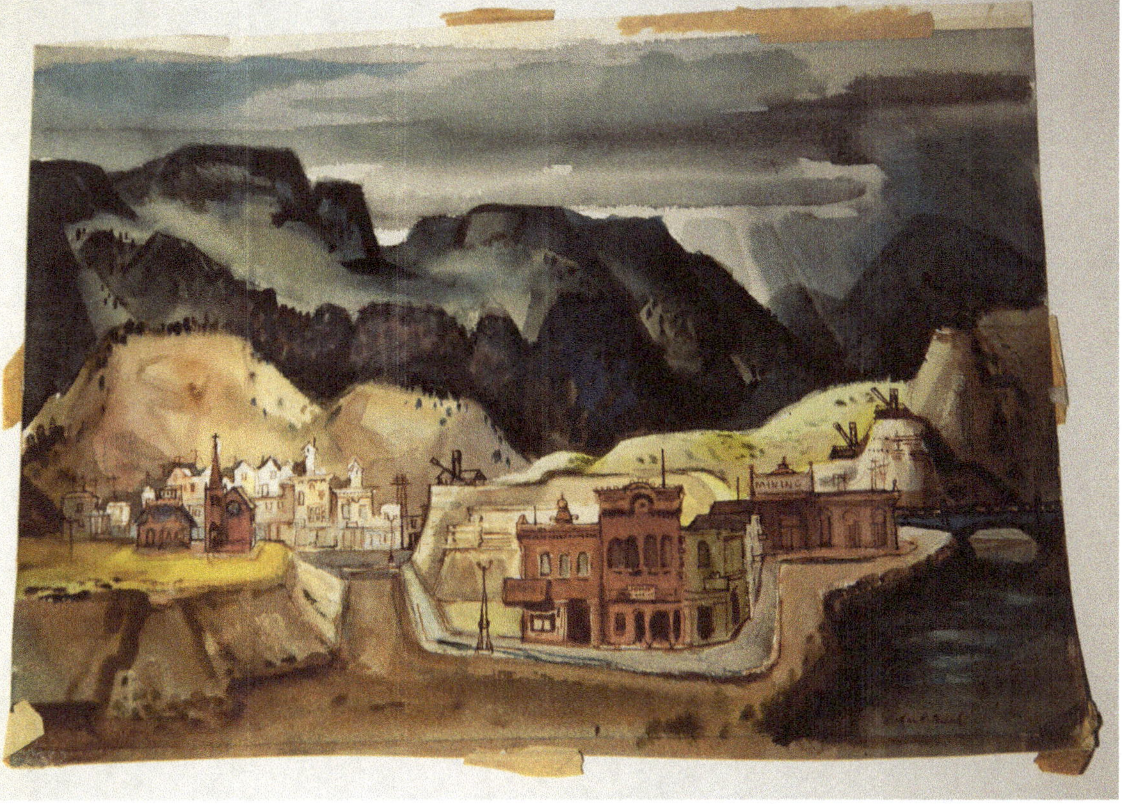

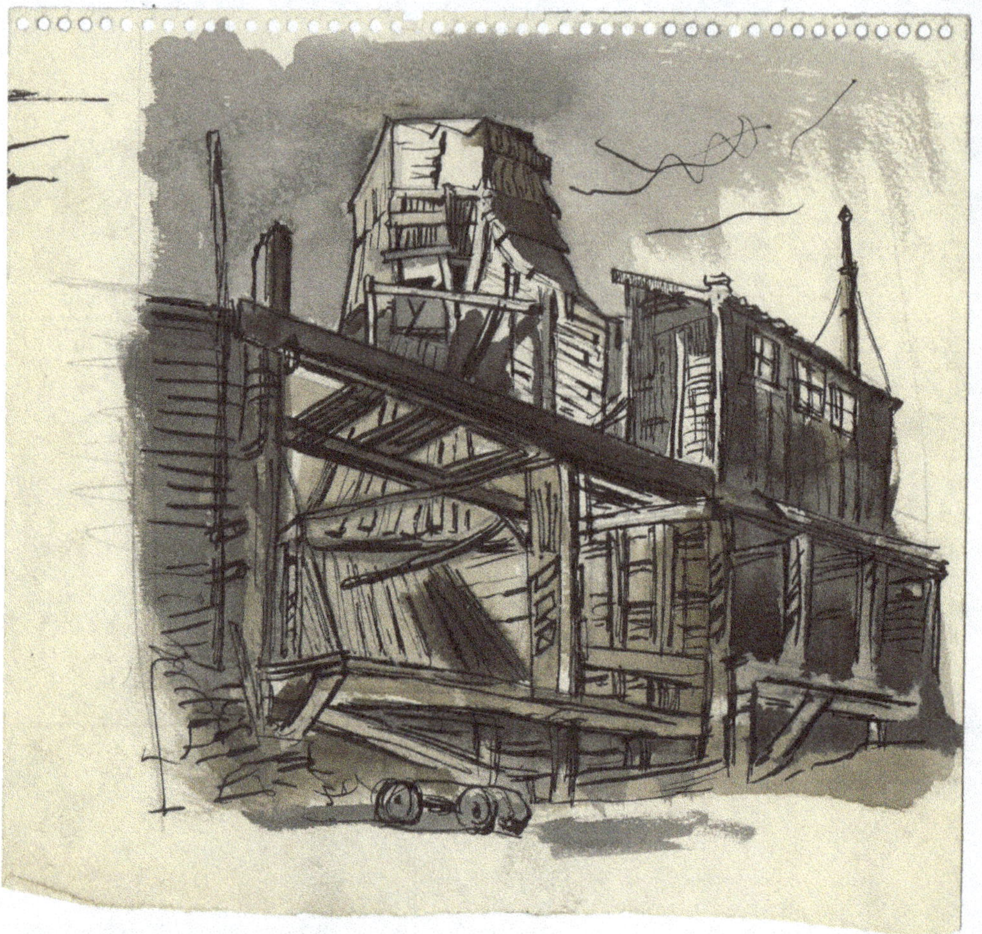

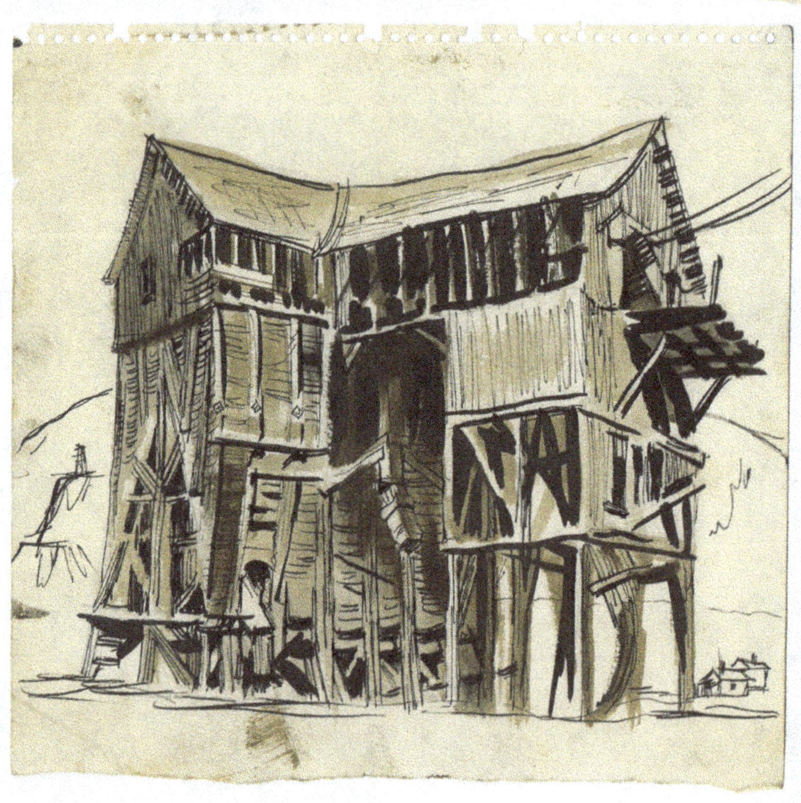

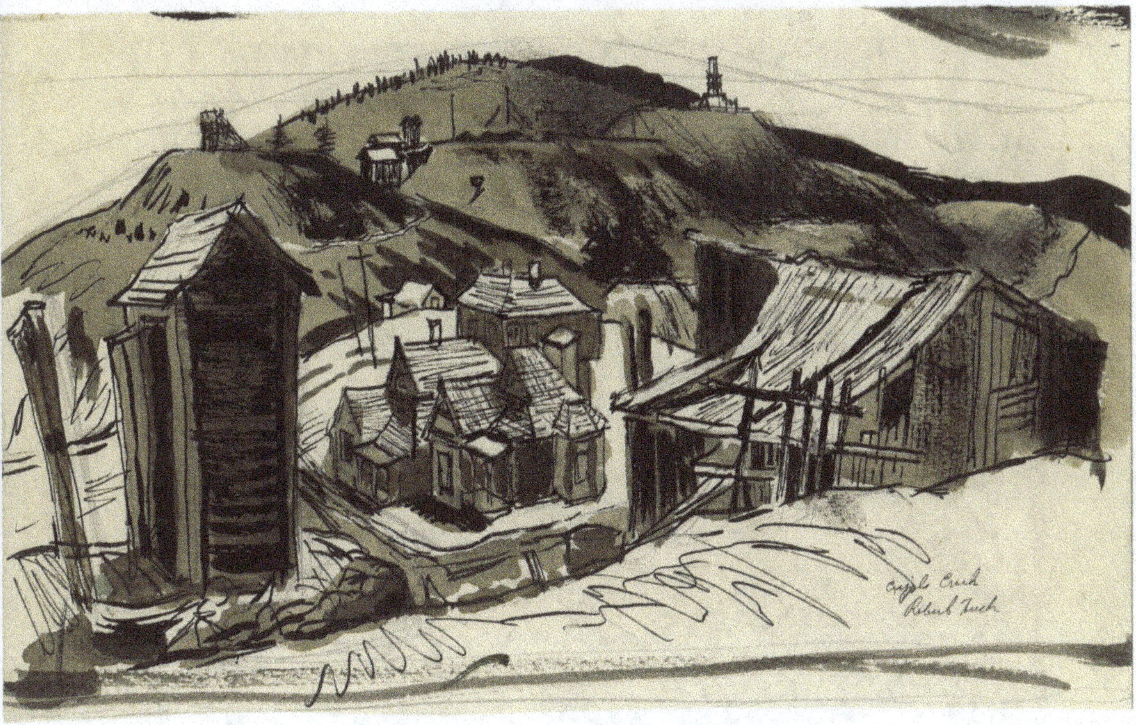

Colorado.   Above: Cripple Creek   Below: Boarding House

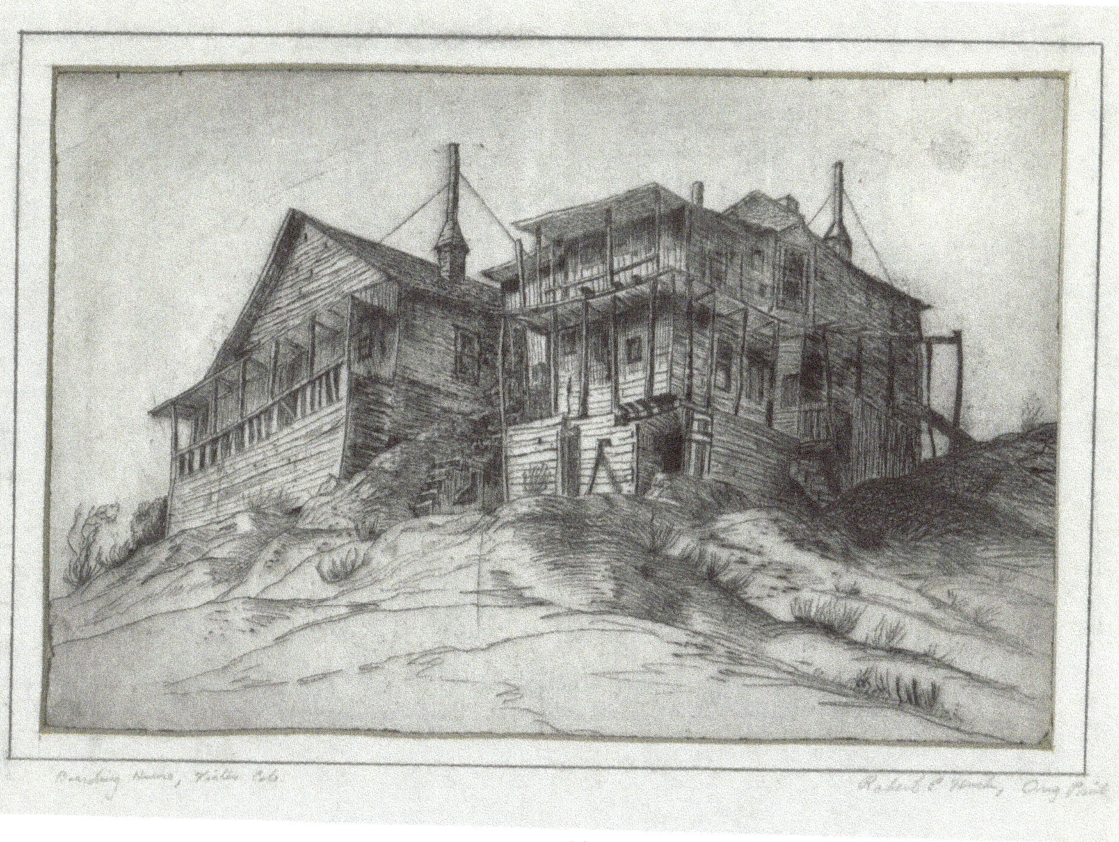

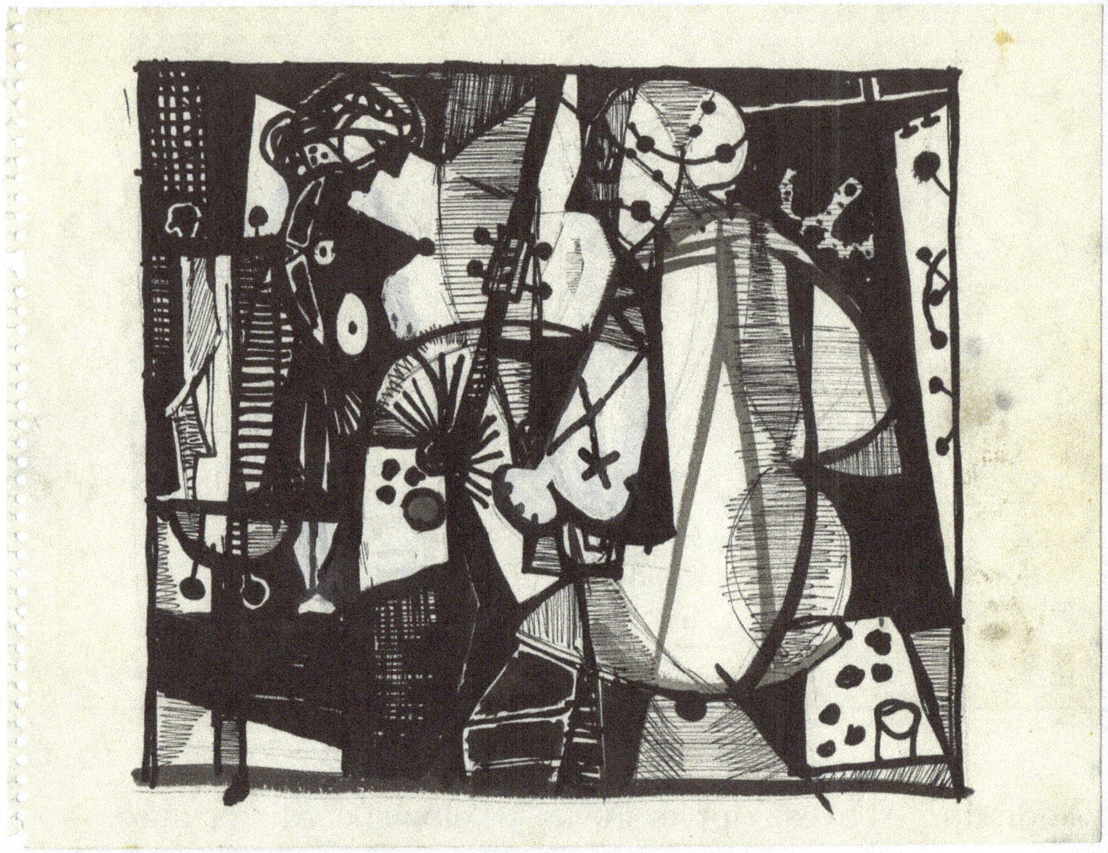

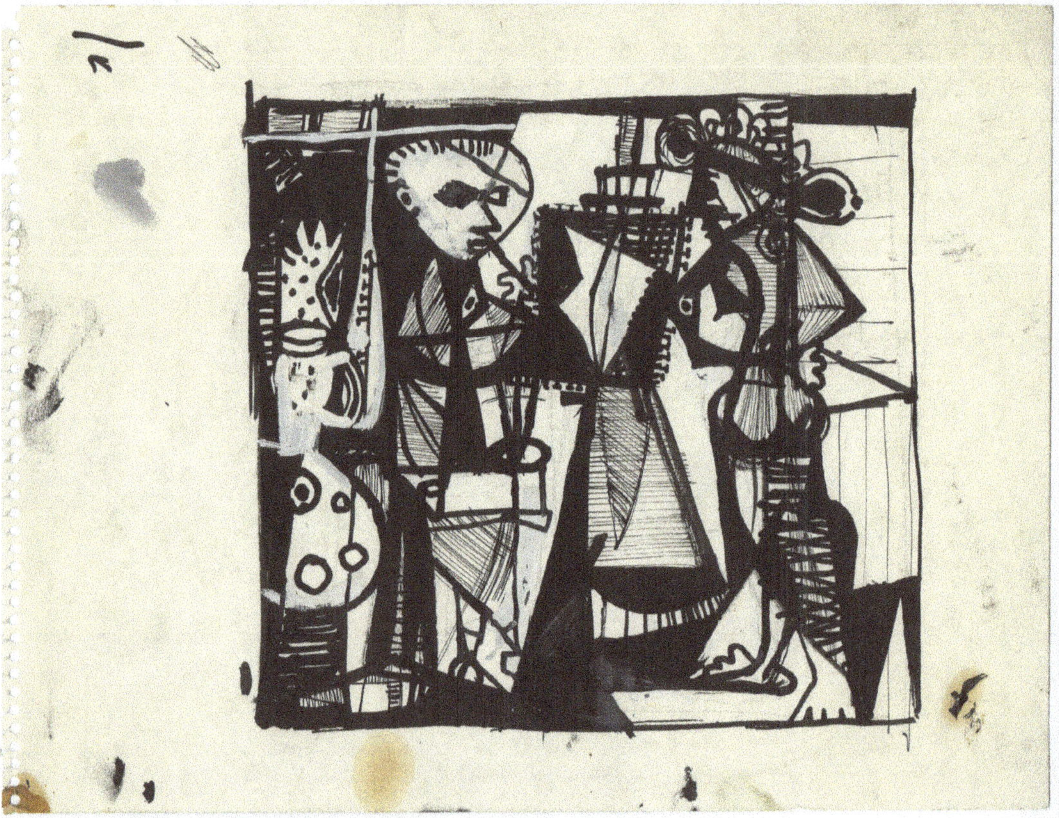

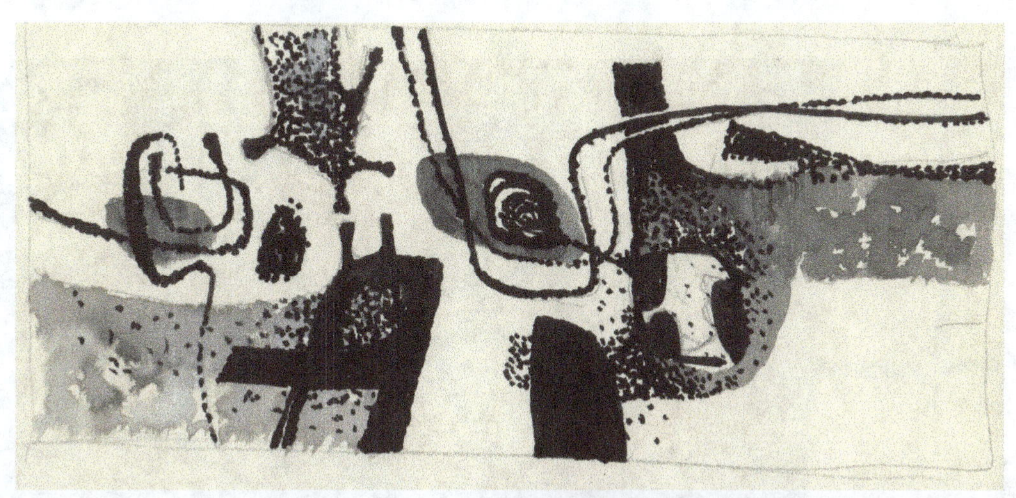

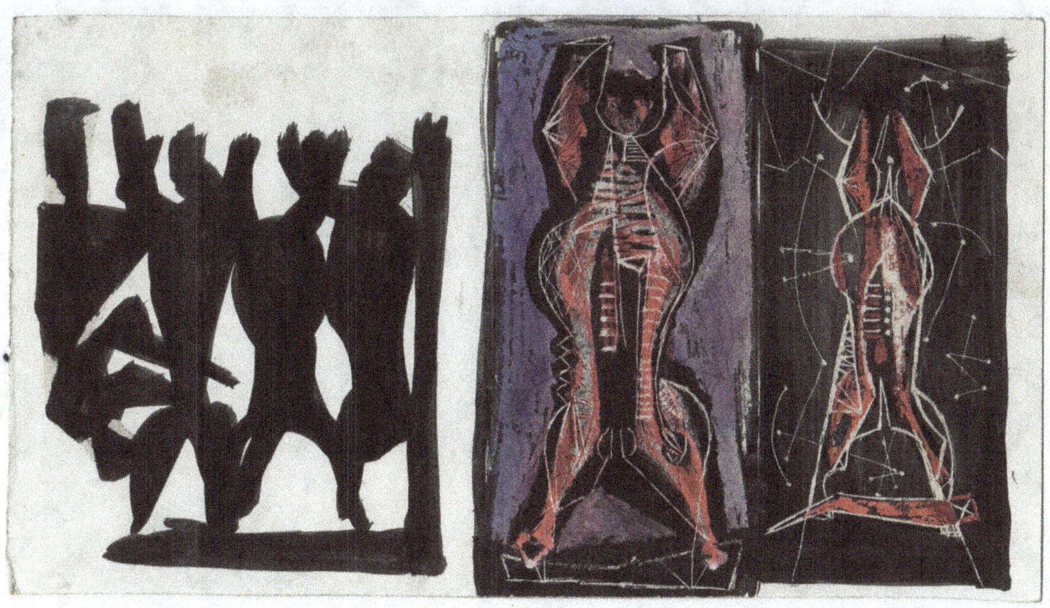

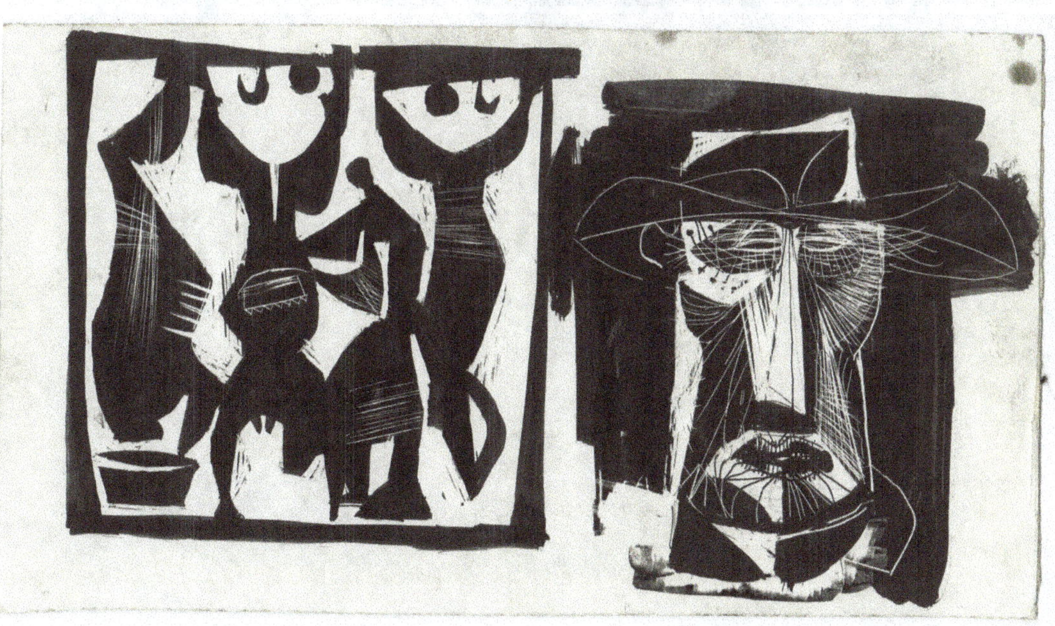

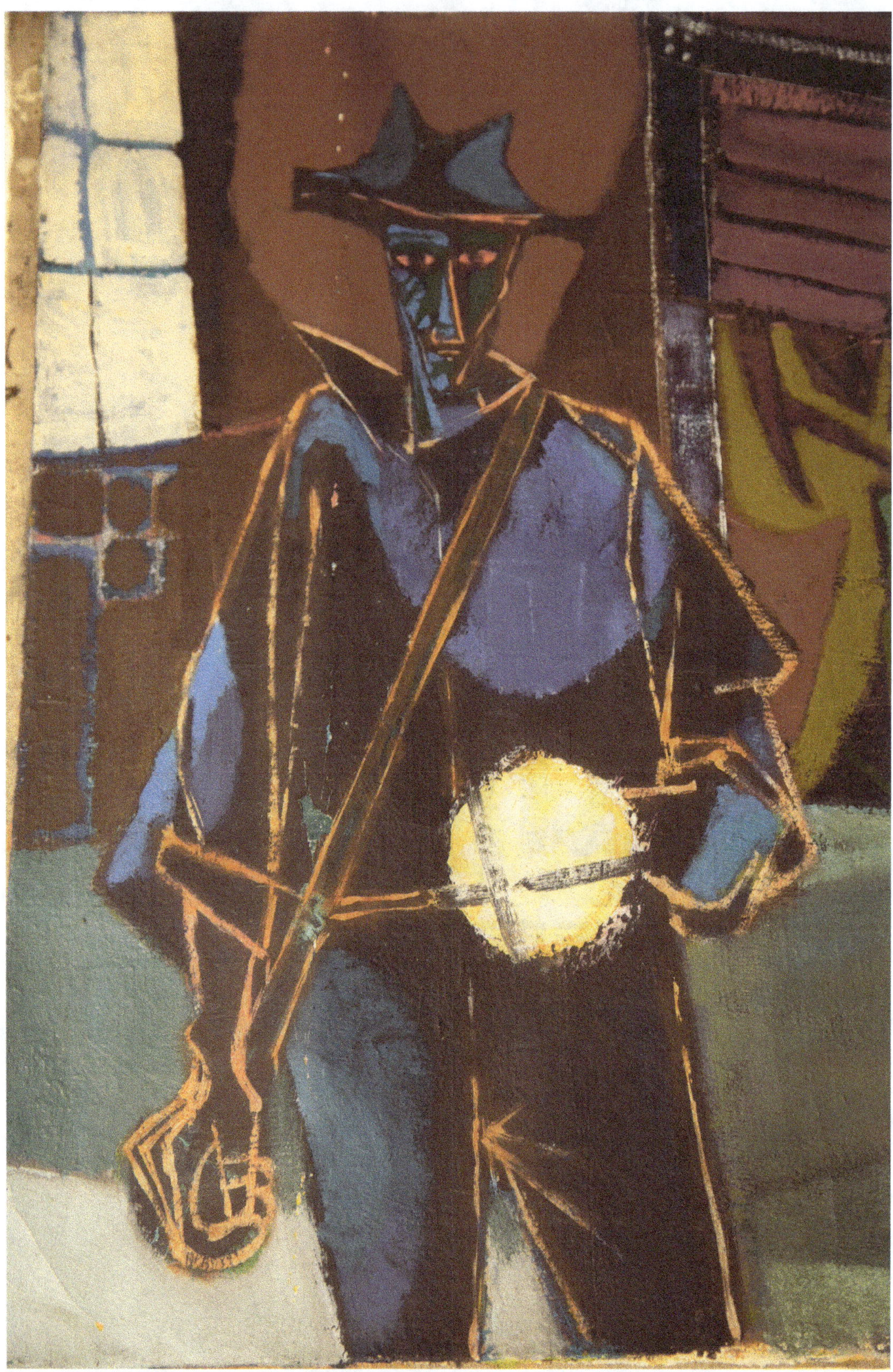

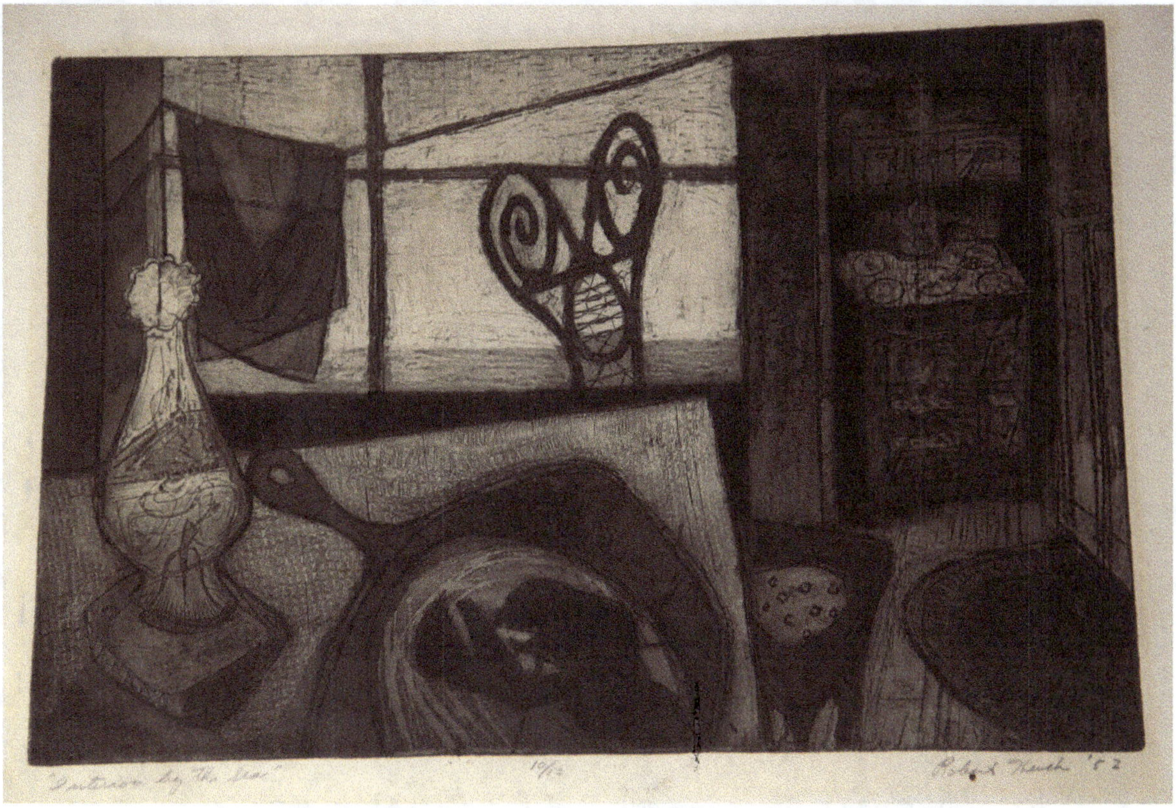

"Interior by the Sea" & "Fisherman and Catch" (1952)

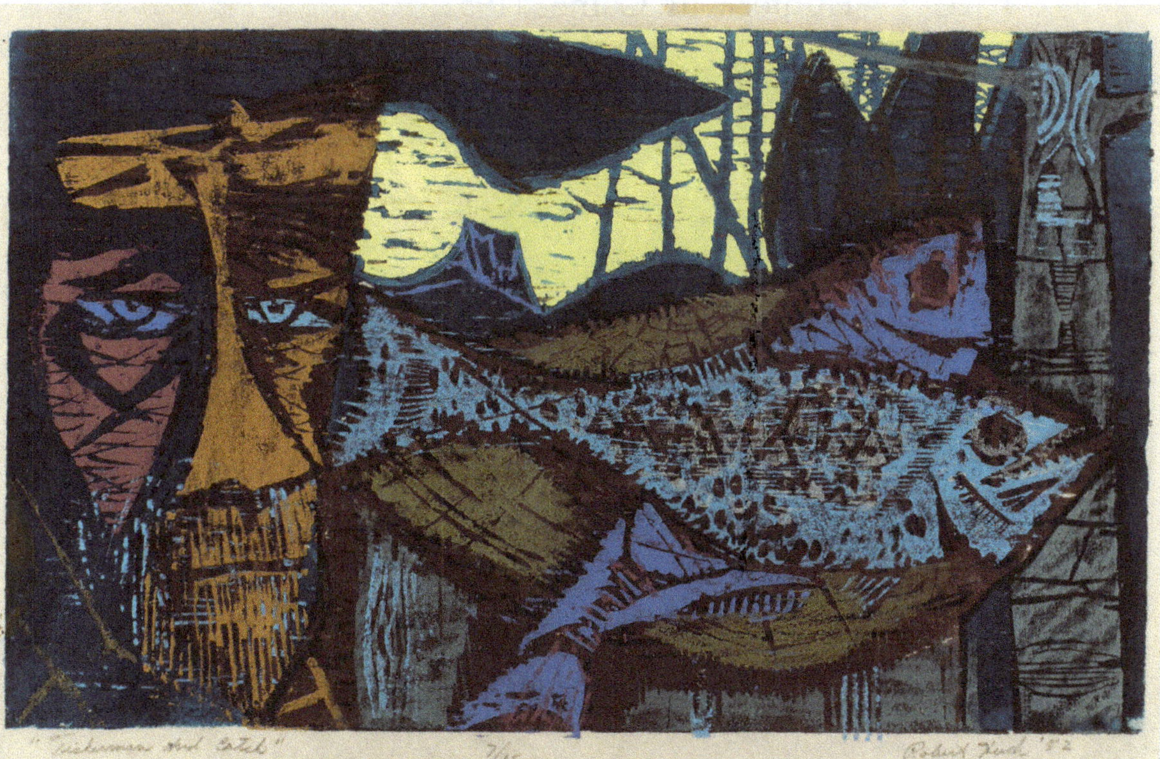

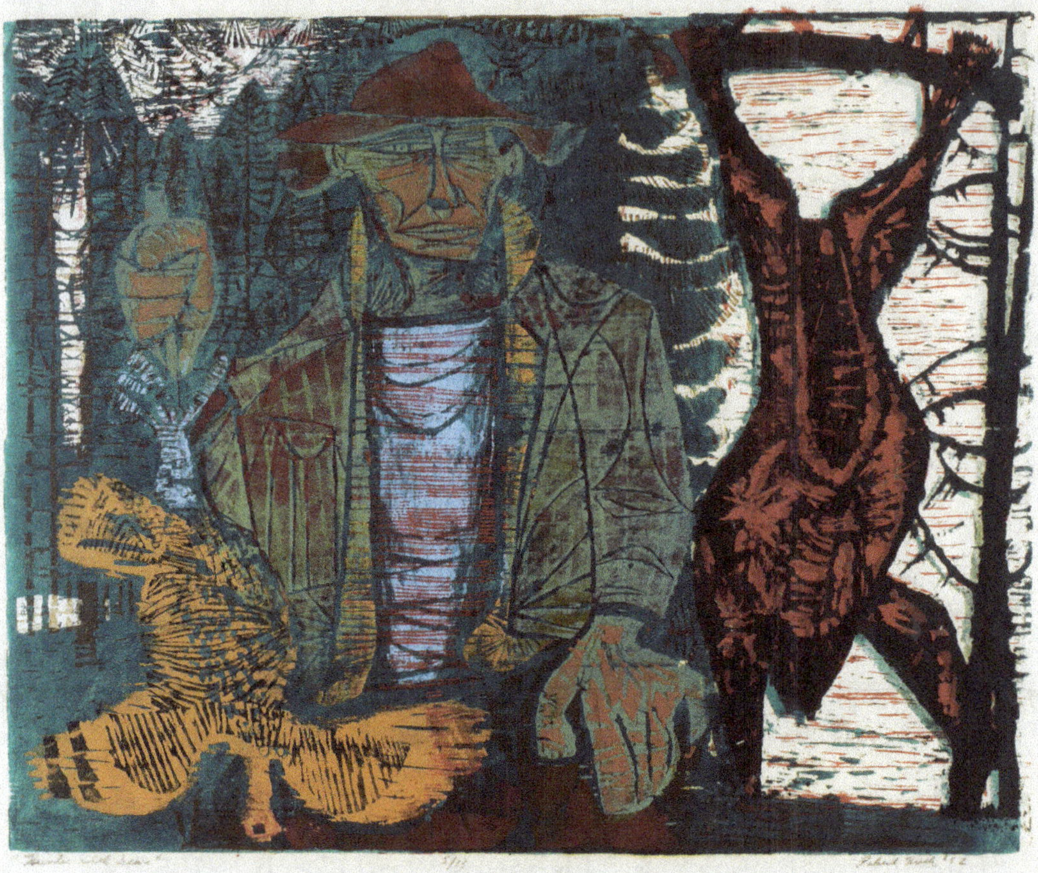

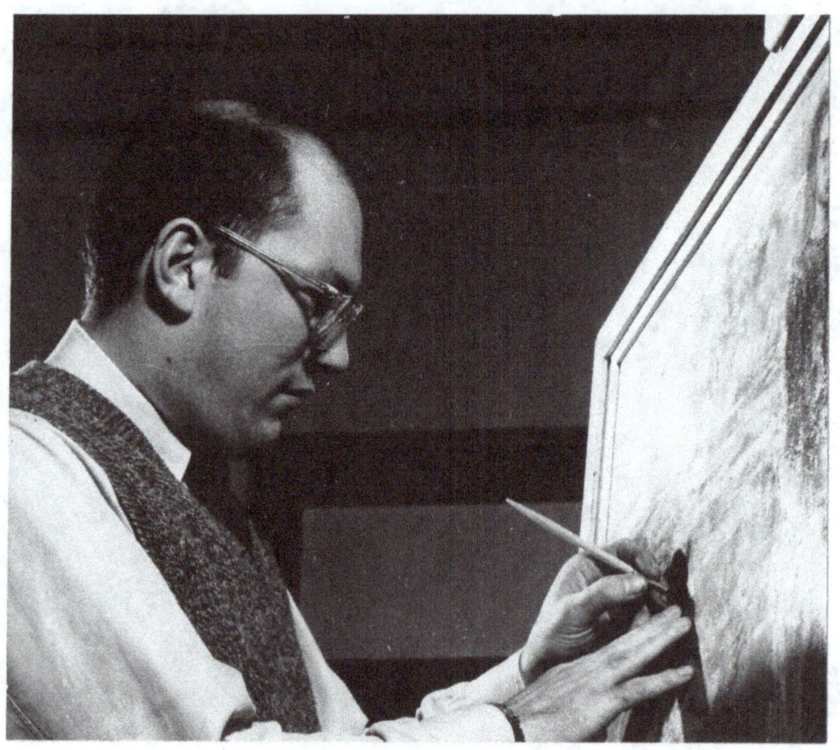

"Hunter with Game" (1952)

Huck and
painting
from p.30

May 22, 1952, Robert Huck's MFA thesis at the University of Colorado is approved. Entitled, *An Approach to a Painting Problem*, it is "an analysis both written and pictorial of an approach to the act of painting using the still life as a motif," recording in detail the three phases of creation: idea, experiment, and final statement. The following six illustrations from his thesis provide a unique understanding of the way Huck created a work of art.

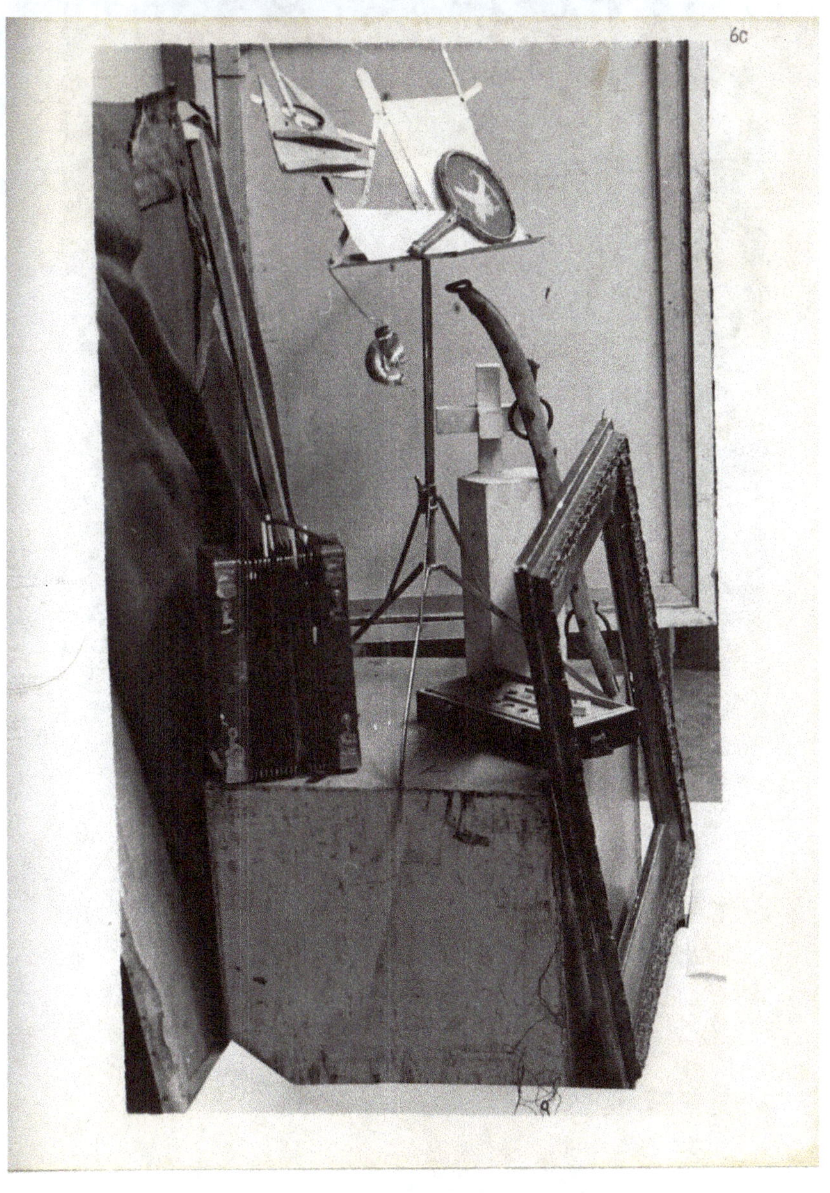

"Photograph of the Motif"

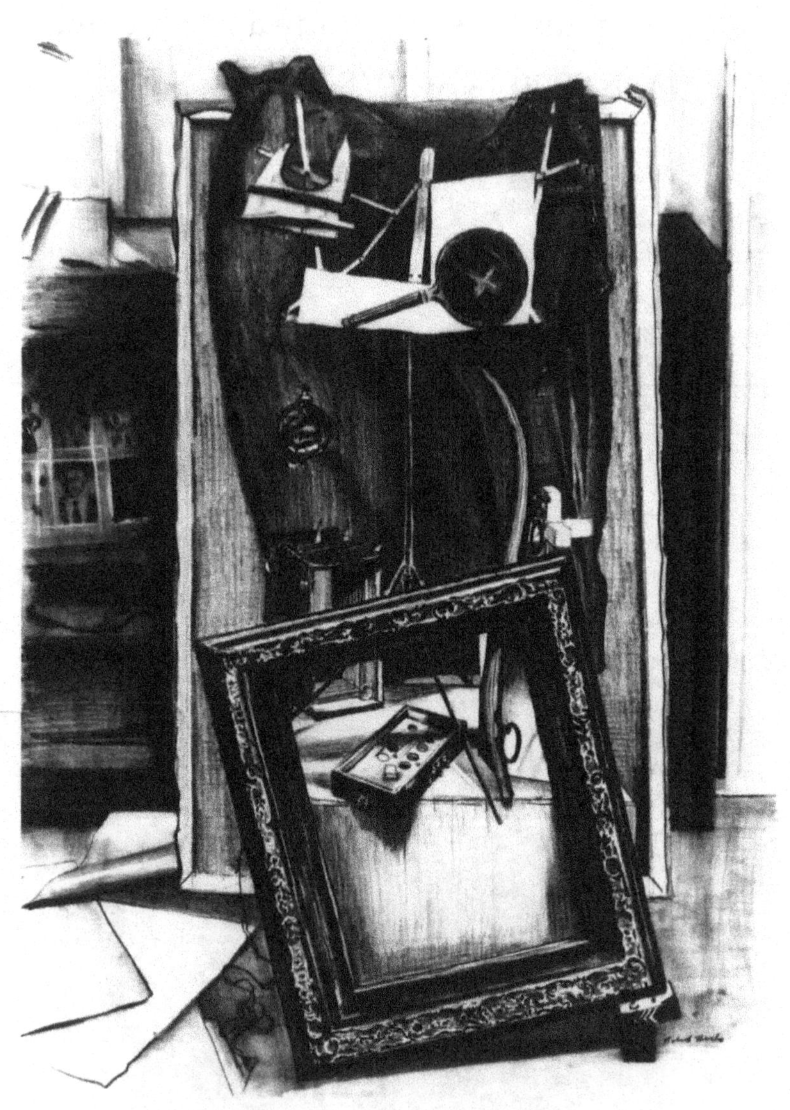

"Naturalistic Study"

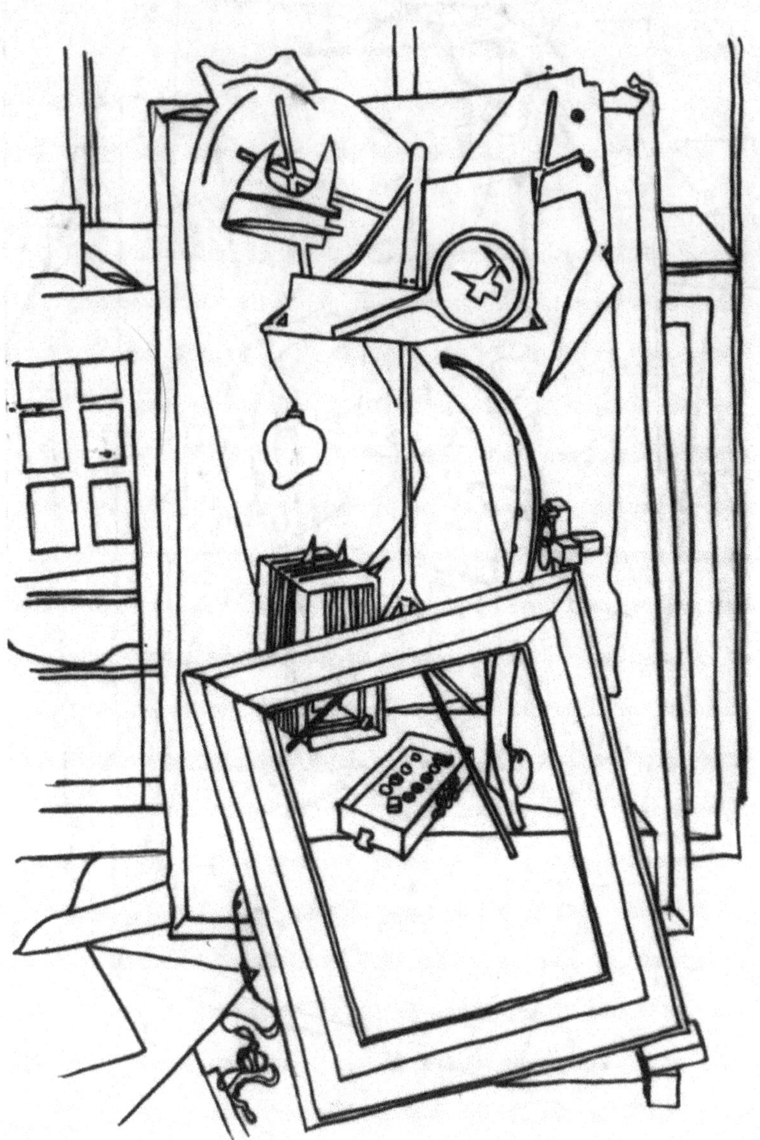

"Line Study"

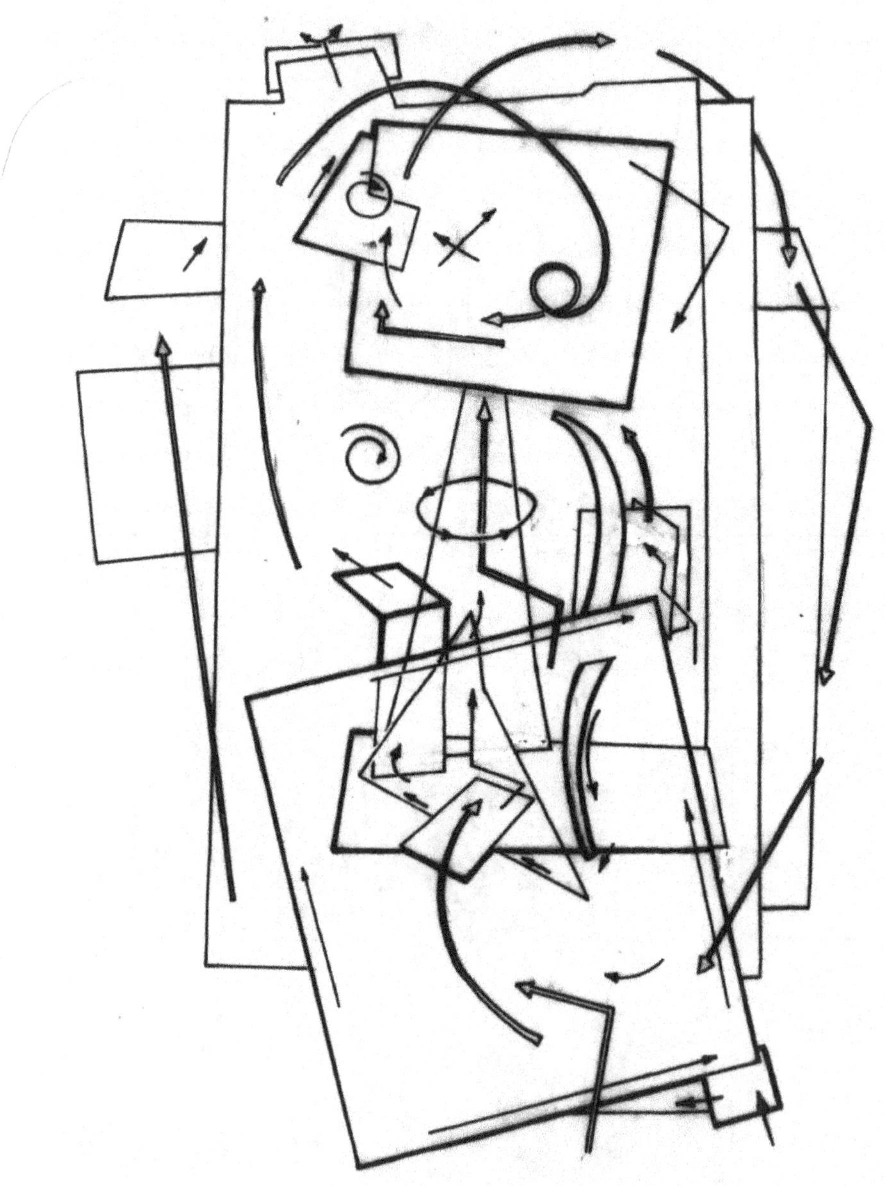

"Movement Study"

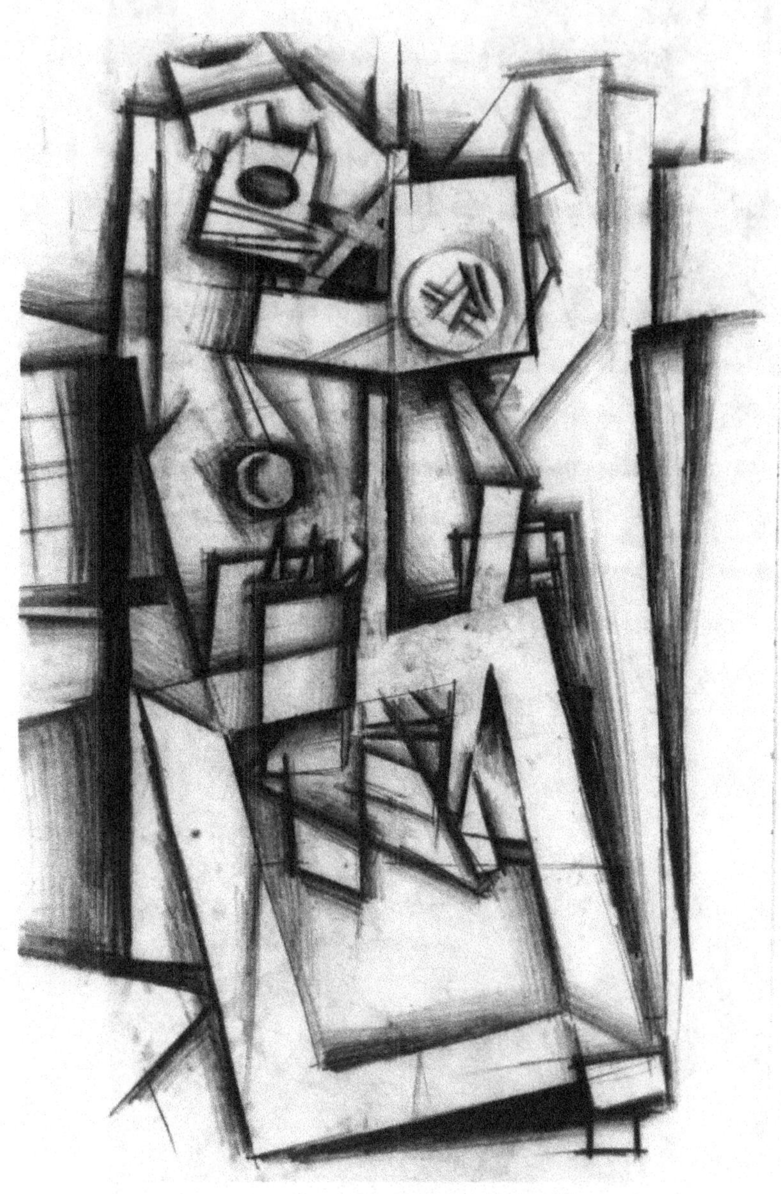

"Overlapping Plane Study"

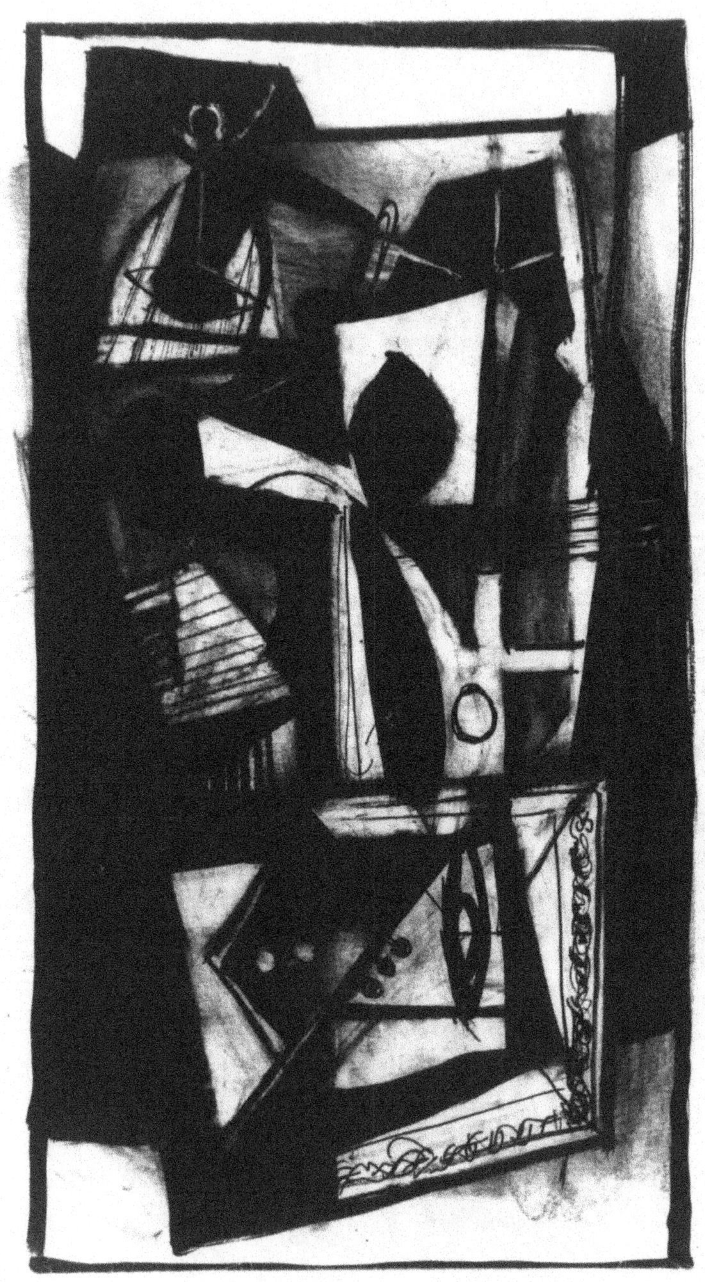

"Final Drawing"

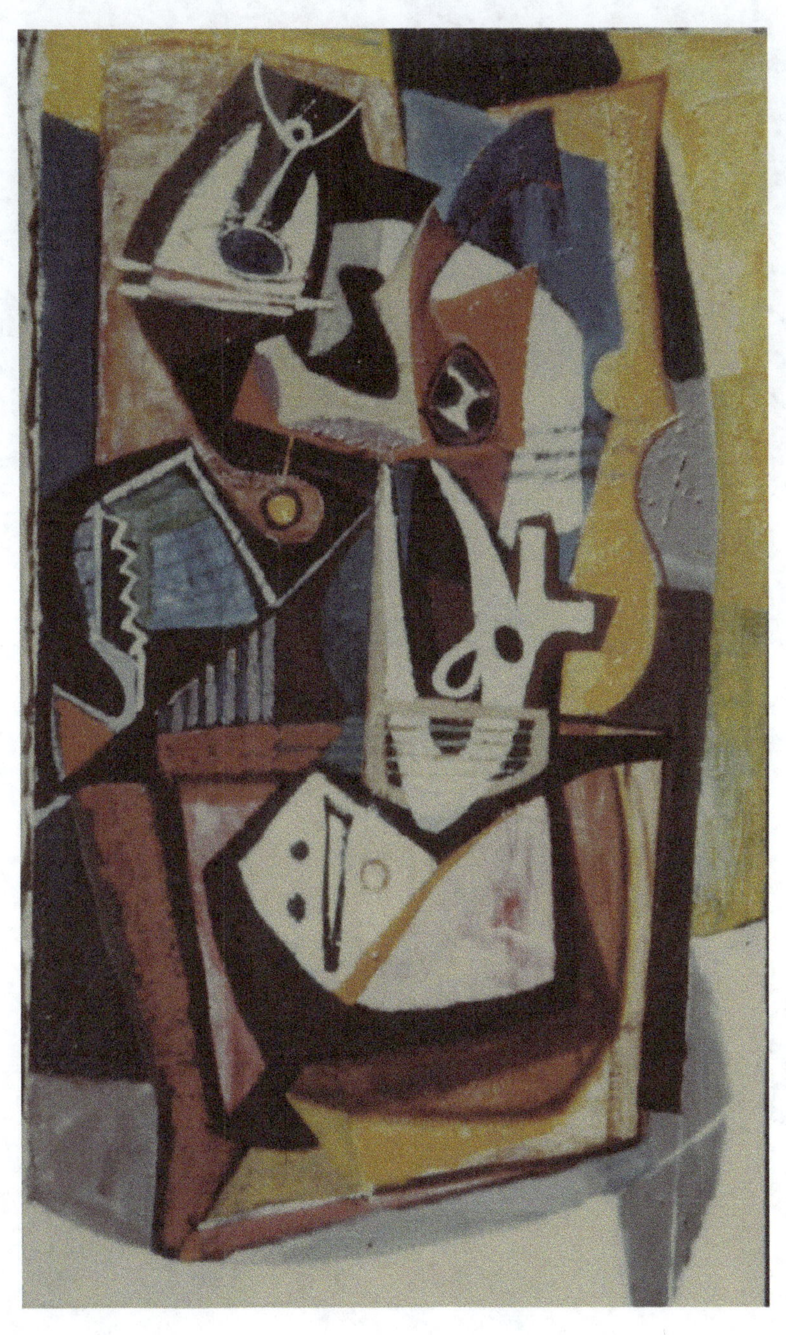

"Final Painting"

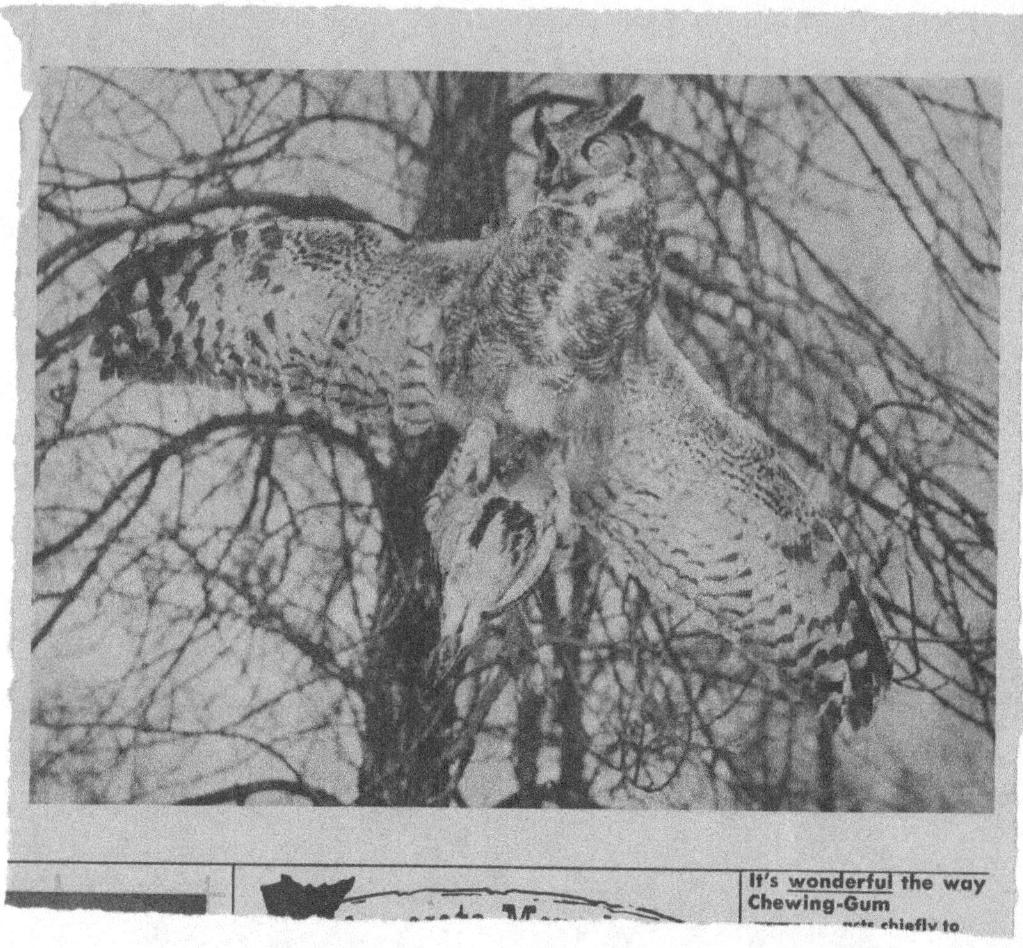

It's wonderful the way
Chewing-Gum
gets chiefly to

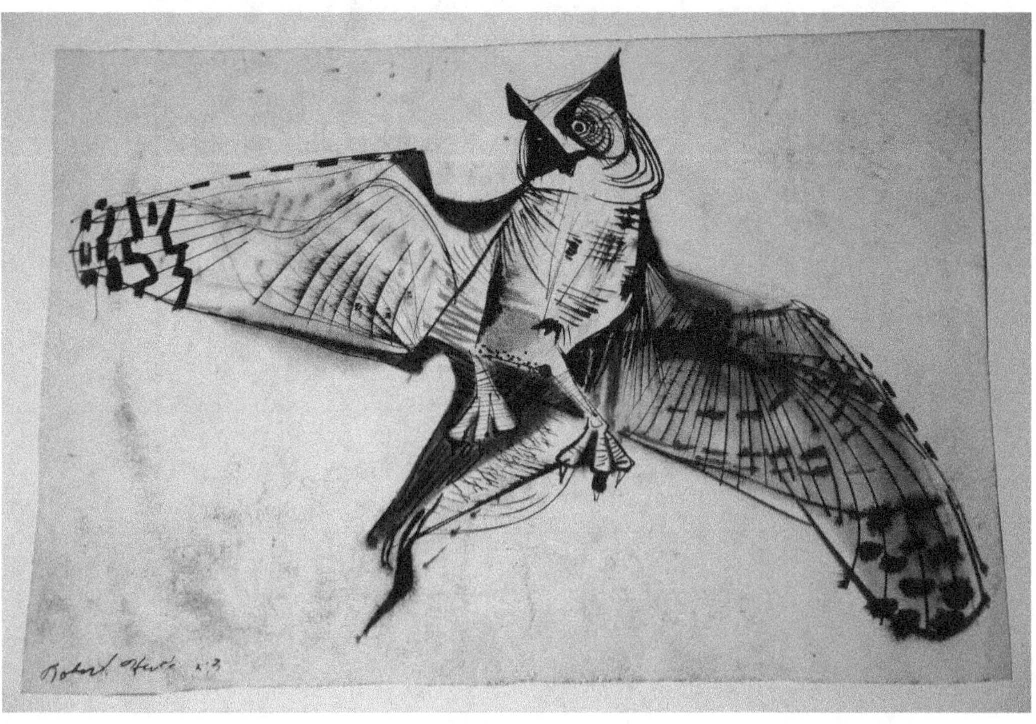

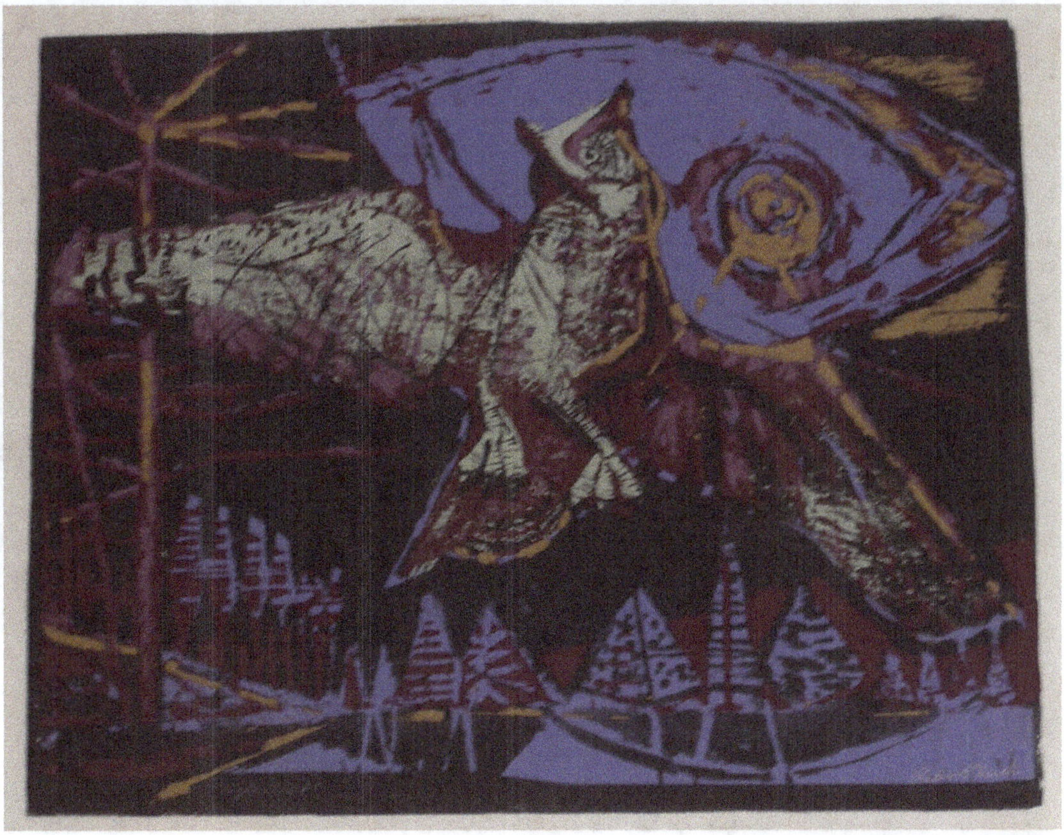

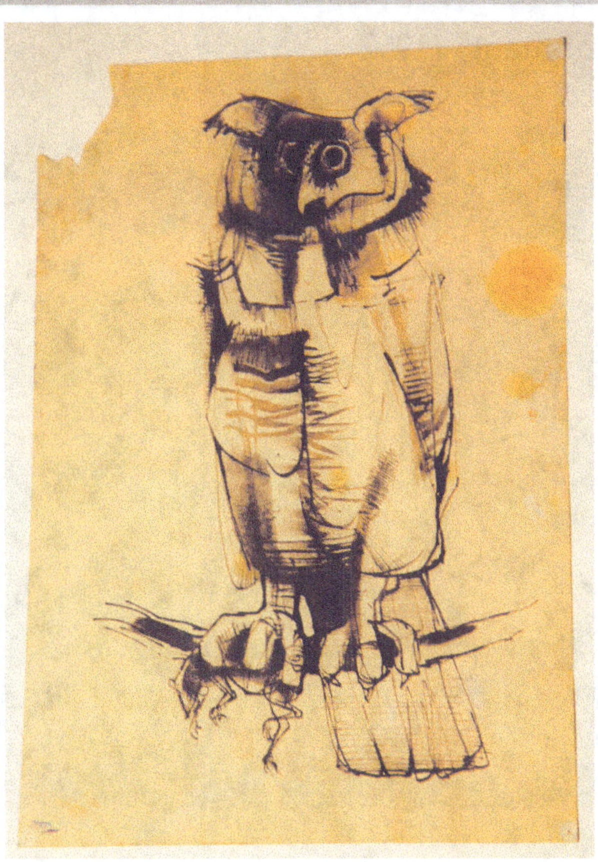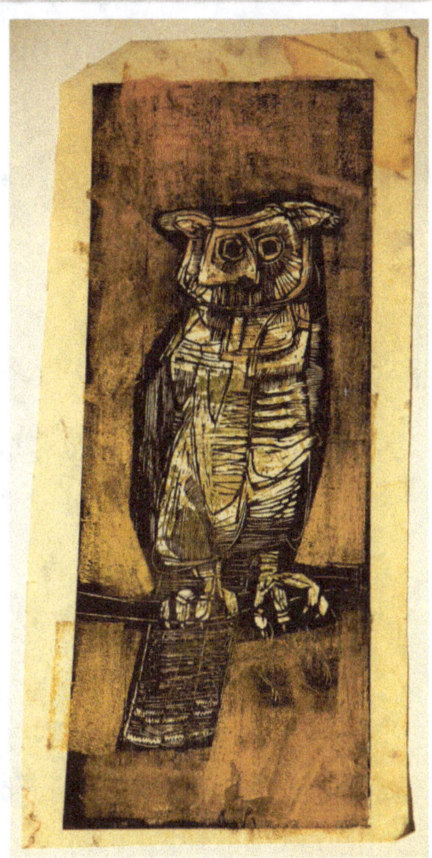

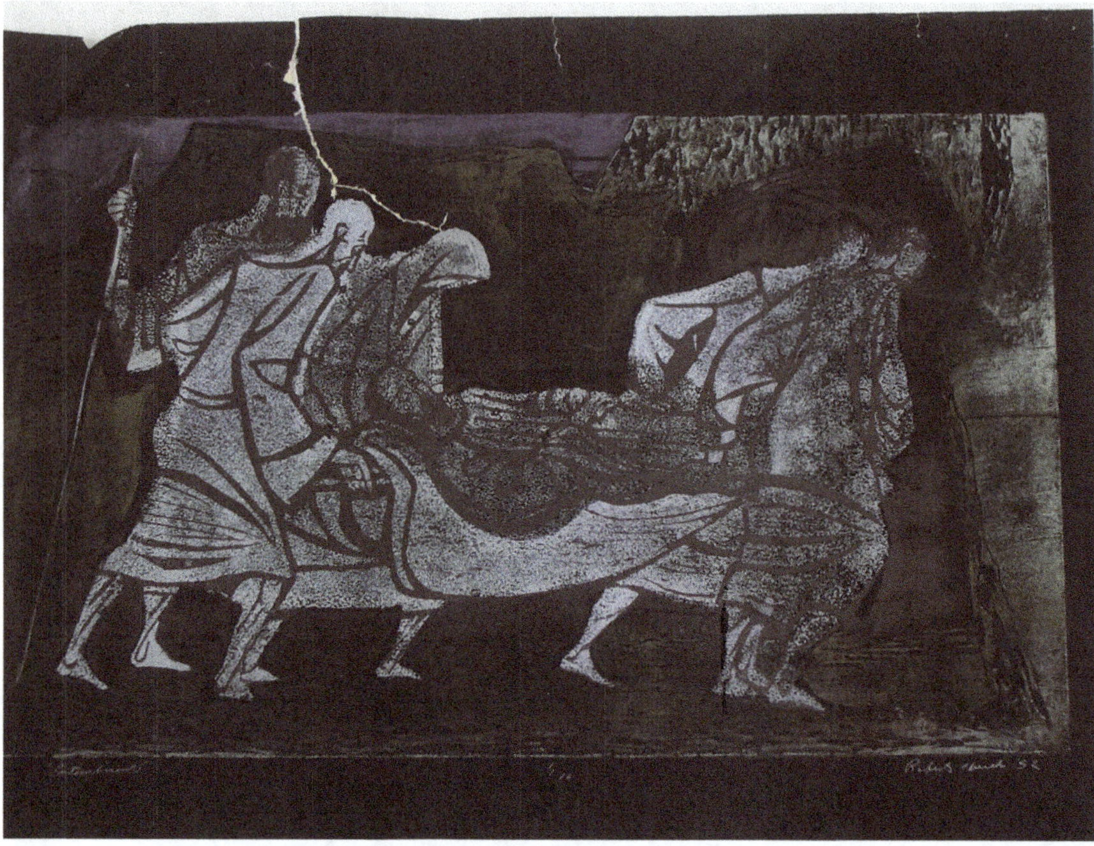

"Entombment" (1952)

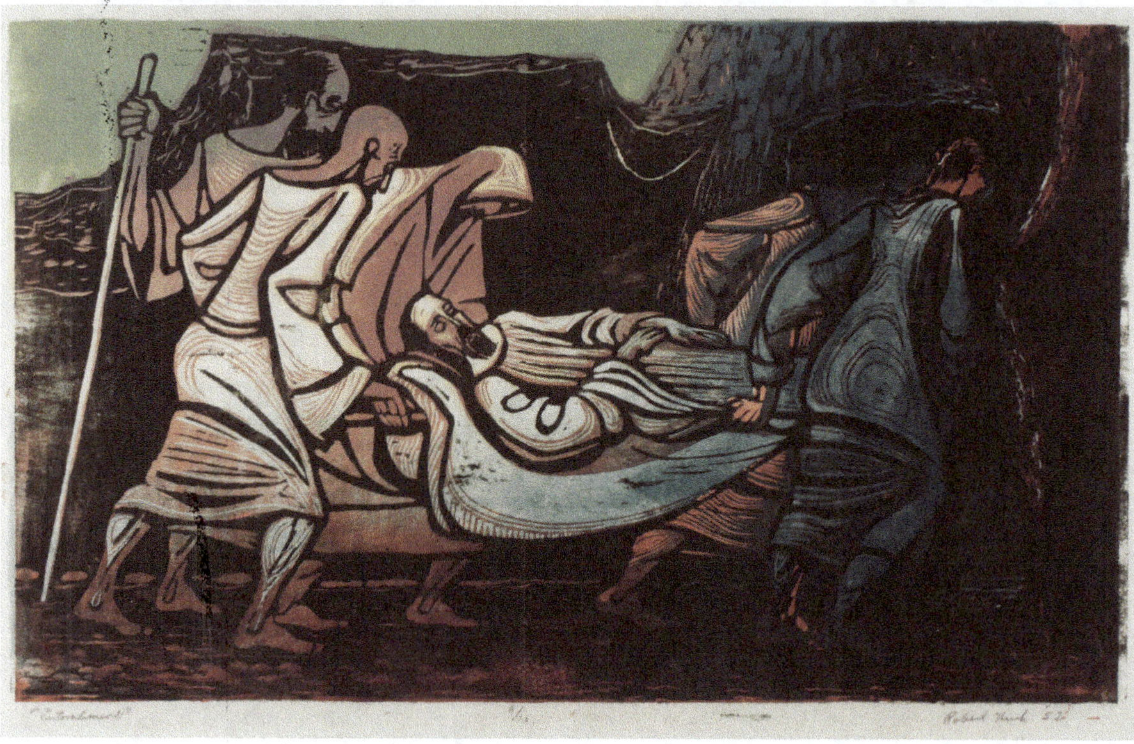

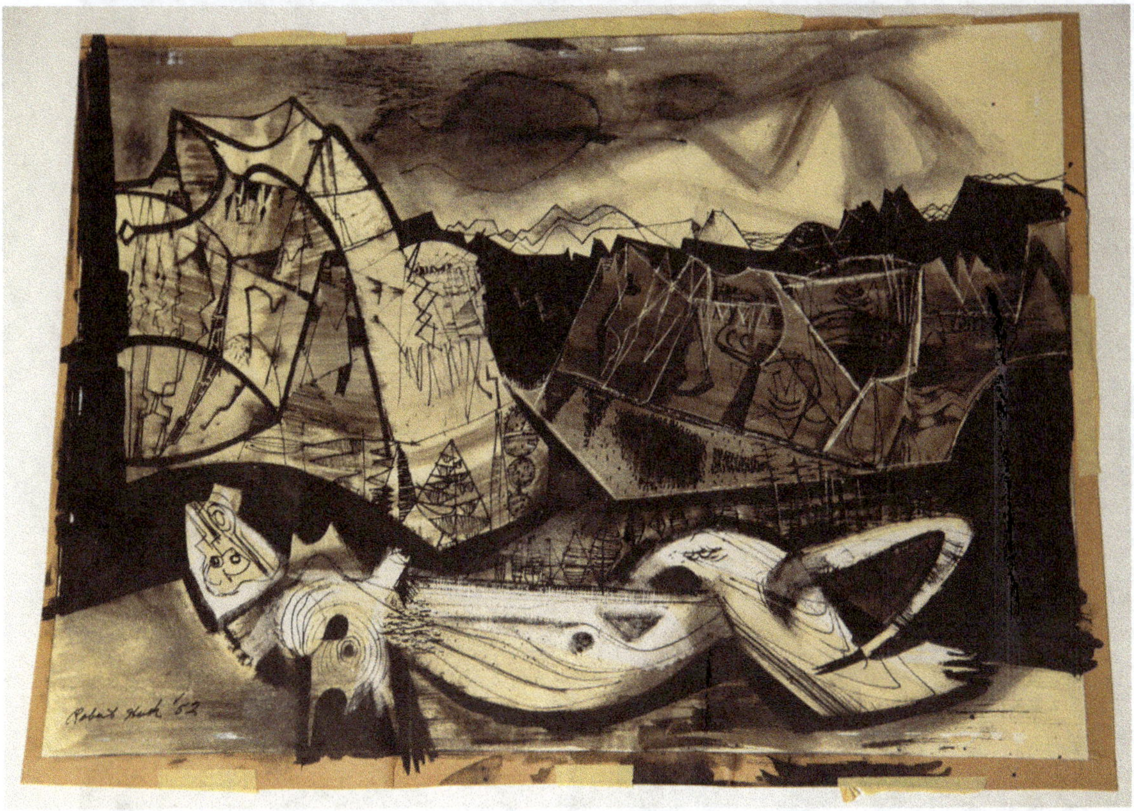

"Old Mountains" (1953)

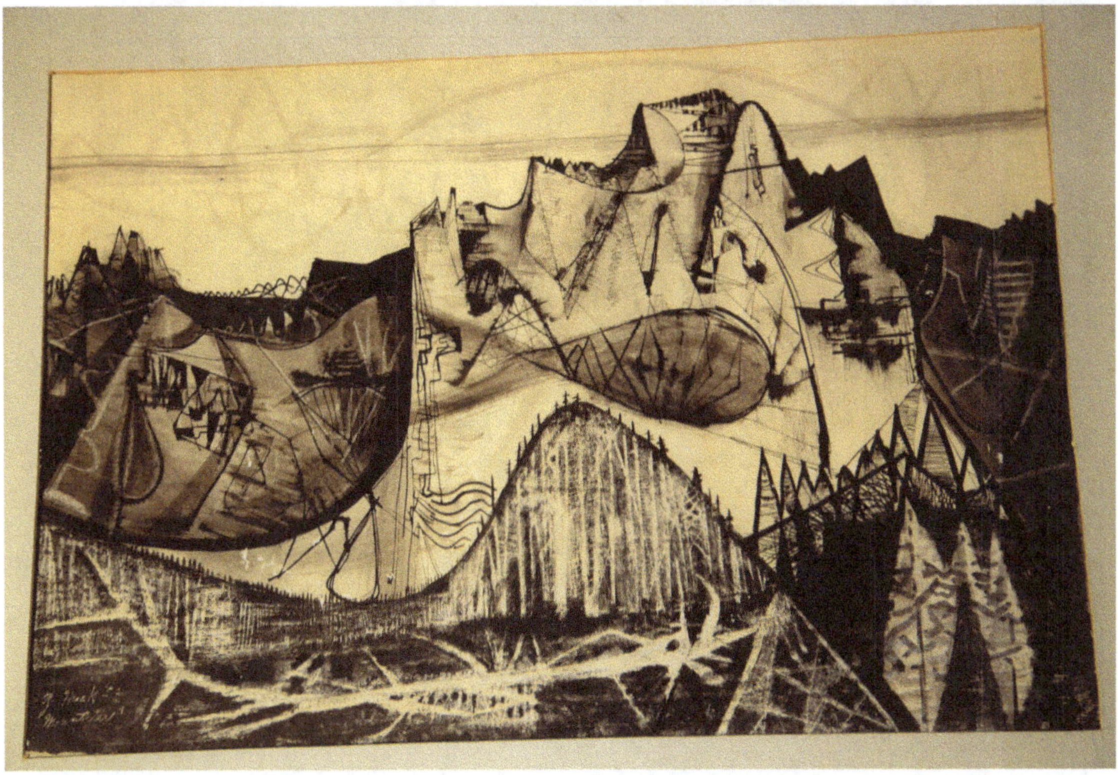

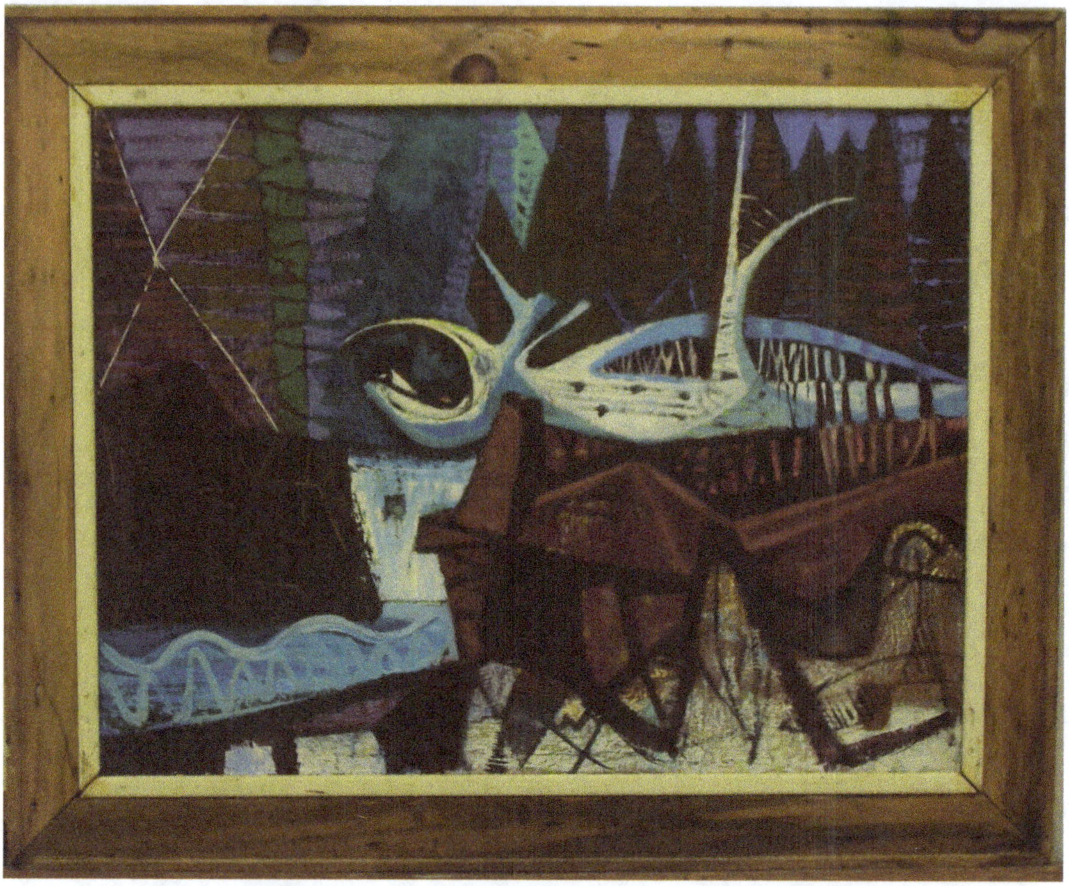

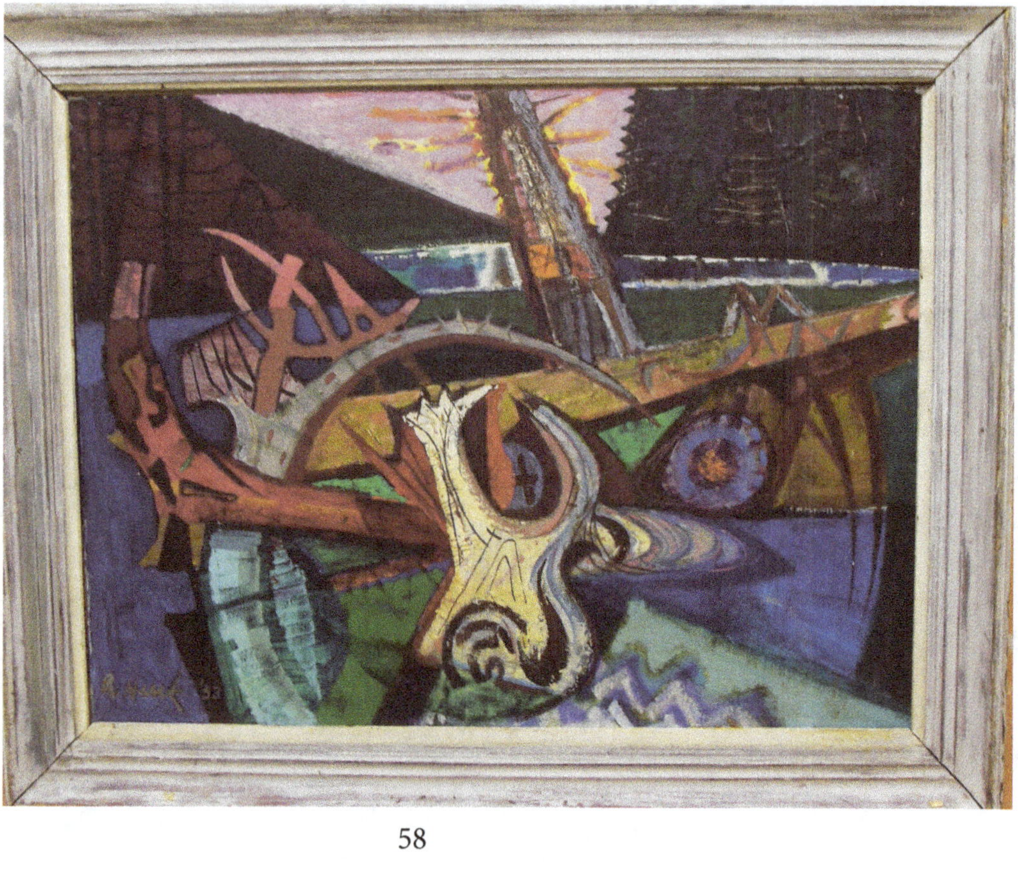

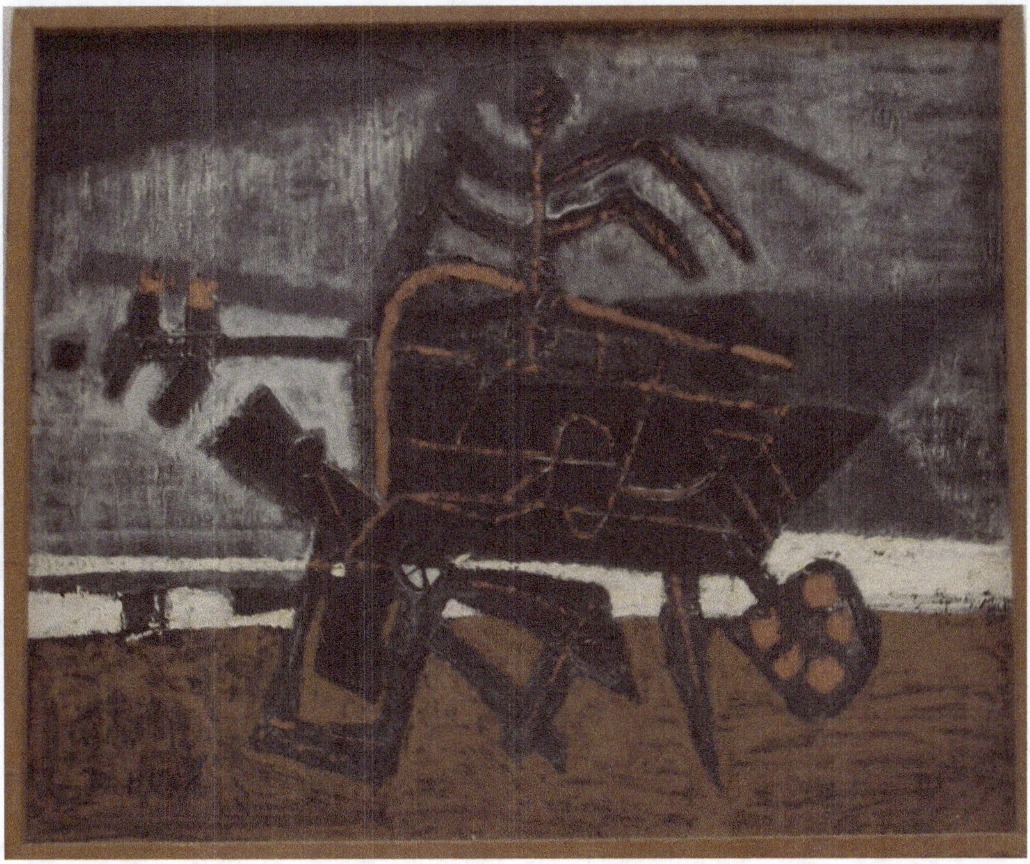

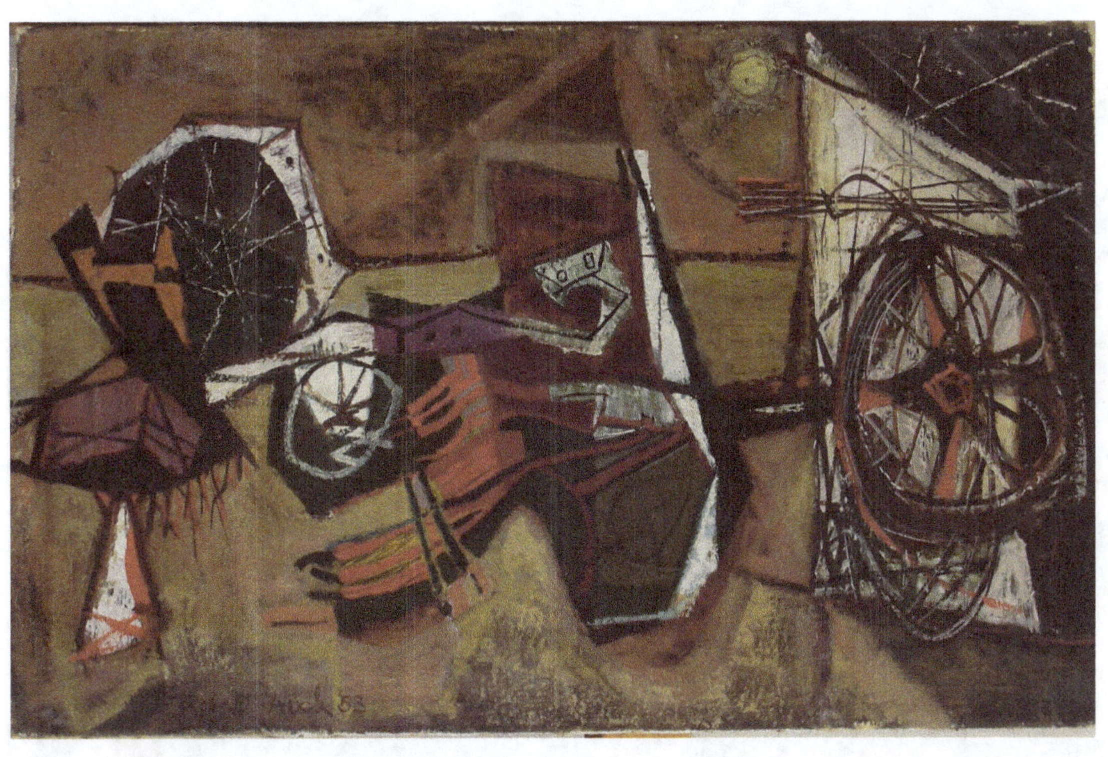

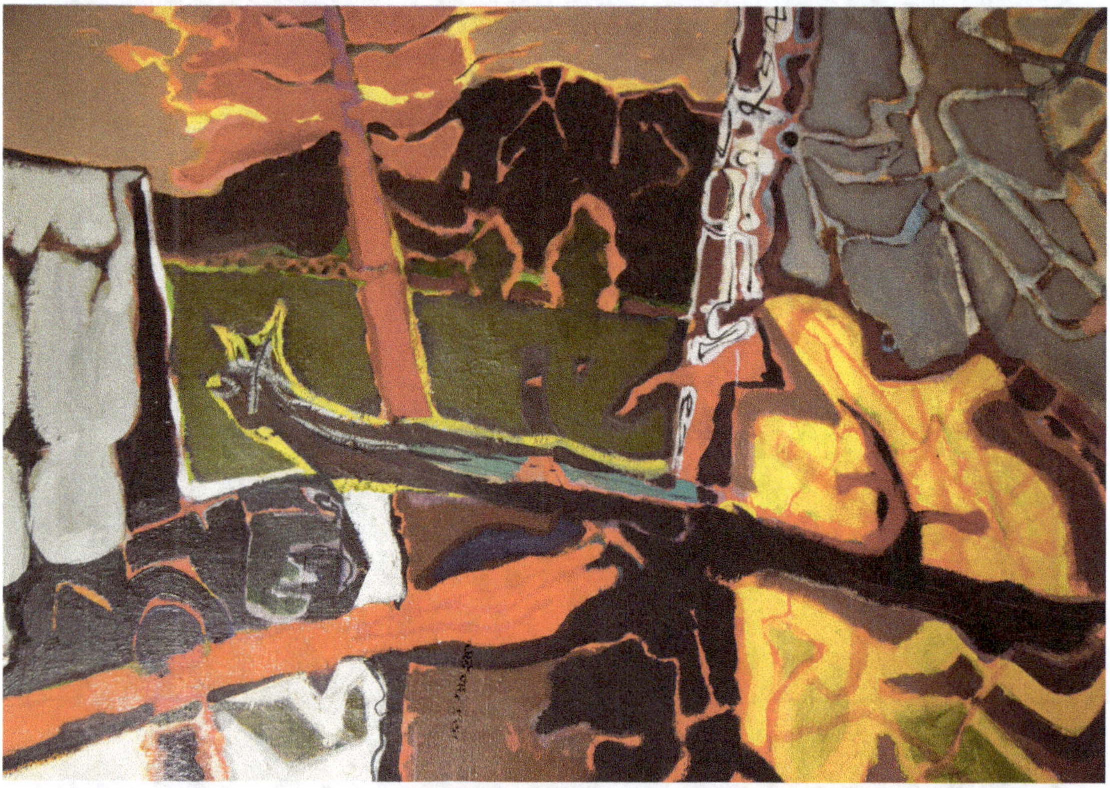

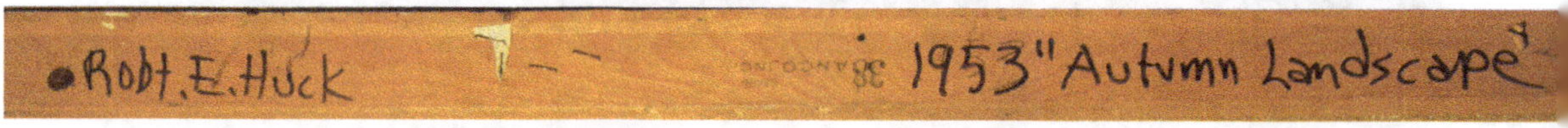

Robt. E. Huck
1953 "Autumn Landscape"

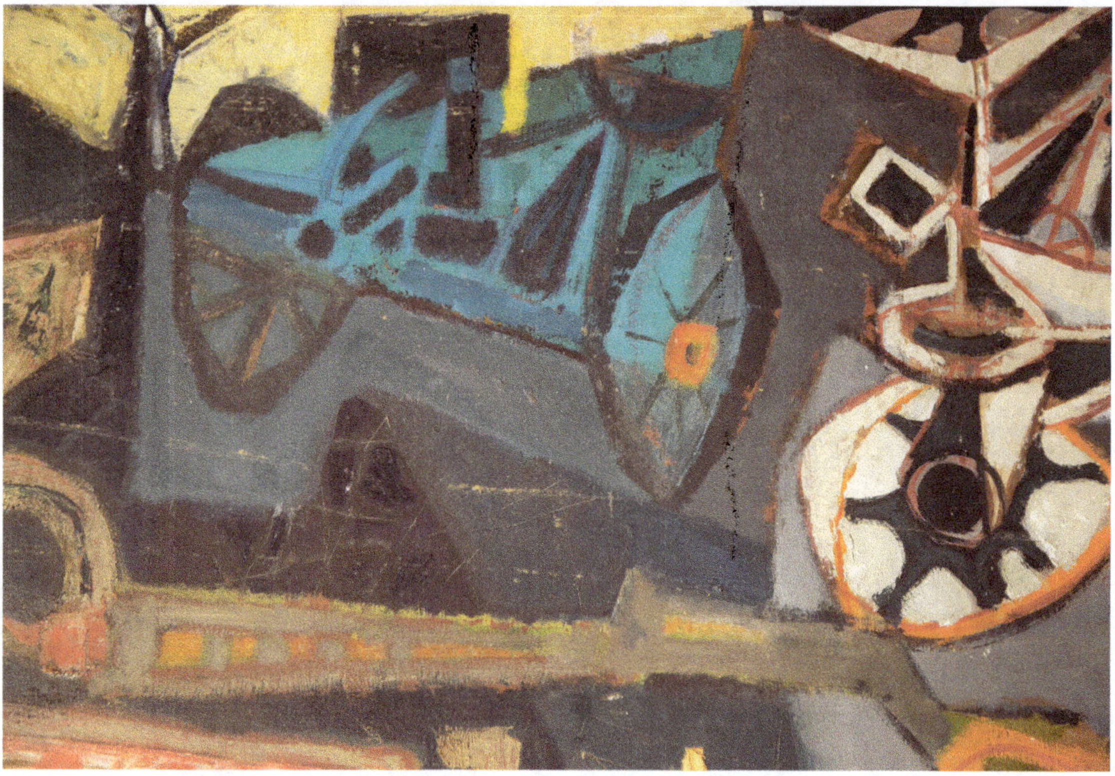

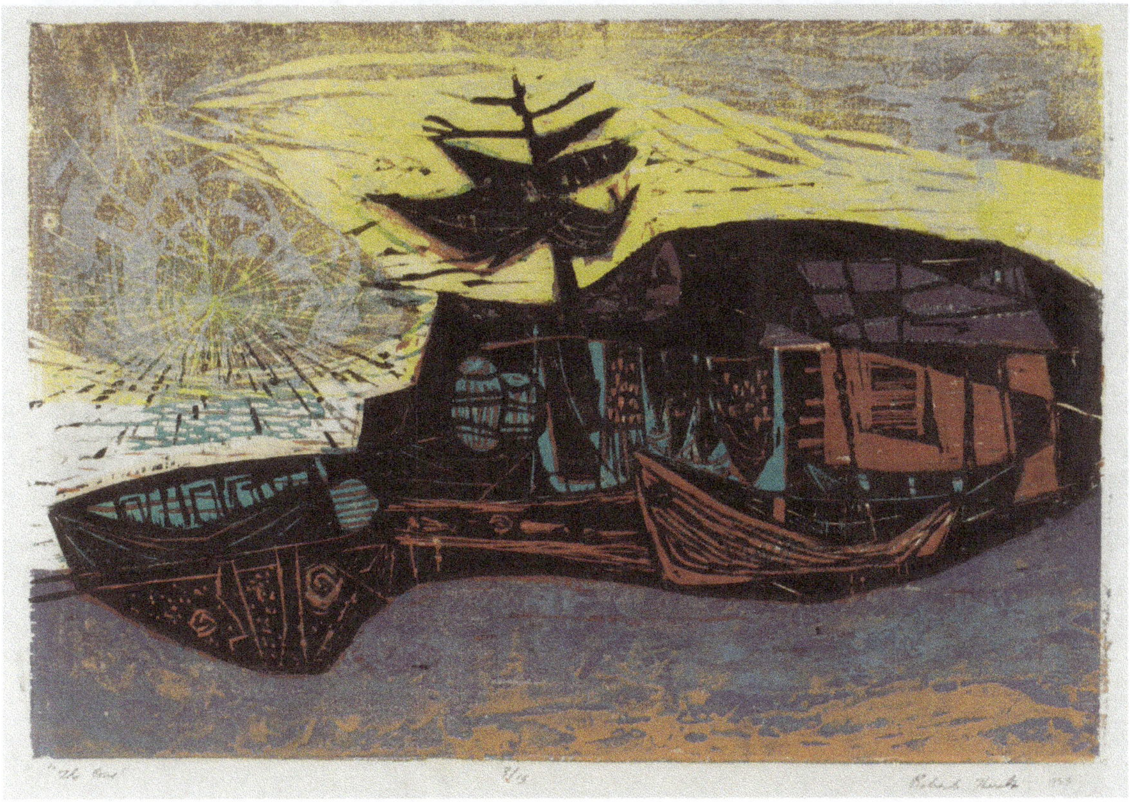

"The Cove" and "Sailor's Cottage" (1953)

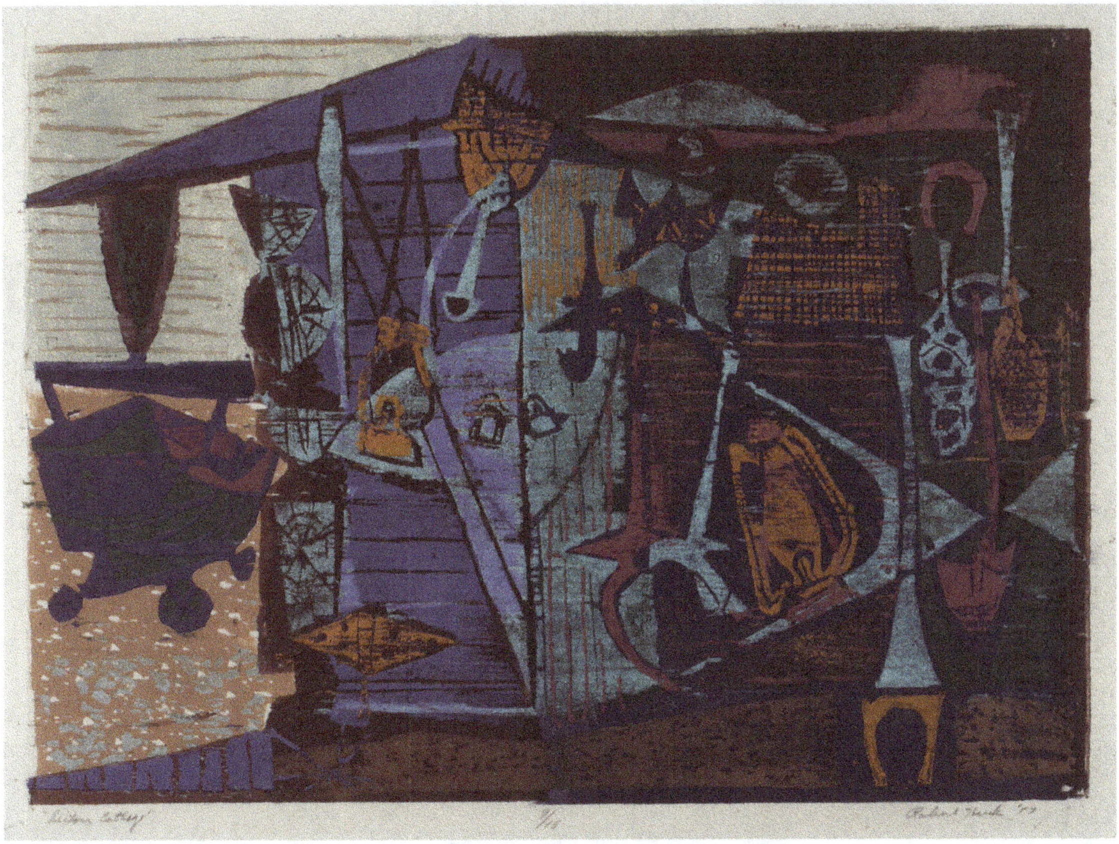

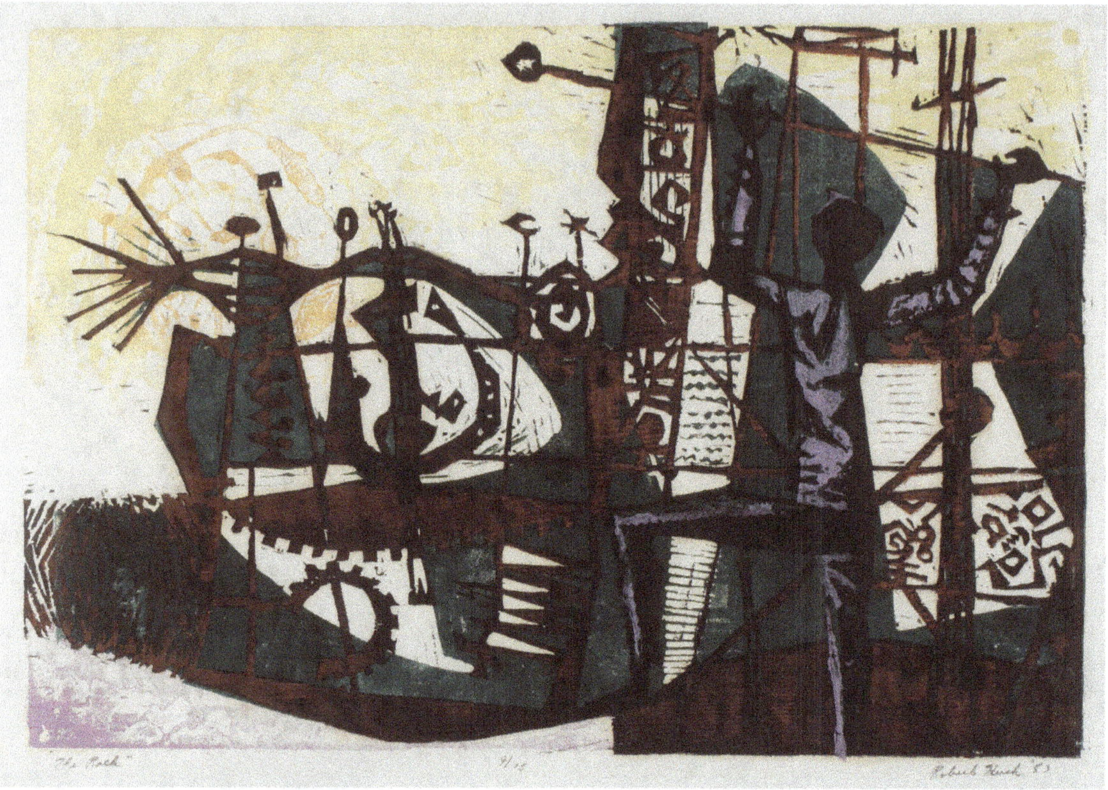

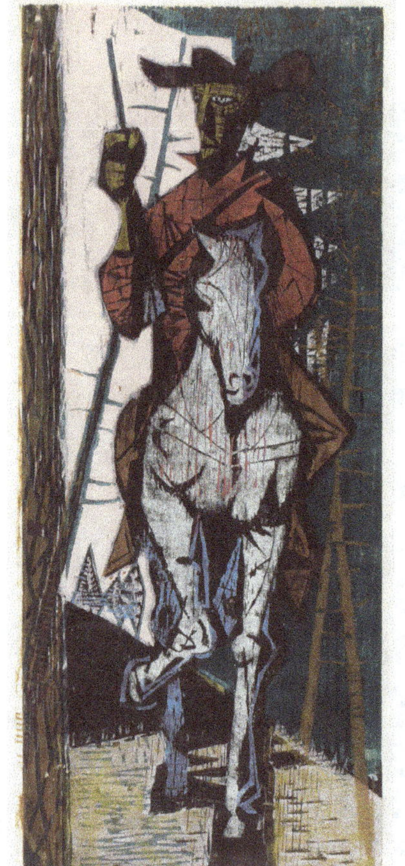

"The Rack" (1953)

"Equestrian" (1953)

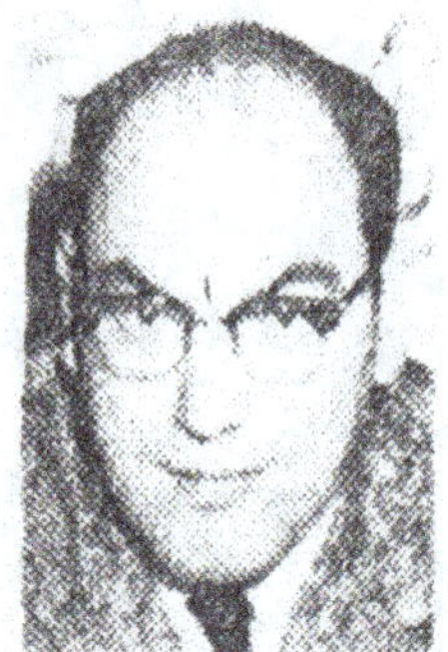

Prof. Huck

Since 1947, Huck has had 56 art pieces accepted in shows and exhibitions throughout the Midwest and on both coasts. Block prints, oil and water color paintings and sculptures have received national recognition. The Seattle Press Assn. is sponsoring a one-man traveling art show of his paintings as a community cultural project. This show is presently moving through the cities of the state of Washington.

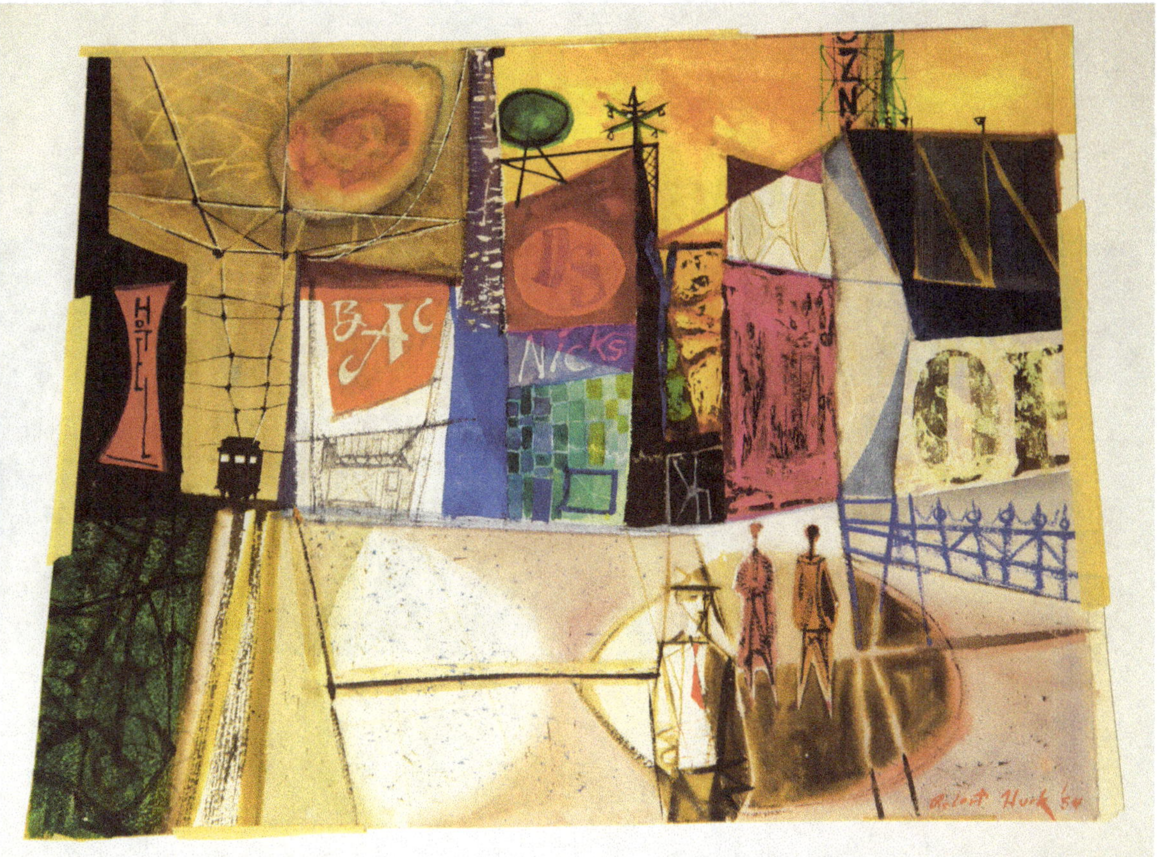

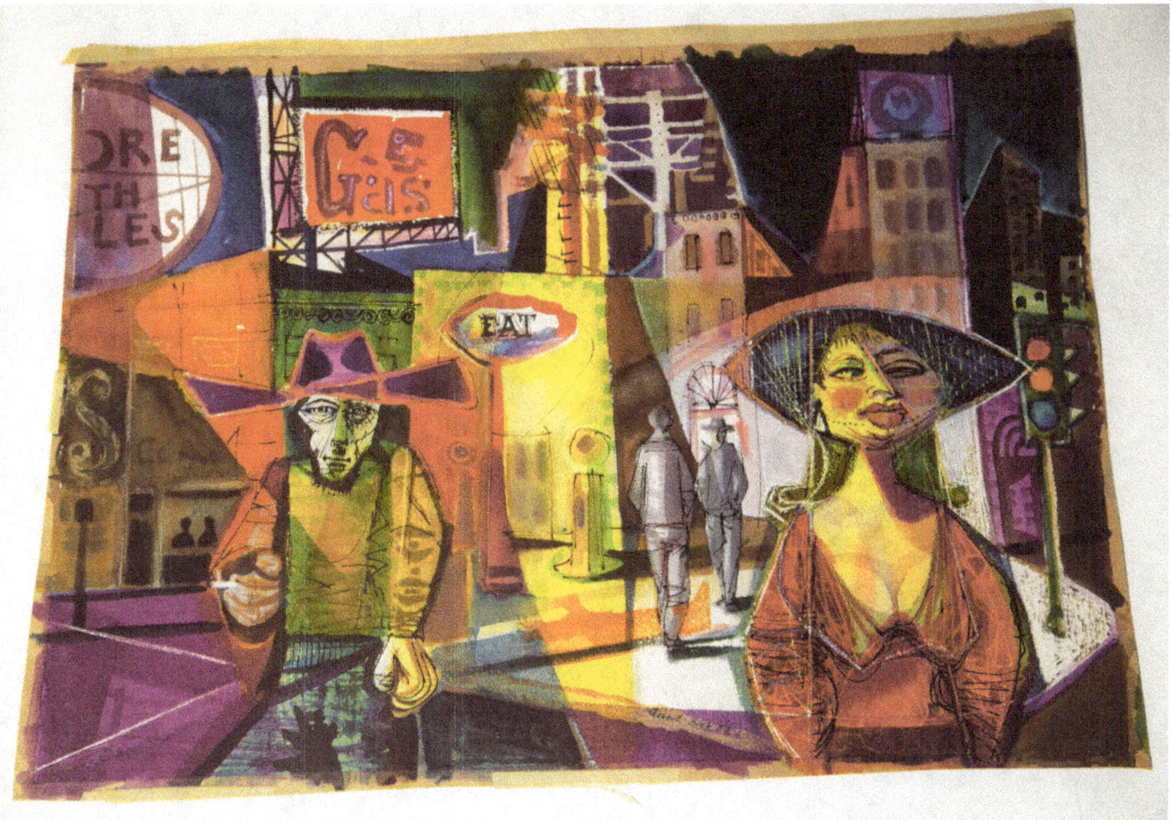

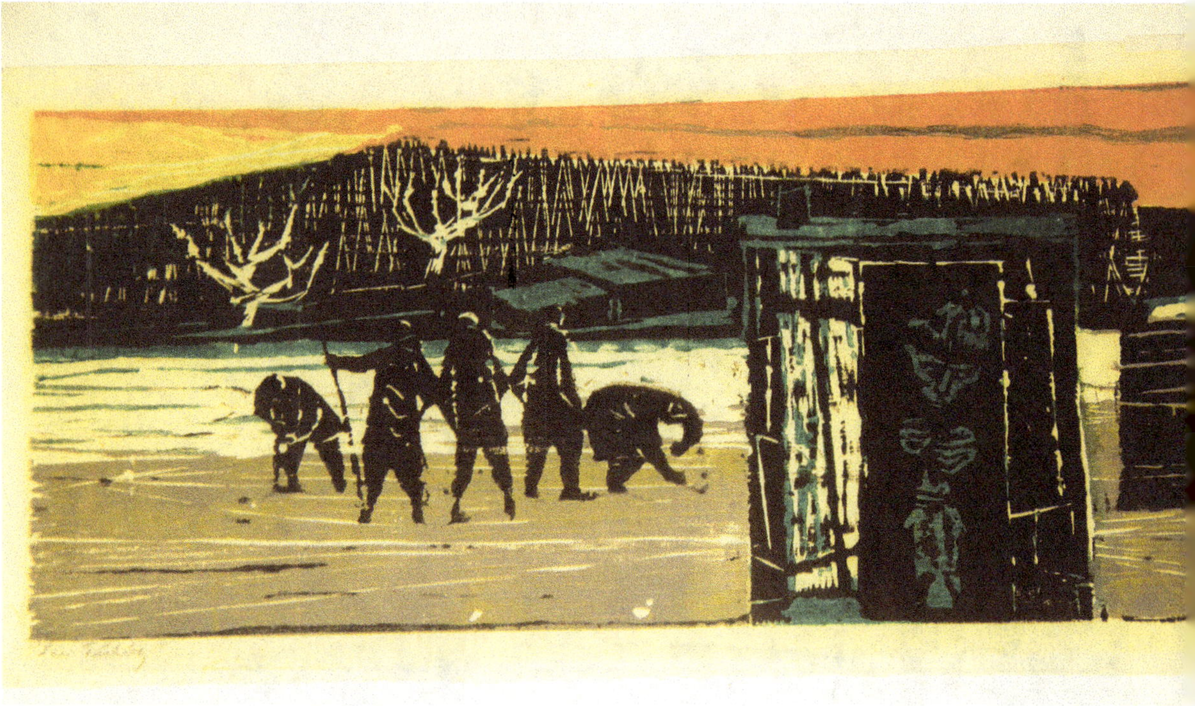

"Ice Fishing" (1954)

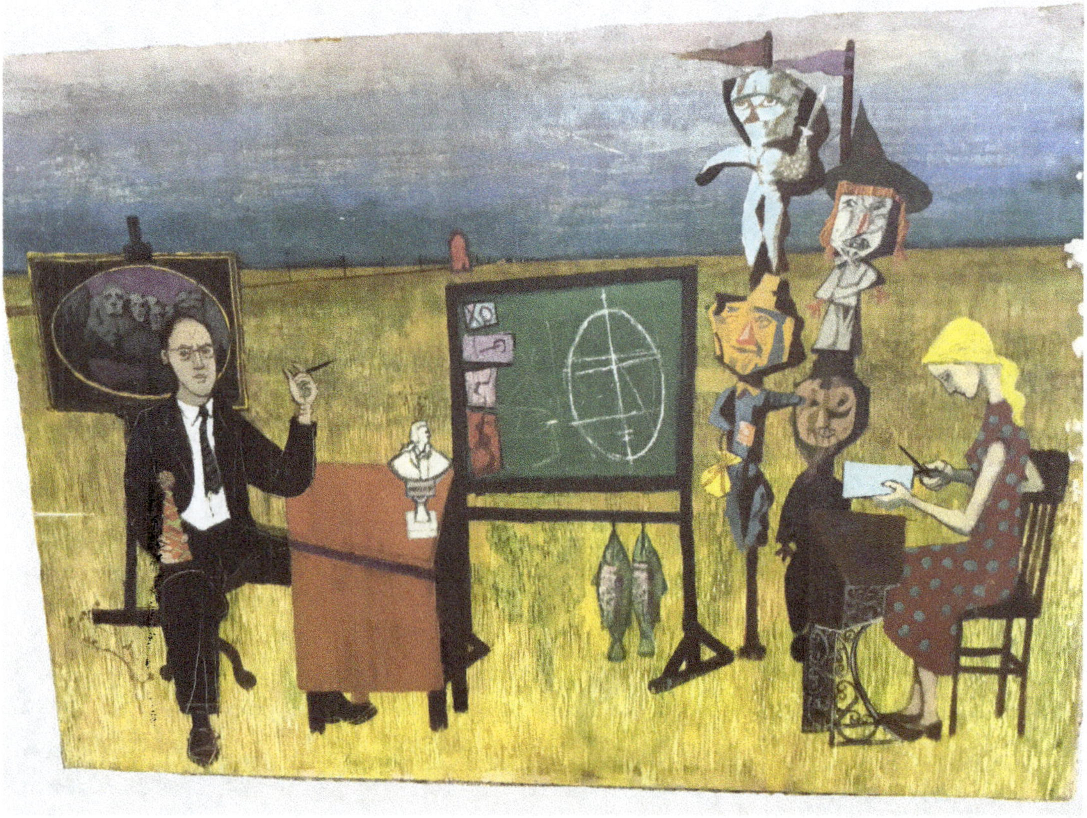

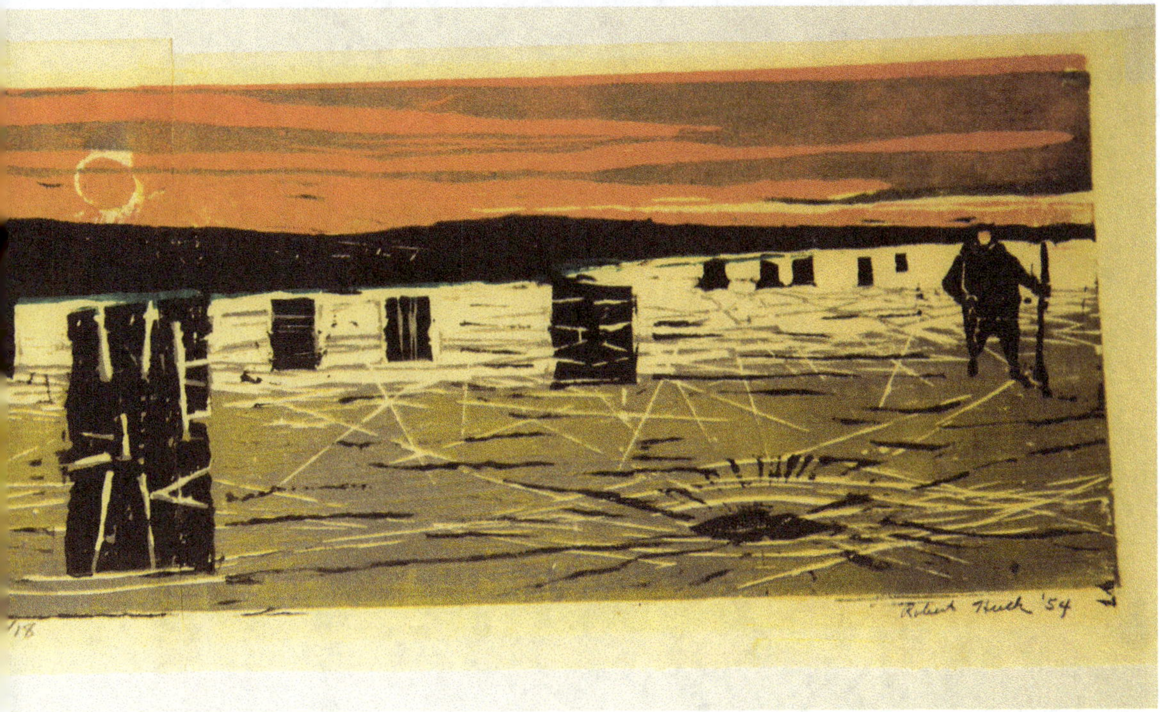

"The Ichthyologist" (1954)

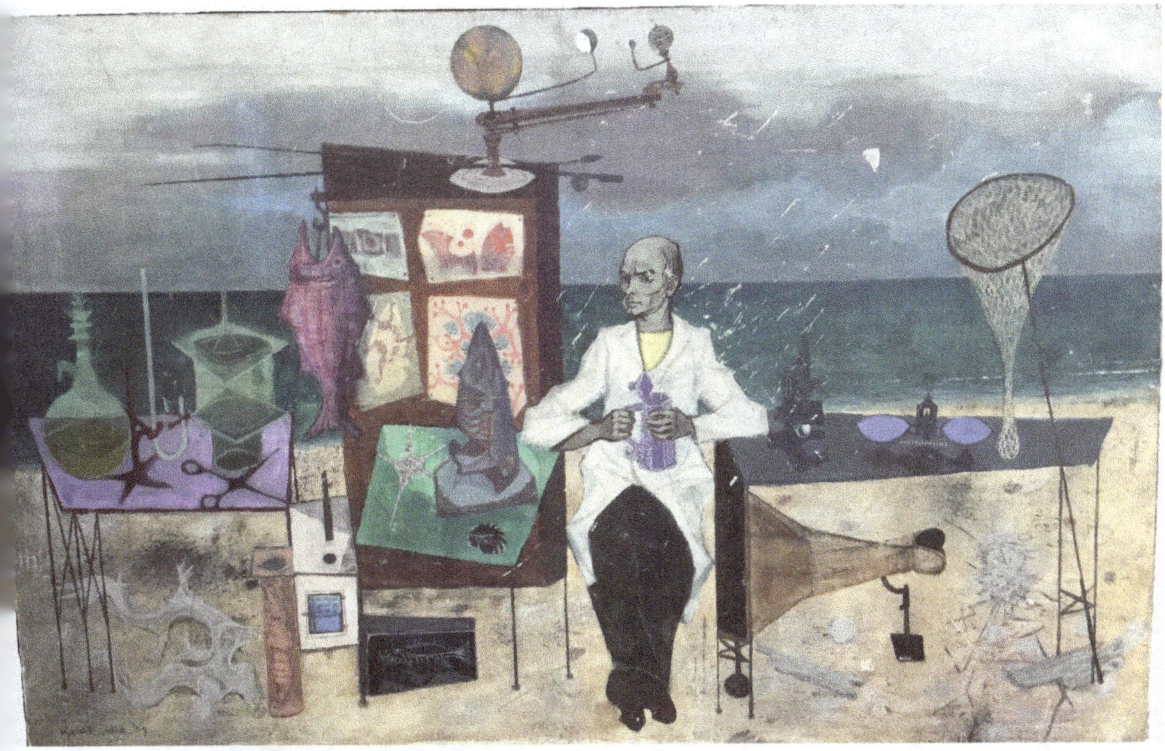

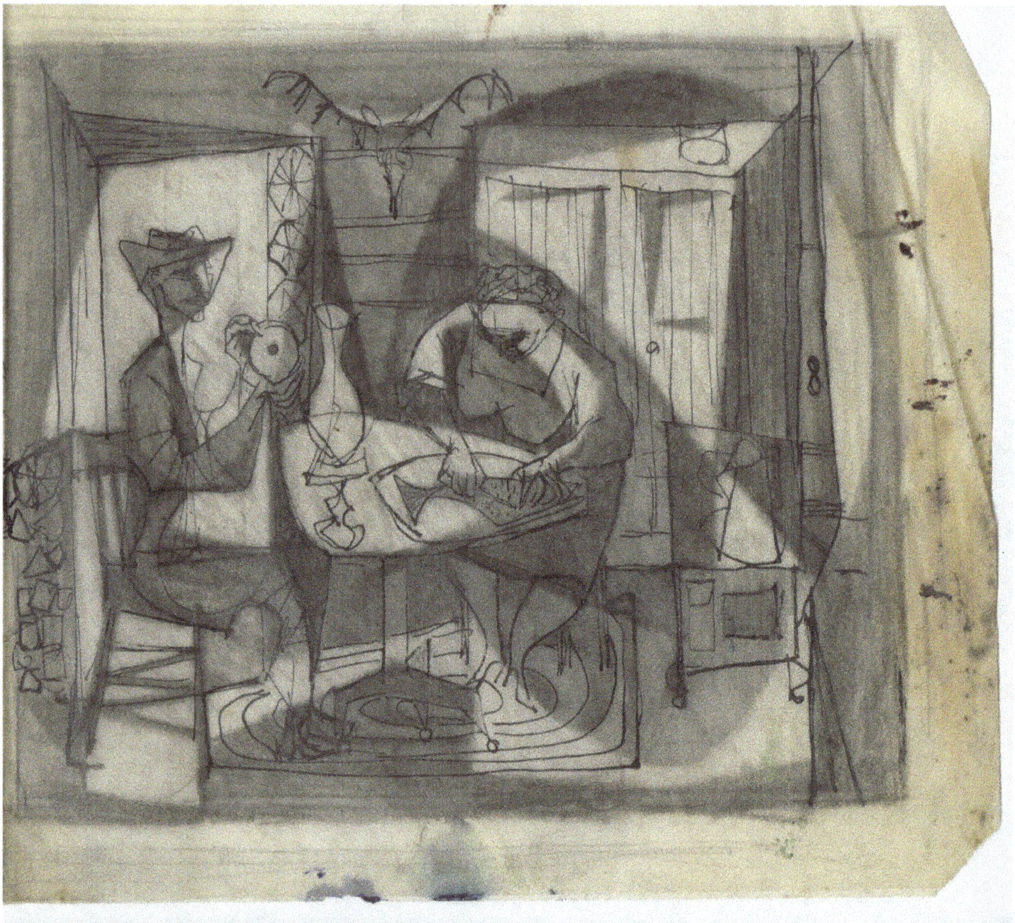

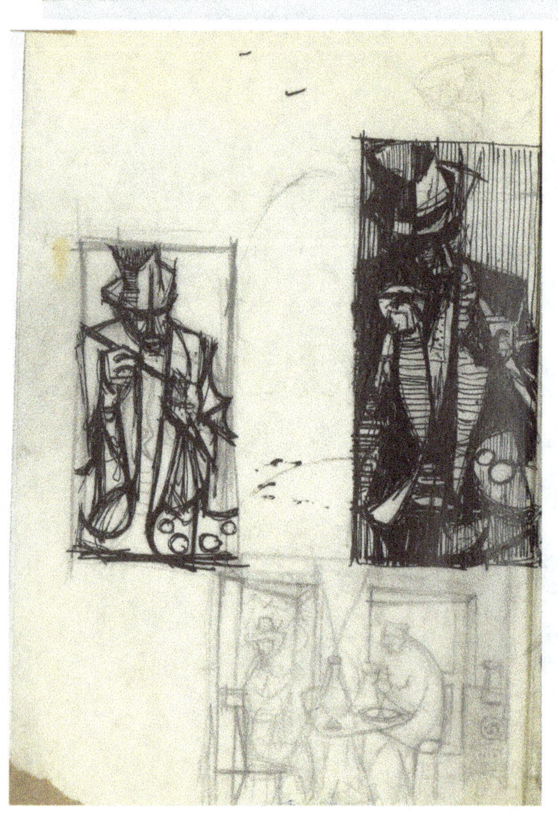

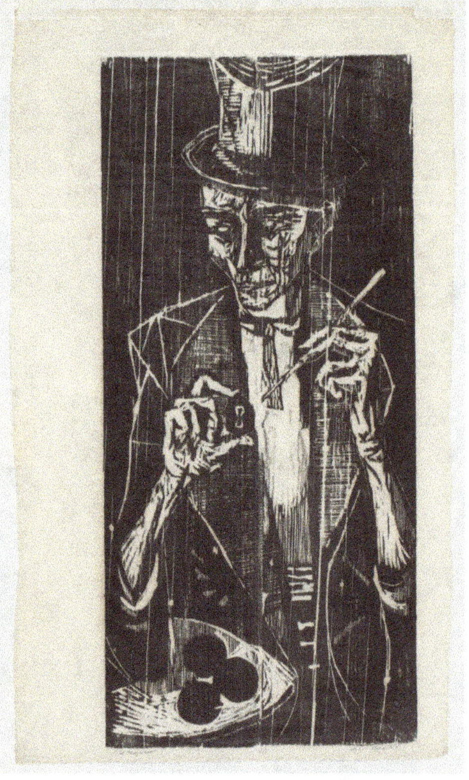

In the **spring of 1954**, Huck receives a Fulbright Scholarship entitling him to study painting in Rome, Italy. He and Dorothy will spend a year in Europe, returning to America in August, 1955.

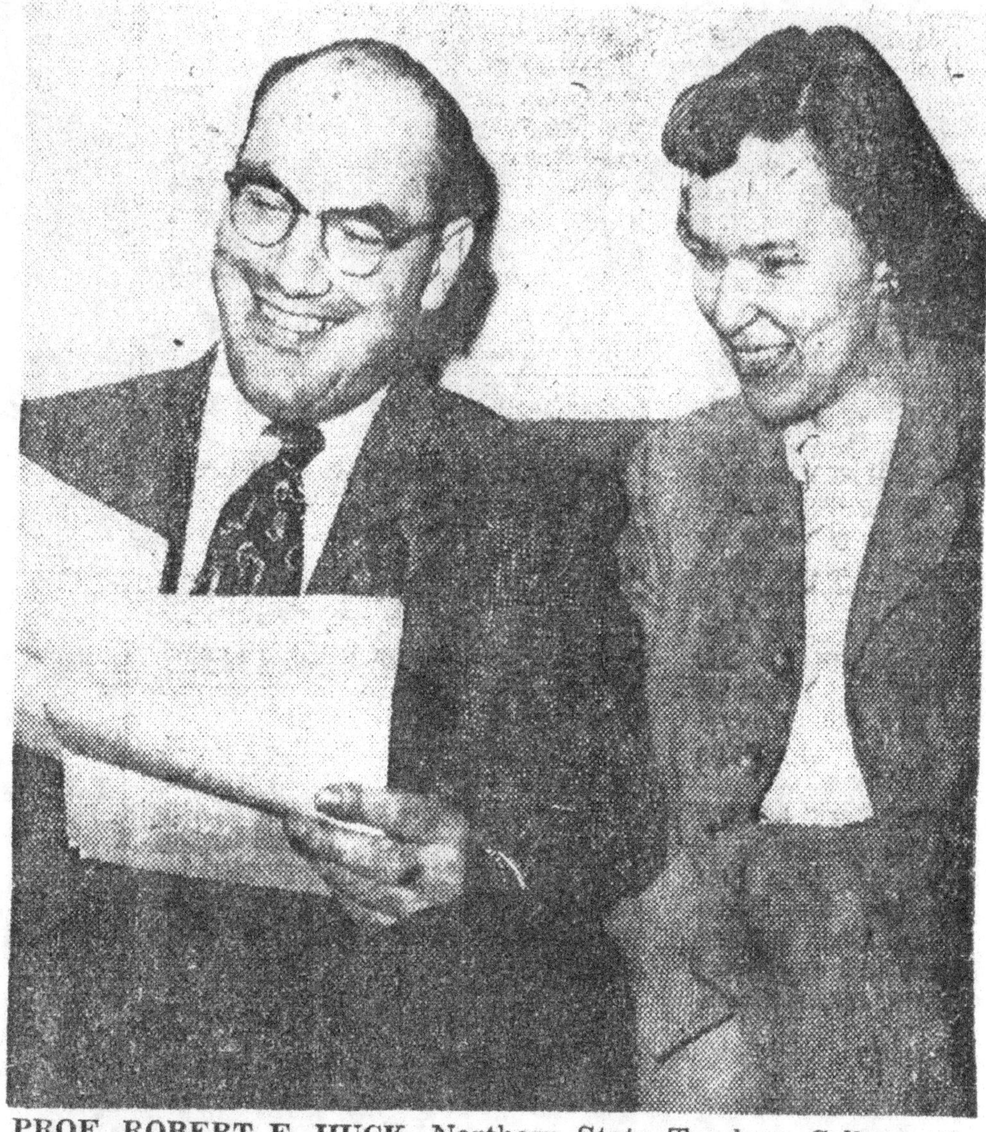

PROF. ROBERT E. HUCK, Northern State Teachers College art instructor and his wife, Dorothy, read a letter from the Department of State informing Prof. Huck that he is a recipient of a Fulbright Scholarship which entitles him to study in Rome, Italy, for one year.

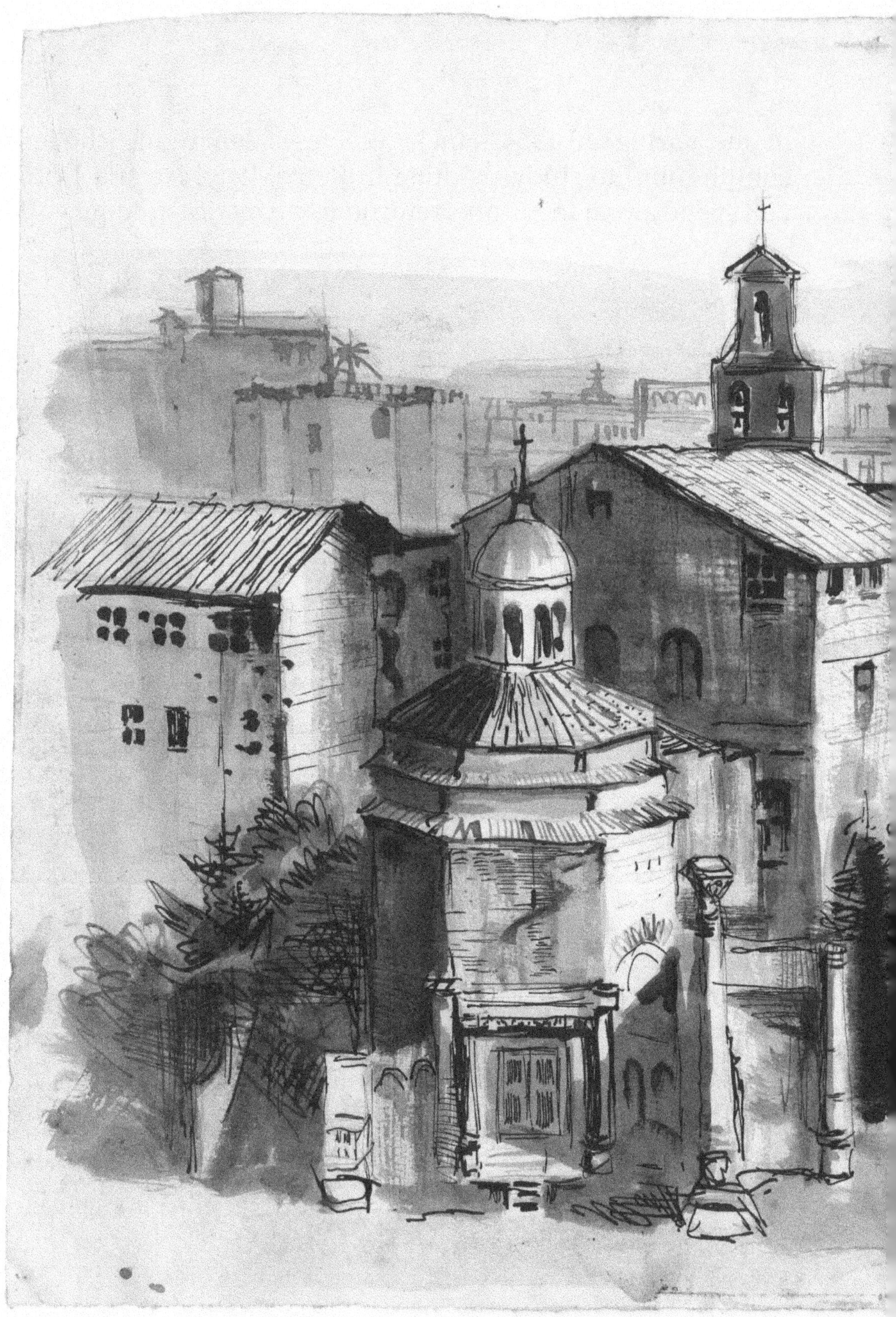

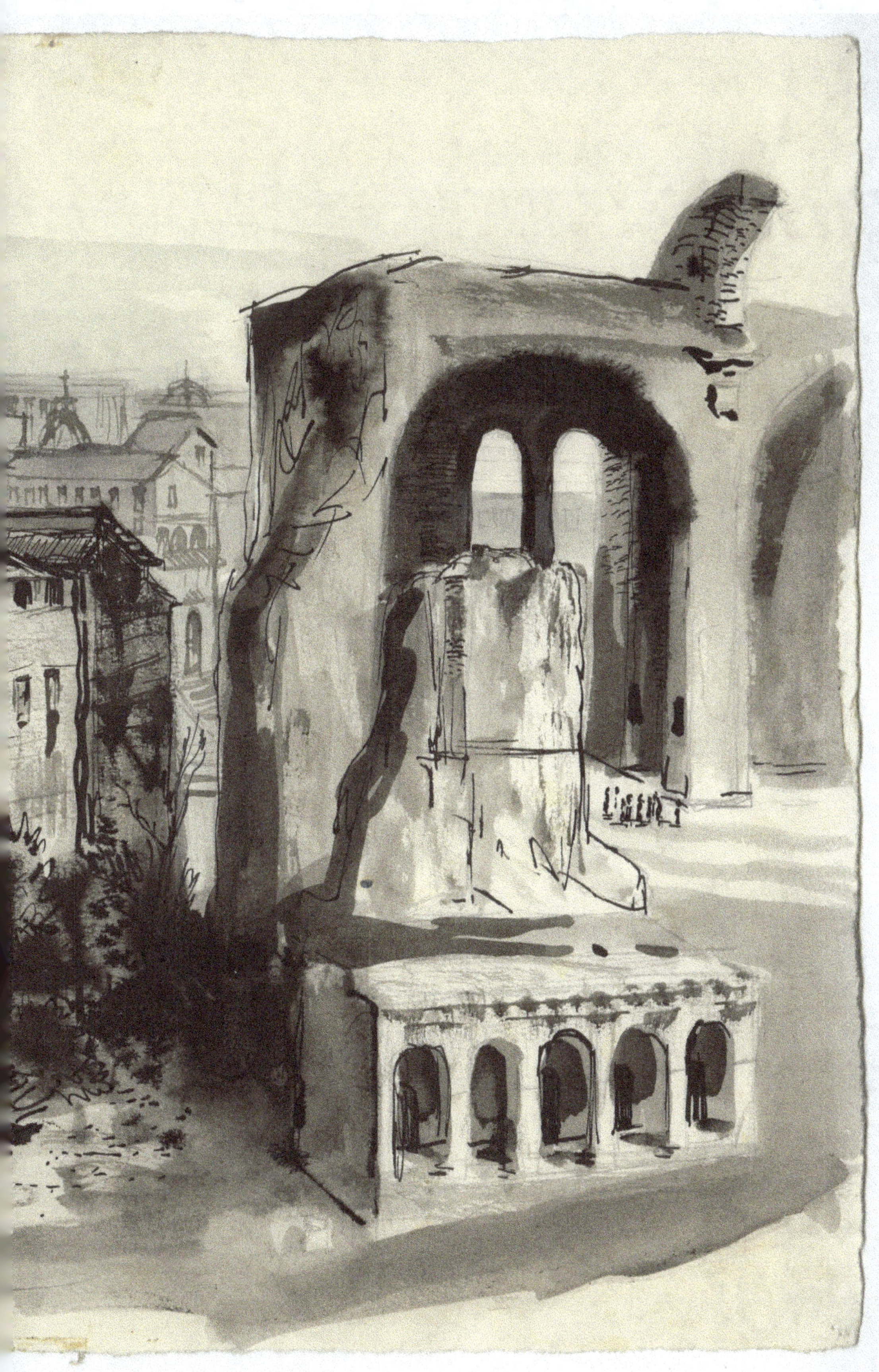

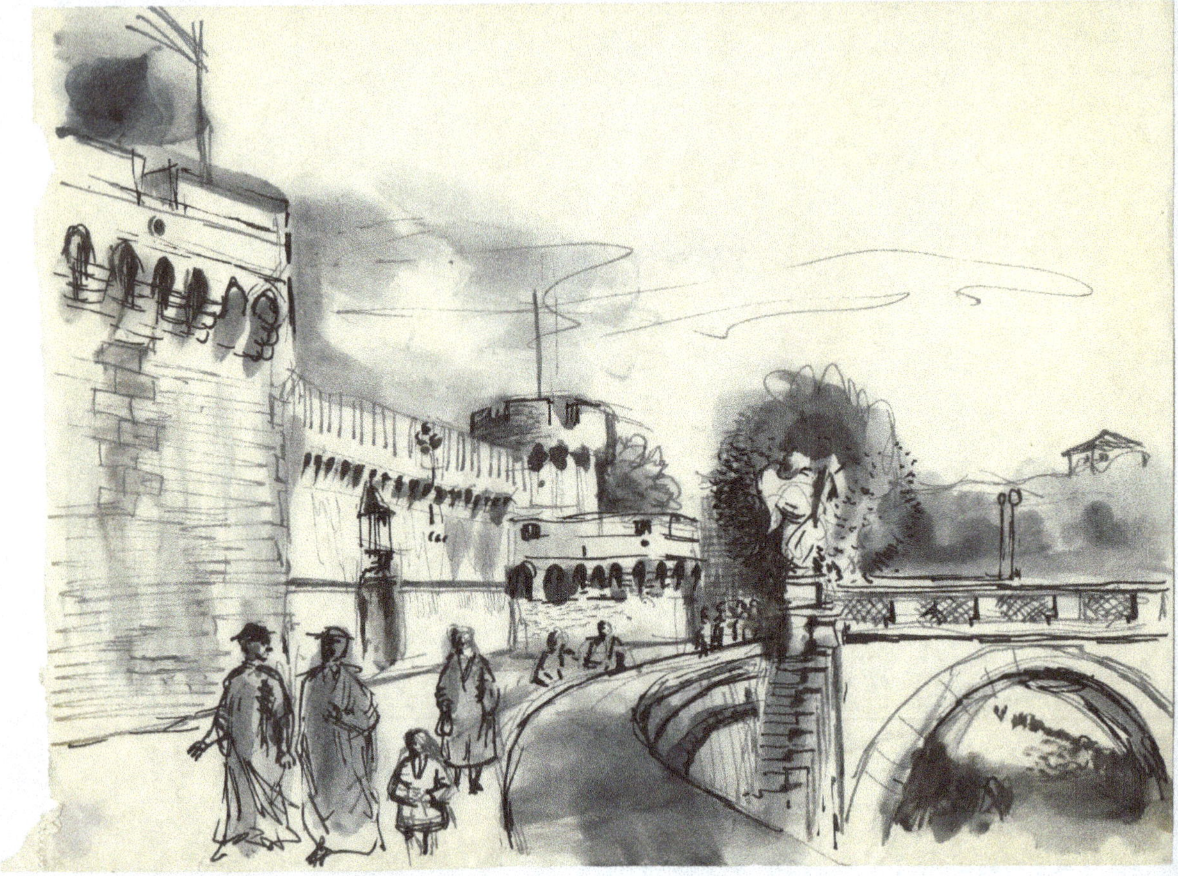

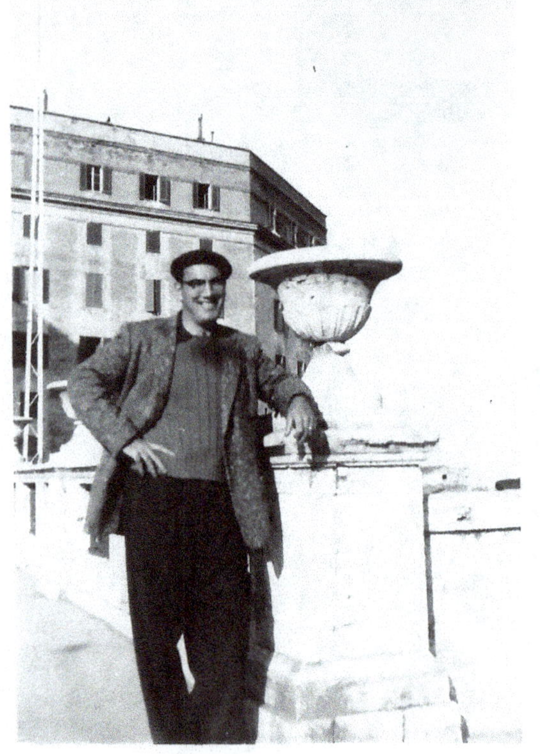

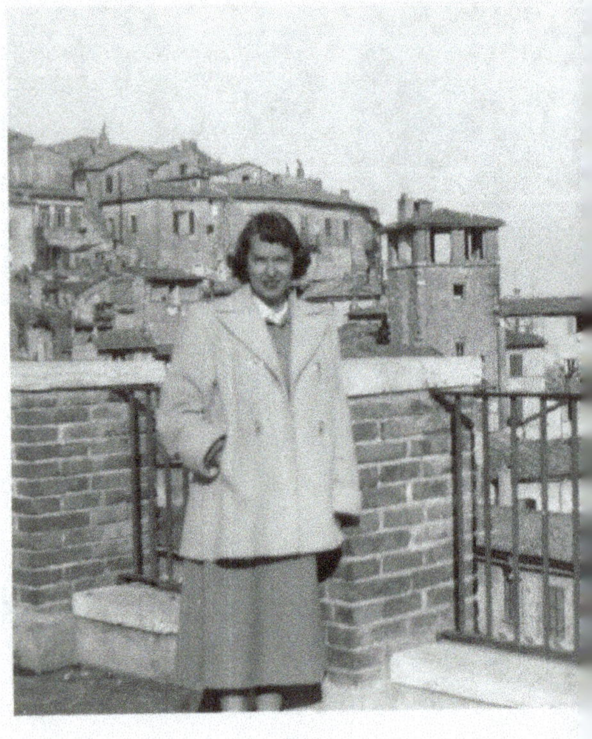

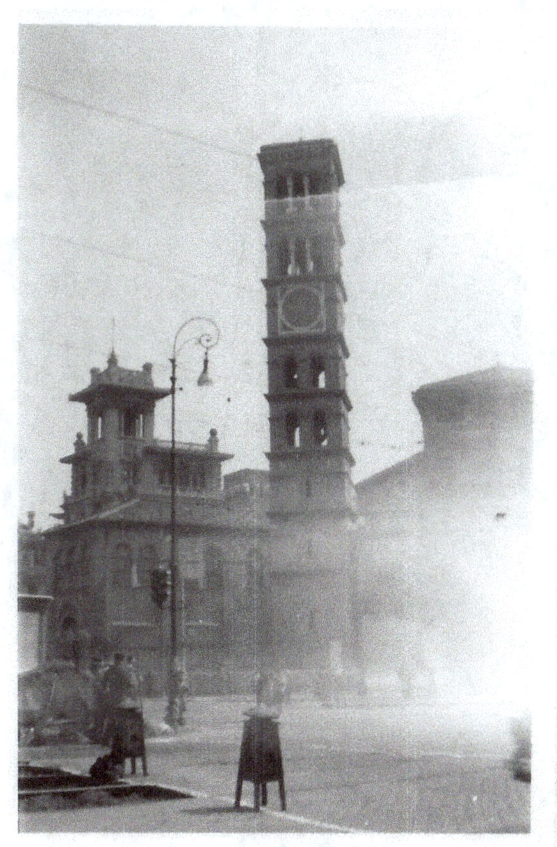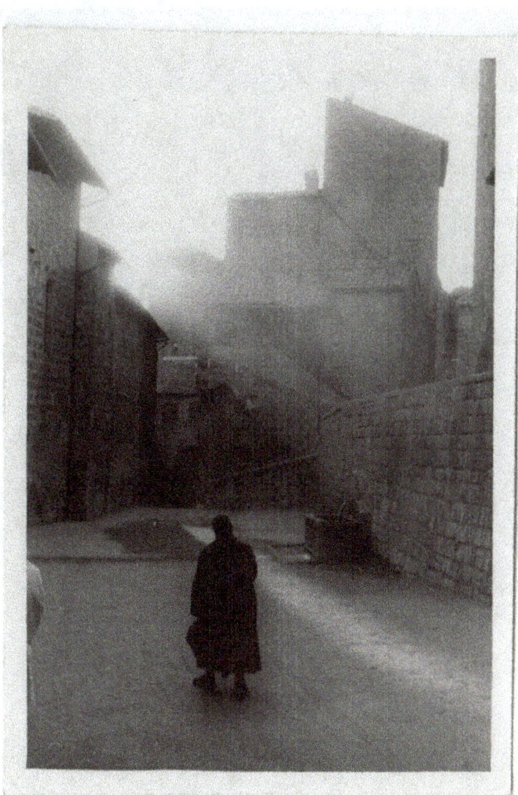

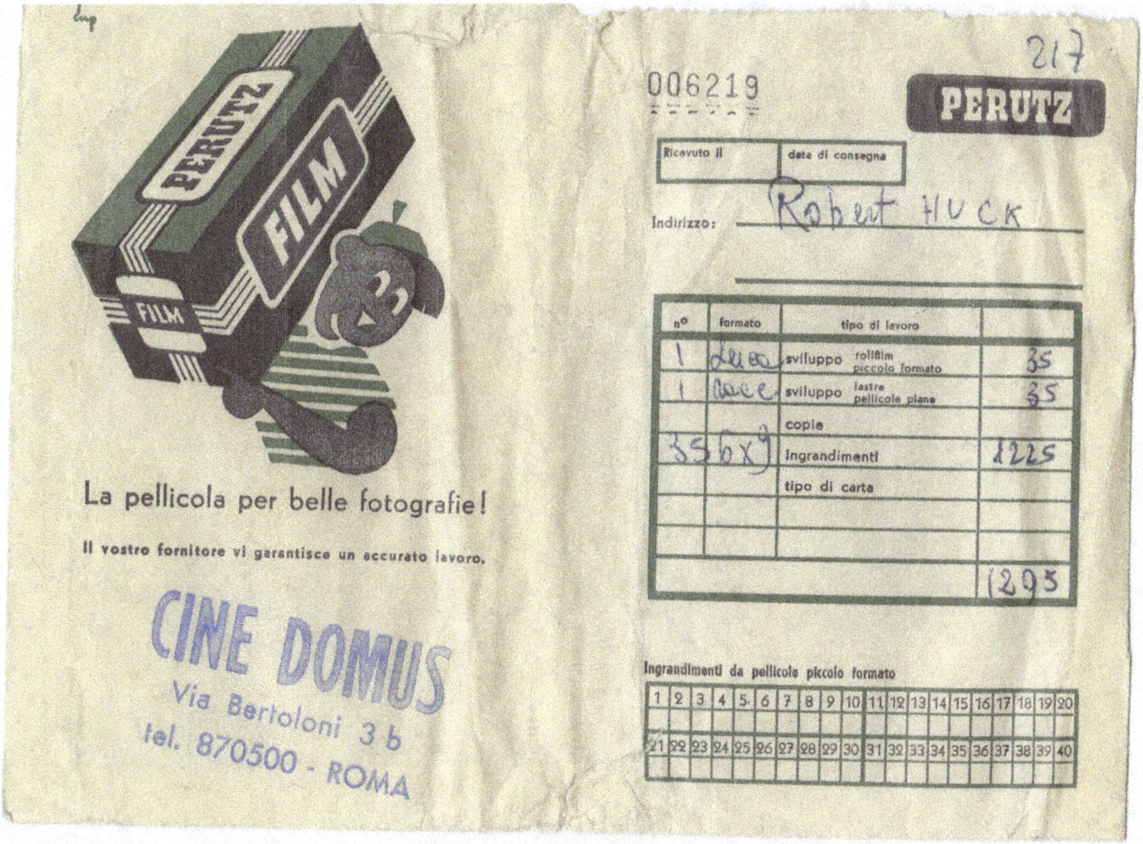

La pellicola per belle fotografie!

Il vostro fornitore vi garantisce un accurato lavoro.

CINE DOMUS
Via Bertoloni 3 b
tel. 870500 - ROMA

006219

PERUTZ

217

Ricevuto il	data di consegna

Indirizzo: Robert HUCK

nº	formato	tipo di lavoro		
1	Leica	sviluppo	rollfilm piccolo formato	35
1	Pace	sviluppo	lastre pellicole piane	35
		copie		
35 6x9		ingrandimenti		1225
		tipo di carta		
				1295

Ingrandimenti da pellicole piccolo formato

1	2	3	4	5	6	7	8	9	10	11	12	13	14	15	16	17	18	19	20
21	22	23	24	25	26	27	28	29	30	31	32	33	34	35	36	37	38	39	40

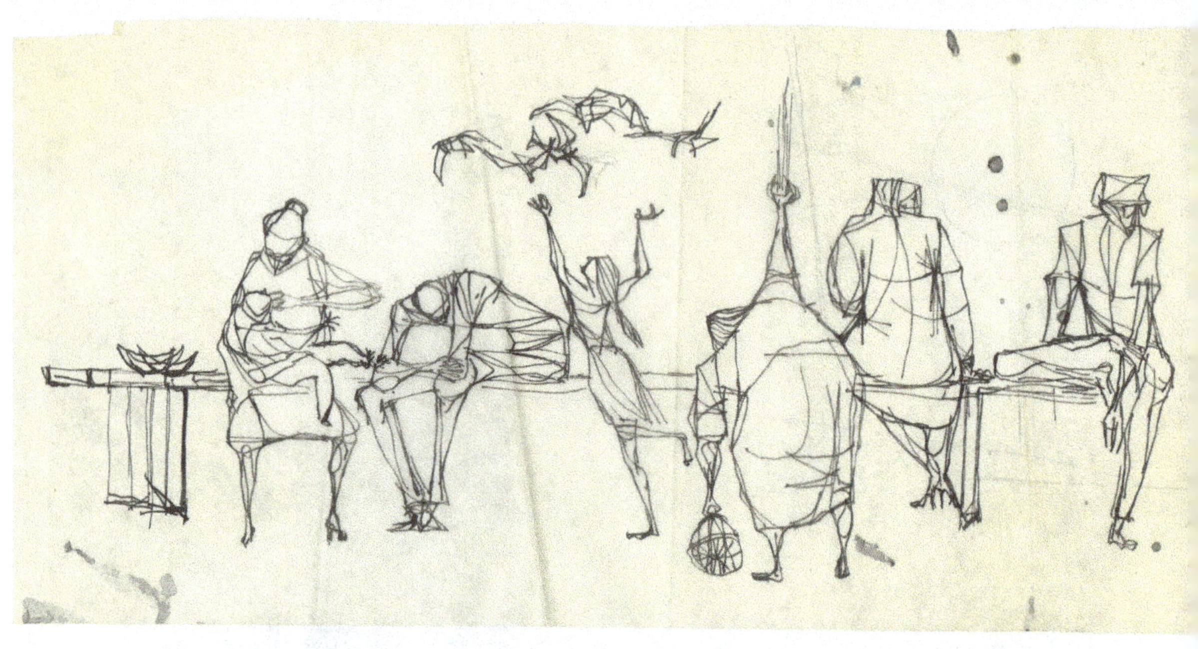

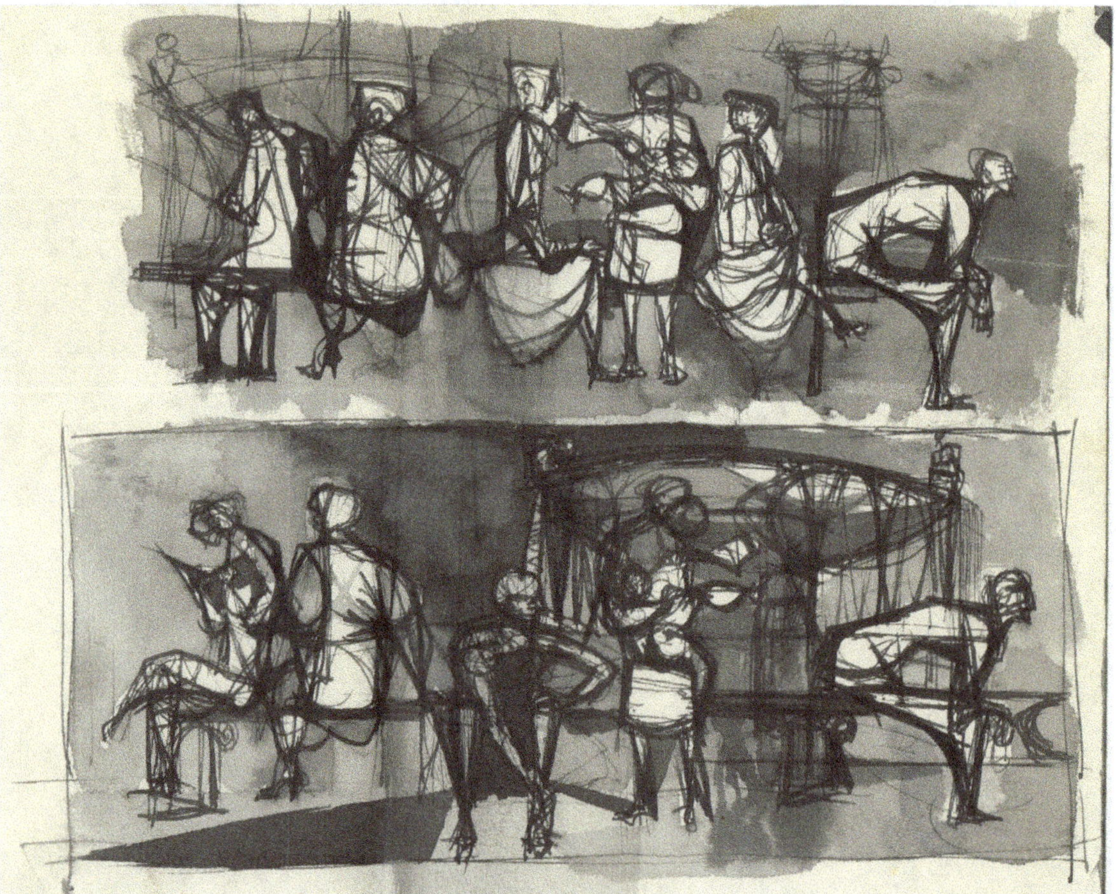

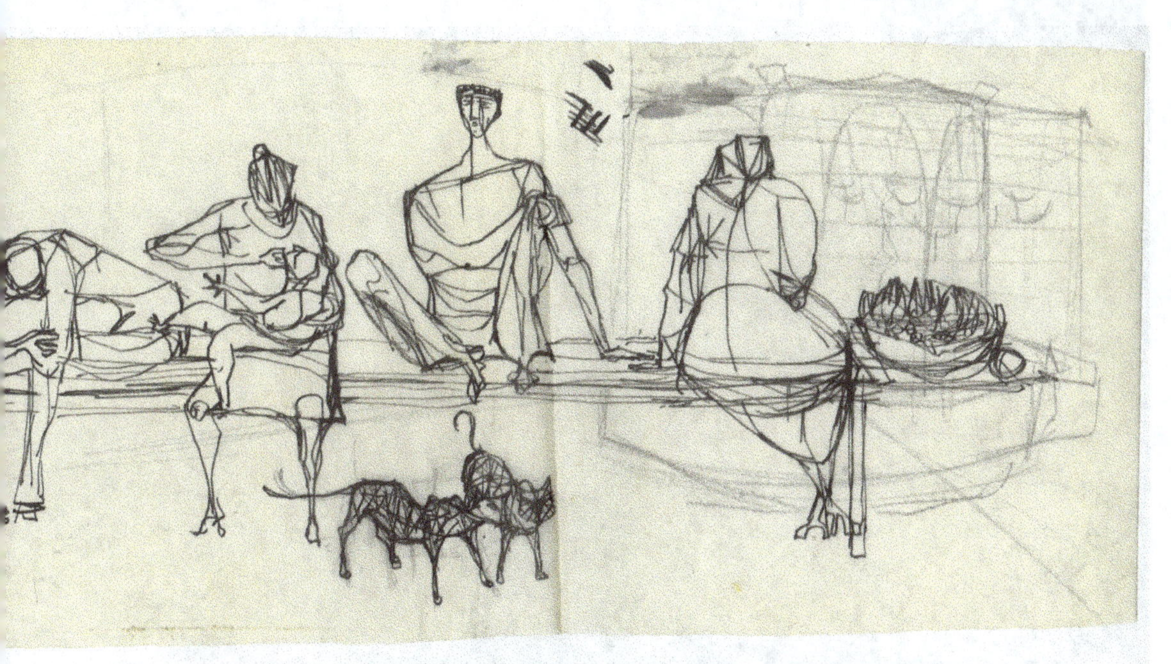

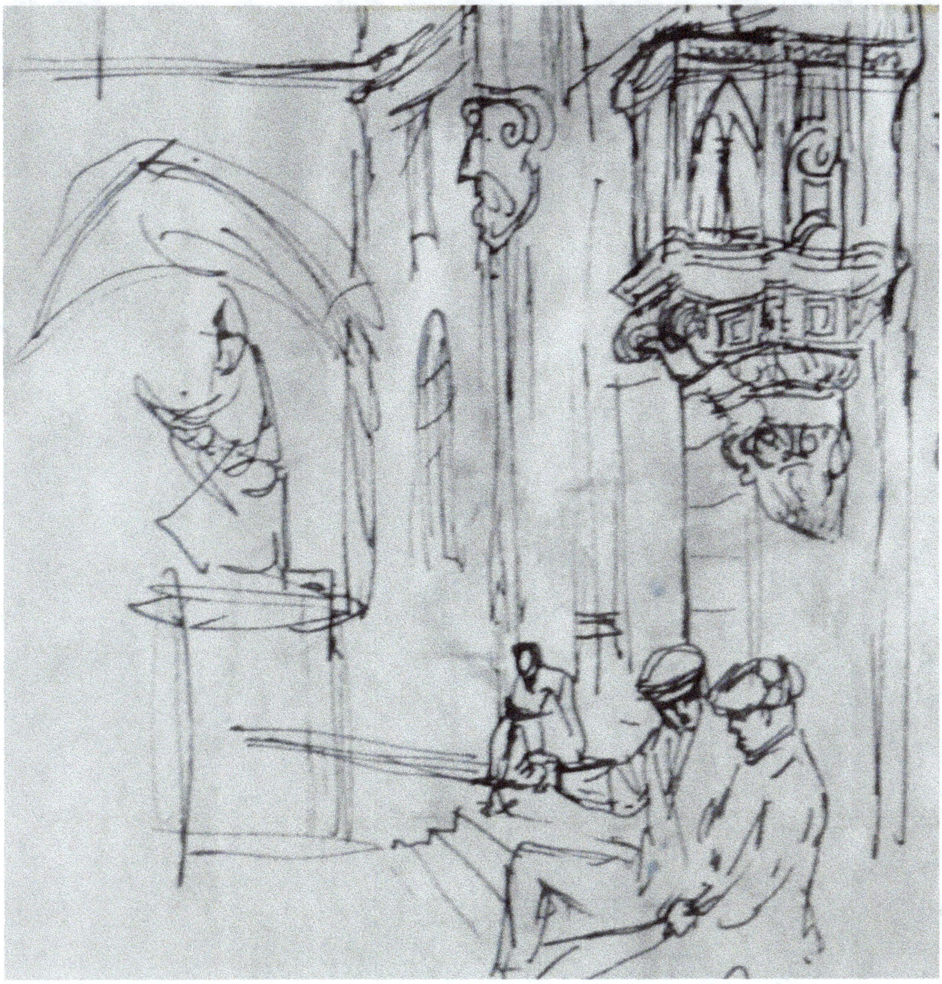

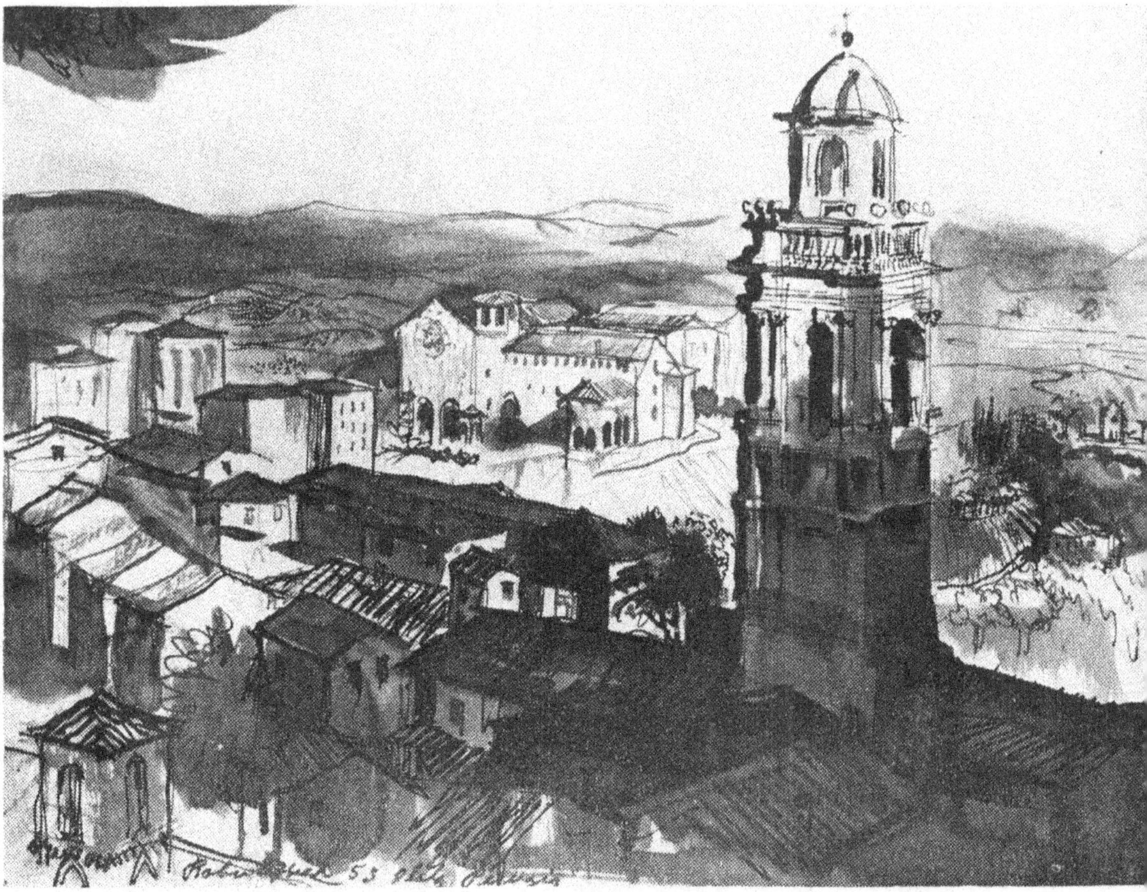

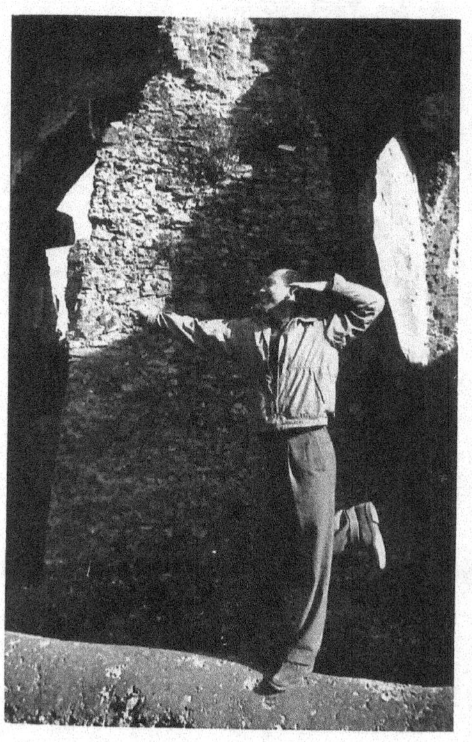

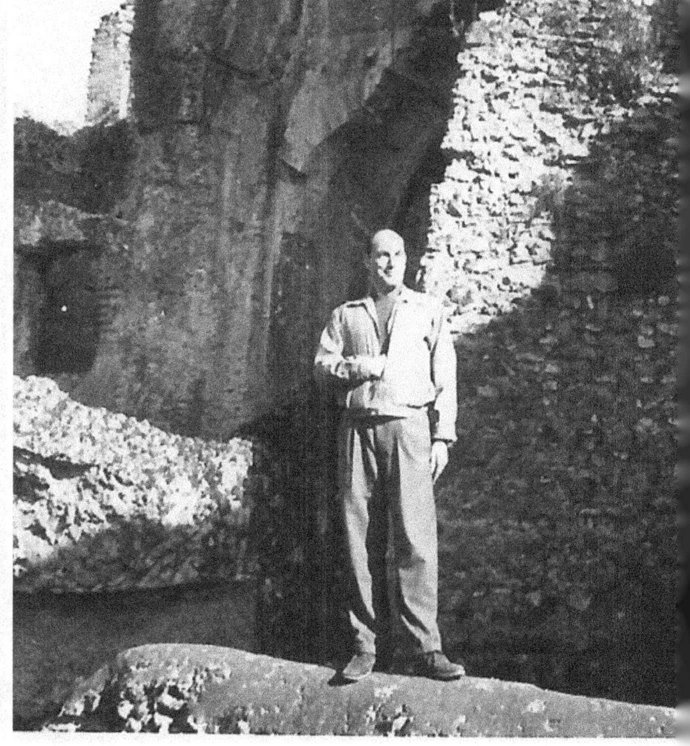

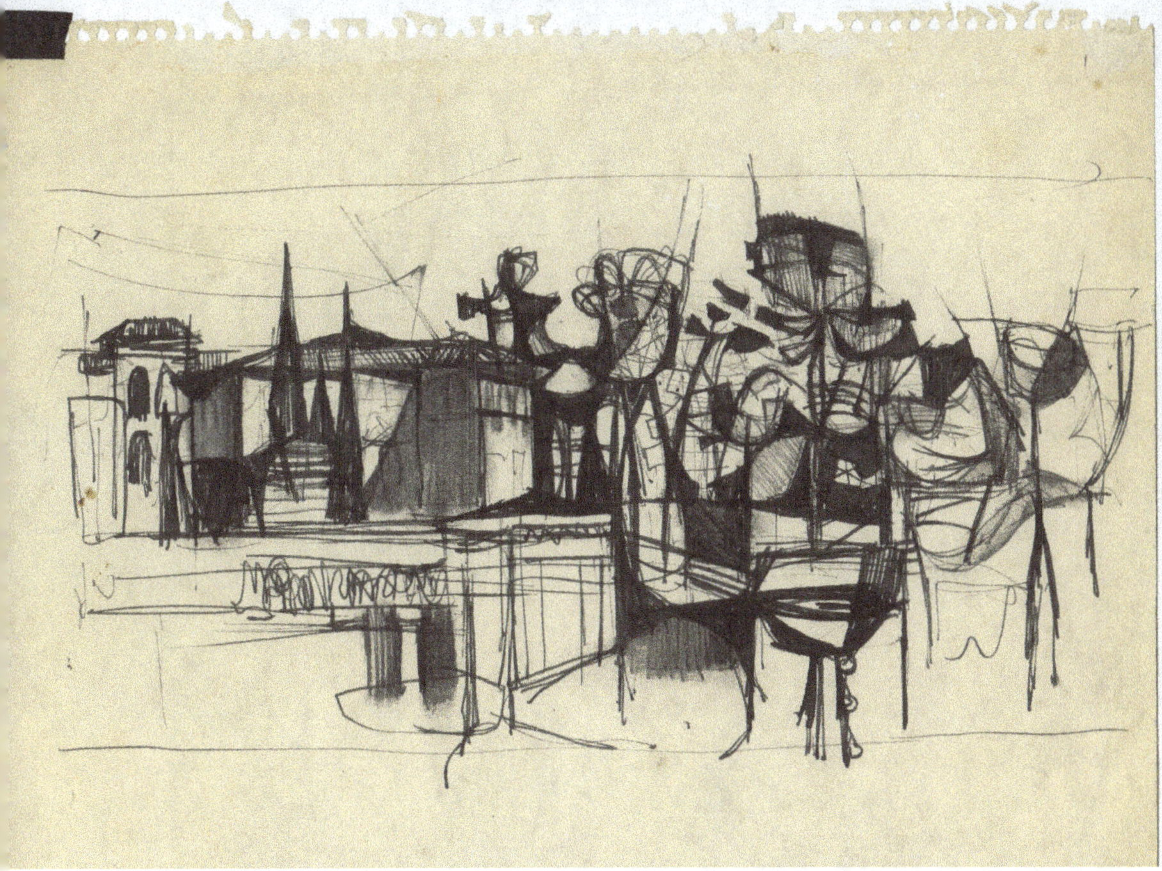

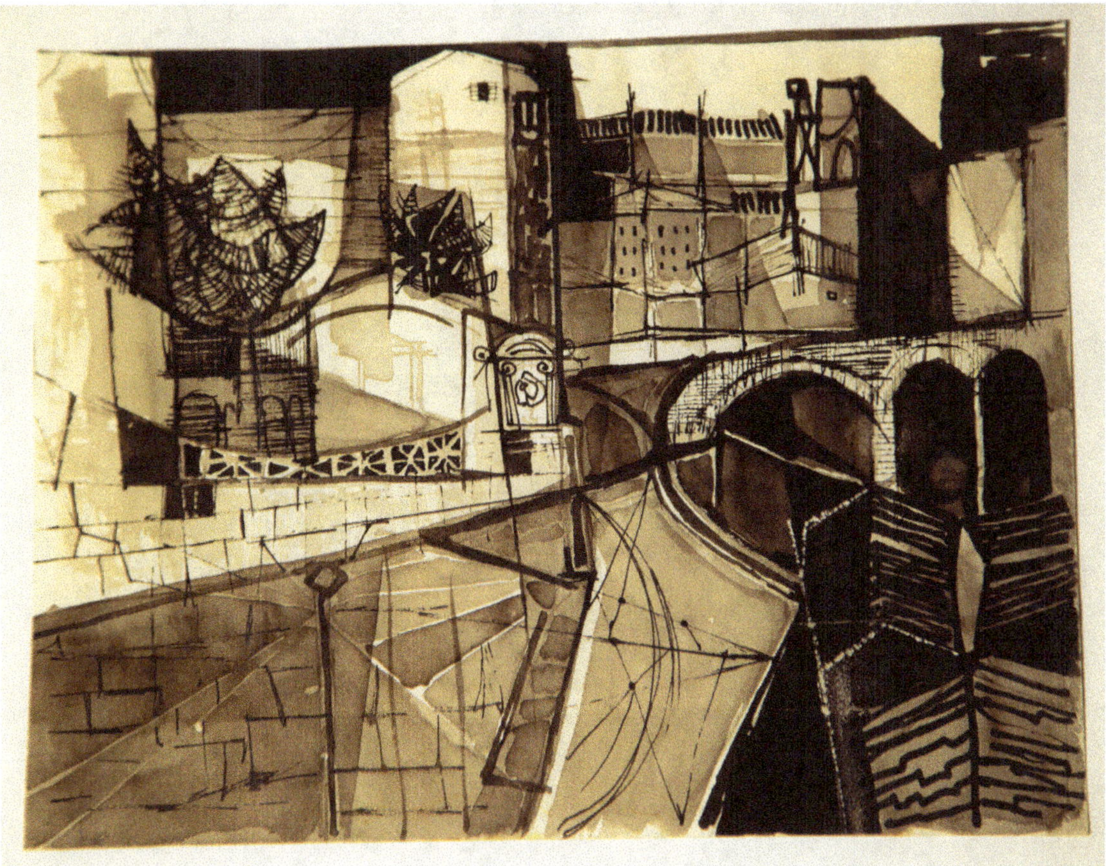

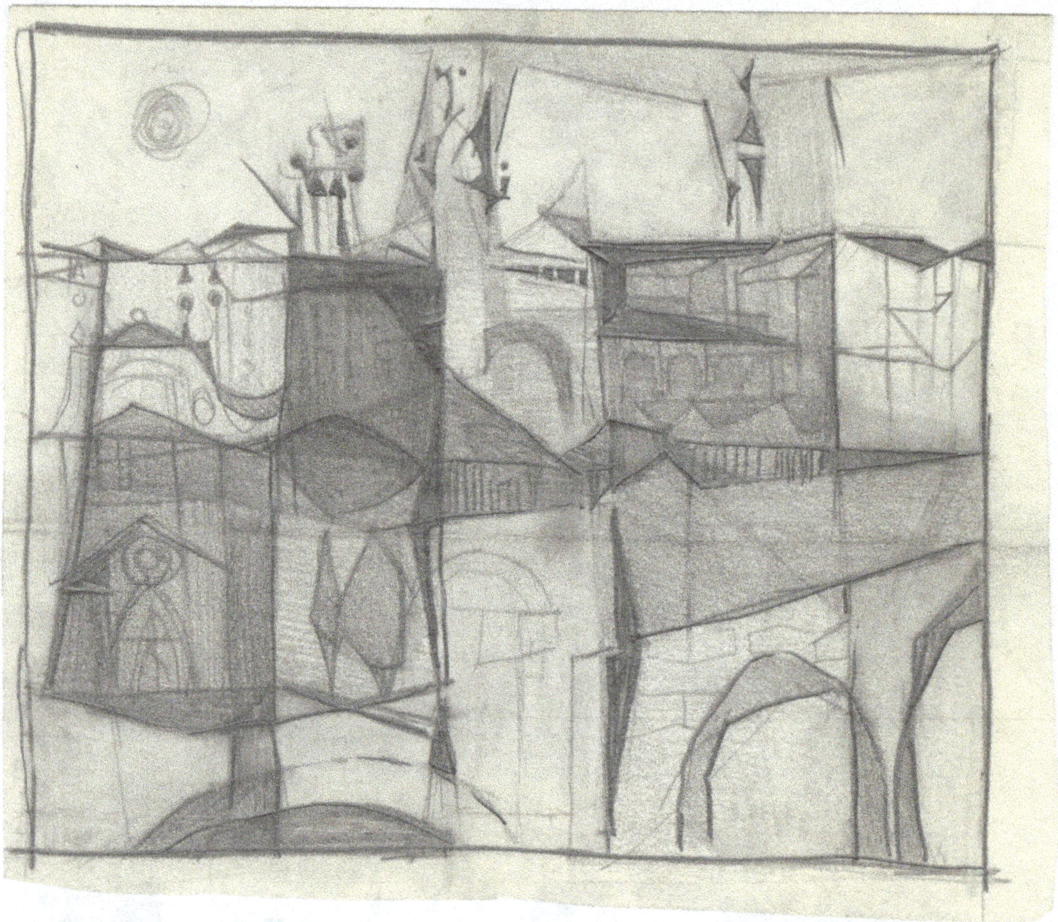

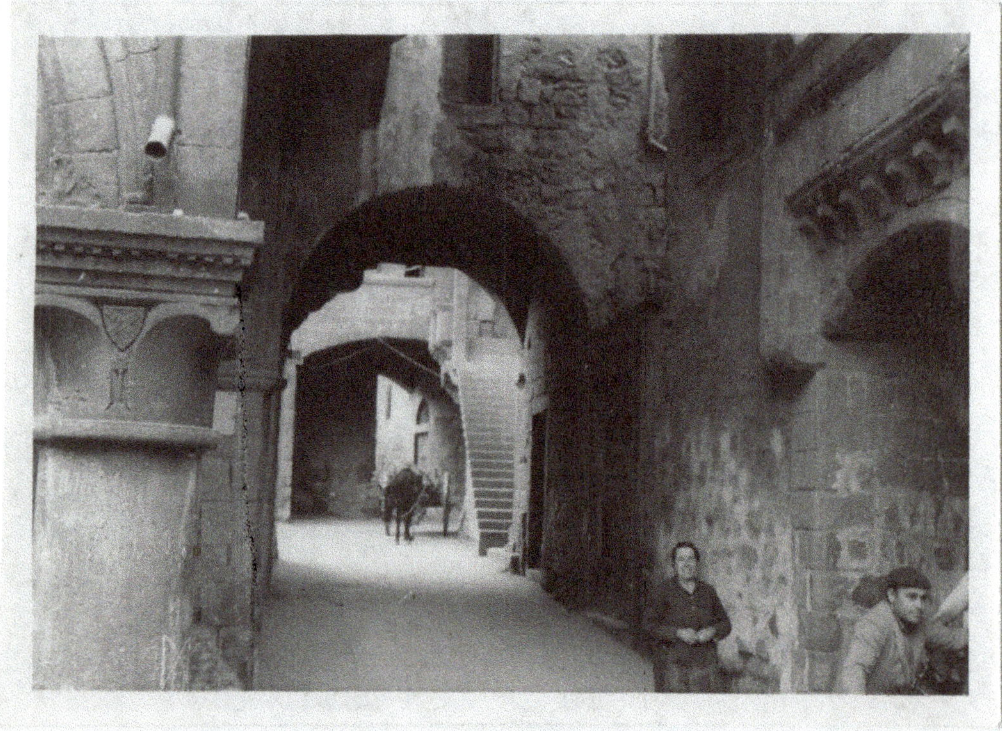

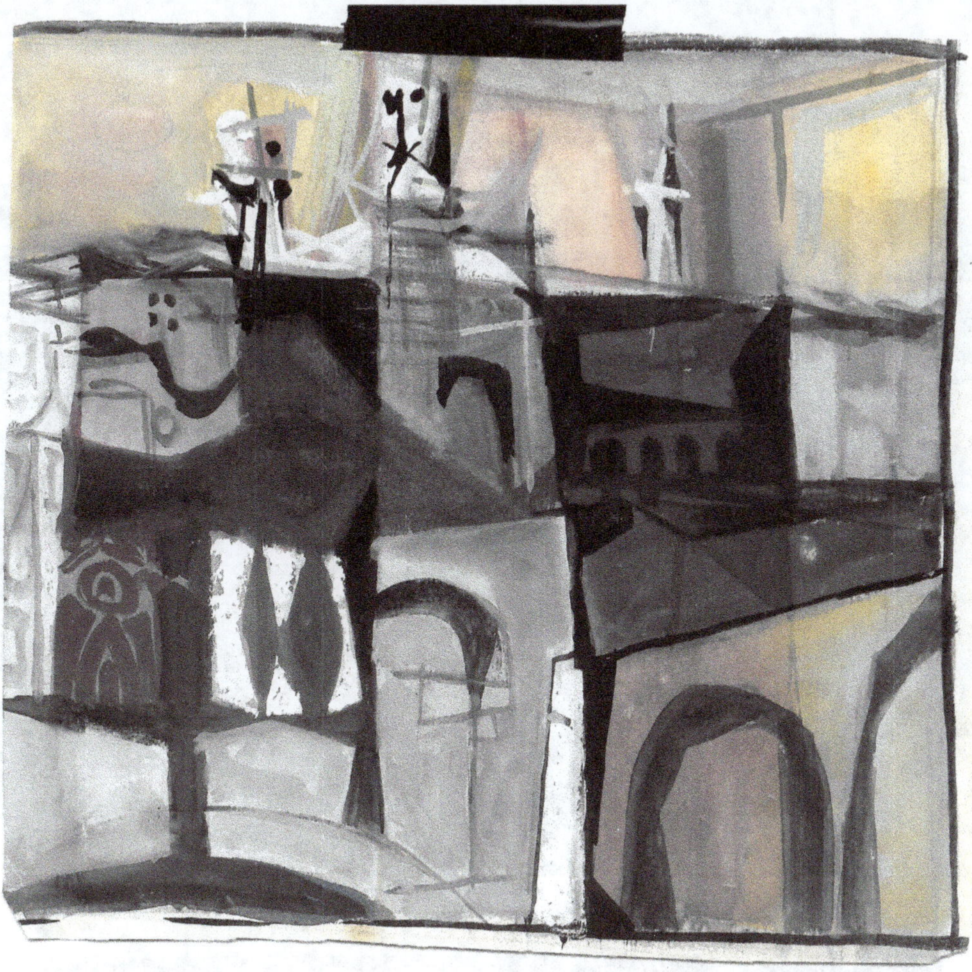

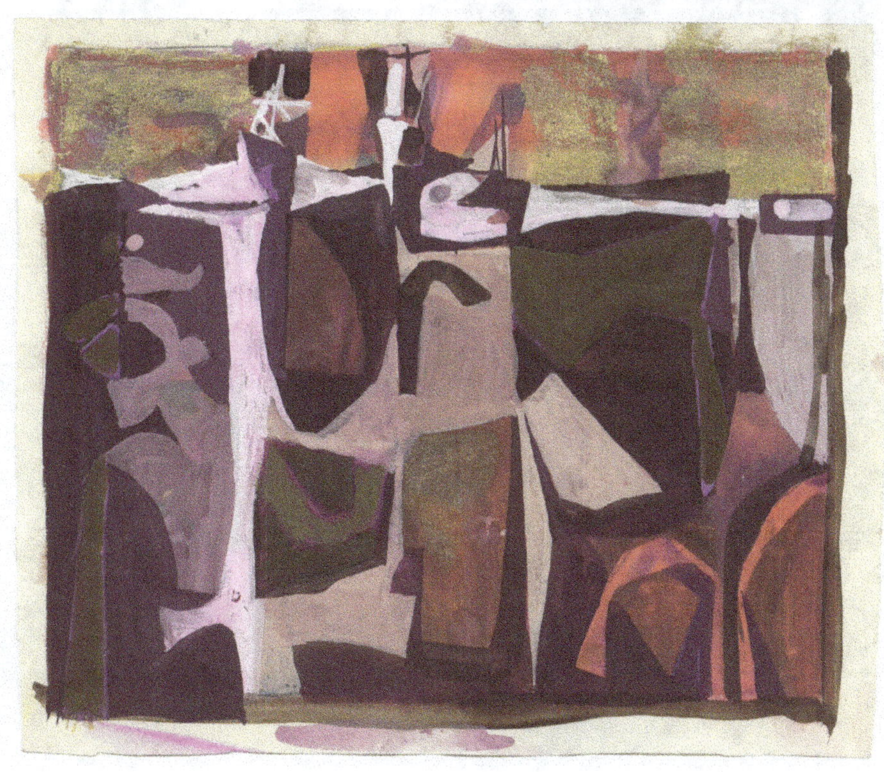

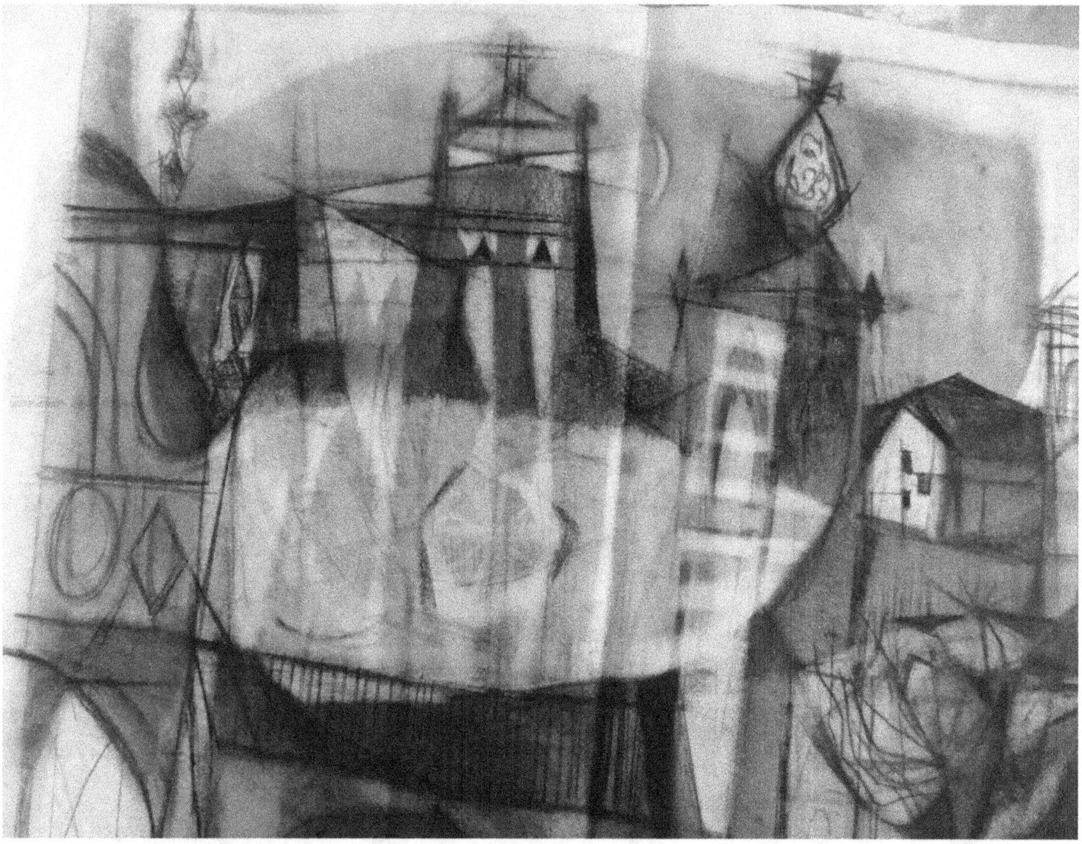

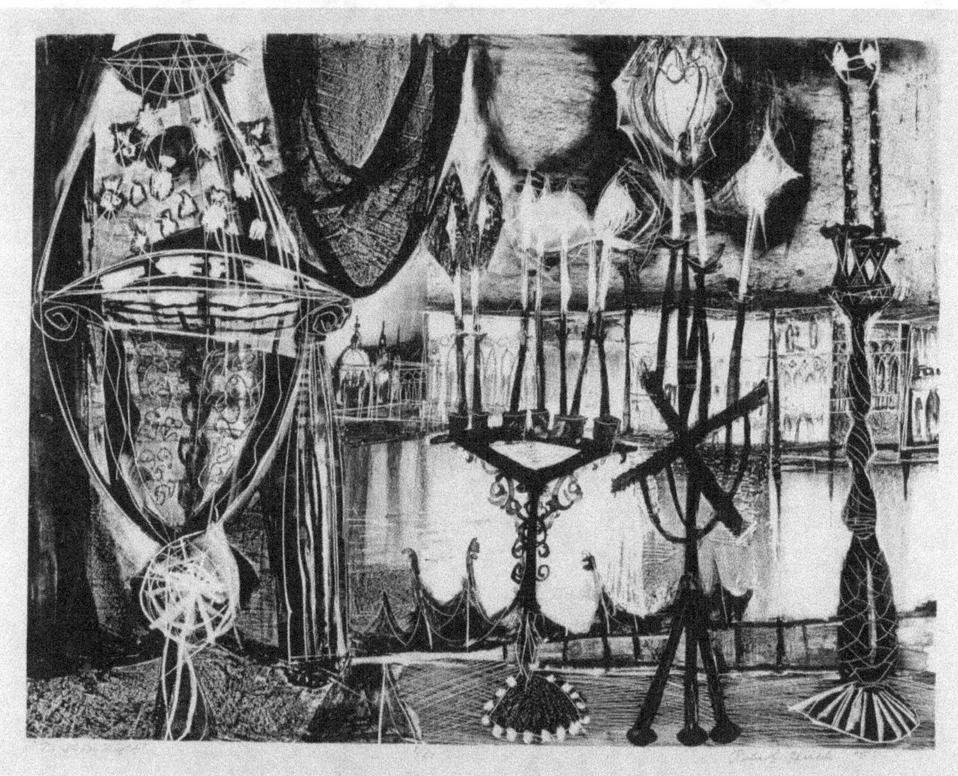

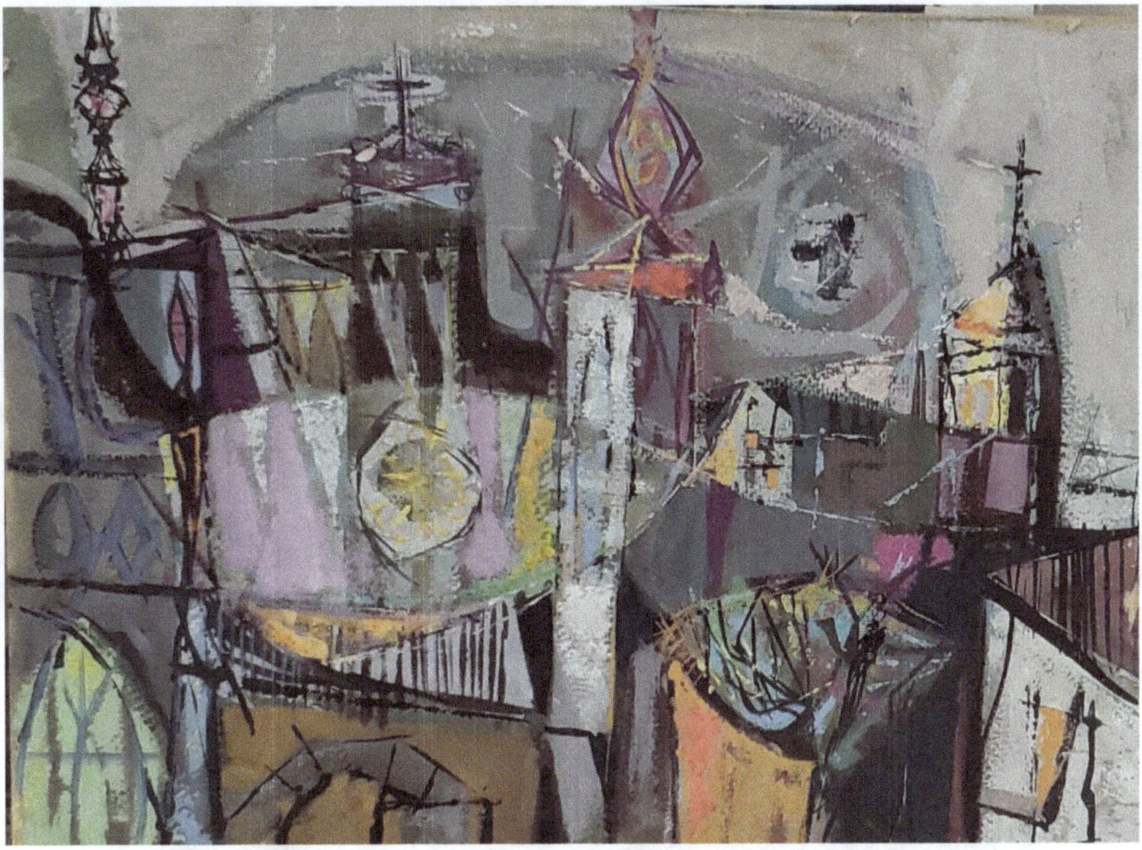

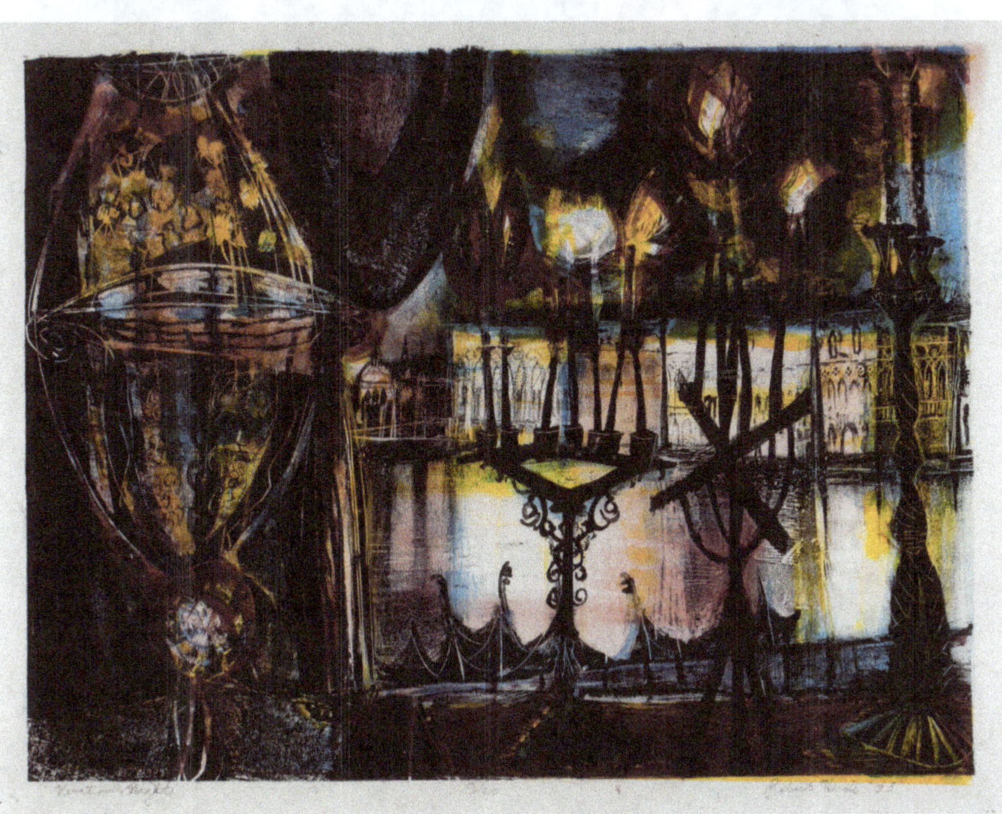

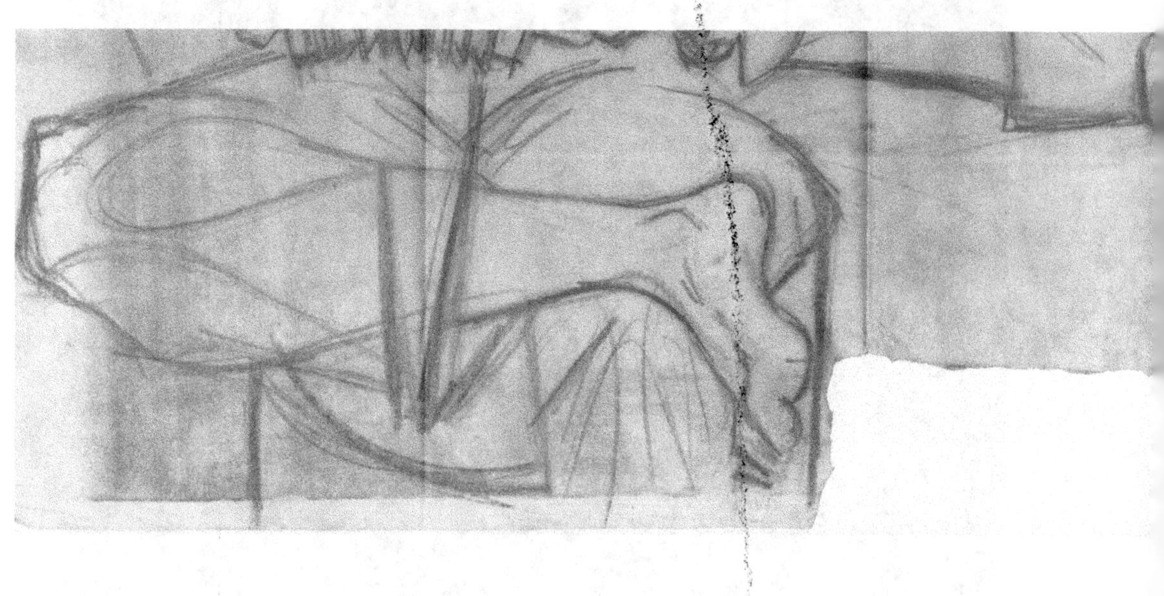

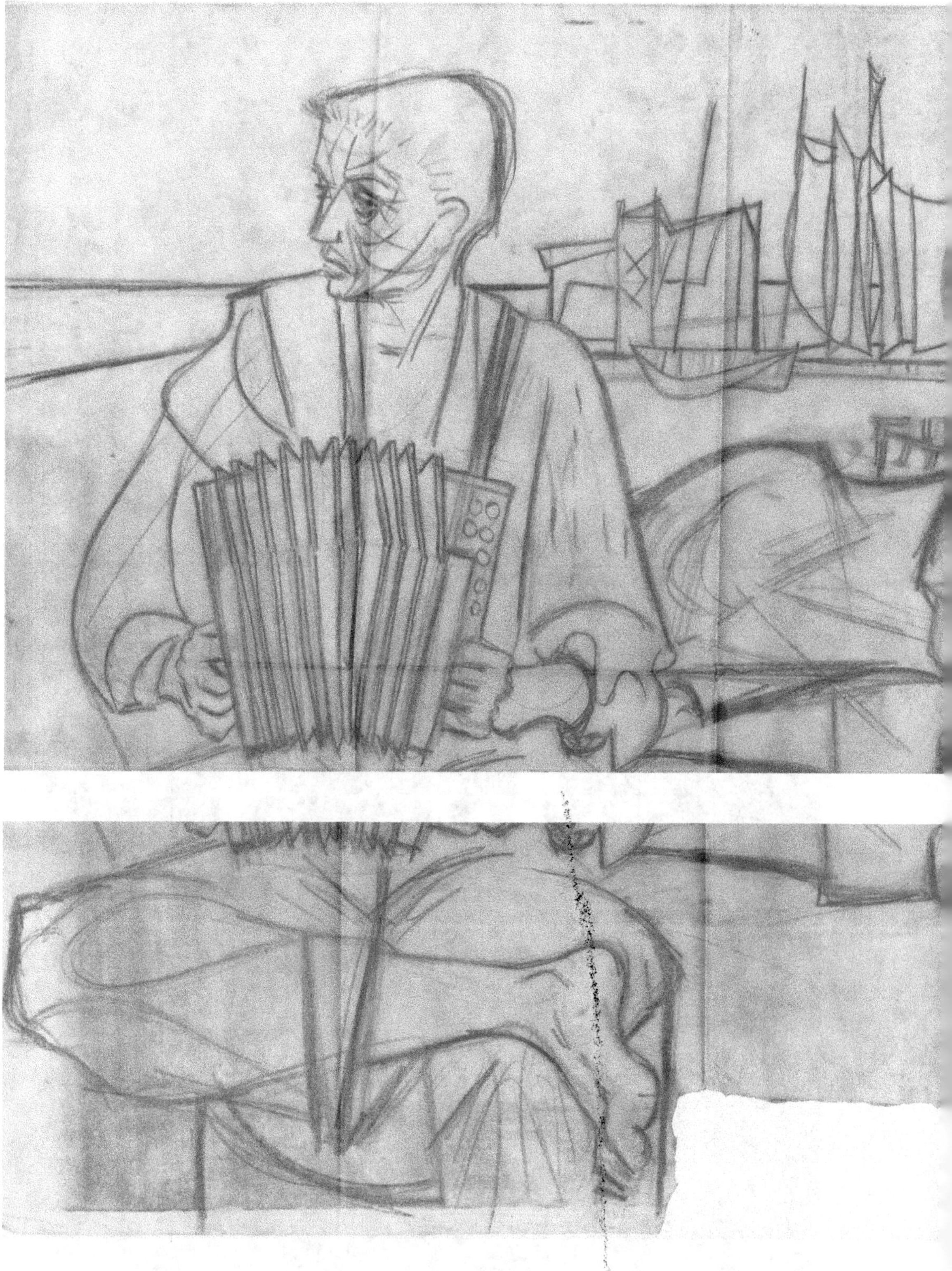

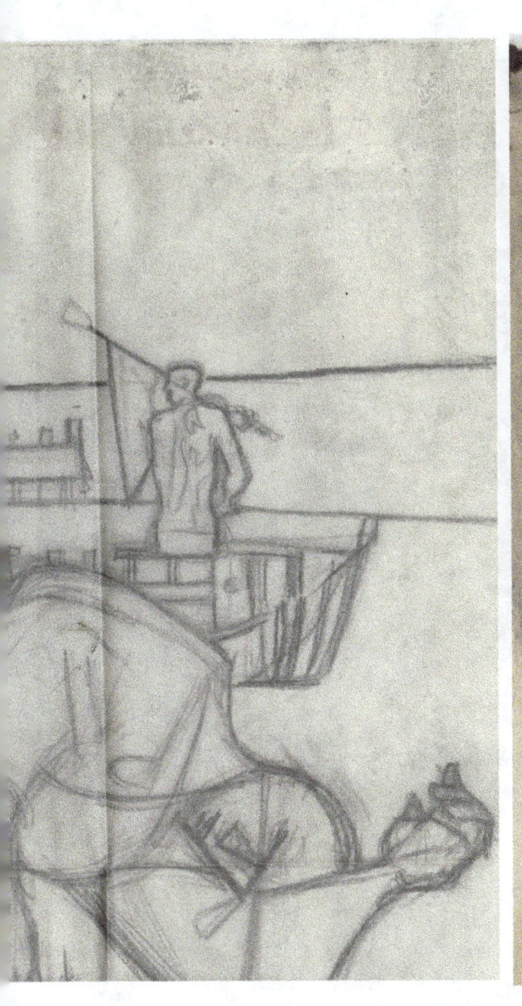

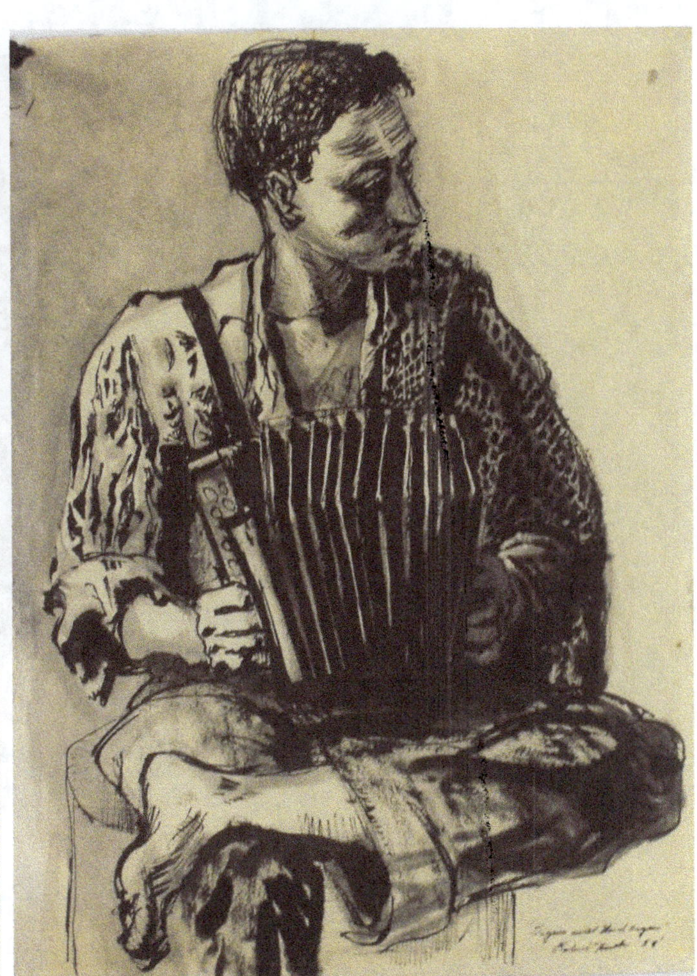

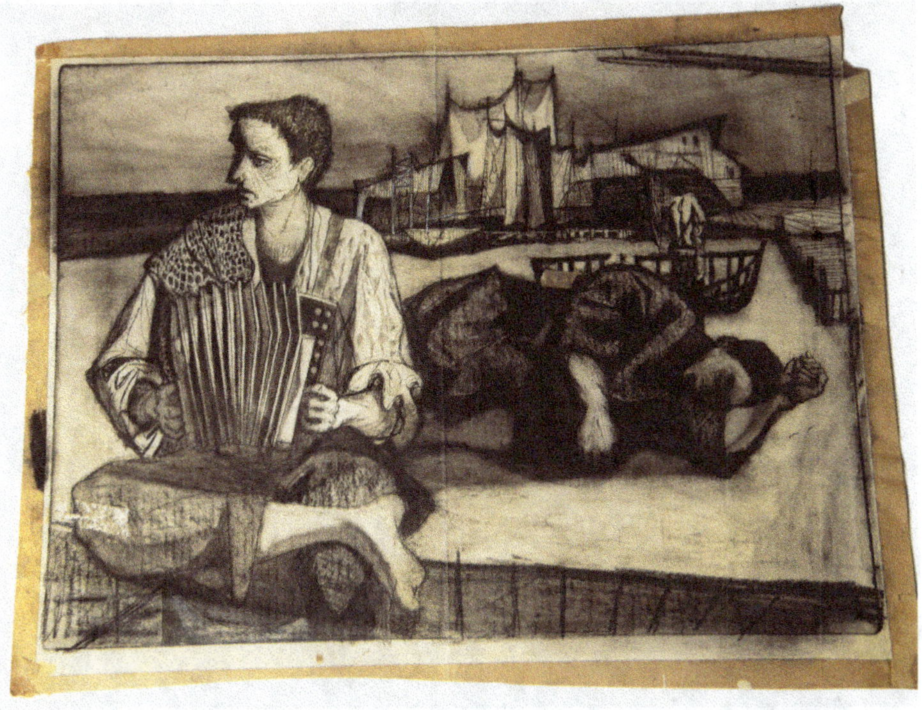

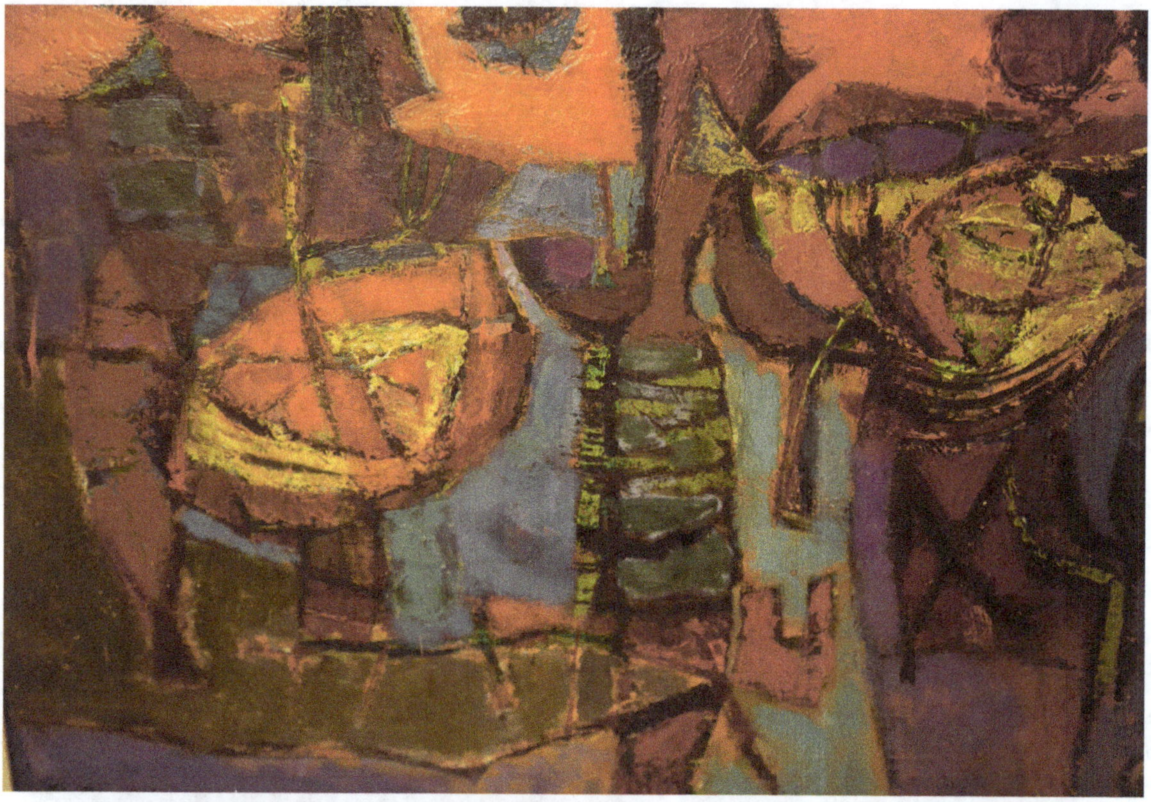

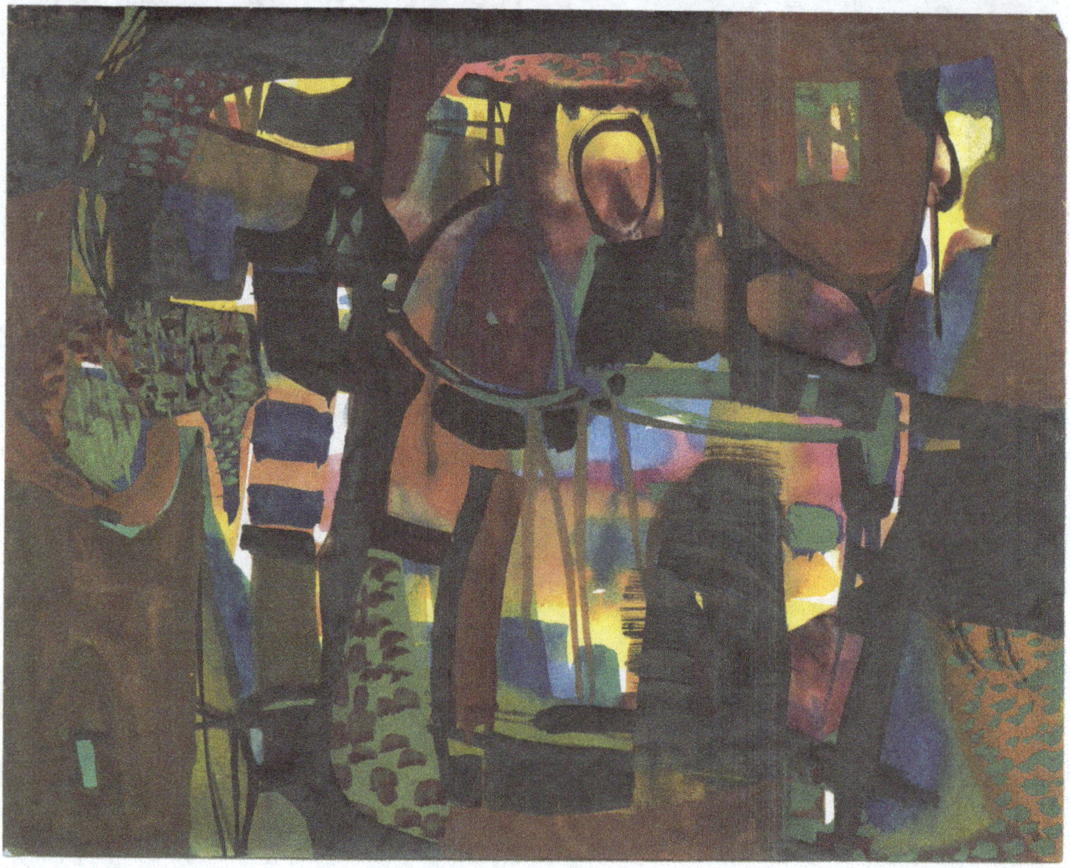

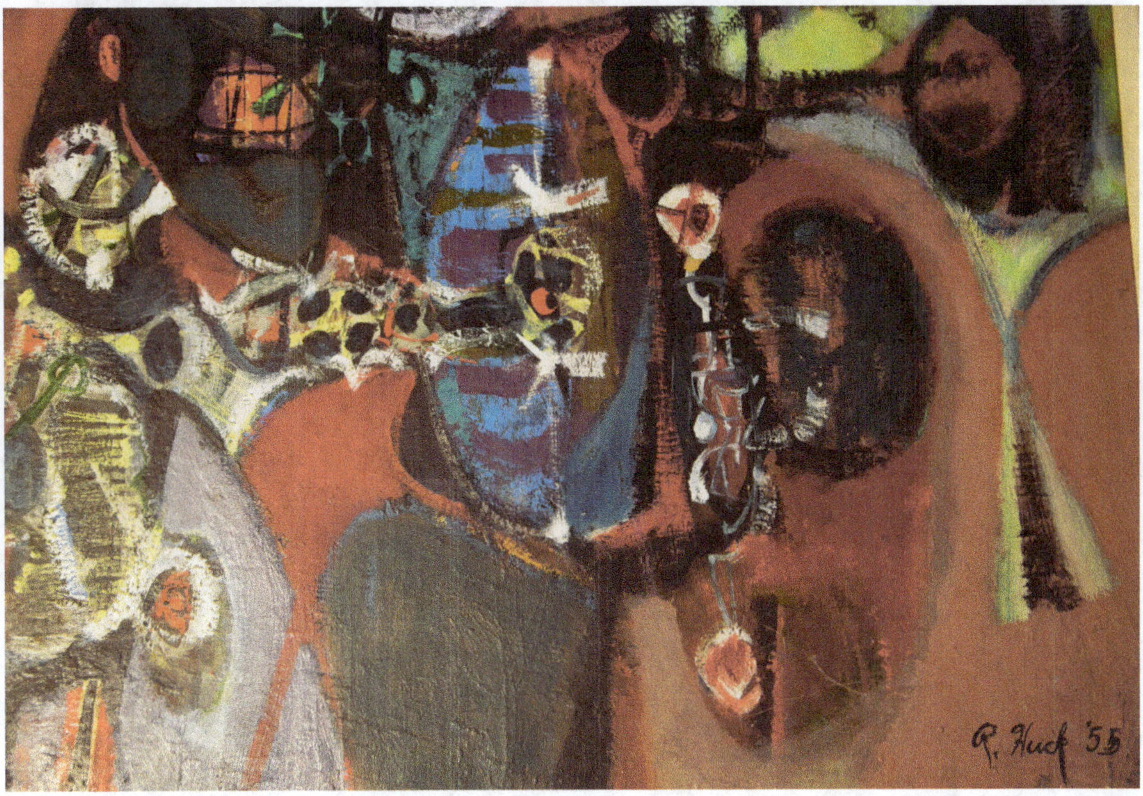

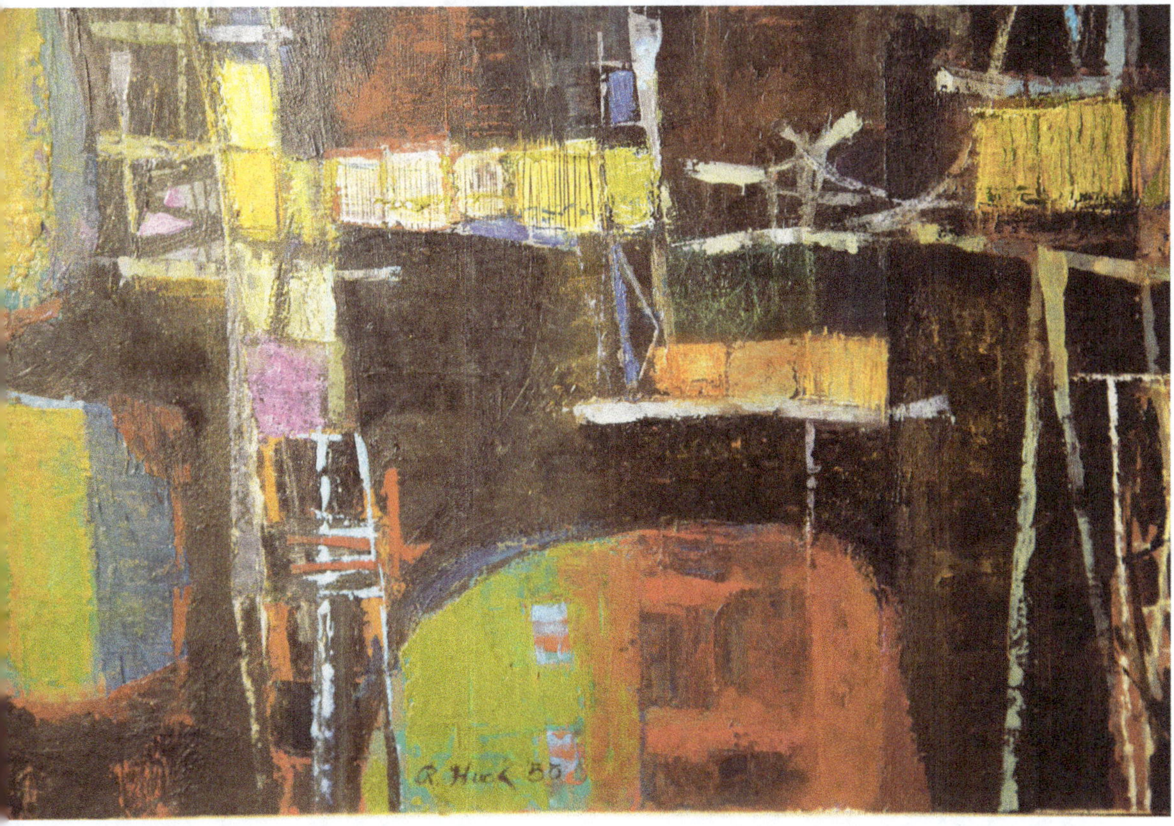

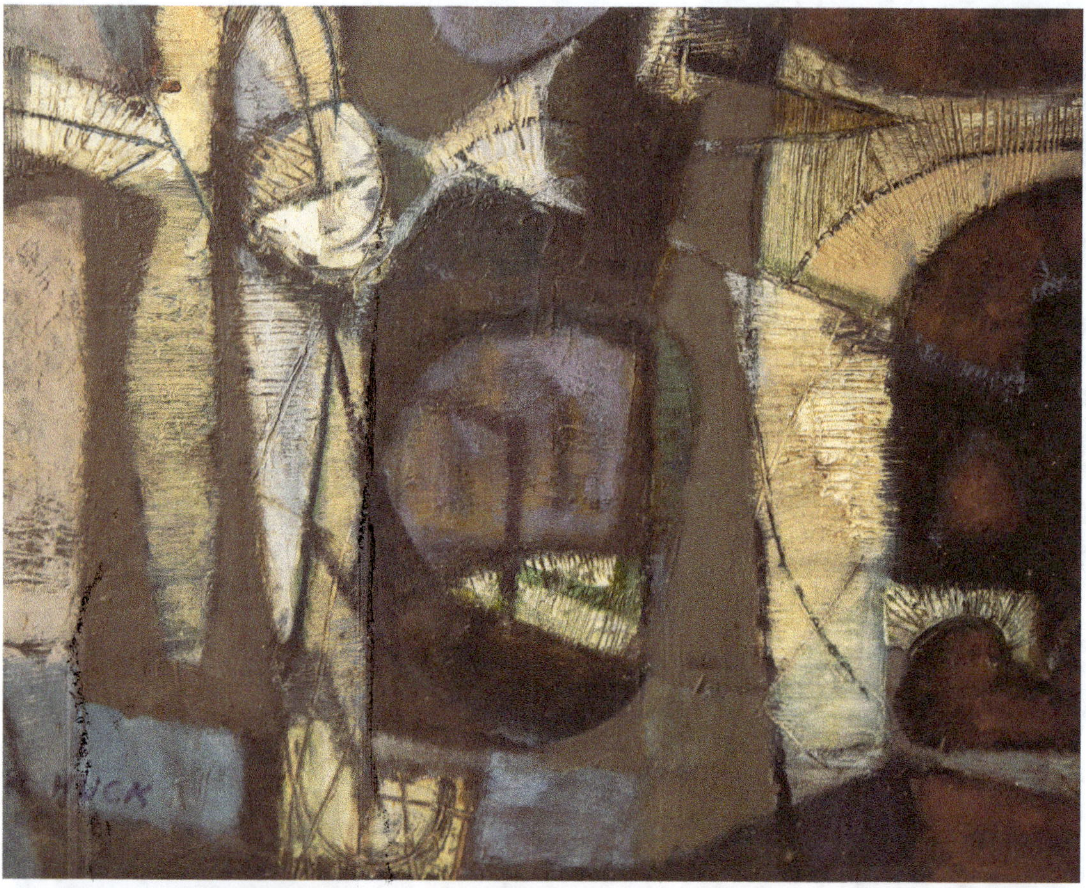

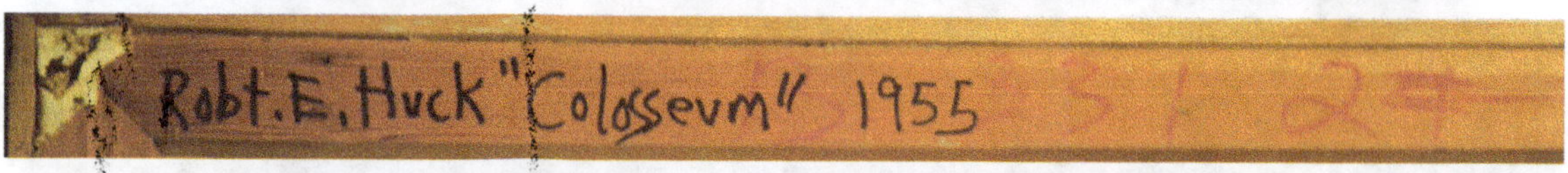

Robt. E. Huck "Colosseum" 1955

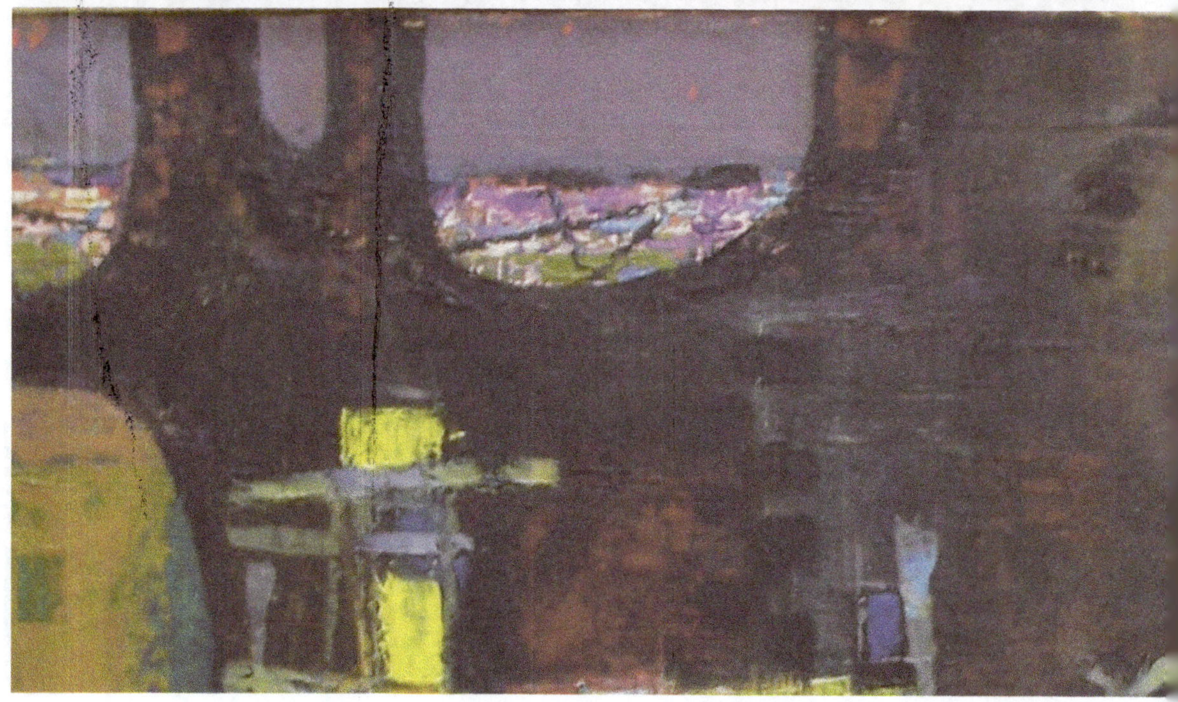

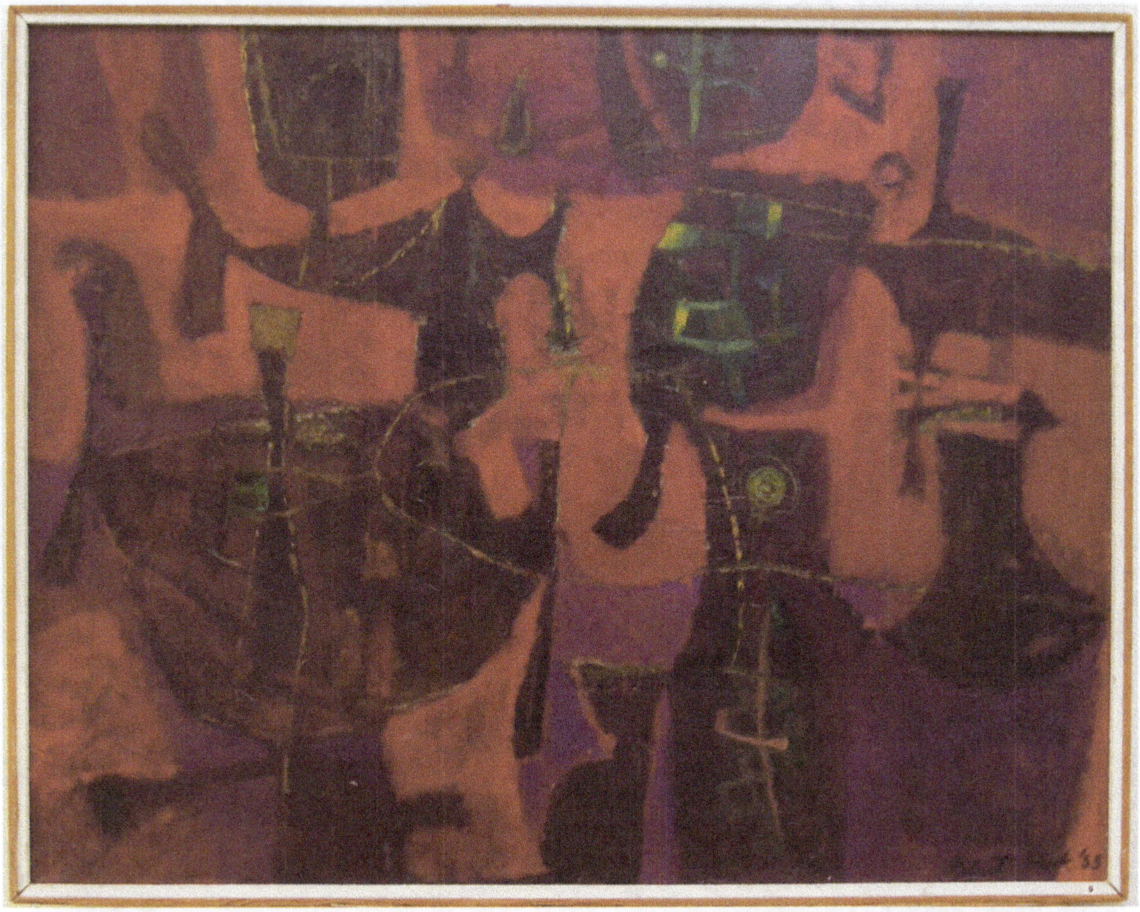

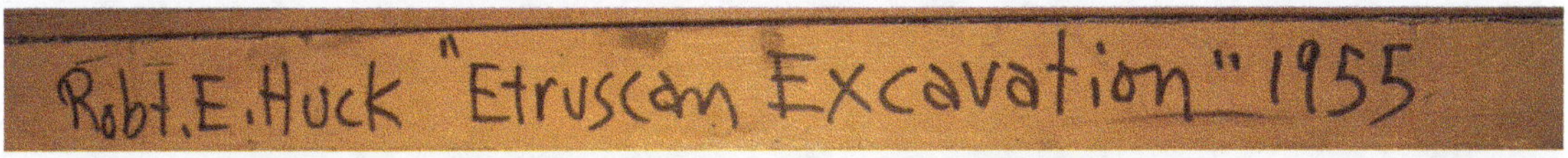

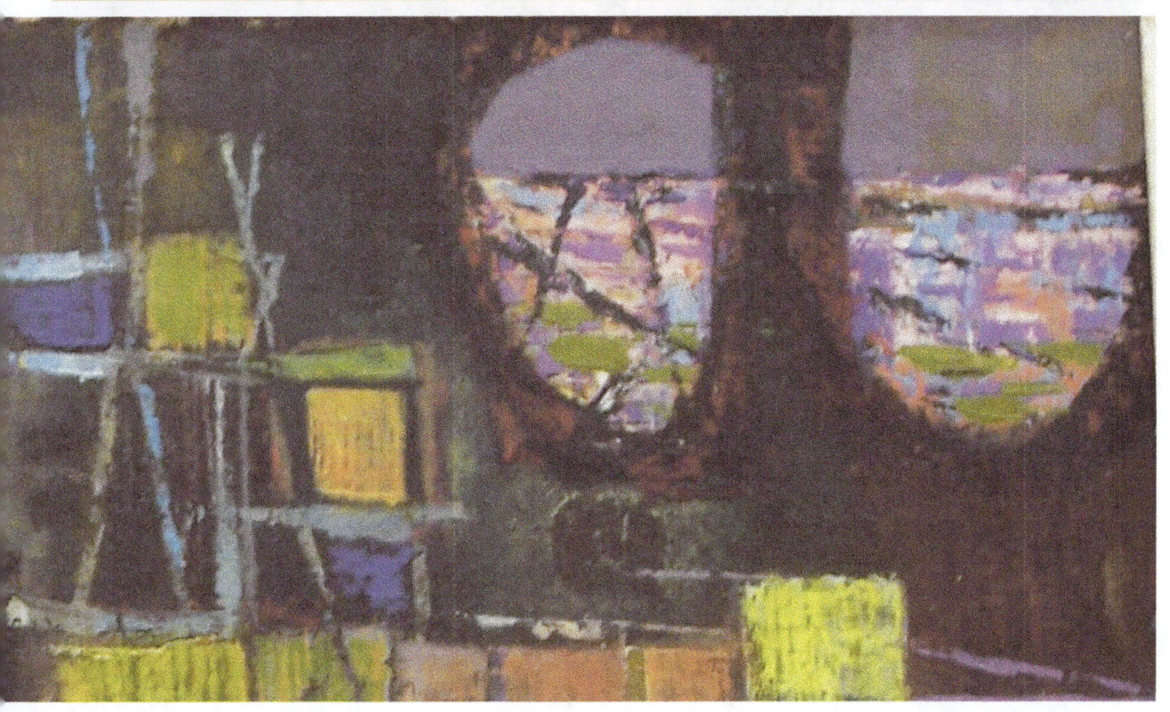

Robt. E. Huck "Etruscan Excavation" 1955

June 1955, while still living in Rome, Huck applies for an art teaching position at Oregon State College, citing his interest in a "northwest location."

Artist Gordon Gilkey recommends hiring Huck:

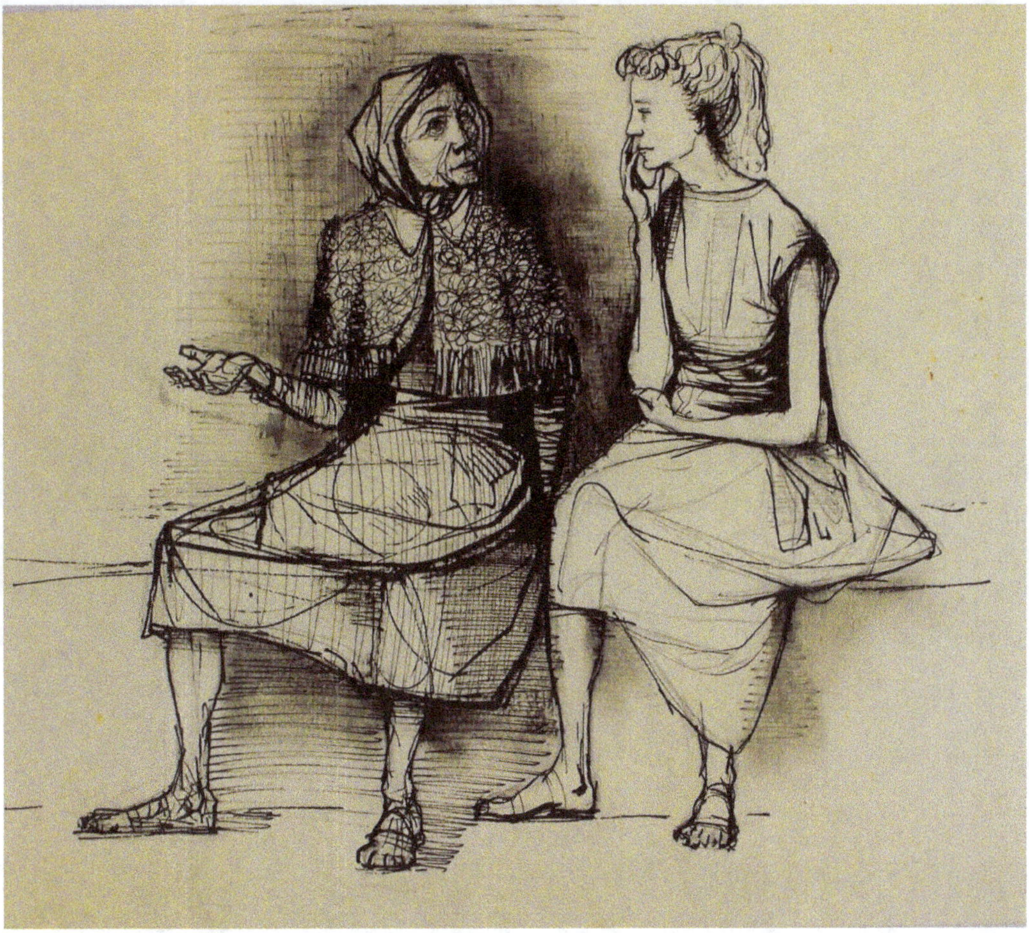

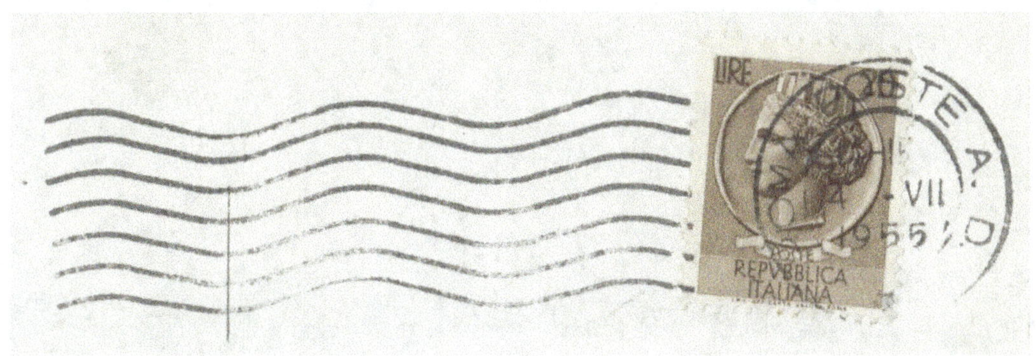

"The greatest value one receives from having been here is the feeling that you have seen and even experienced in a vicarious way western man's visual record of beliefs and triumphs, frailties and ambitions, as it comes down through history from civilization to civilization." (6)

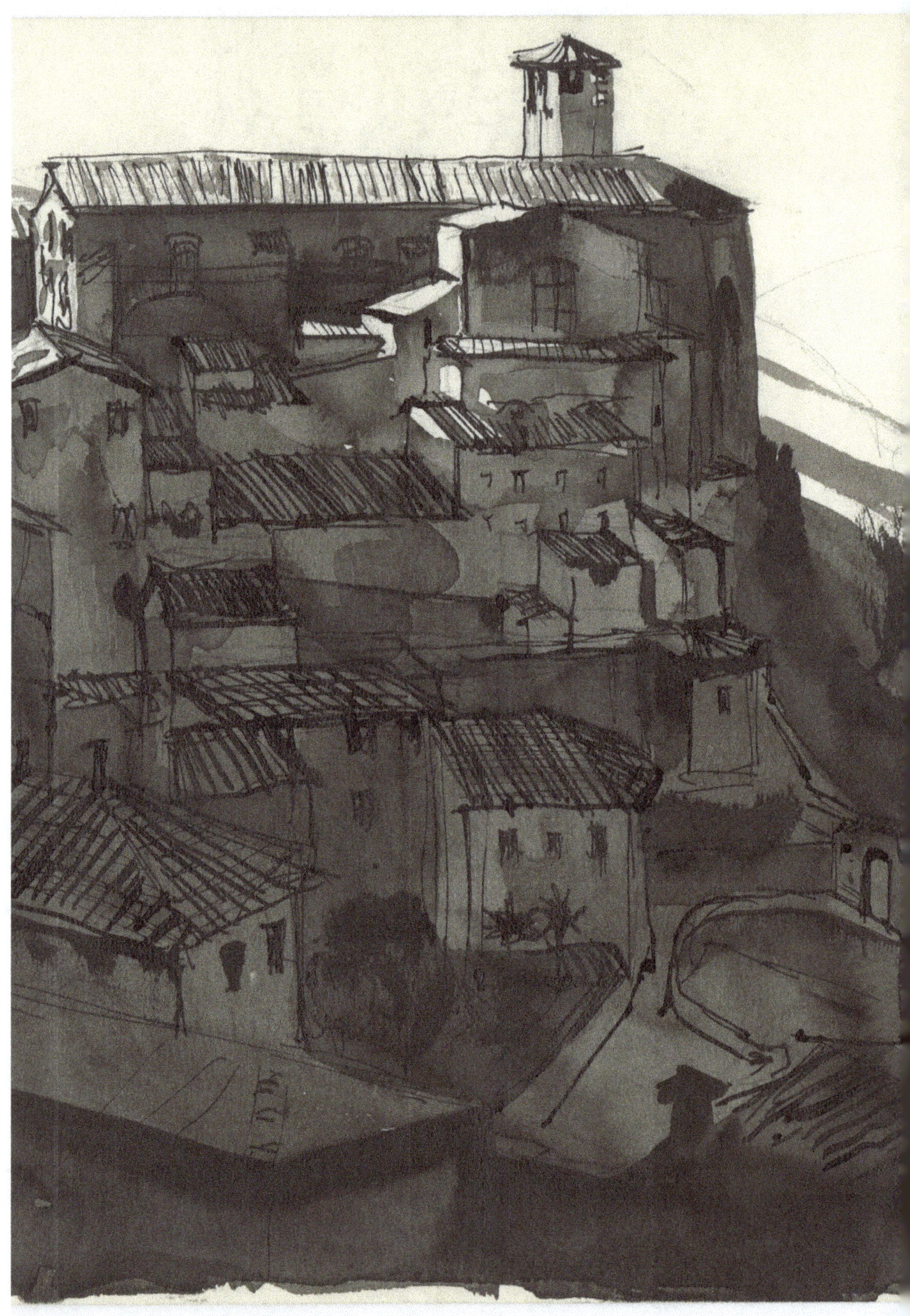

Department of Higher Education
(Oregon State System of Higher Education)

No. ....

PUBLIC EMPLOYES RETIREMENT SYSTEM
STATE OF OREGON

369 State Office Building, 1400 S. W. 5th Avenue, Portland 1, Oregon

PERSONNEL RECORD AND CLAIM FOR PRIOR SERVICE IF ANY

Instructions: All statements must be printed in ink or typed. Please use extreme care in filling in this questionnaire. Accuracy will reduce the amount of work necessary to secure confirmation of statements made herein. Return the completed blank to the department head or the official from whom you received it. Promptness in completing this blank is essential. Extreme care should be used in naming a beneficiary. Do not name estate. Only a person having an insurable interest in the life of the member qualifies to be a beneficiary. Generally speaking this will limit the choice of a beneficiary to a spouse or blood relation.

Name ...... ROBERT ...... EMERSON ...... HUCK ......
First / Middle / Last

☒ Male
☐ Female

Residence Address 827 SOUTH 8TH
No. and Street or R. F. D.

City, Town or Village CORVALLIS
Zone

County BENTON   State OREGON

Date of birth FEB 26 1923
Month / Day / Year

Place of birth KALISPELL
City or Town

FLATHEAD   MONTANA
County   State or Country

Full **Given** Name of Beneficiary

DOROTHY S. HUCK

Address 827 SOUTH 8TH

CORVALLIS, OREGON

Date of Birth of Beneficiary MARCH 6, 1925

Relationship WIFE

Are you a certificated teacher? Yes ✓   No ....

By whom are you employed STATE OF OREGON

In what capacity ASSISTANT PROF. OF ART   Date employed SEPT. 15, 1955

What is your annual salary $4,500

If you receive any allowance for living quarters, etc., state how much per year $ —

Describe the nature of your major duties, such as teaching, clerical, maintenance, mechanical, inspecting, law enforcement (police), fire fighting (paid fireman), janitor, etc. TEACHING

Do your duties normally require more than six hundred hours of work per year? Yes ✓   No ....

Are you employed as an independent contractor? Yes ....   No ✓

Do you hold an elective office, or an appointive office with a fixed term? Yes ....   No ....

RECORD OF EMPLOYMENT—Furnish in blanks below all periods of public employment in Oregon including all service in state departments, public institutions of learning, counties, cities or other political sub-divisions of the state, and including all U. S. Military Service since 1-1-40. Begin with earliest employment. Identify completely such as State Department, Number and Location of School District, or Branch of Military Force.

| DATES OF EMPLOYMENT | | | NAME AND ADDRESS OF EMPLOYER | YOUR NAME AS IT APPEARED ON PAYROLL |
Month	Day	Year		
From SEPT.	15	1955	OREGON STATE COLLEGE	ROBERT E. HUCK
To		19		
From		19		
To		19		
From		19		
To		19		
From		19		
To		19		

IF ADDITIONAL SPACE NEEDED, USE REVERSE SIDE.

I hereby declare that the foregoing statements are full, true and correct to the best of my knowledge and belief.

Date FEB 29, 1956   Signature of Employe Robert Emerson Huck

I hereby certify that the above employe is now employed and has been employed from September 1955 with no more than 30 days absence.

Feb 29, 1956
Date

Mae Mrs [signature]
Signature of Department Head or School Official

Employer No. ....   Title ....

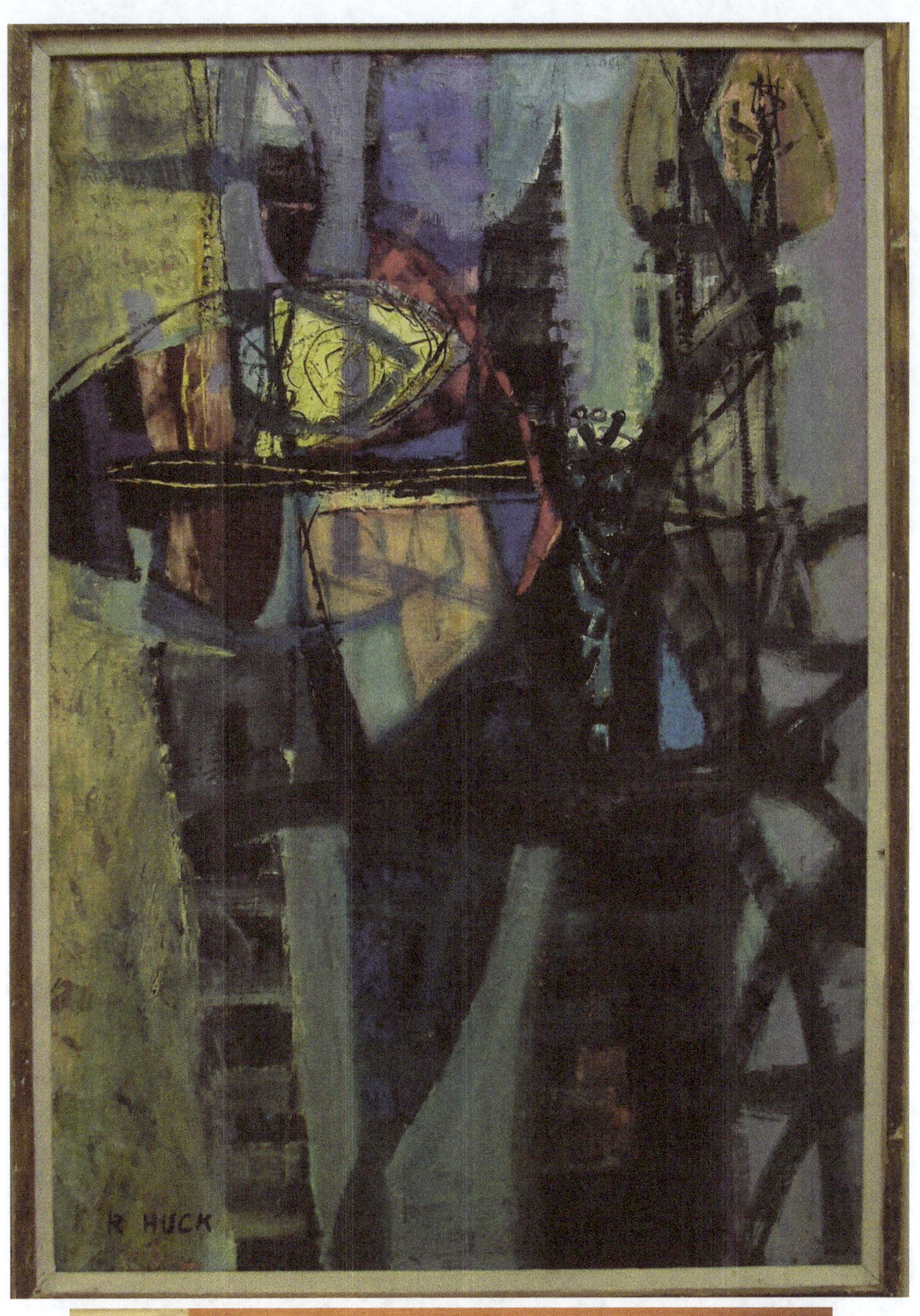

7. CATHEDRAL THEME, 1956, oil on canvas

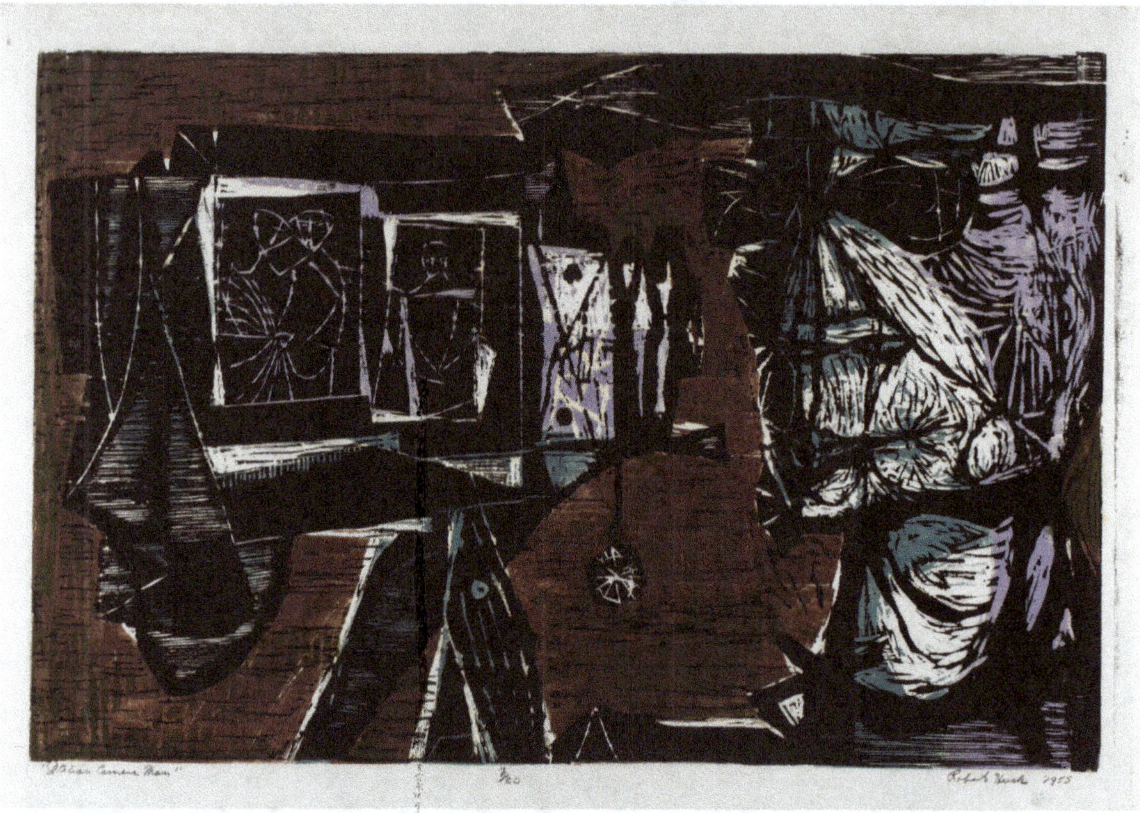

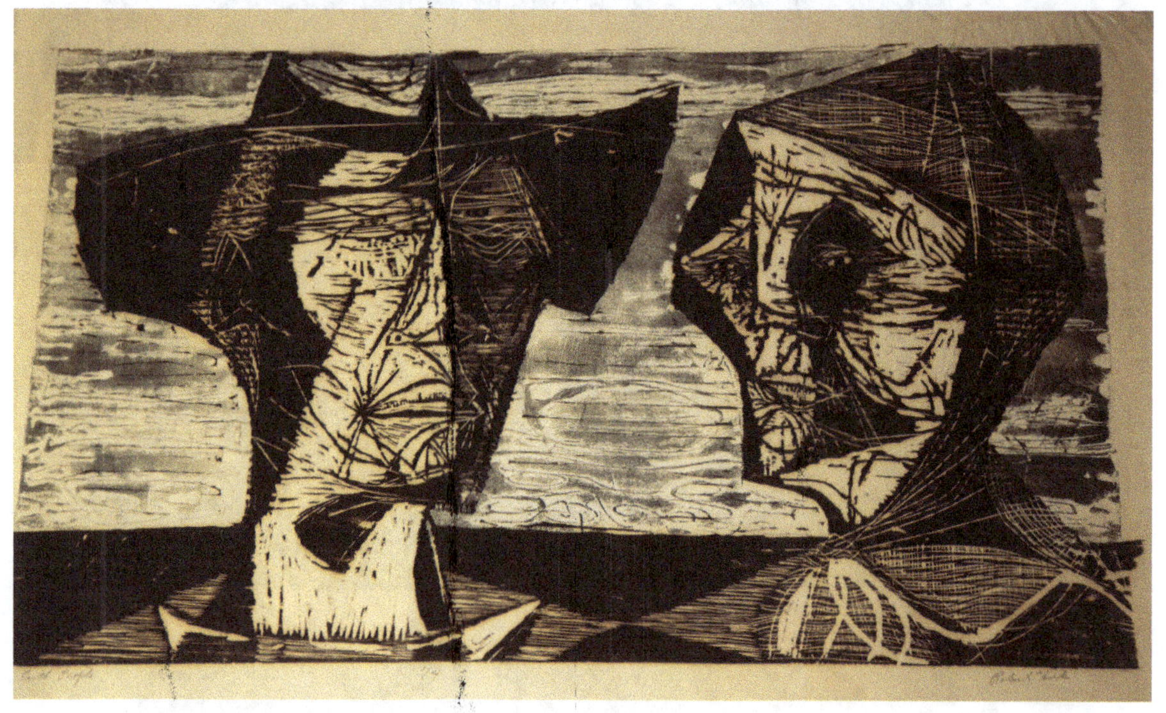

"Italian Camera Man" and "Earth People" (1955)

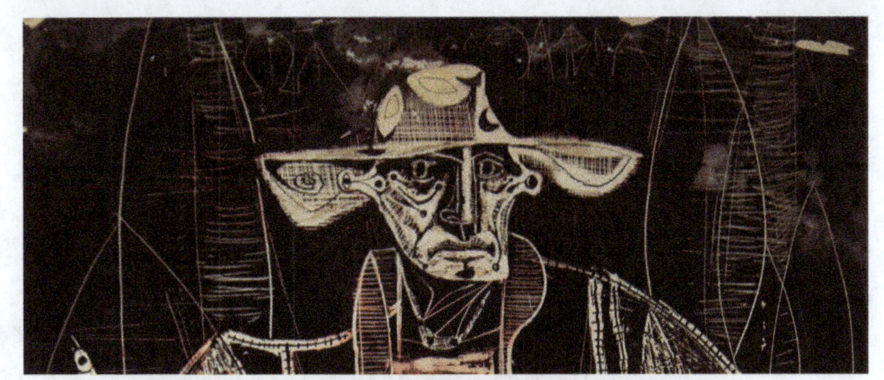

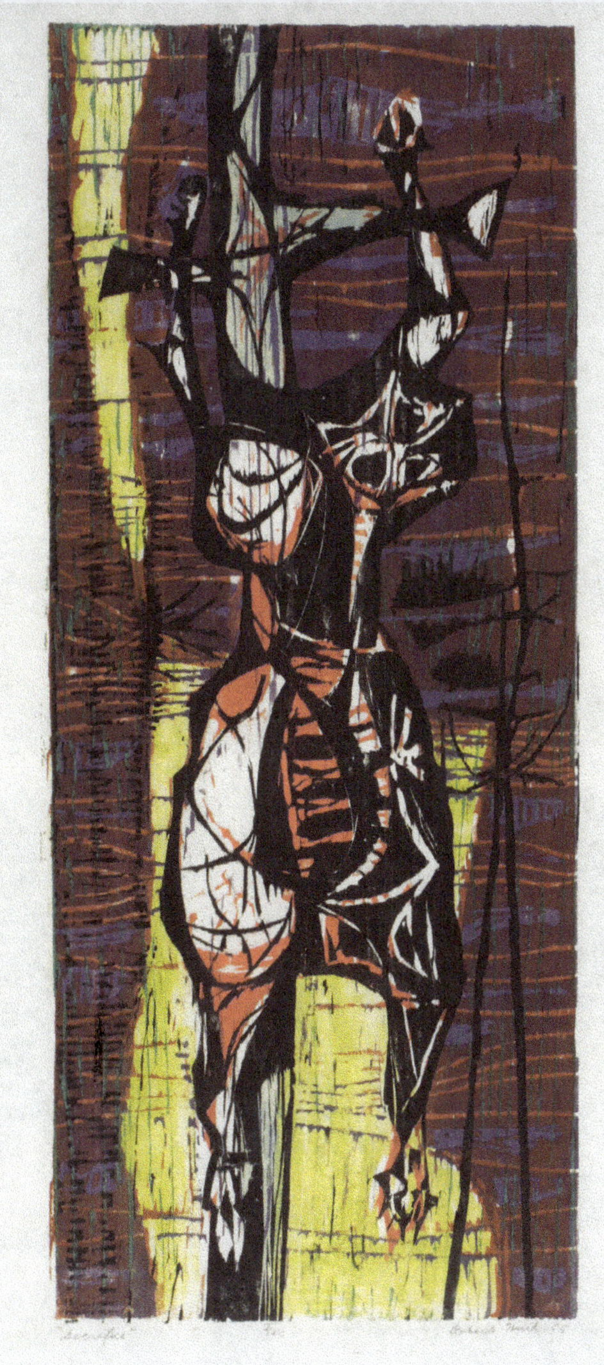

(1956)

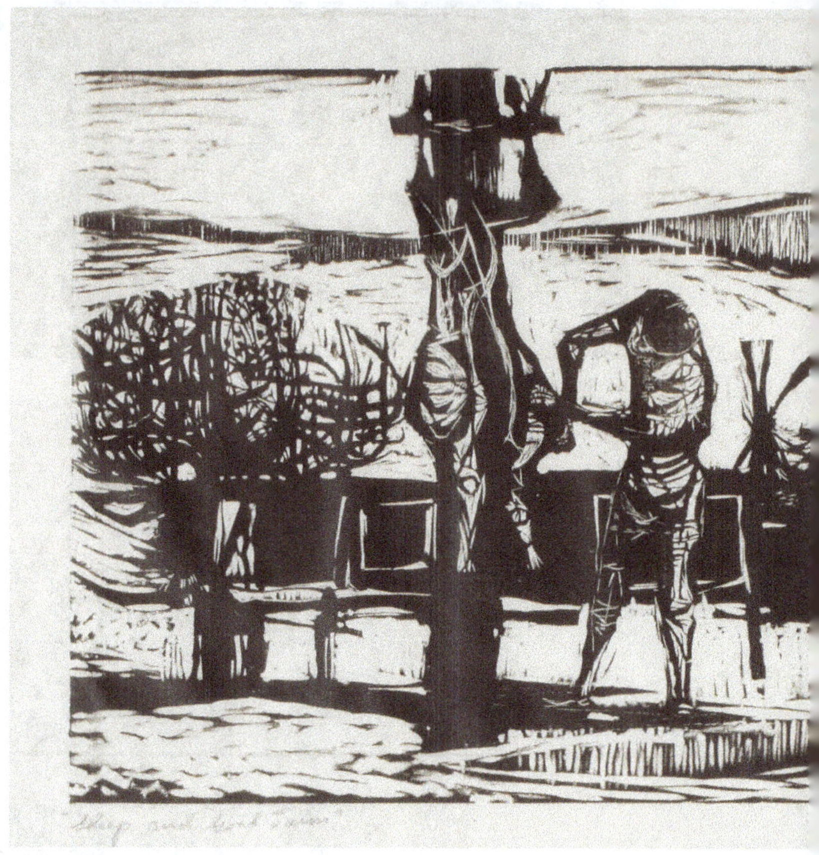

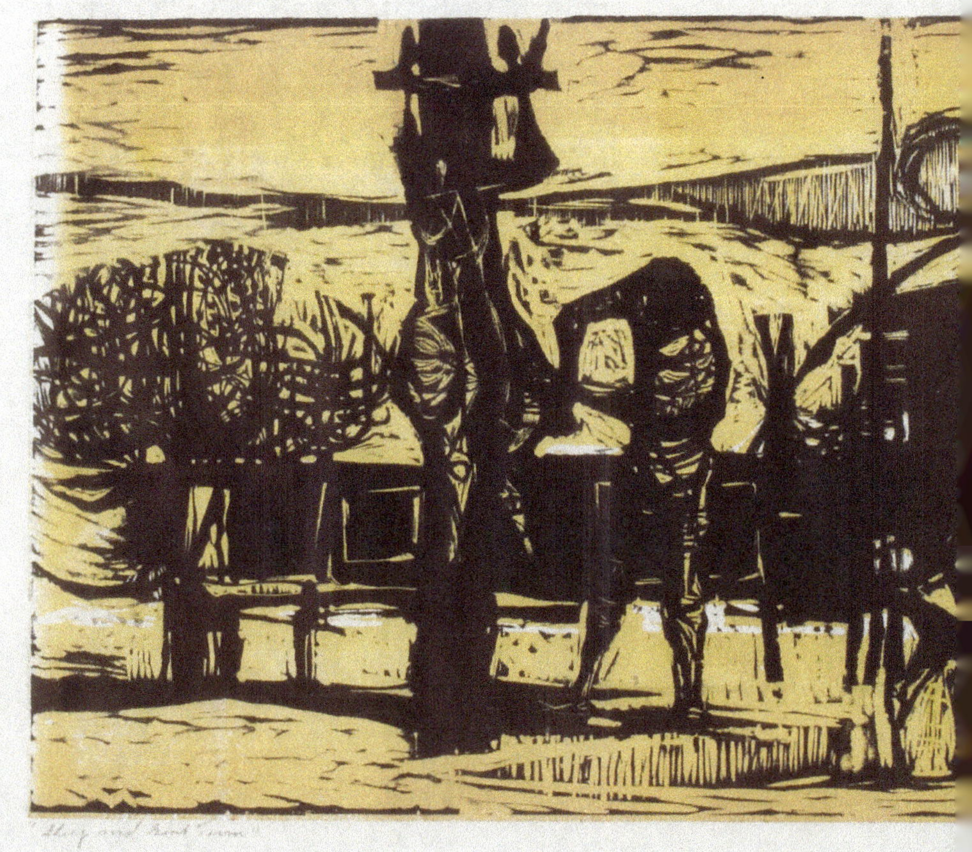

94

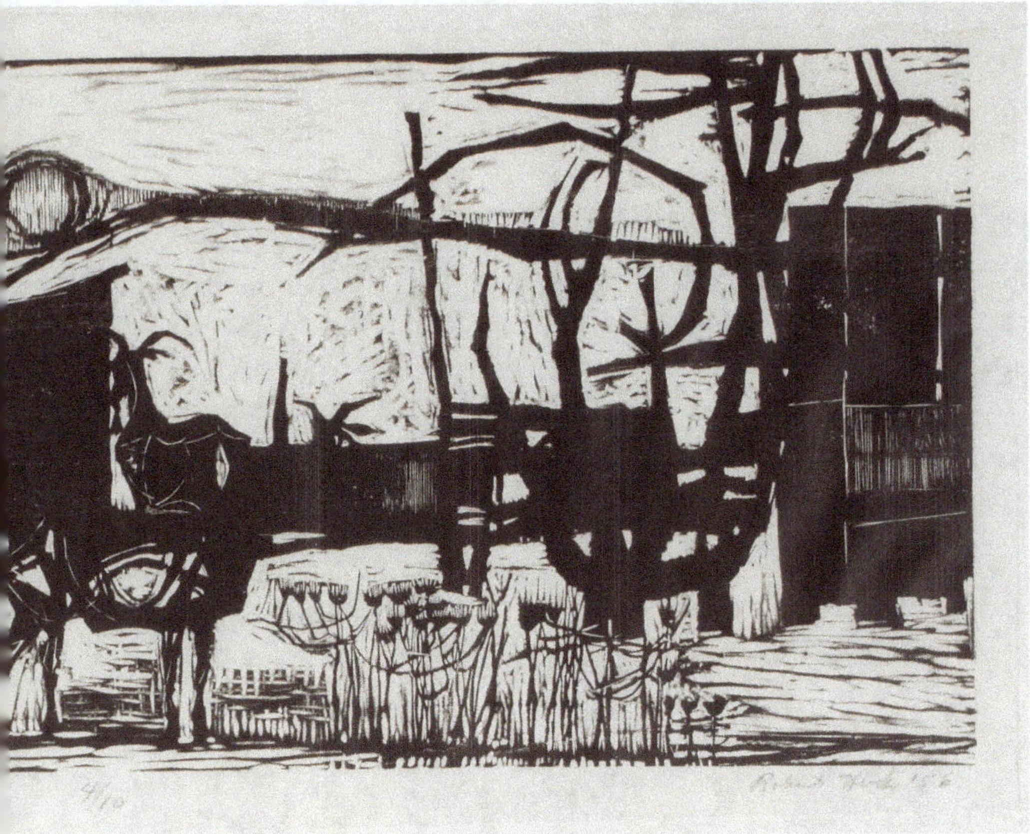

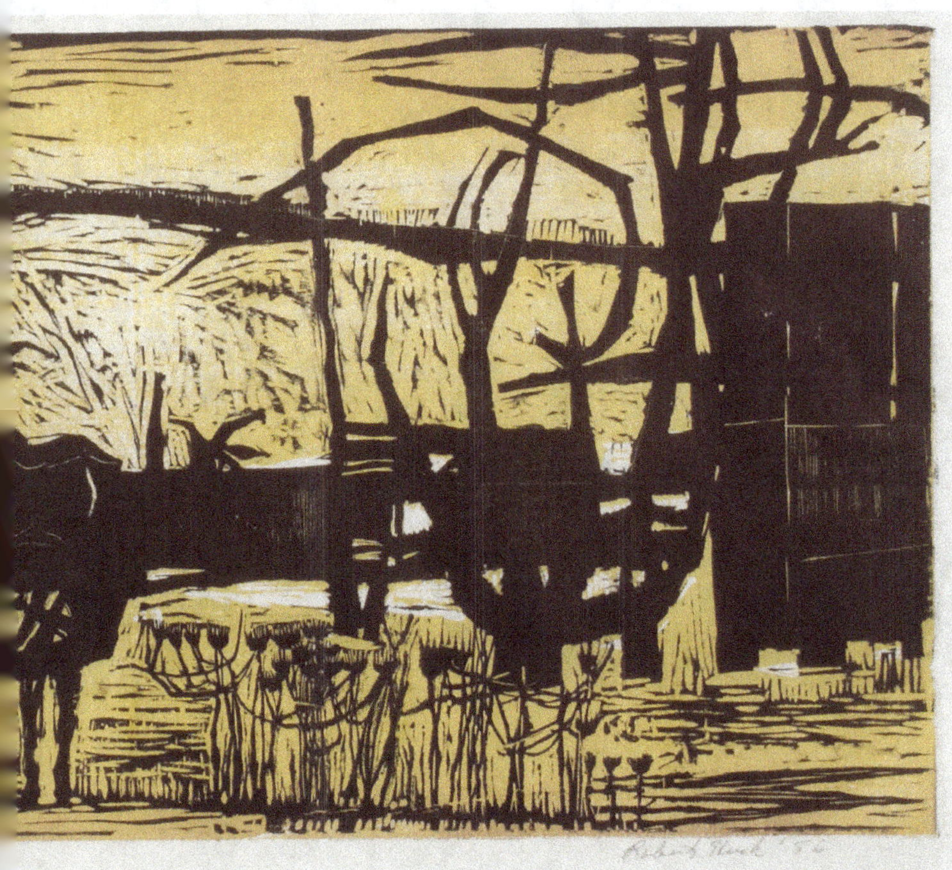

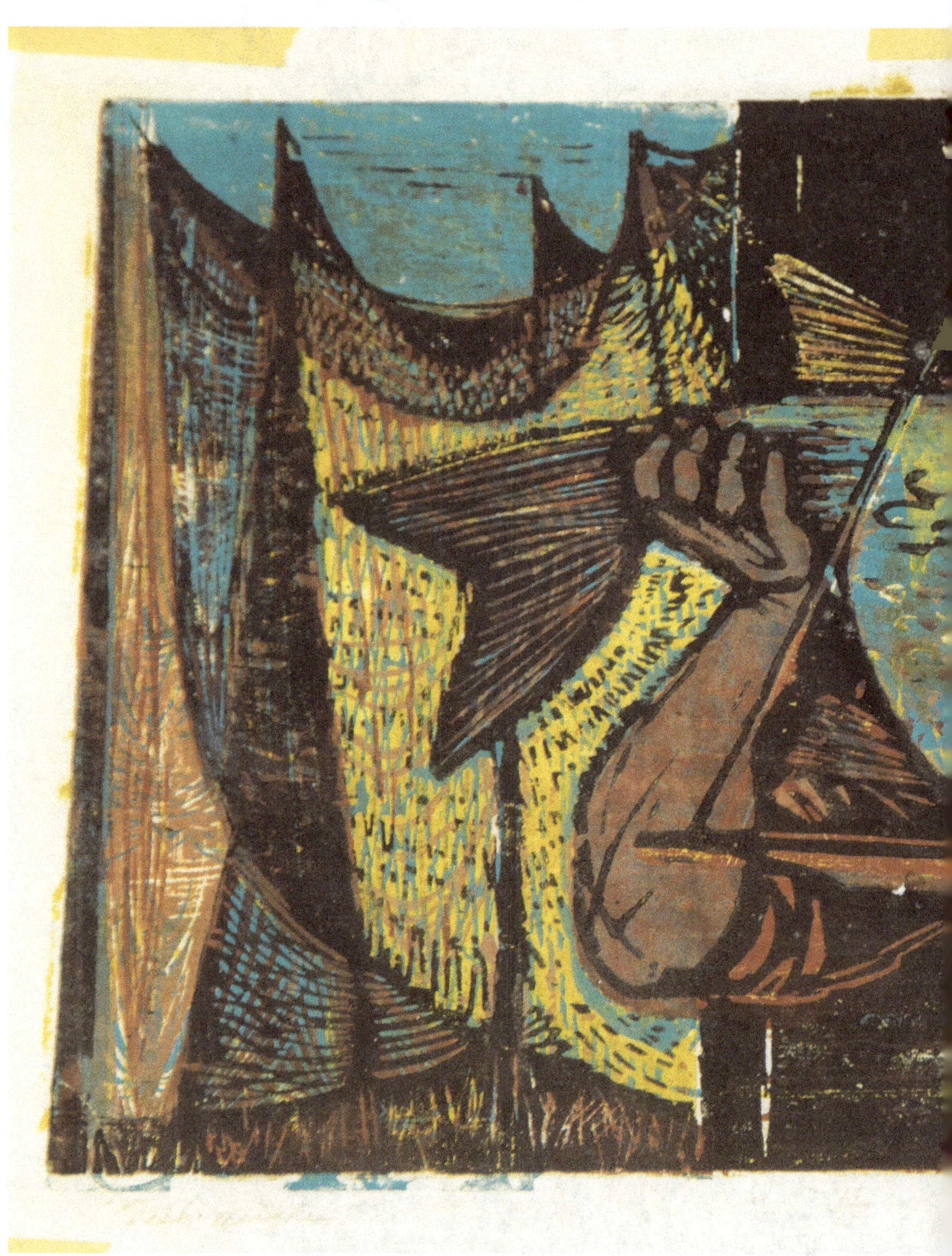

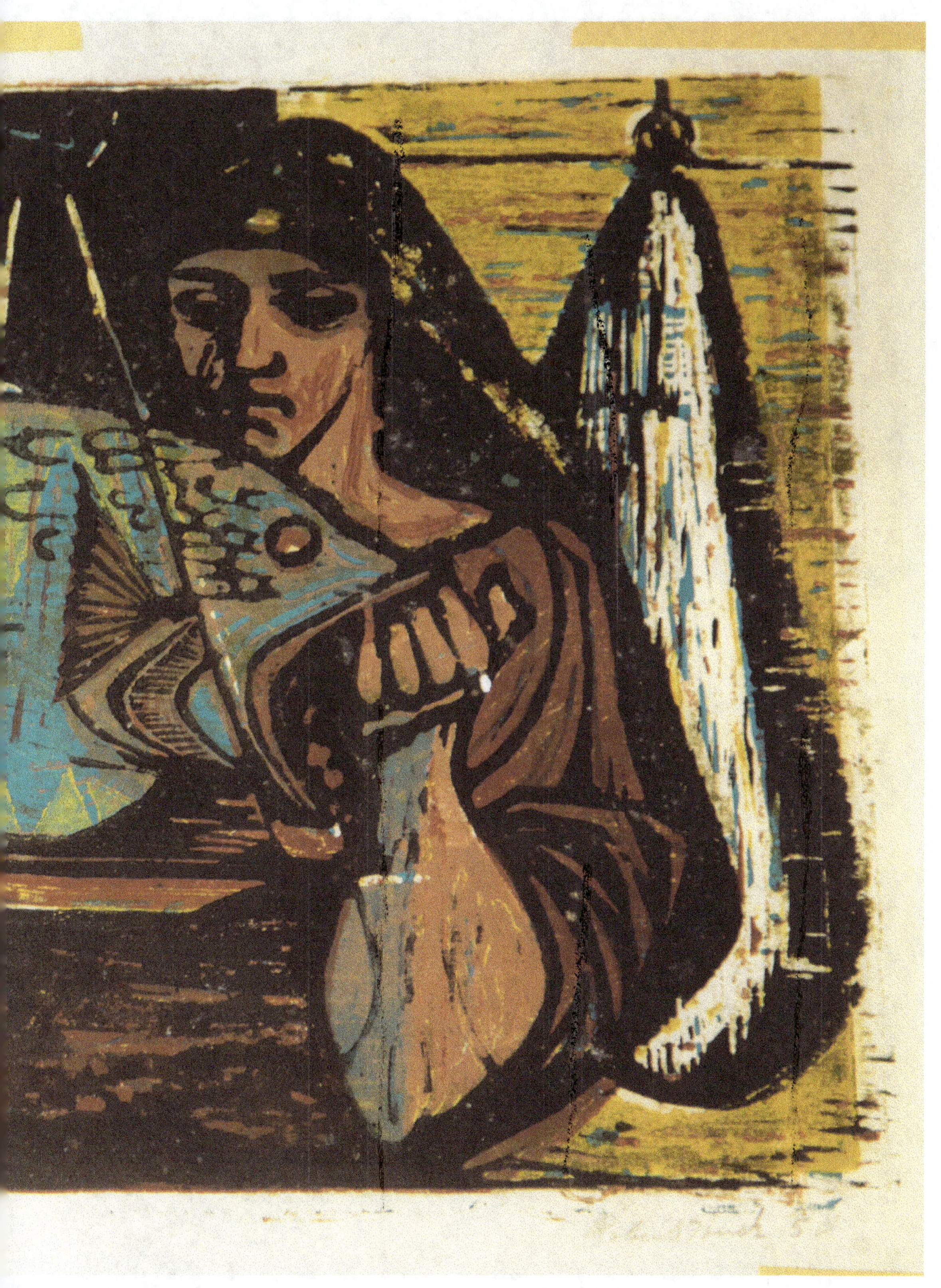

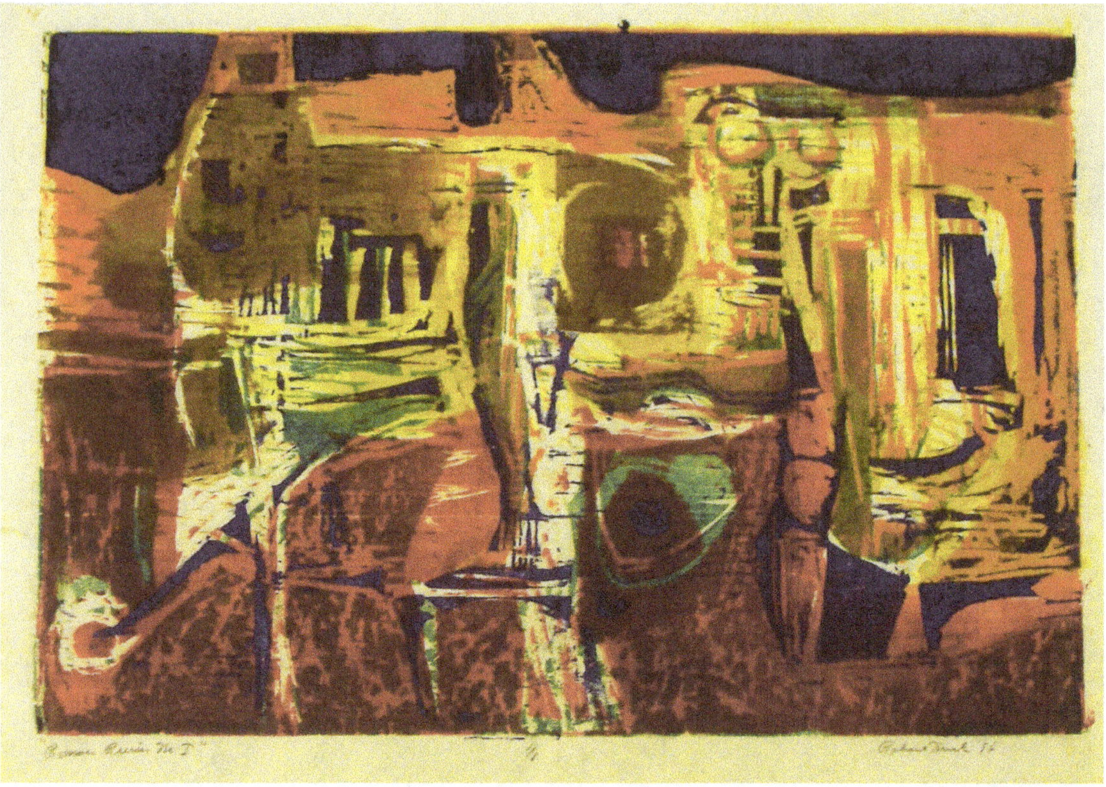

"Roman Ruins" (1956)

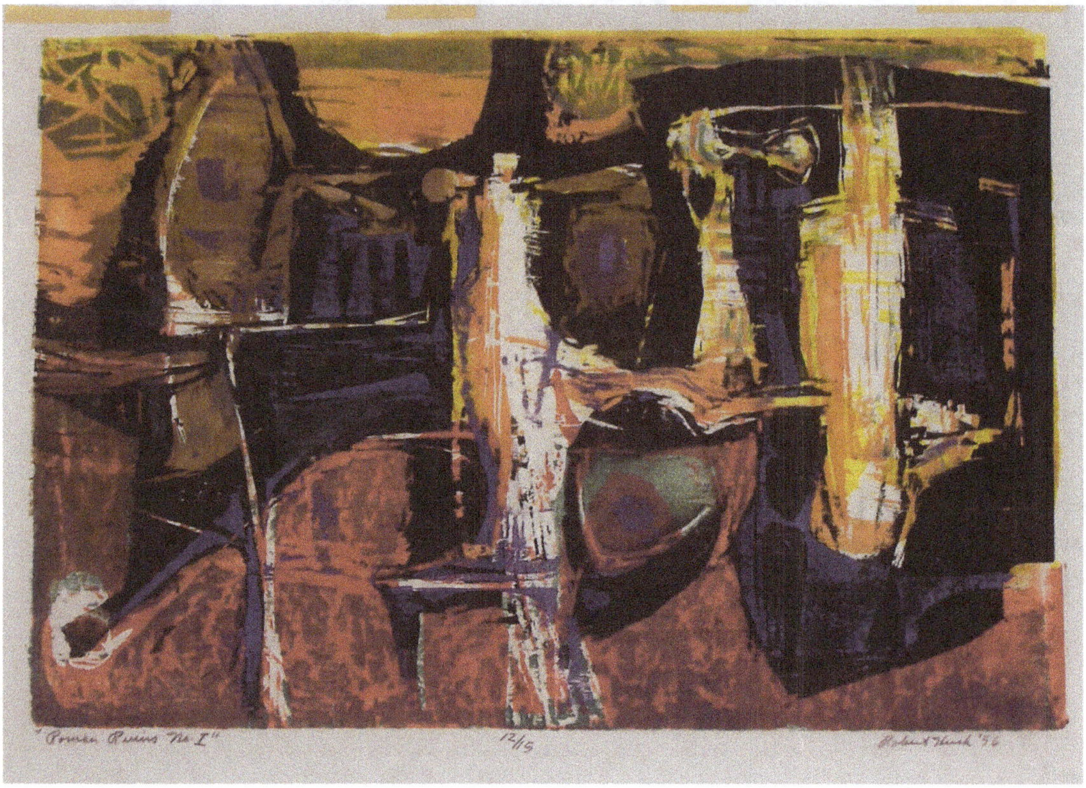

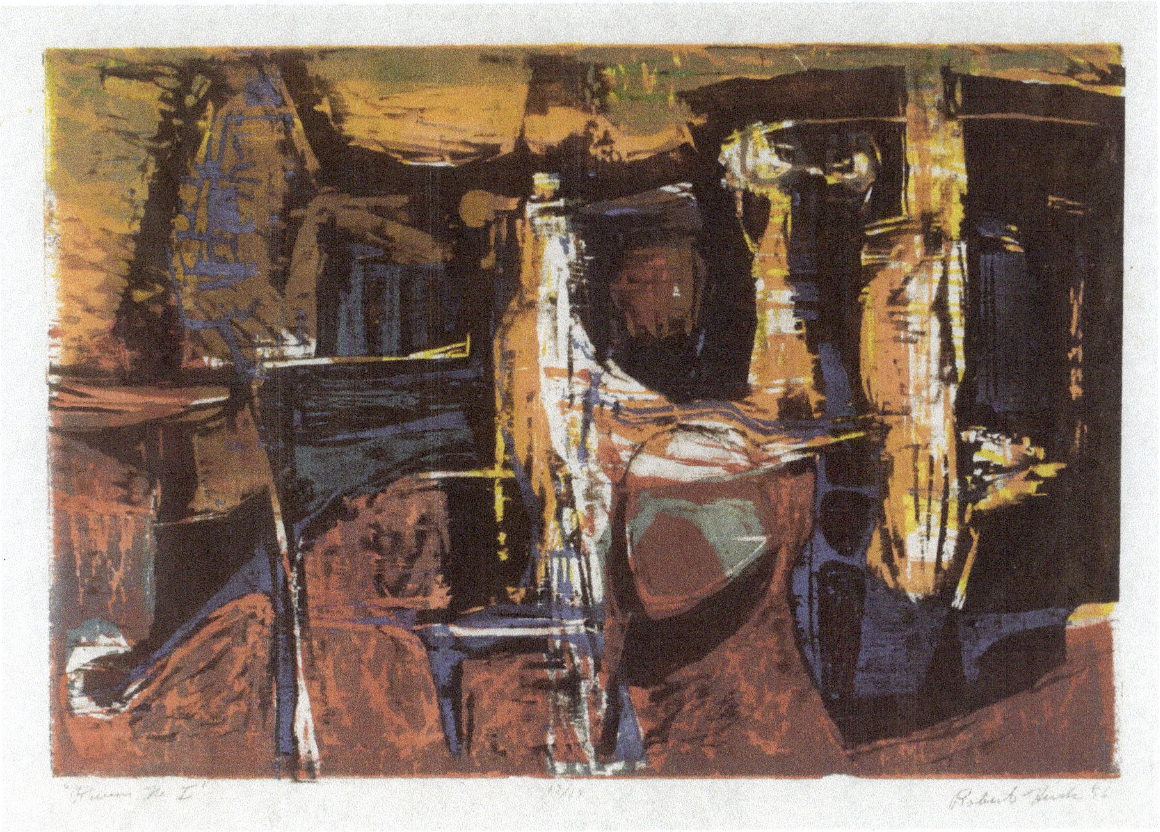

"Theme on H and G" (1956)

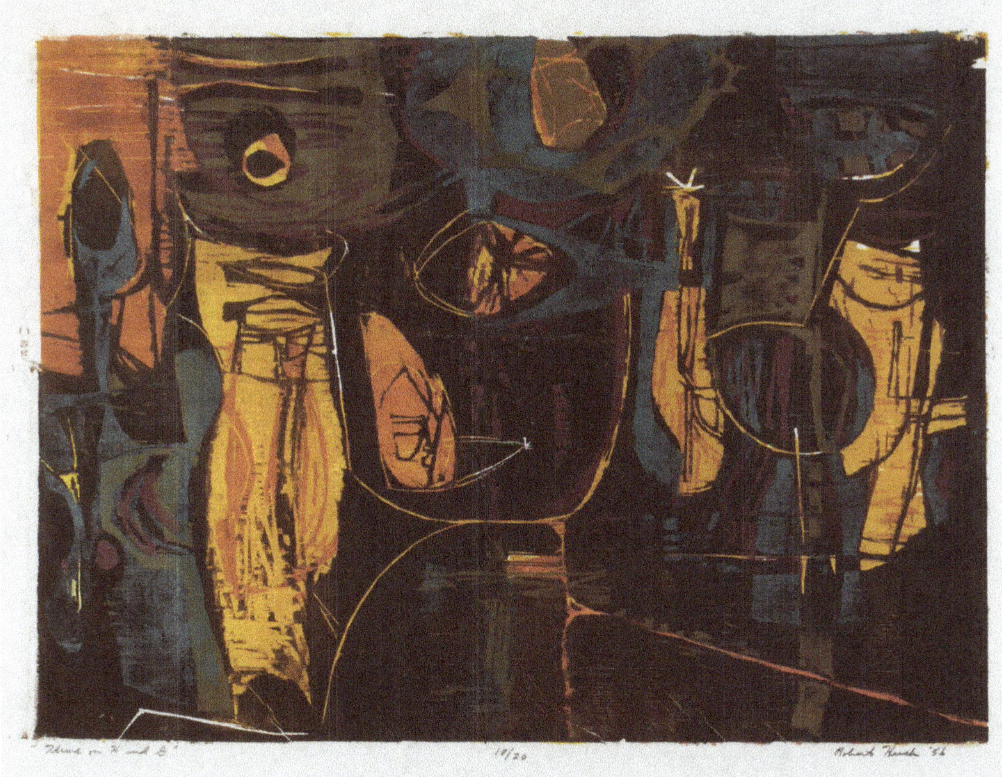

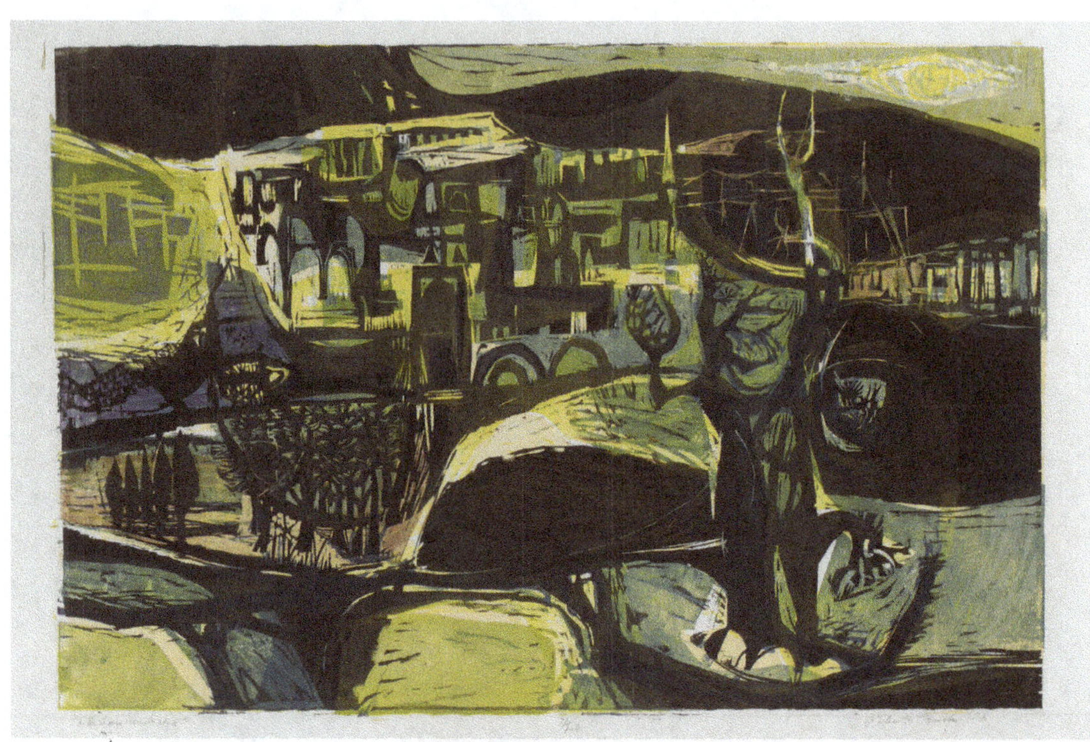

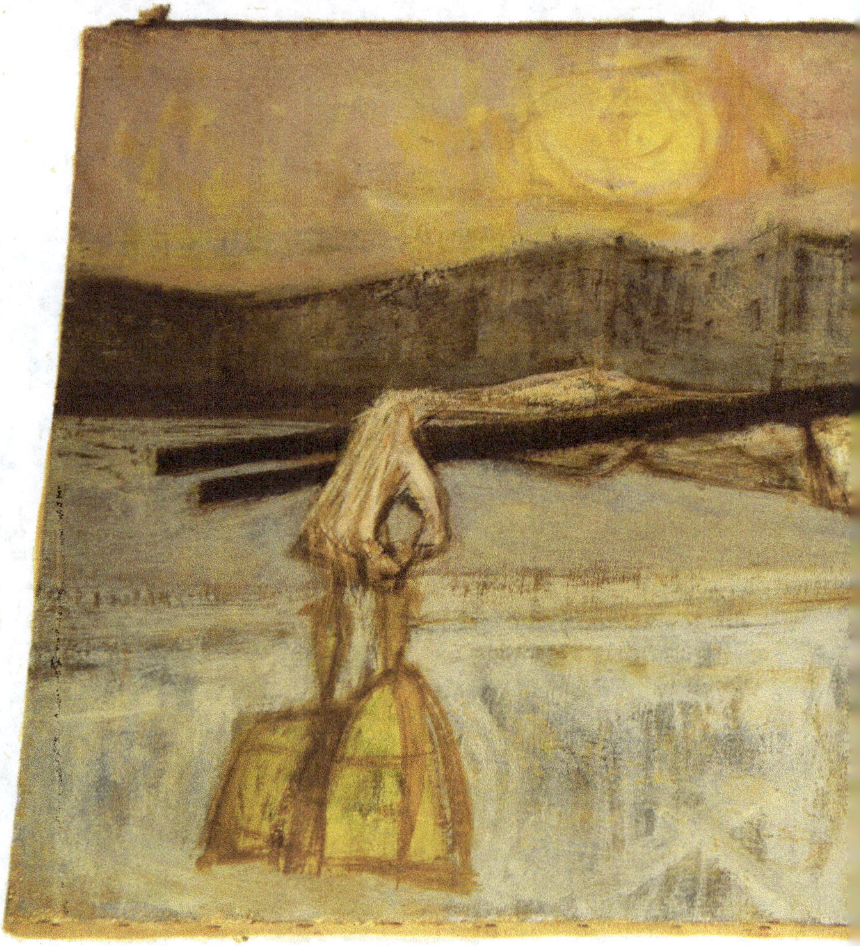

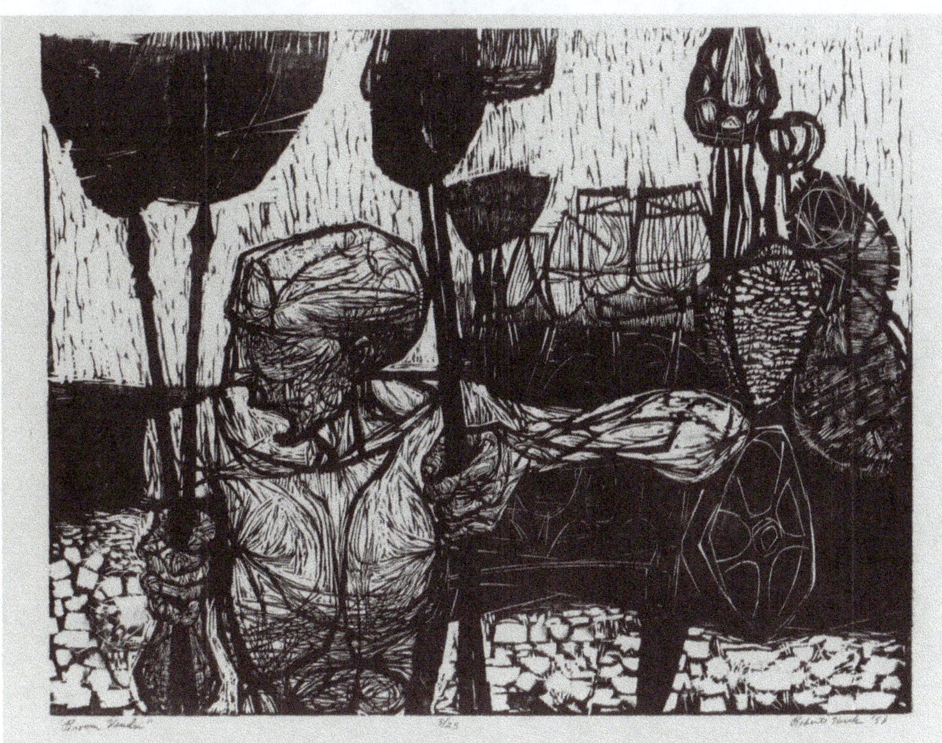

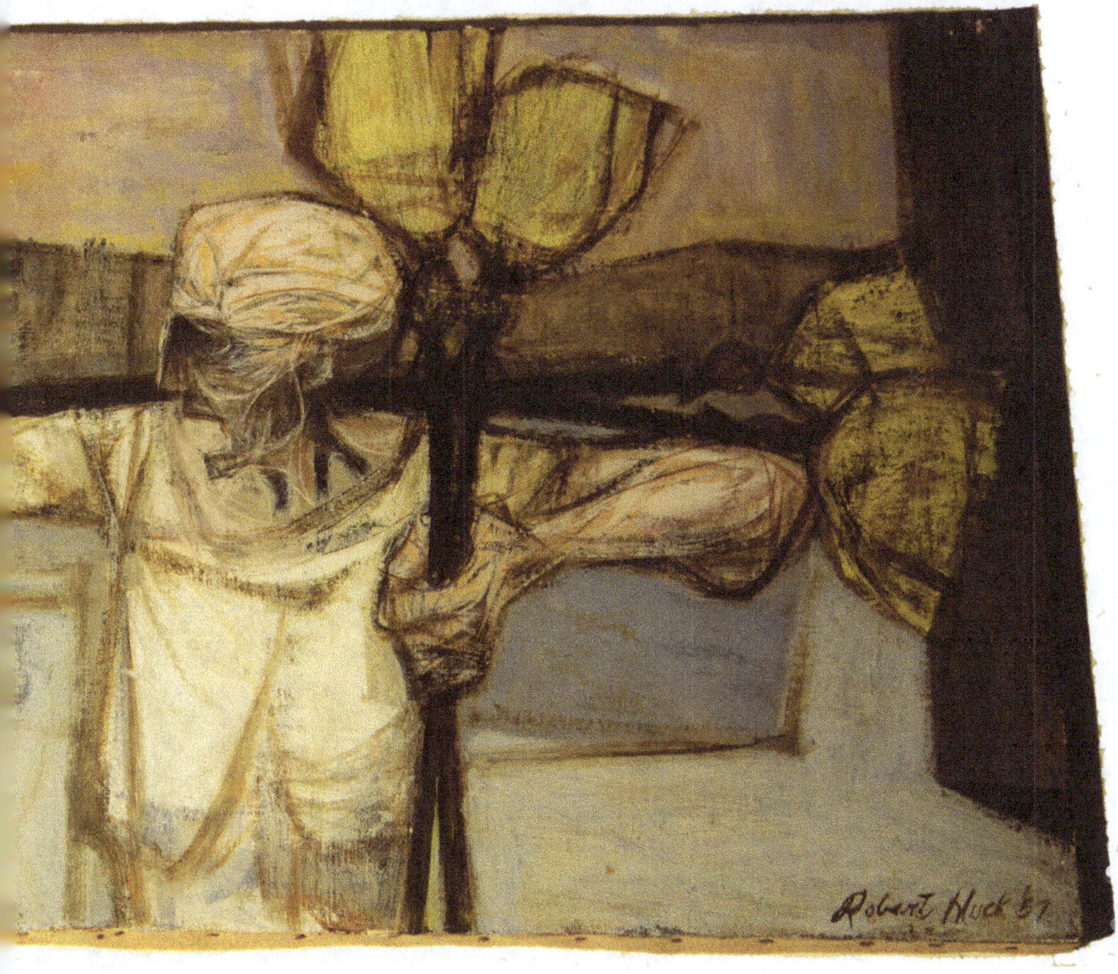

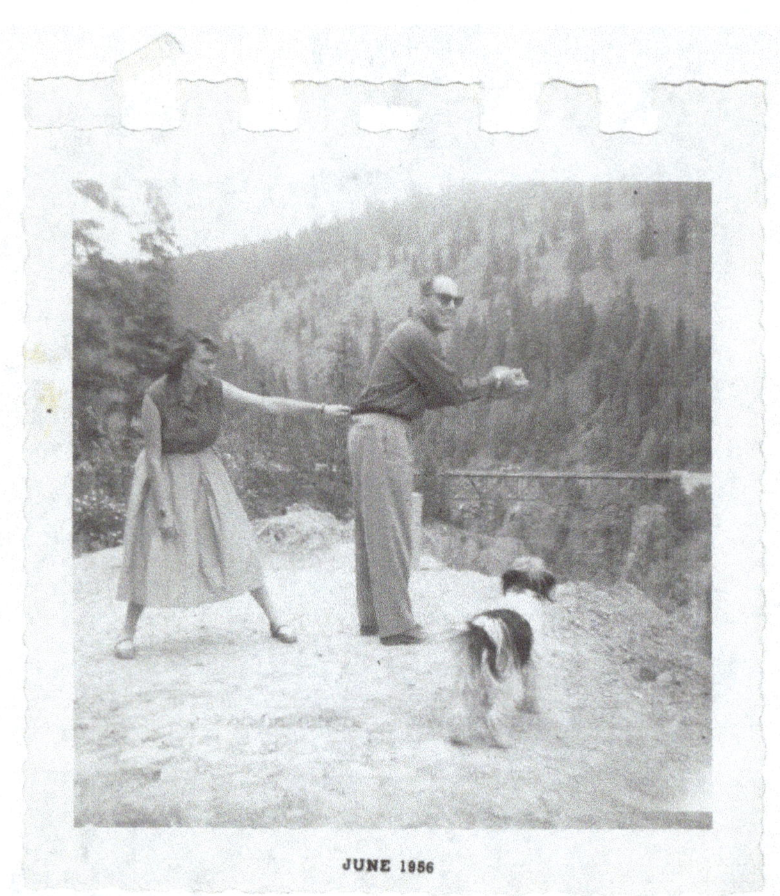

JUNE 1956

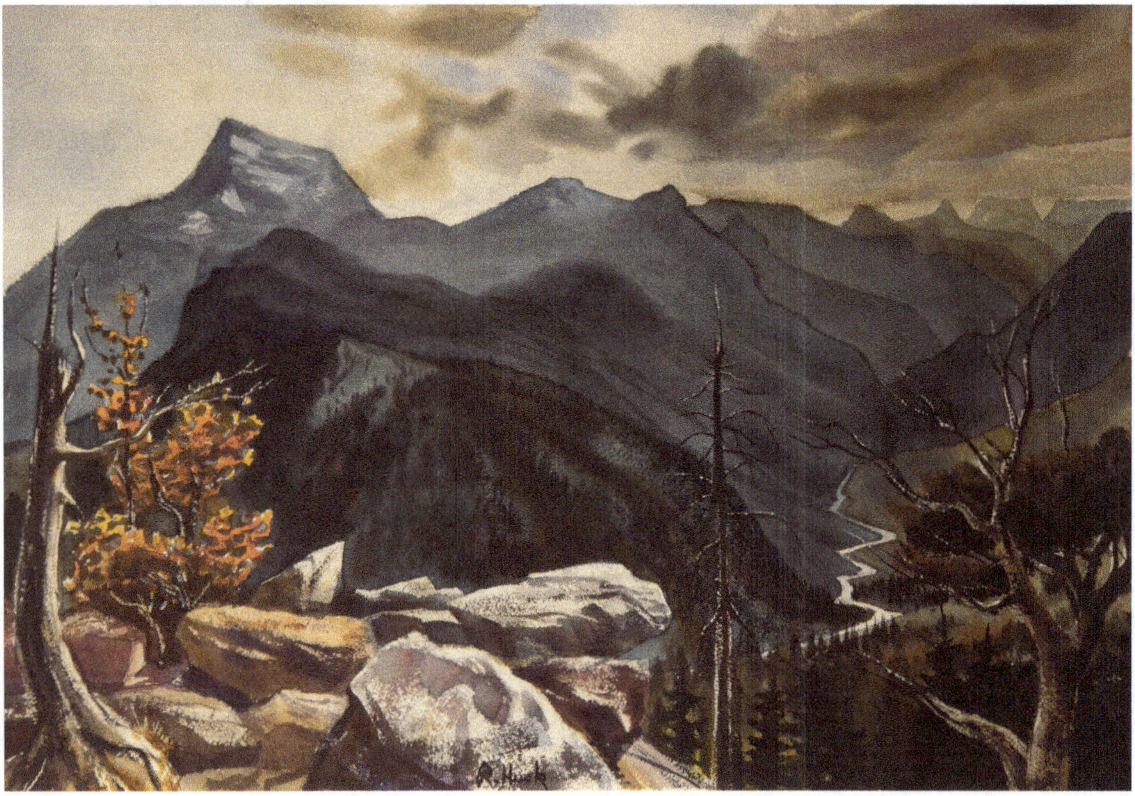

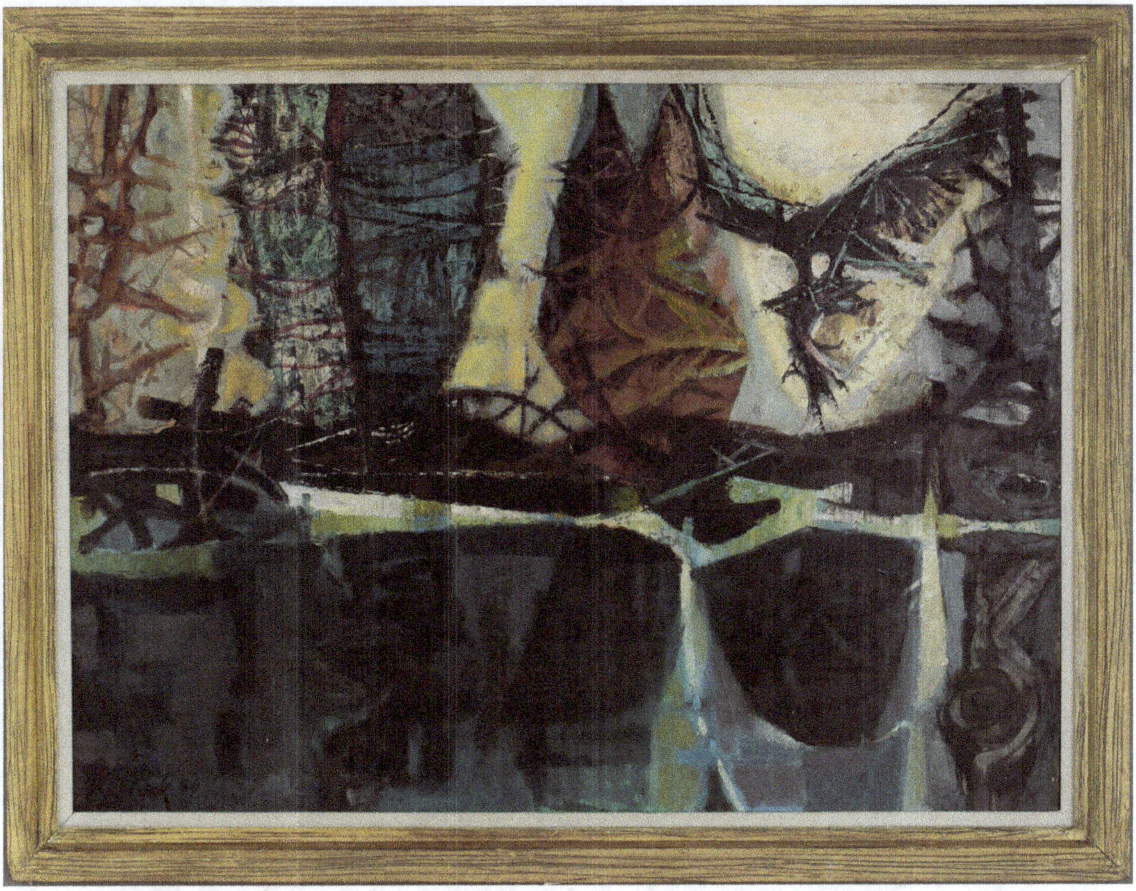

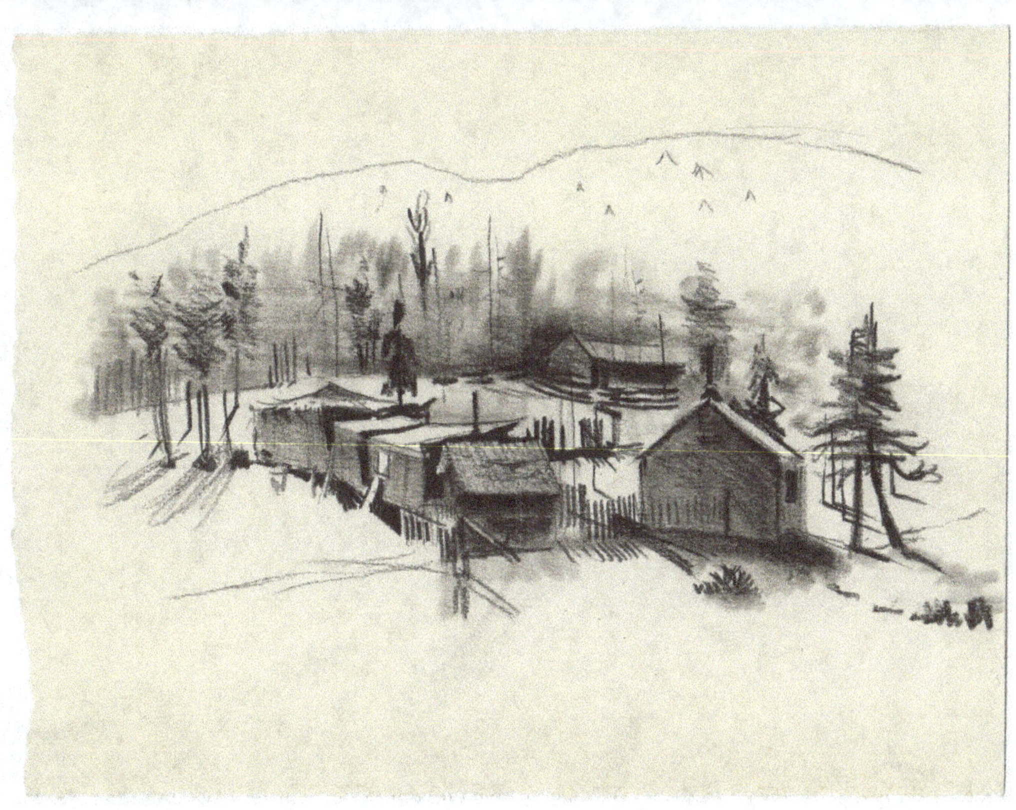

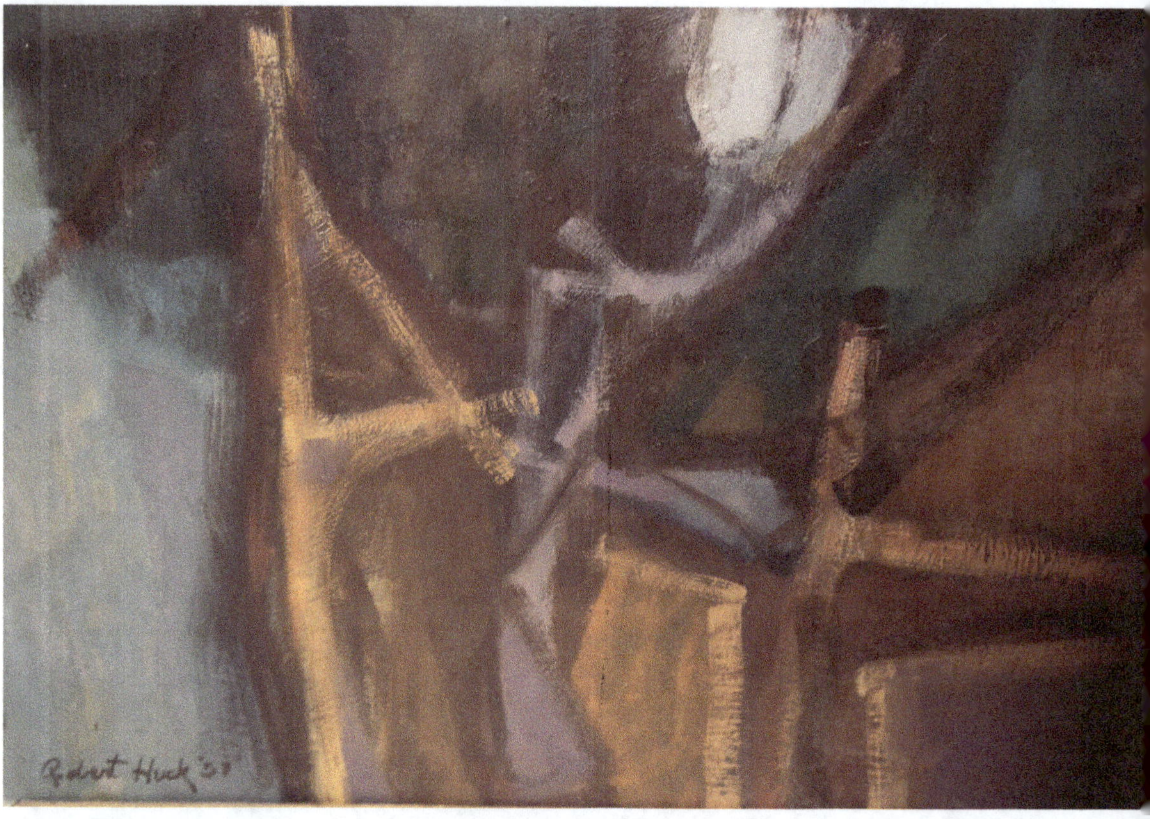

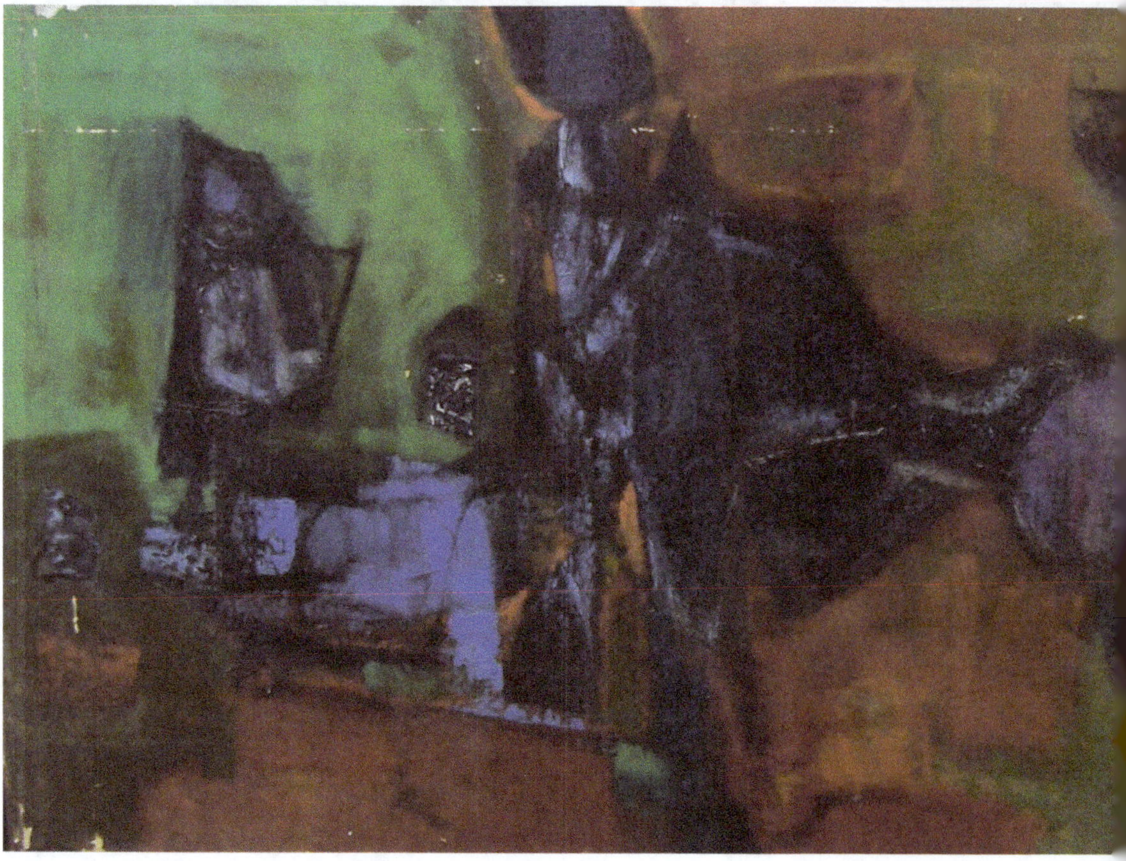

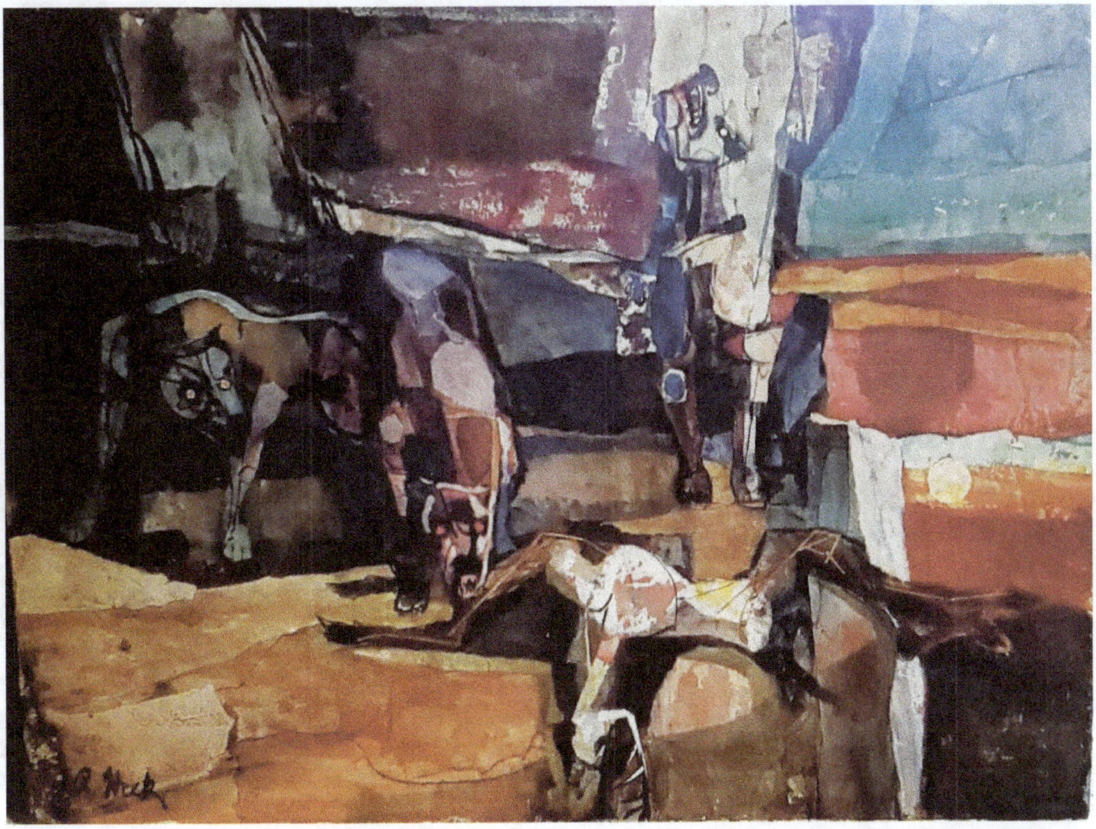

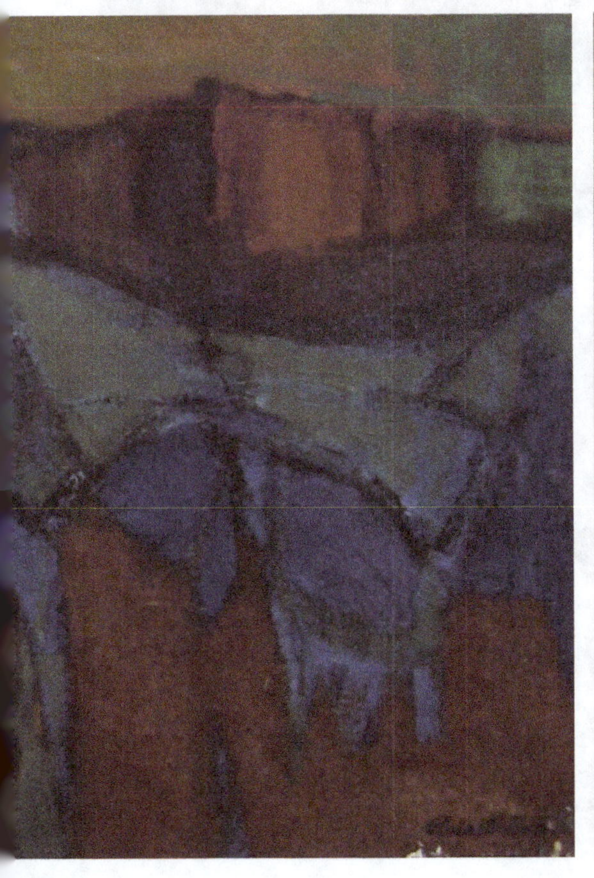

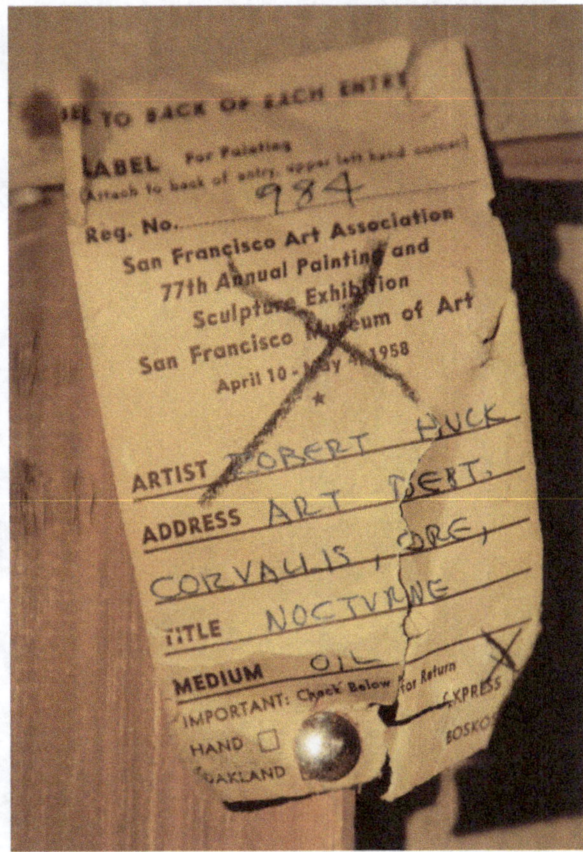
...UE TO BACK OF EACH ENTRY
LABEL   For Painting
(Attach to back of entry, upper left hand corner)
Reg. No.   984
San Francisco Art Association
77th Annual Painting and
Sculpture Exhibition
San Francisco Museum of Art
April 10 - May 11 1958
*
ARTIST   ROBERT HUCK
ADDRESS   ART DEPT,
CORVALLIS, ORE,
TITLE   NOCTURNE
MEDIUM   OIL
IMPORTANT: Check Below For Return
HAND □   EXPRESS
OAKLAND   BOSKO...

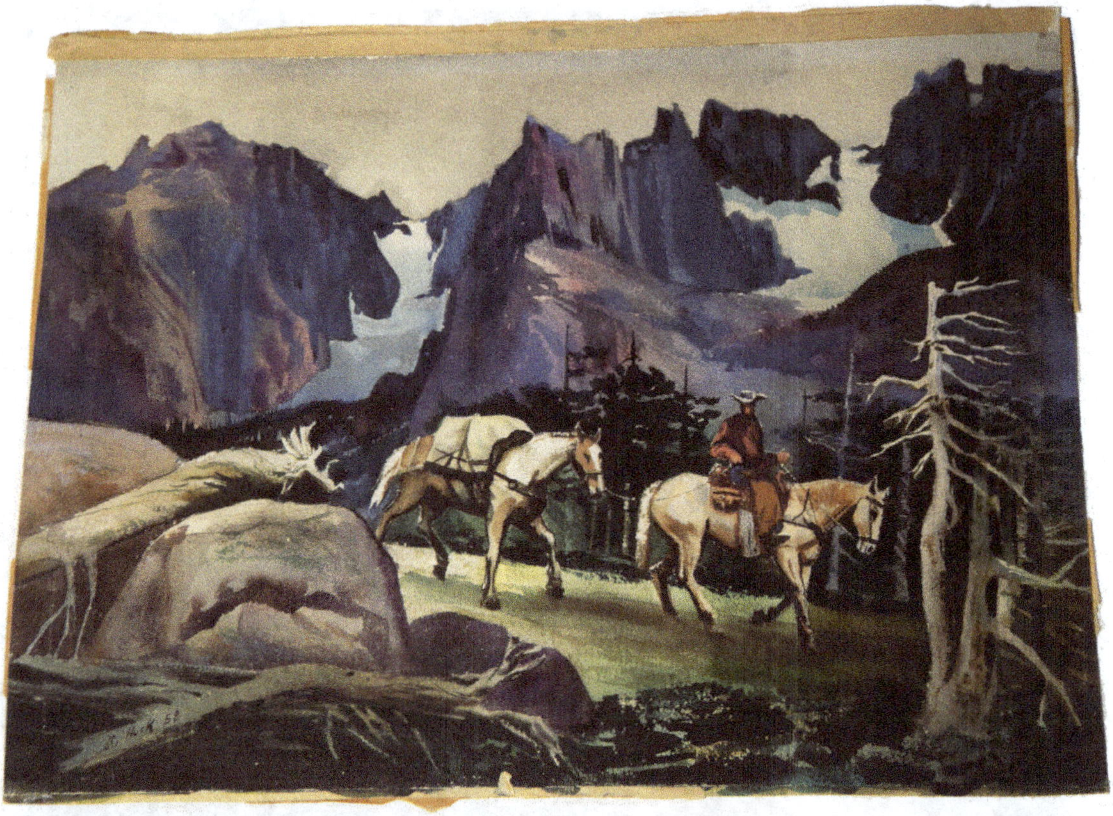

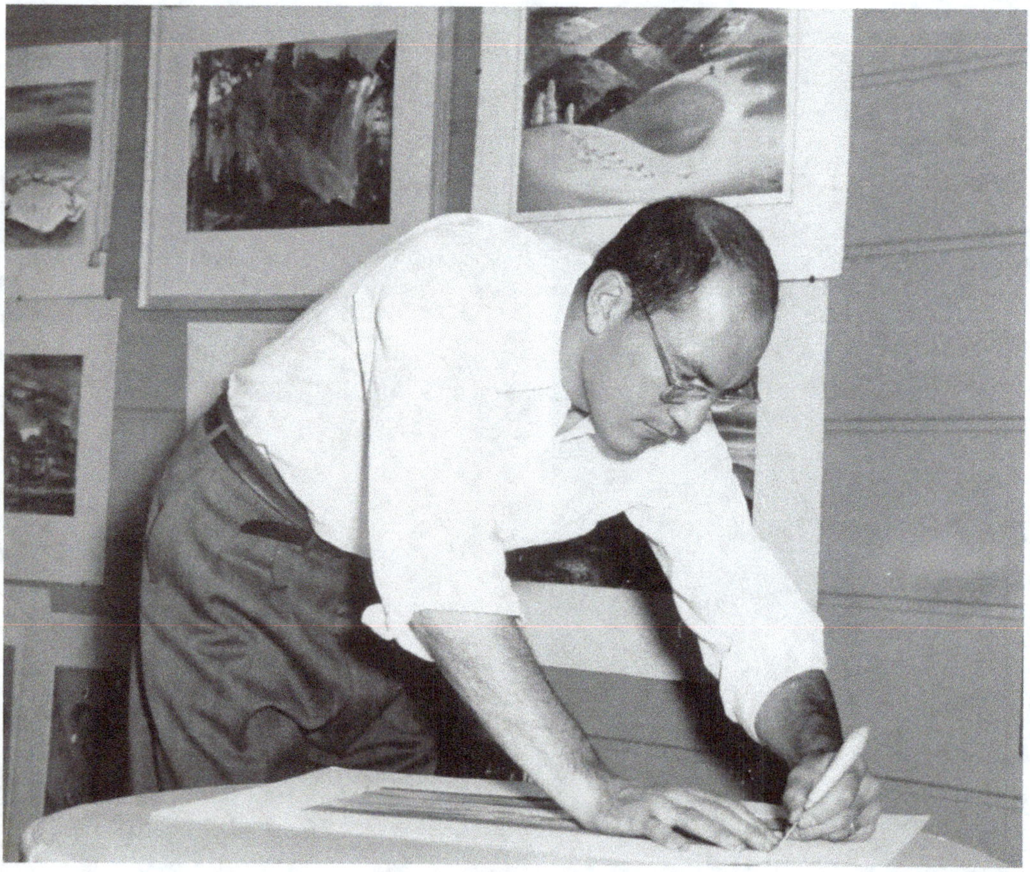

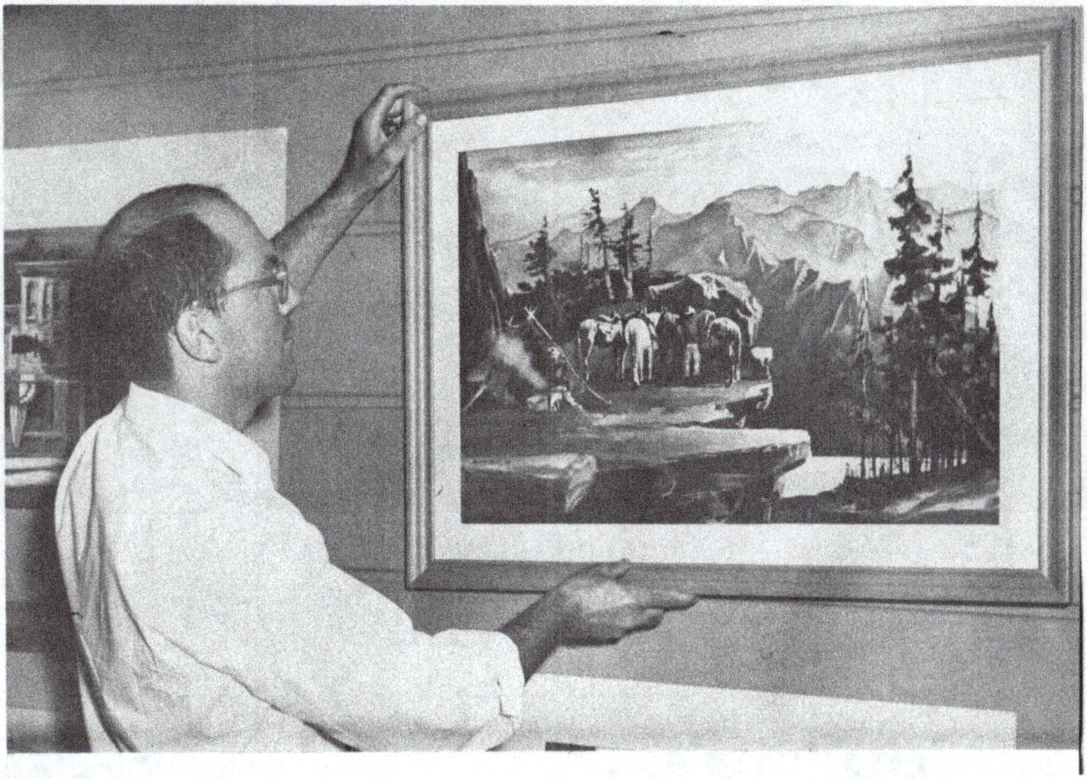

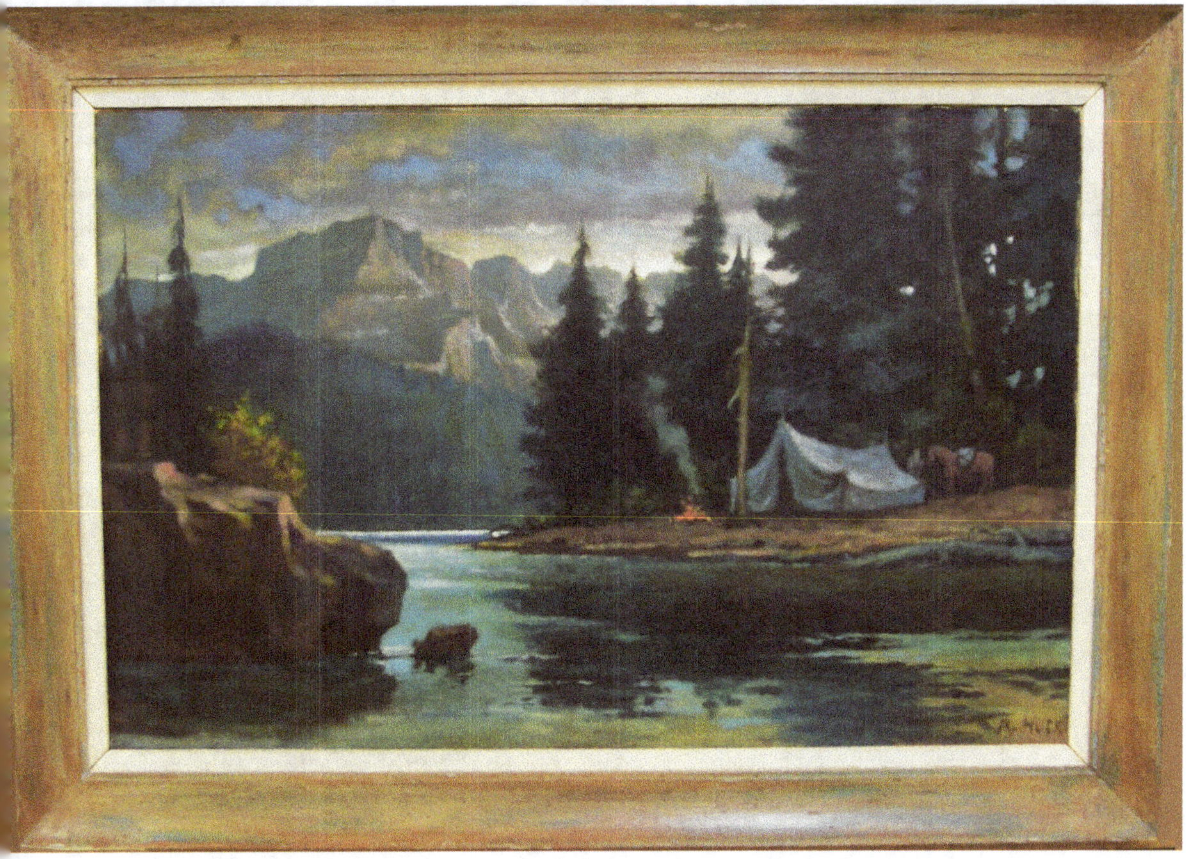

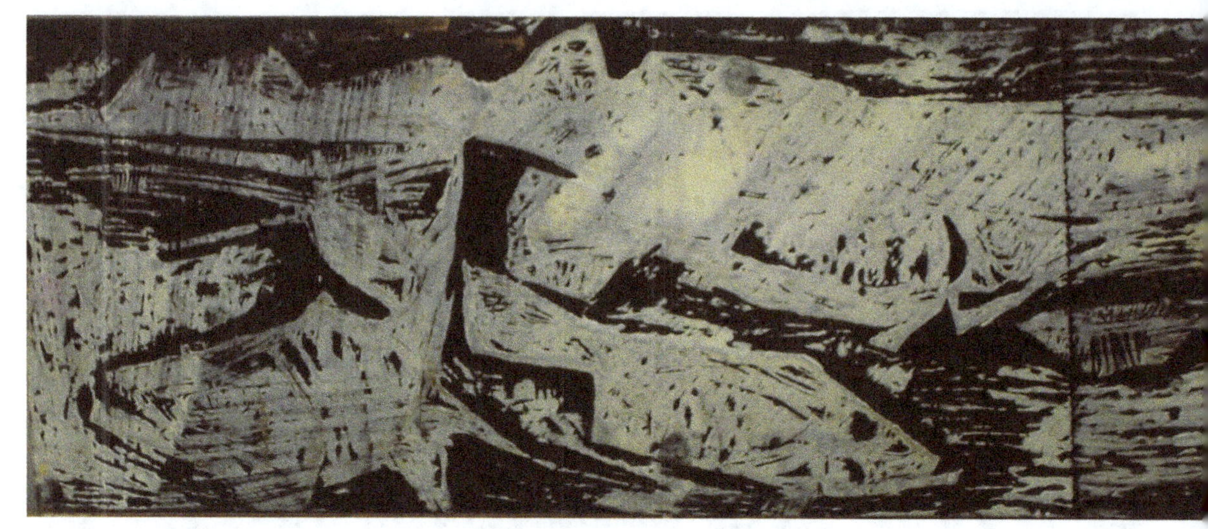

"Mountain Fish" (1957)

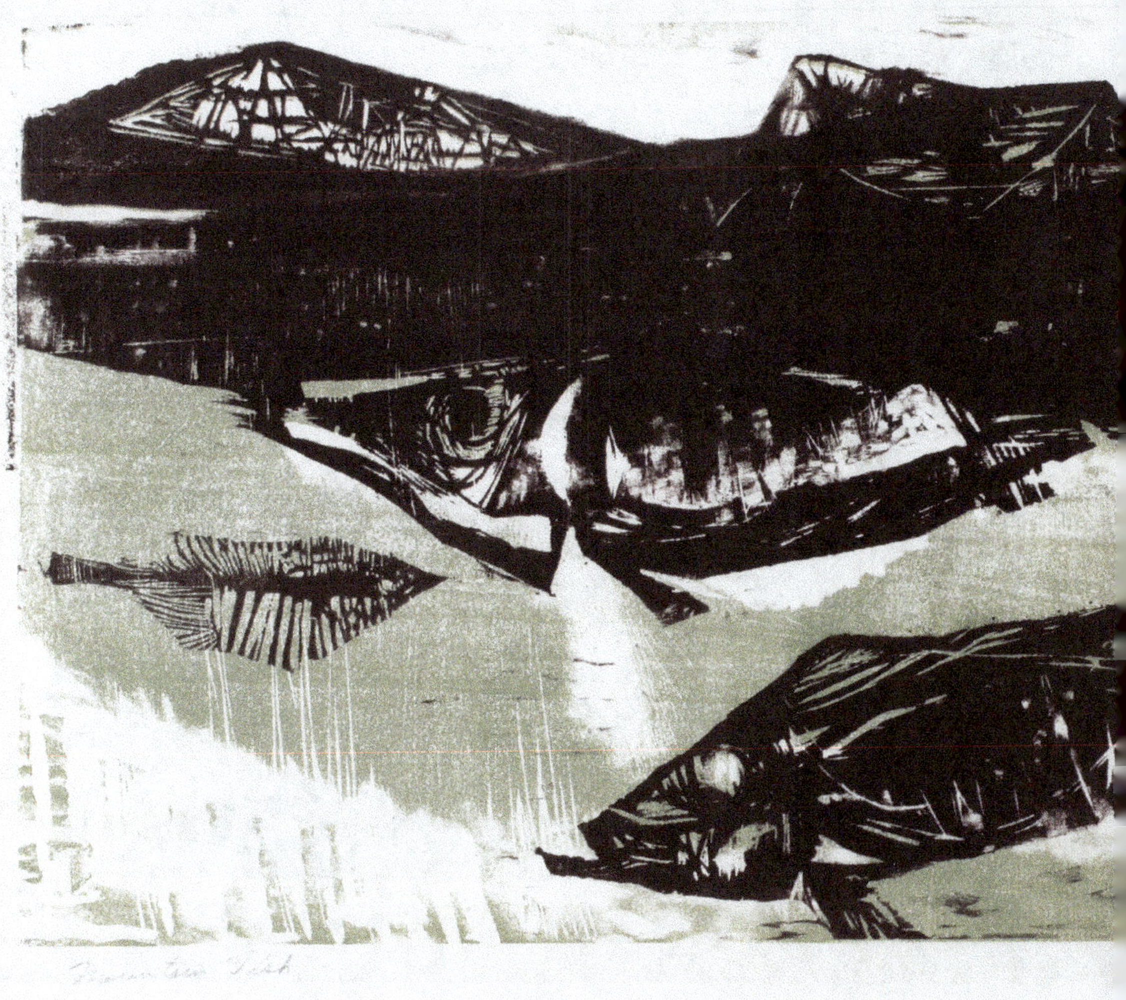

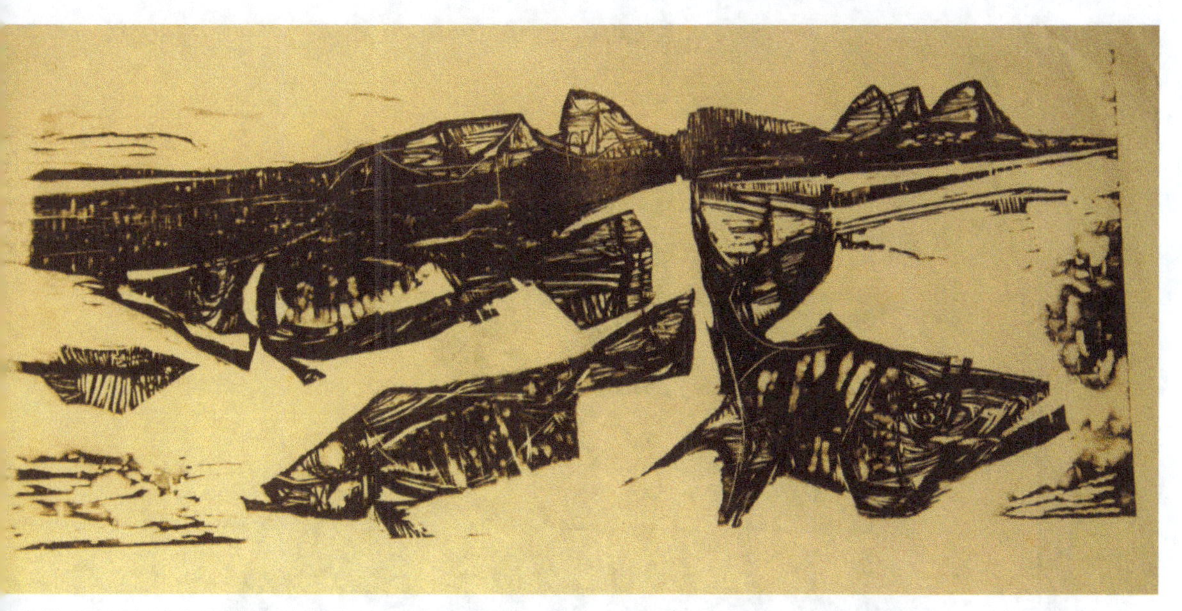

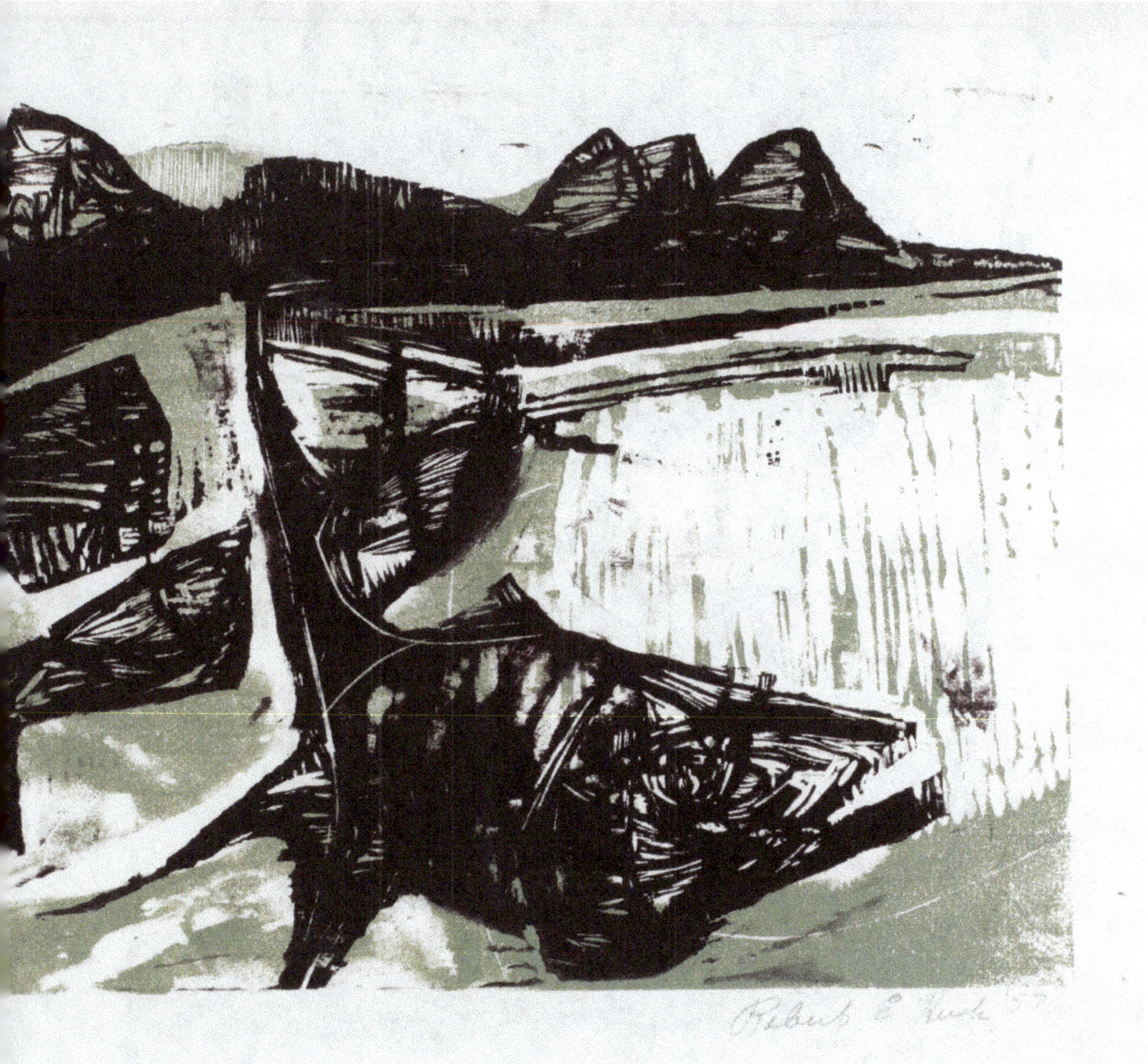

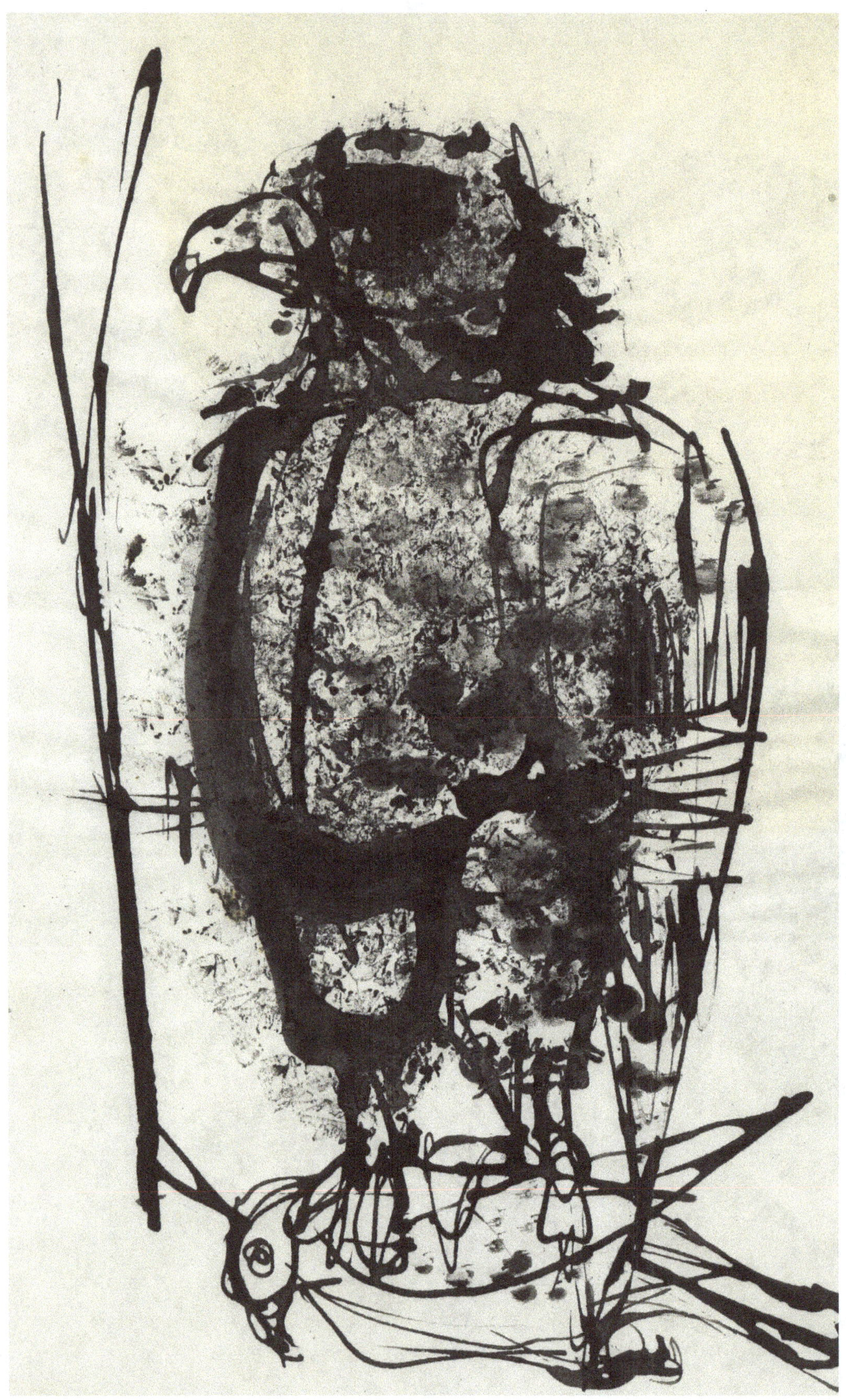

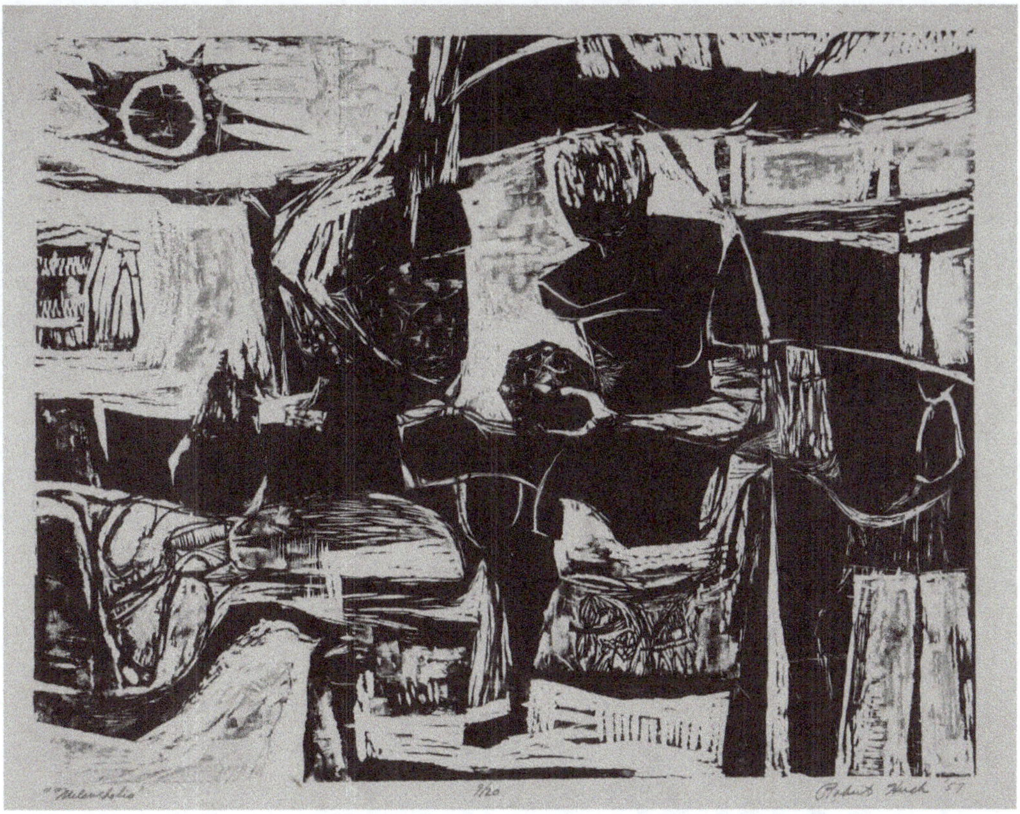

"Melancholia" (1957)

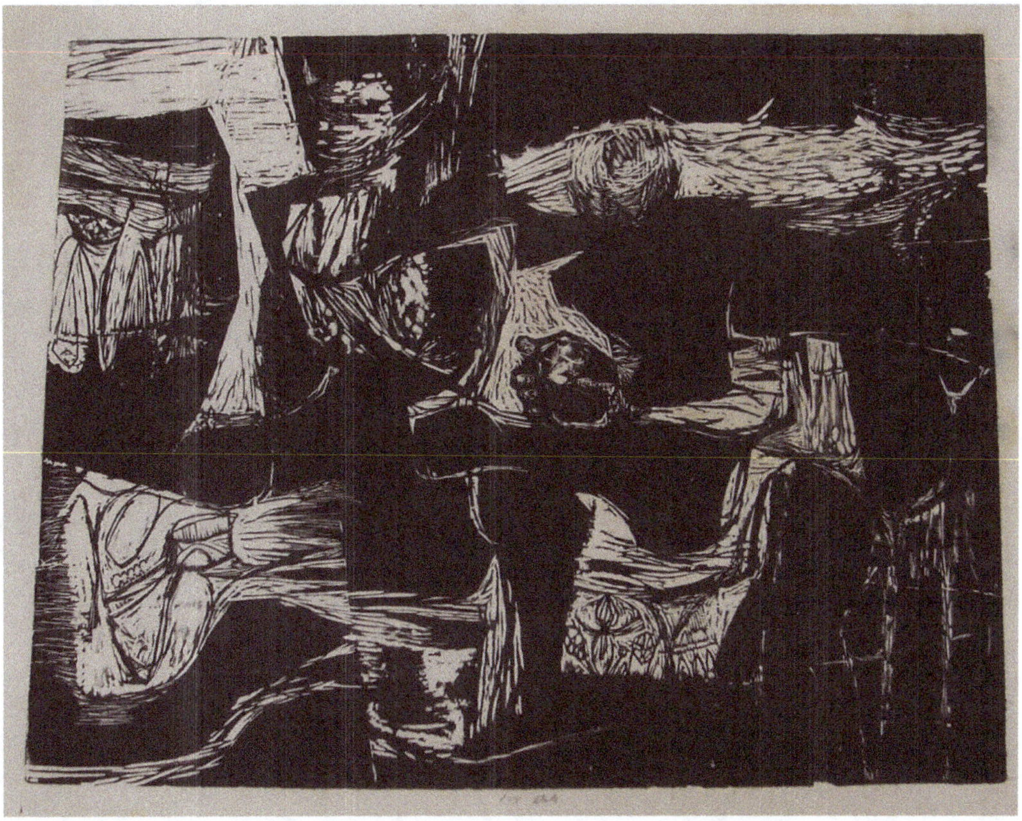

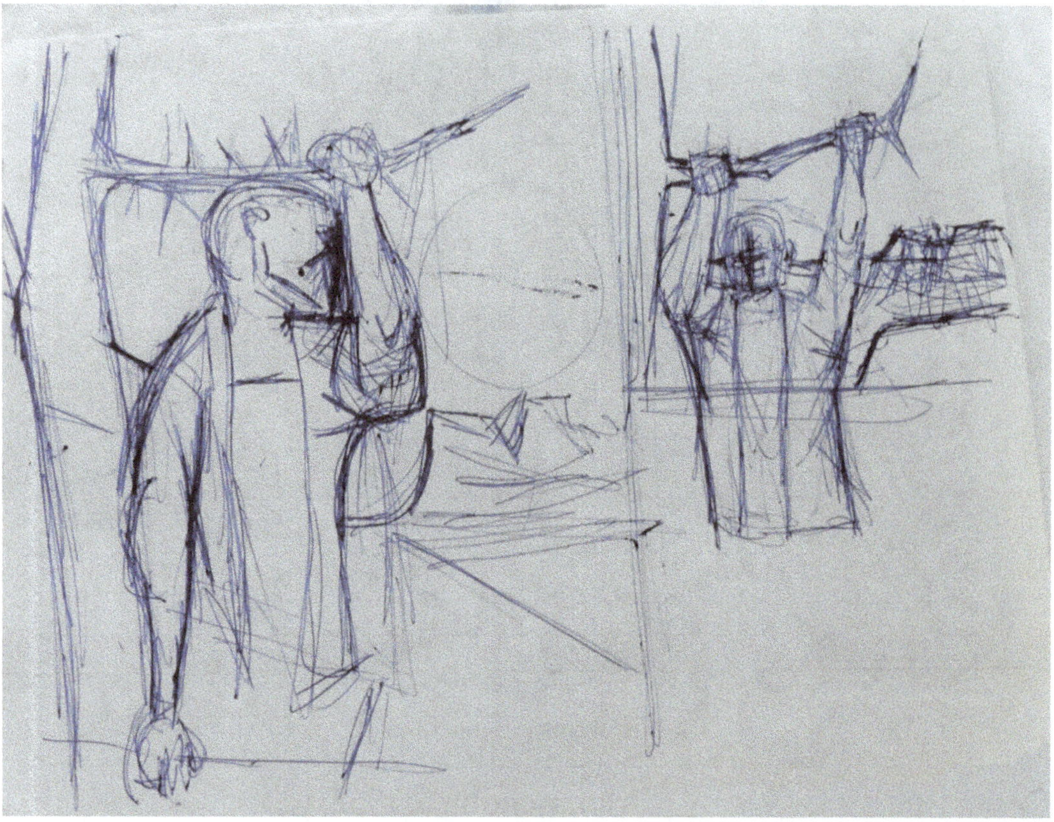

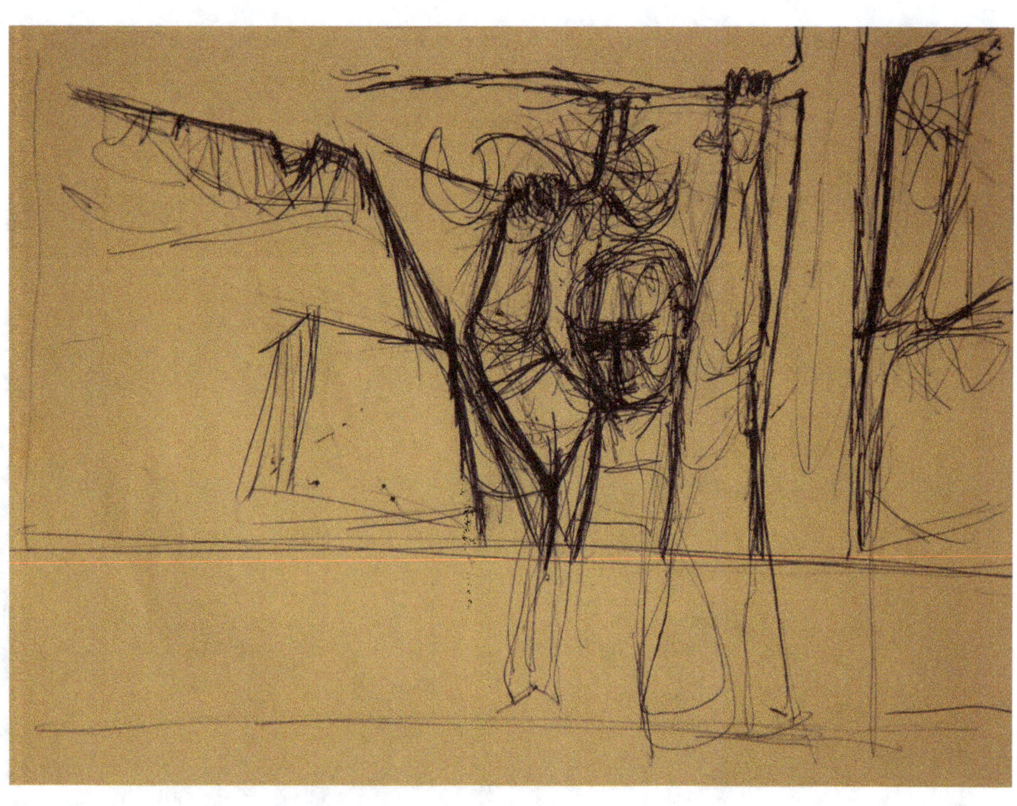

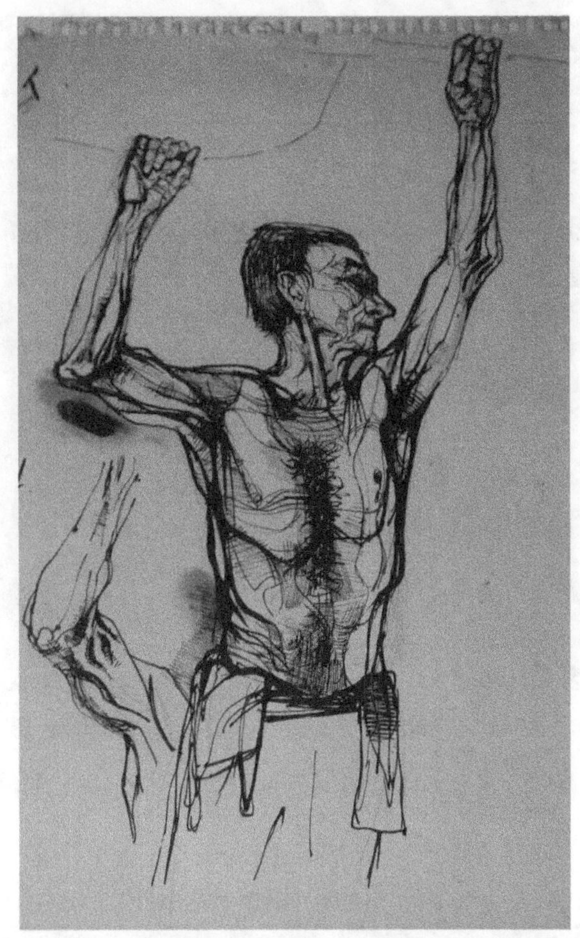

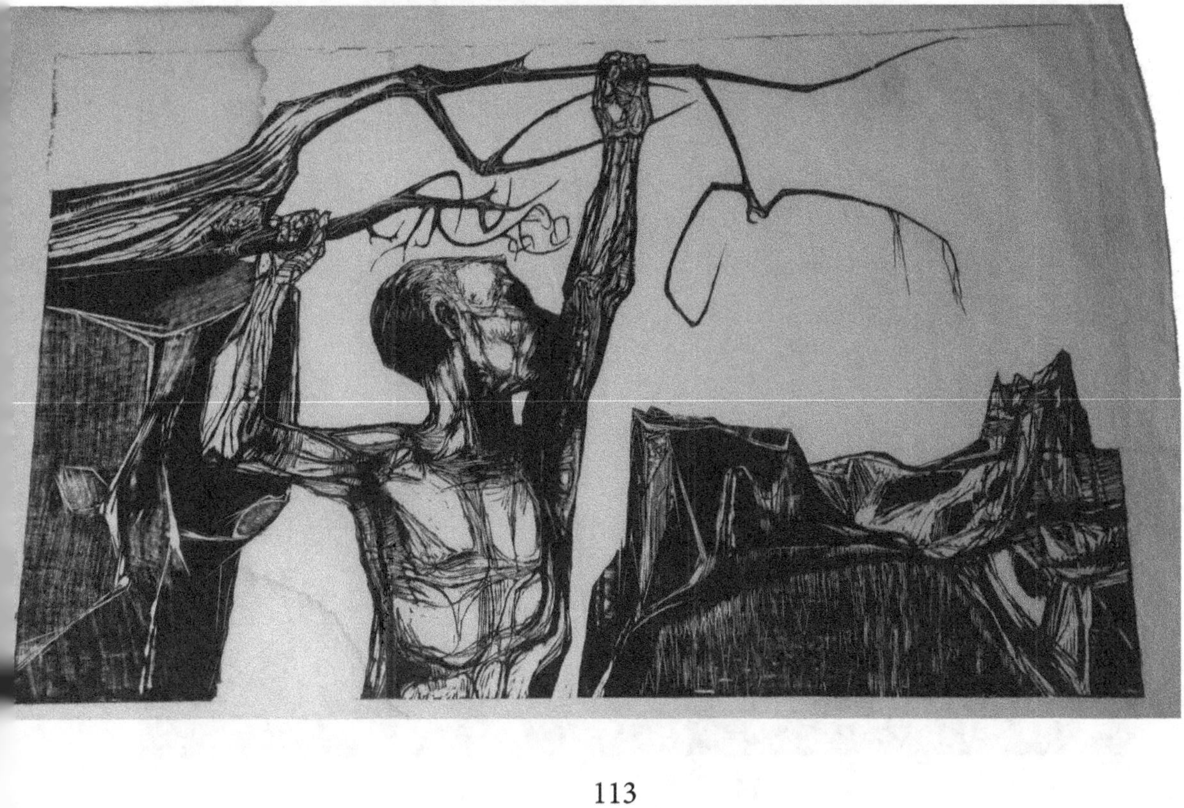

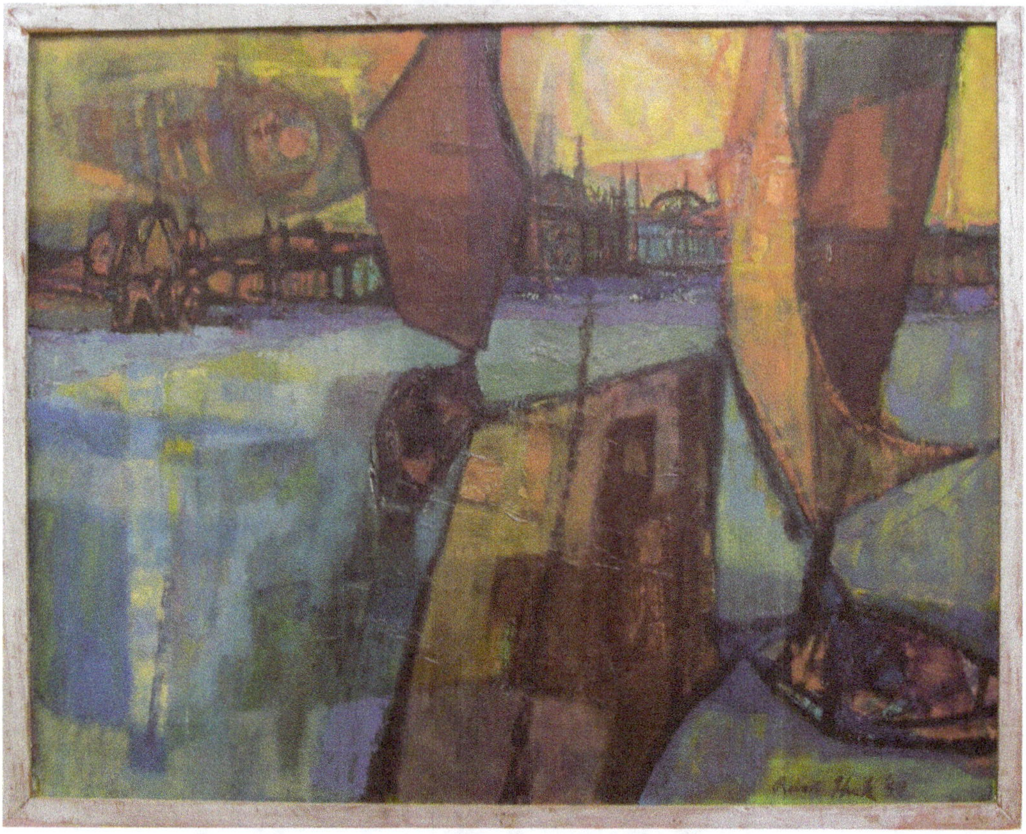

"Toward Venice" and "Venetian Fishing Family" (1957)

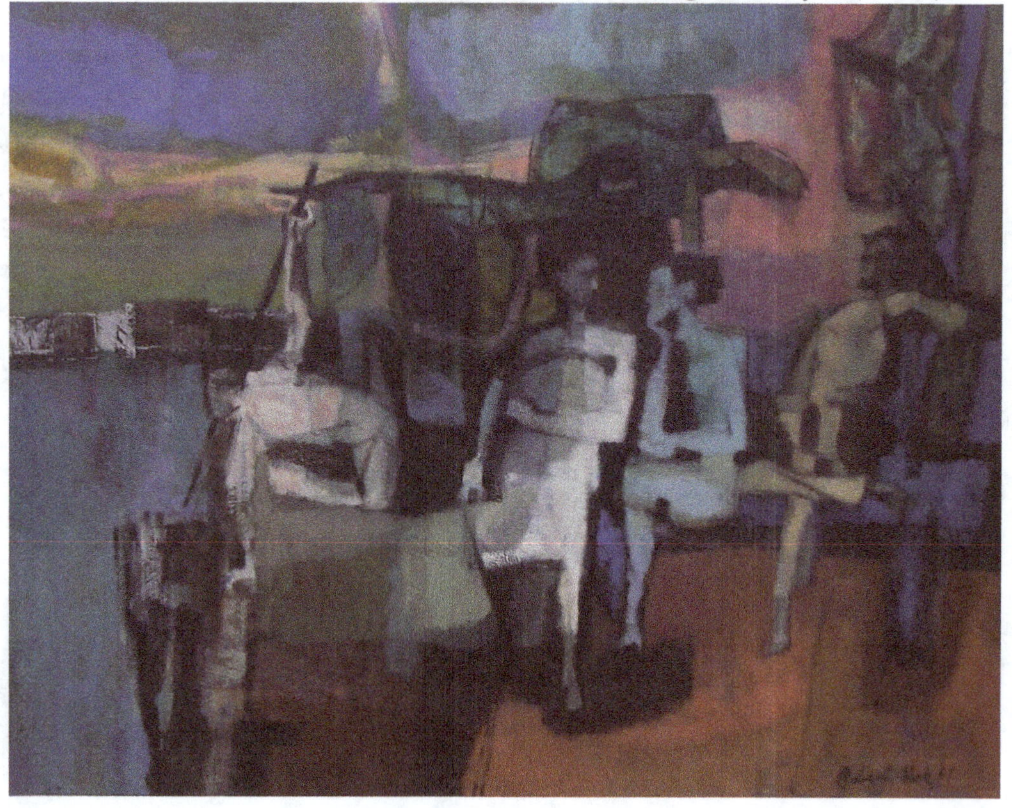

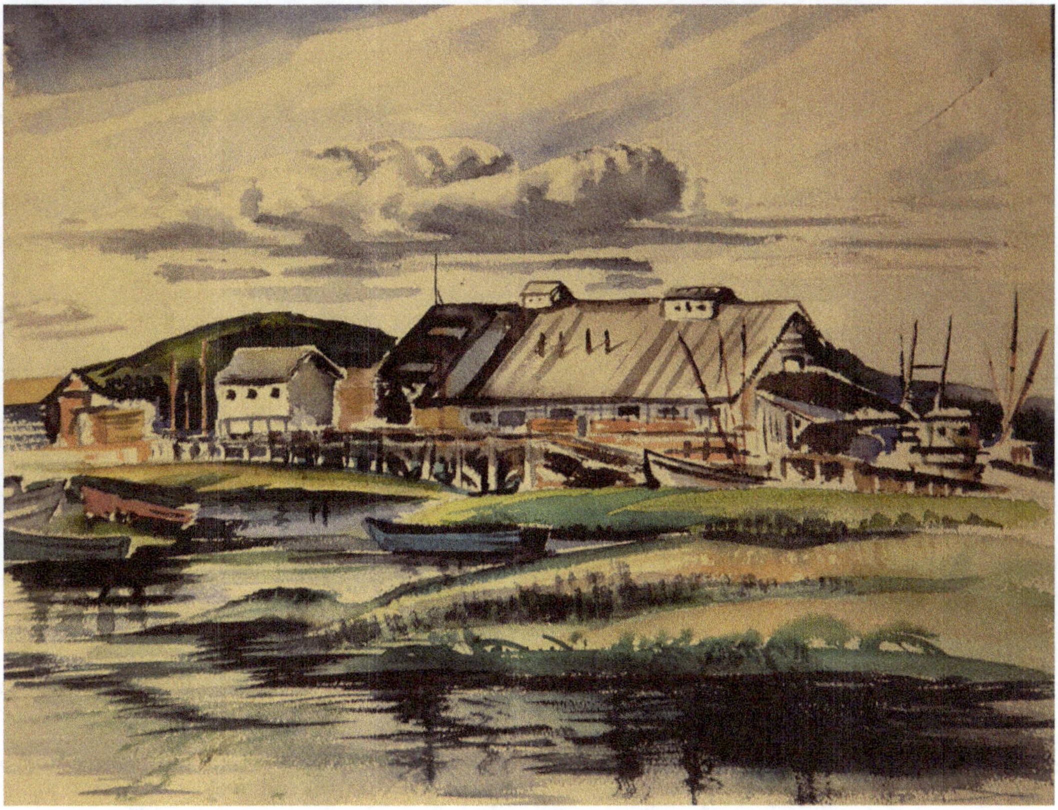

Oregon coastline

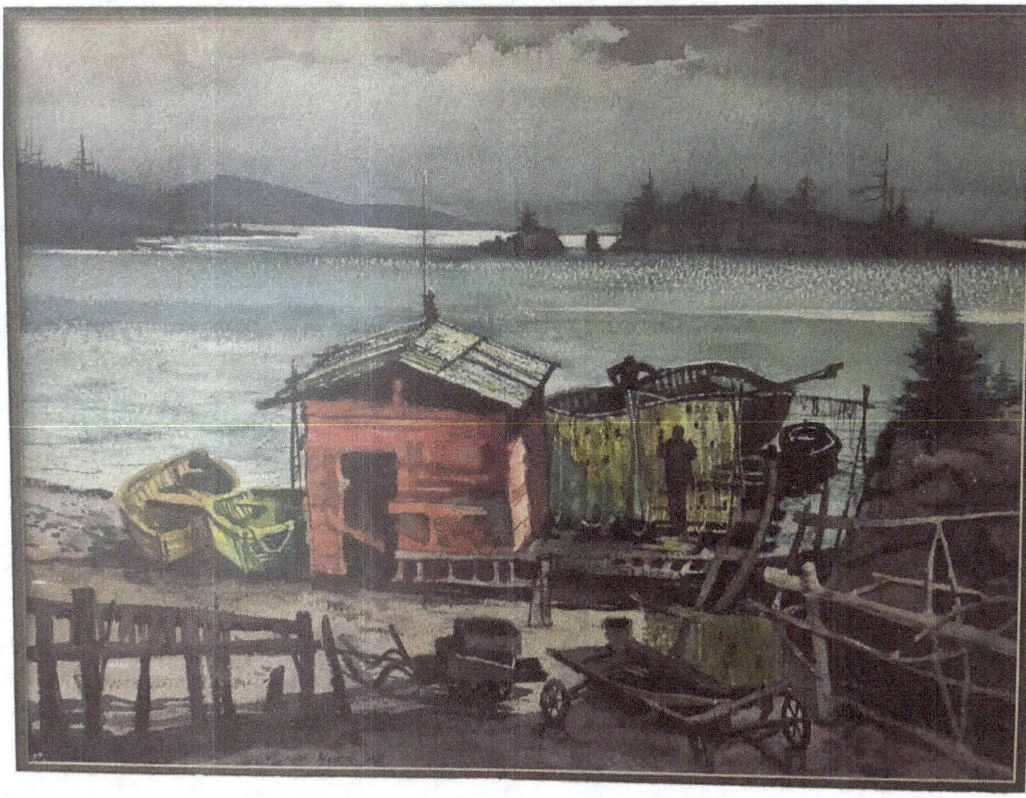

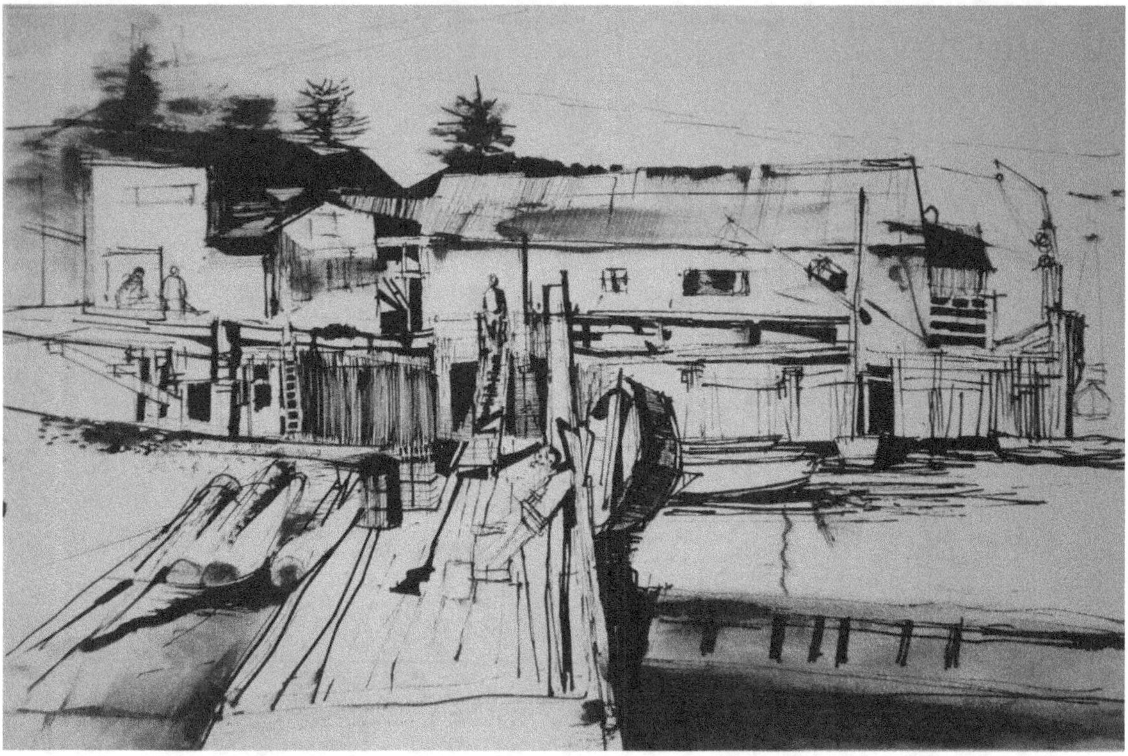

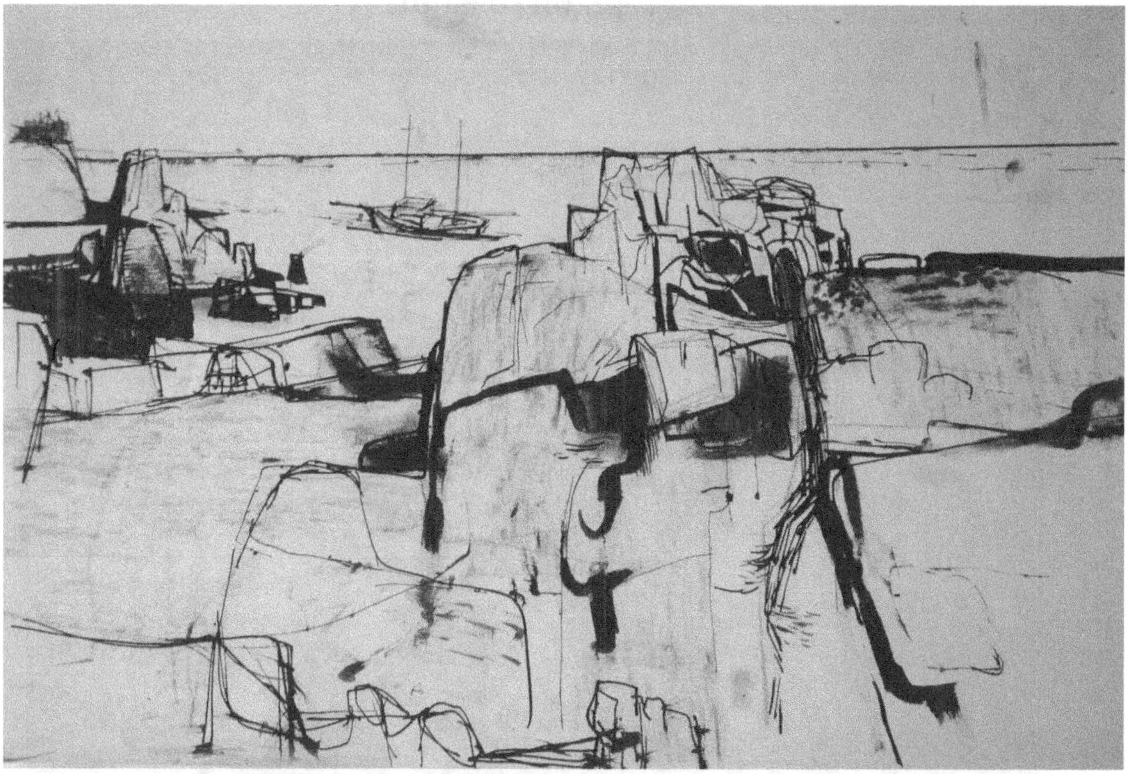

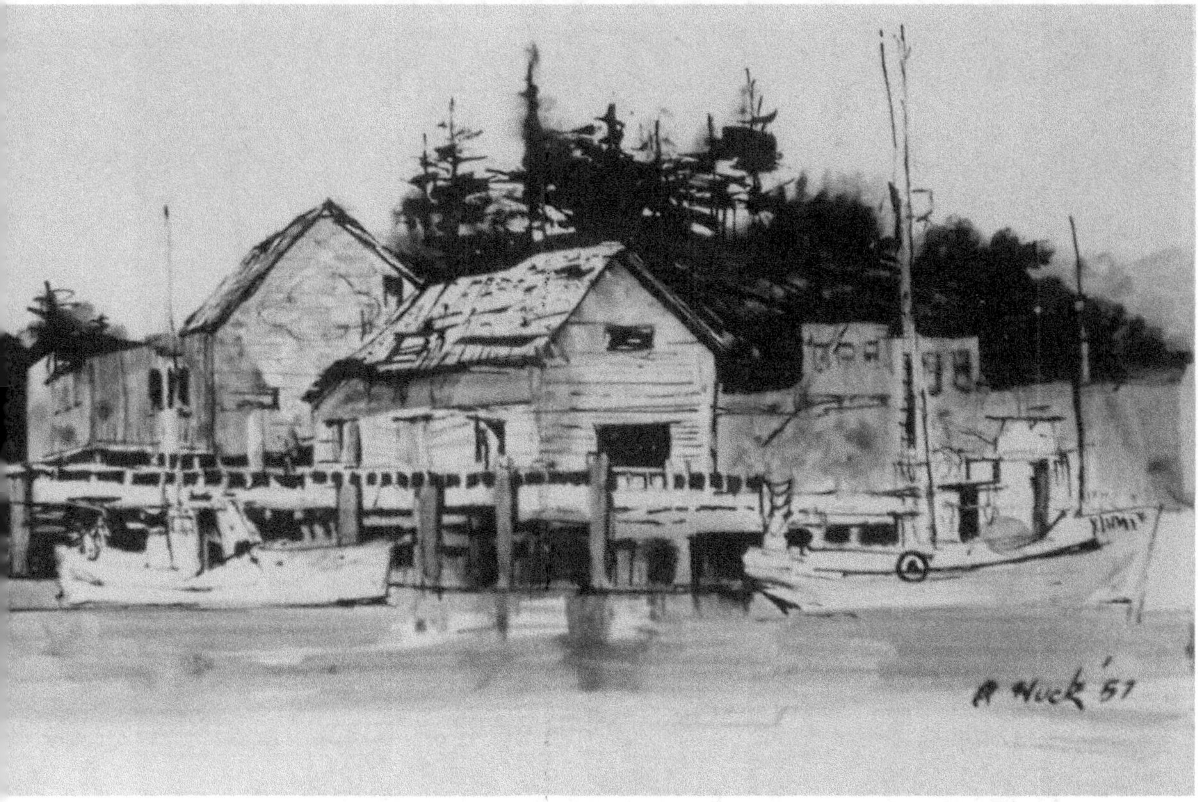

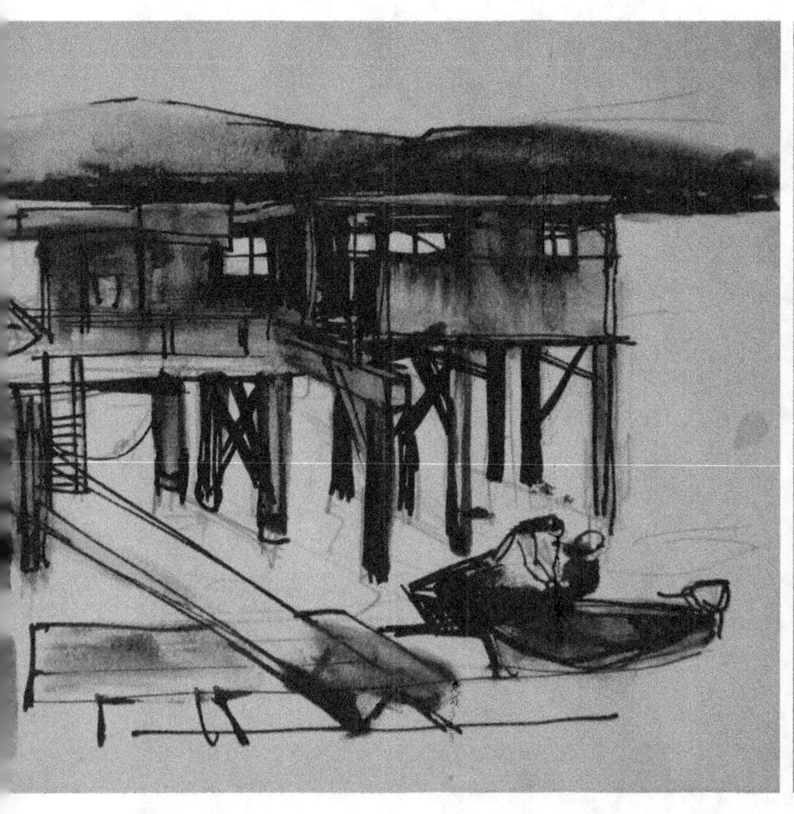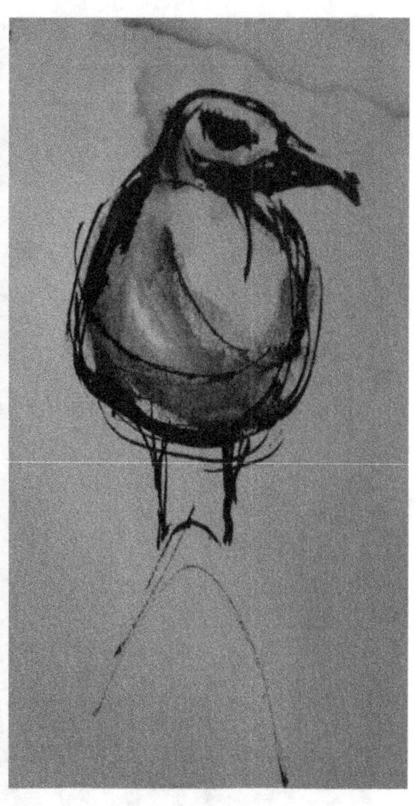

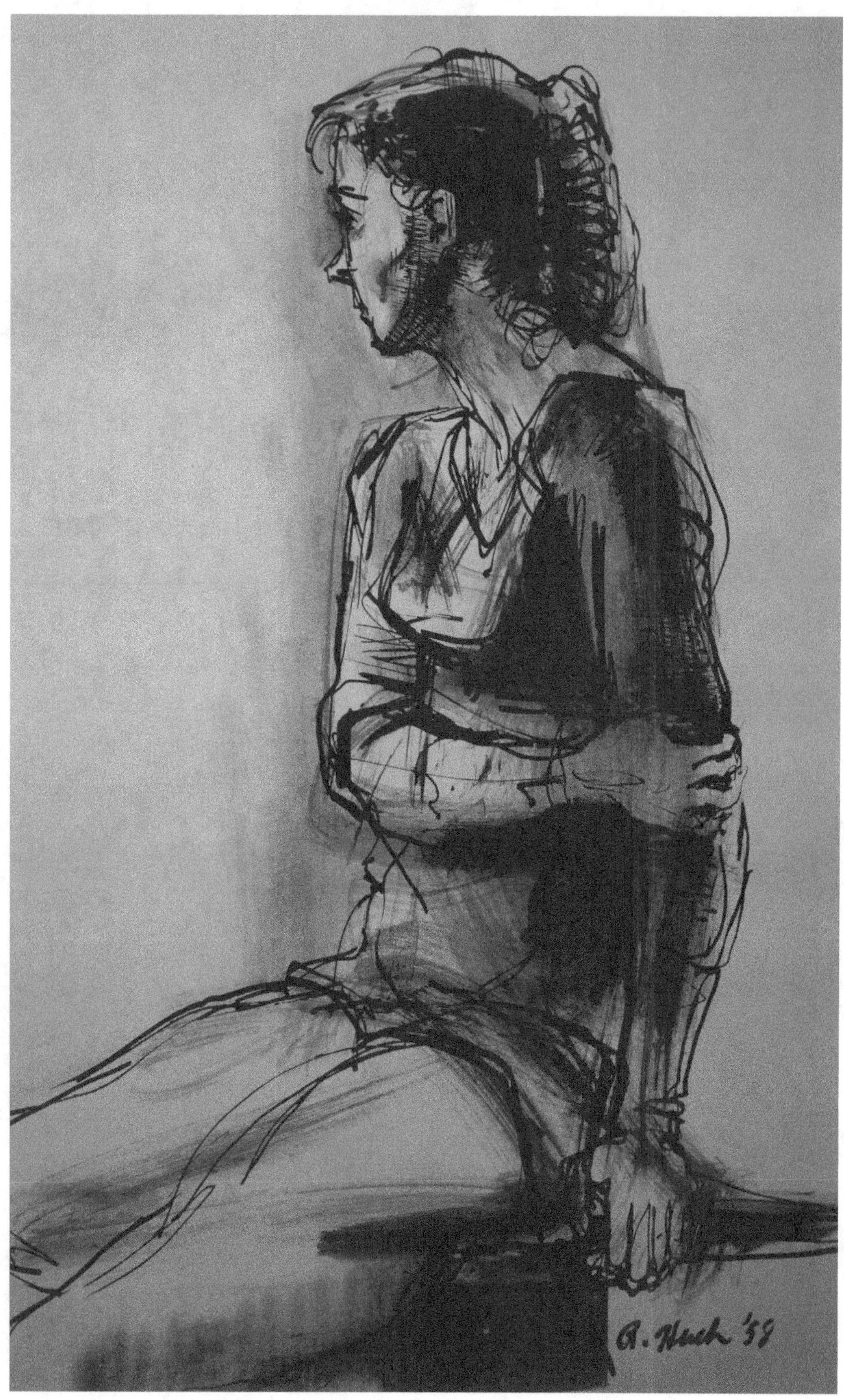

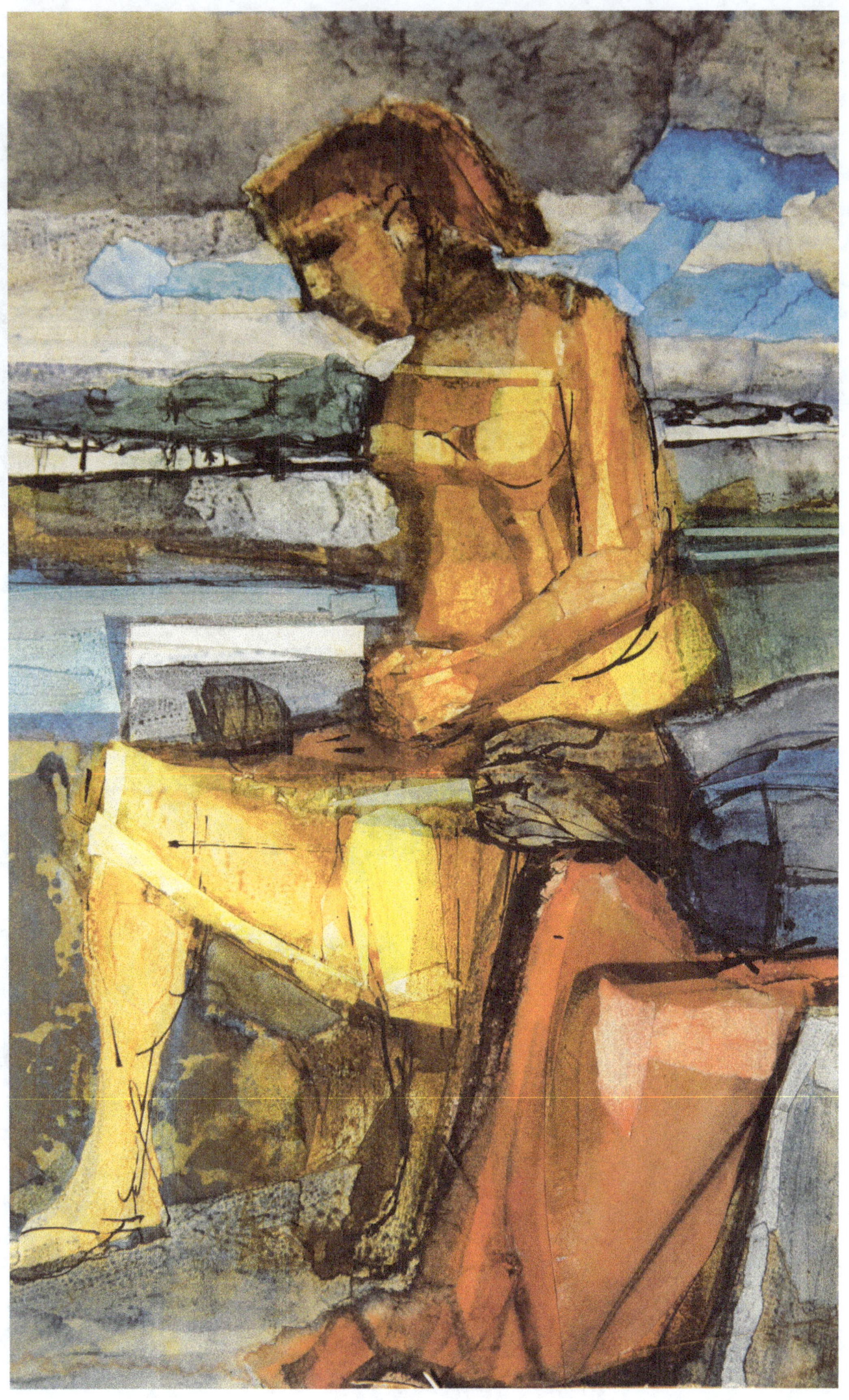

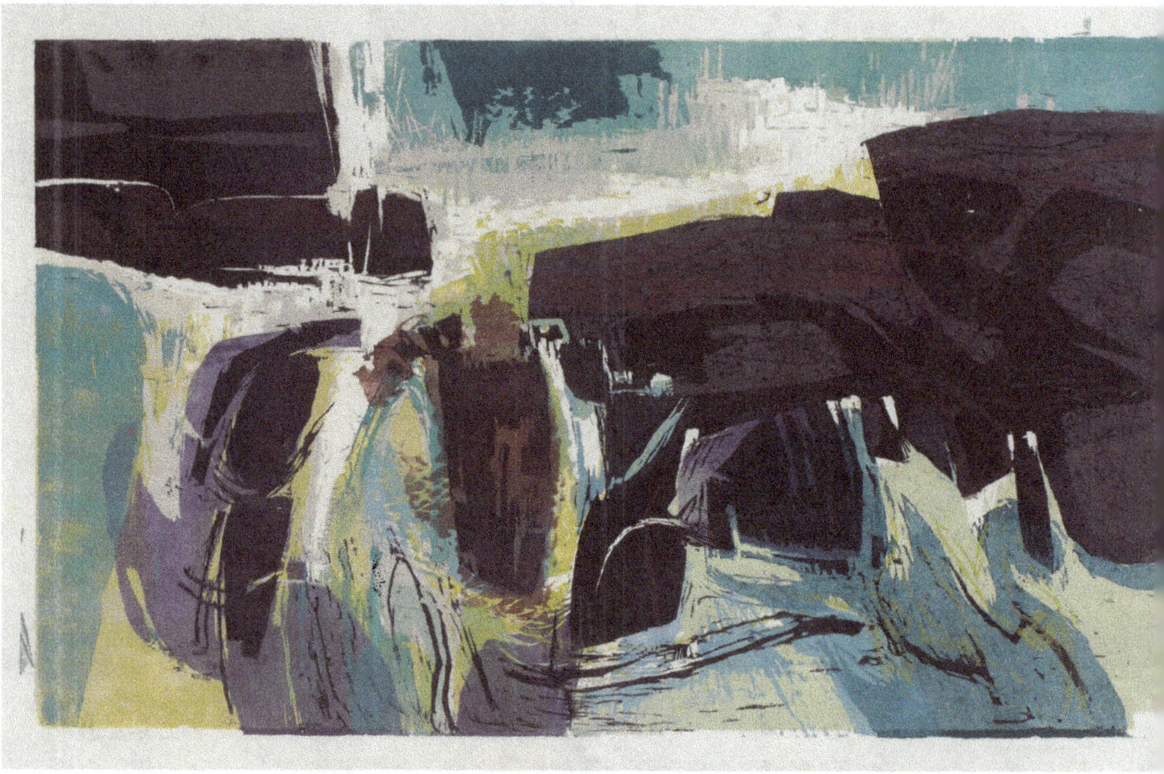

"Coastal Forms" (1958)

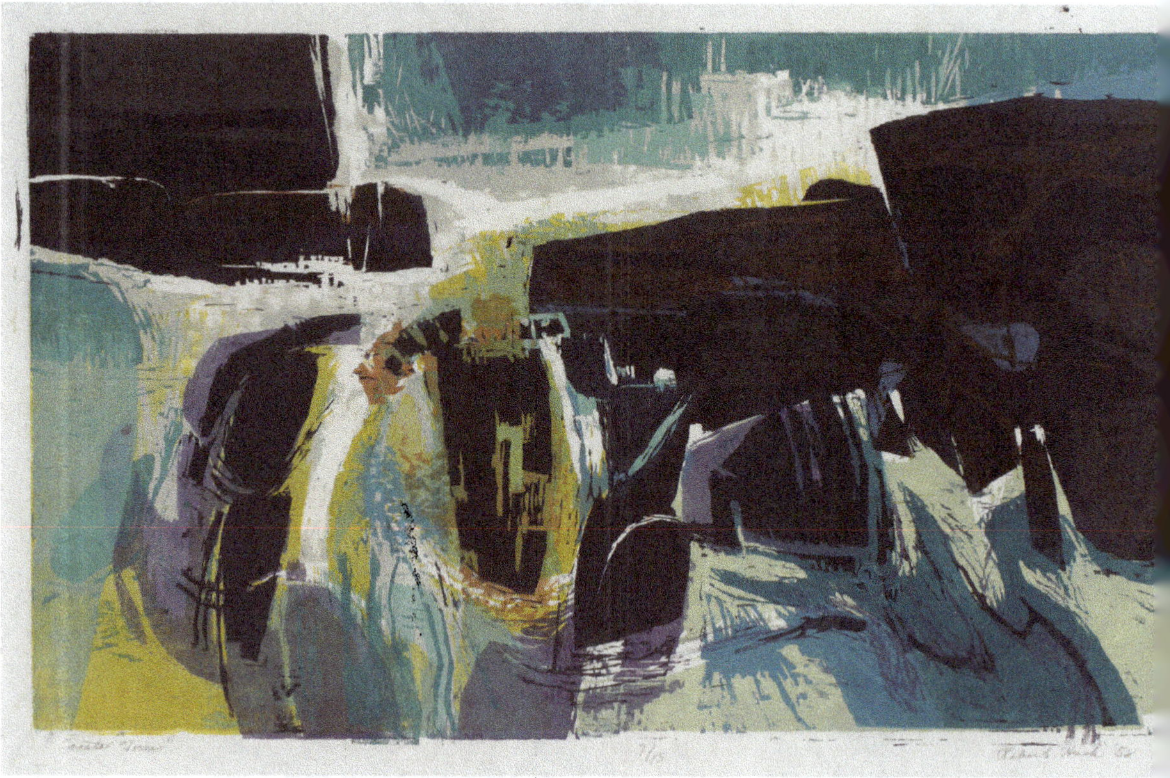

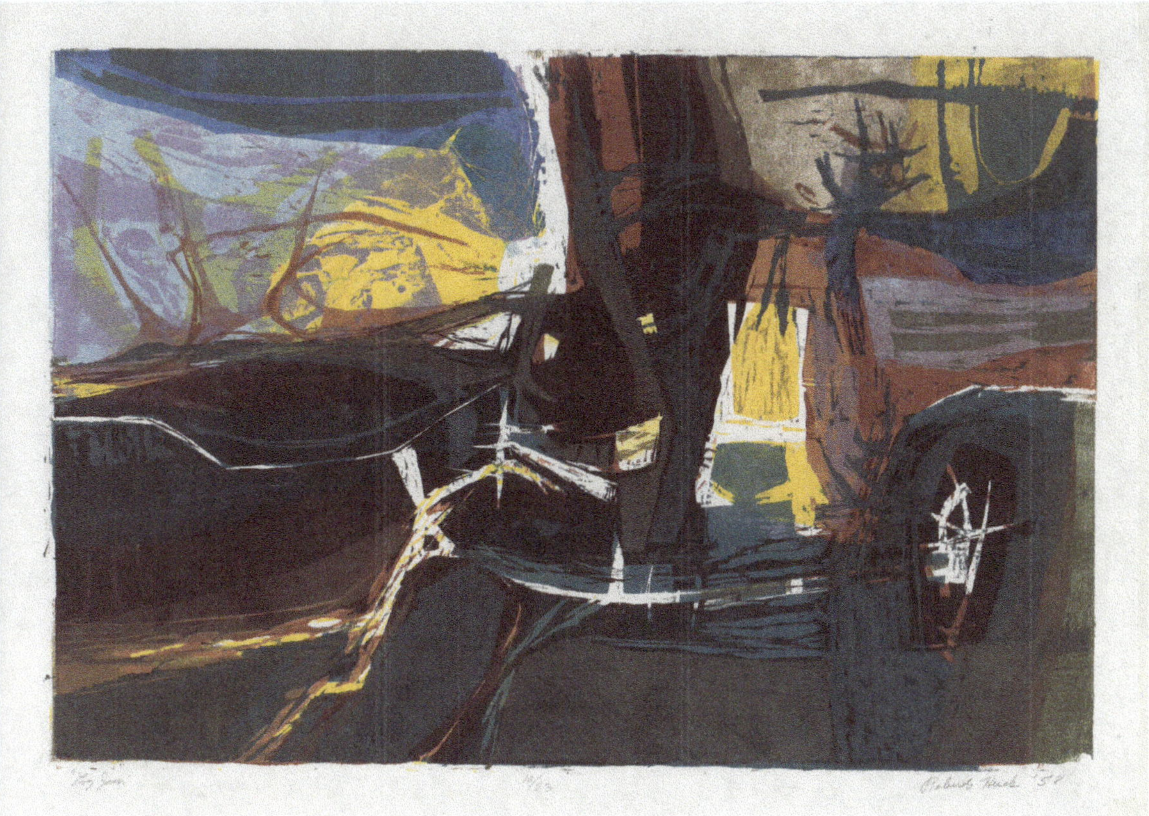

"Log Jam" (1958)

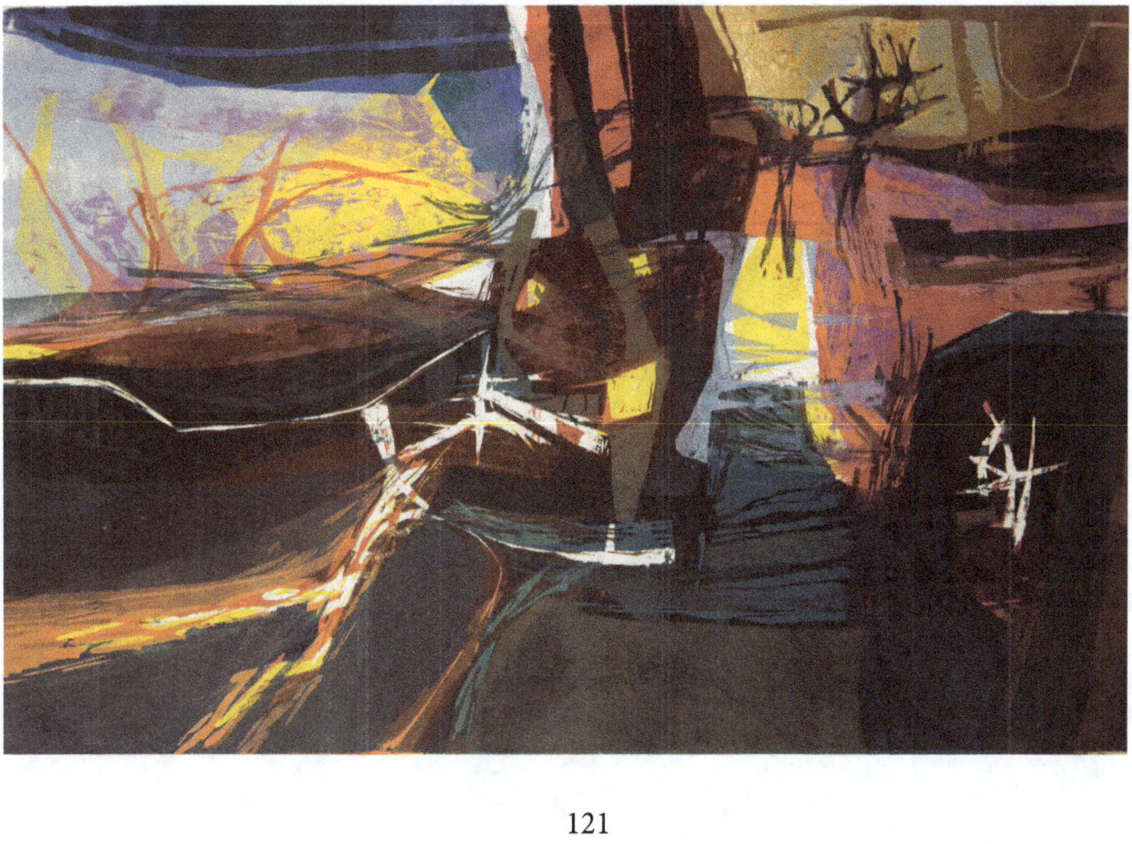

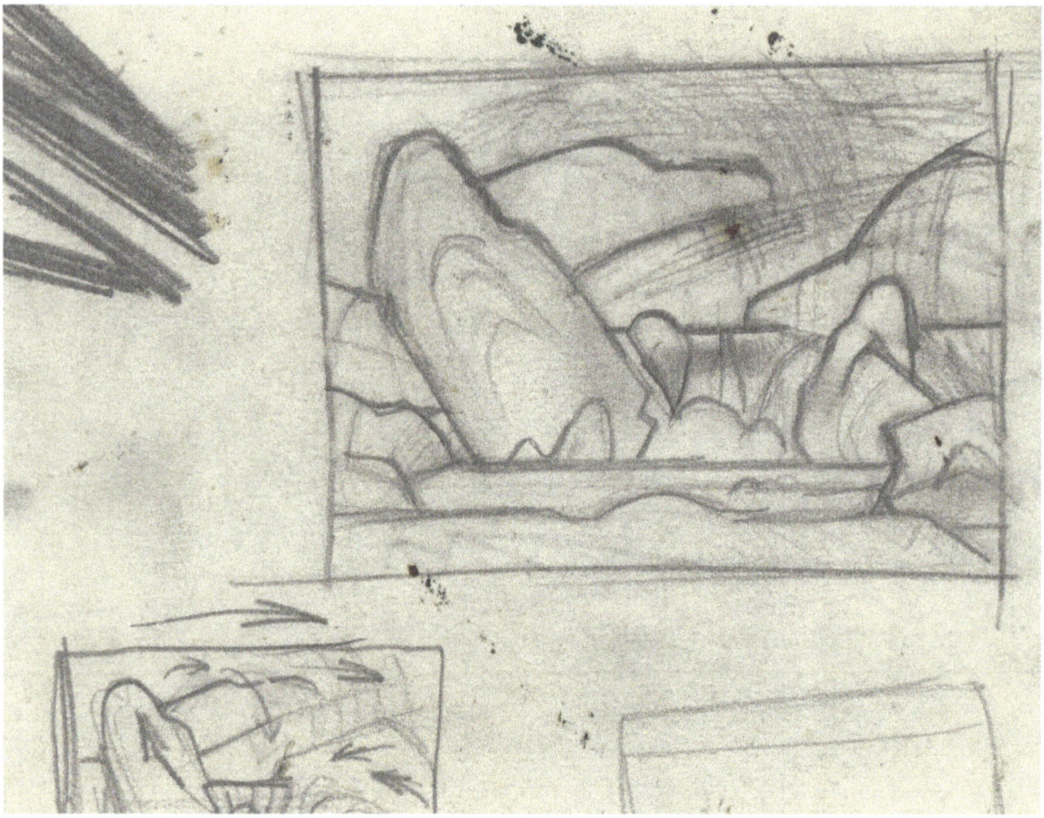

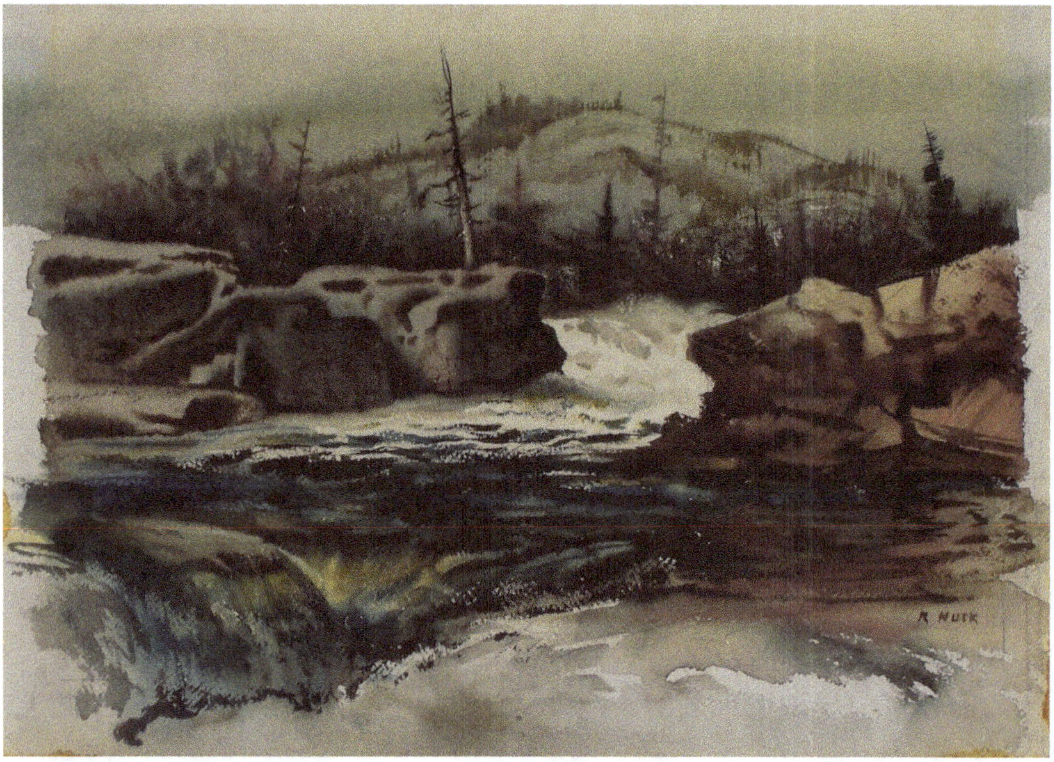

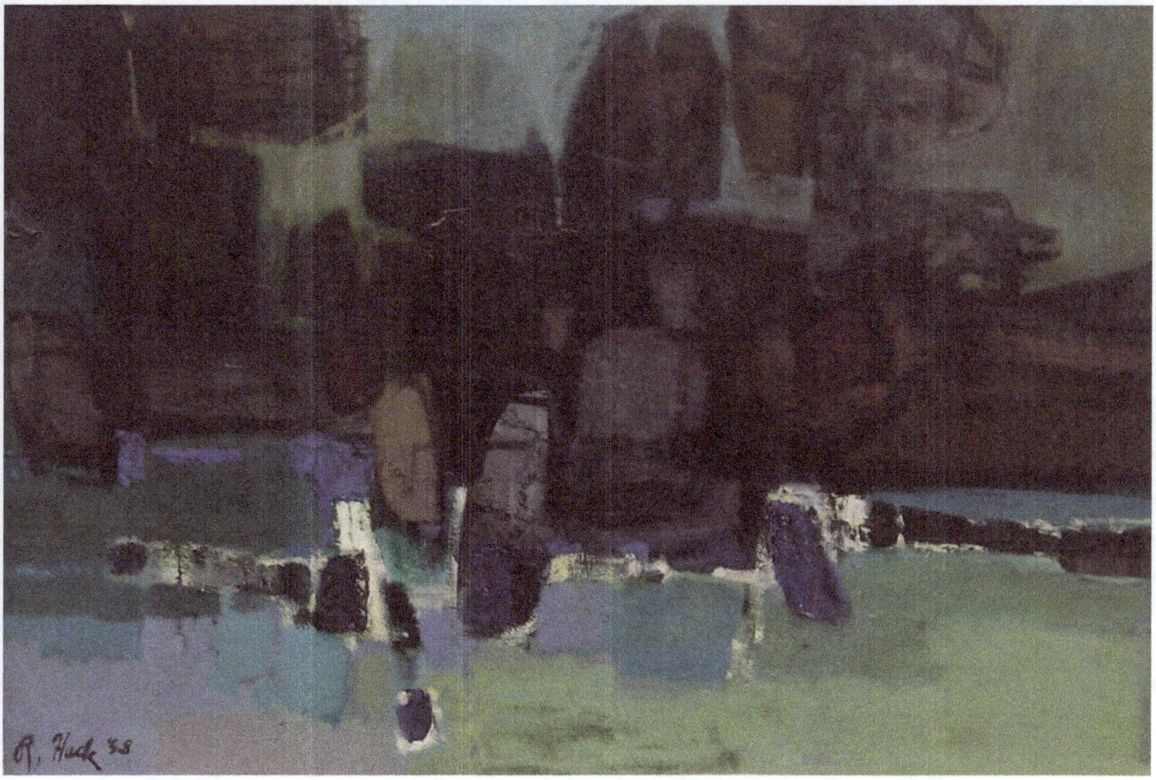

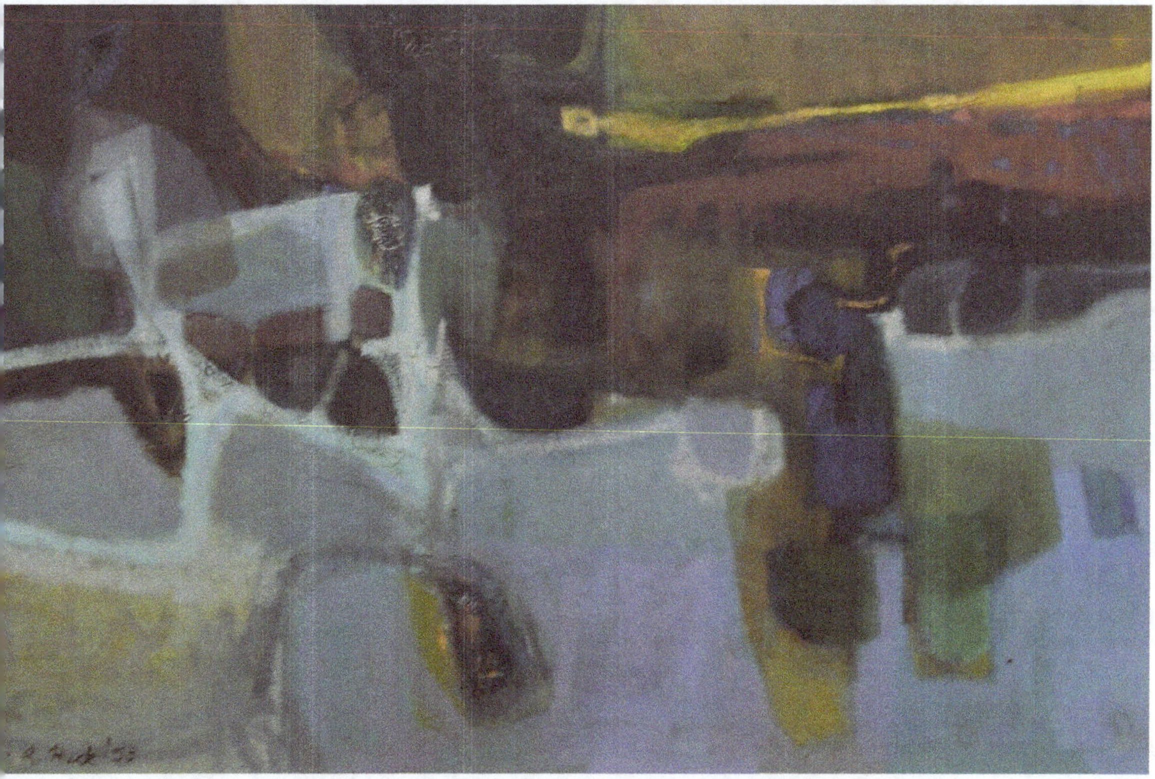

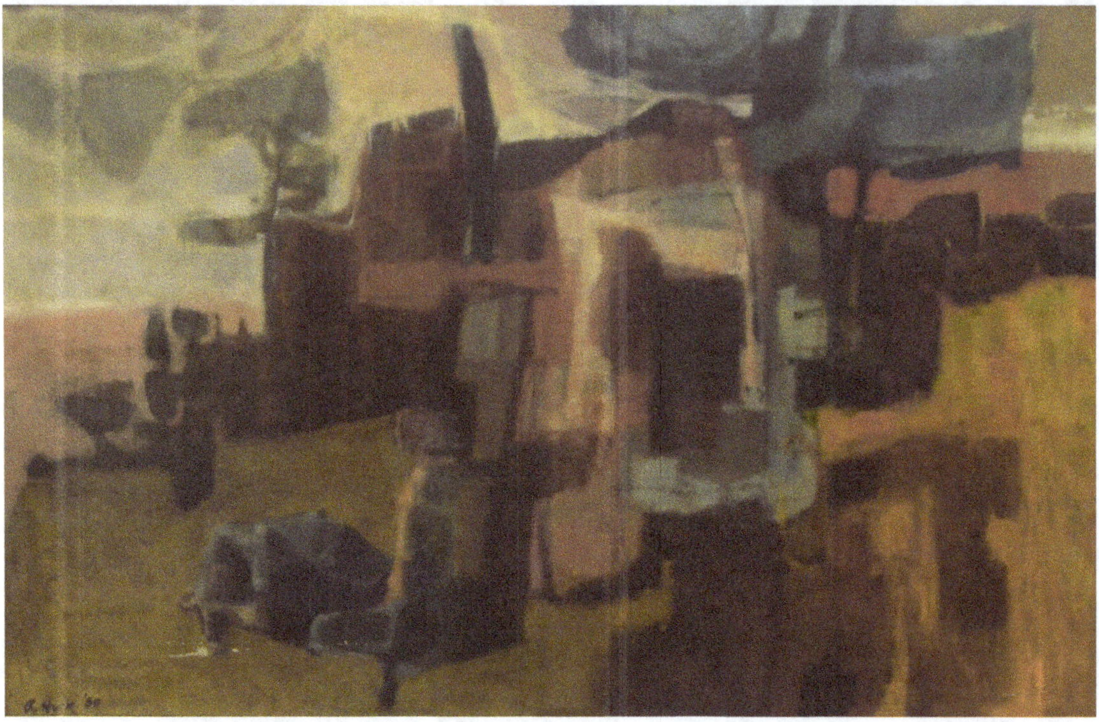

"Chuck Wagon" (1958)

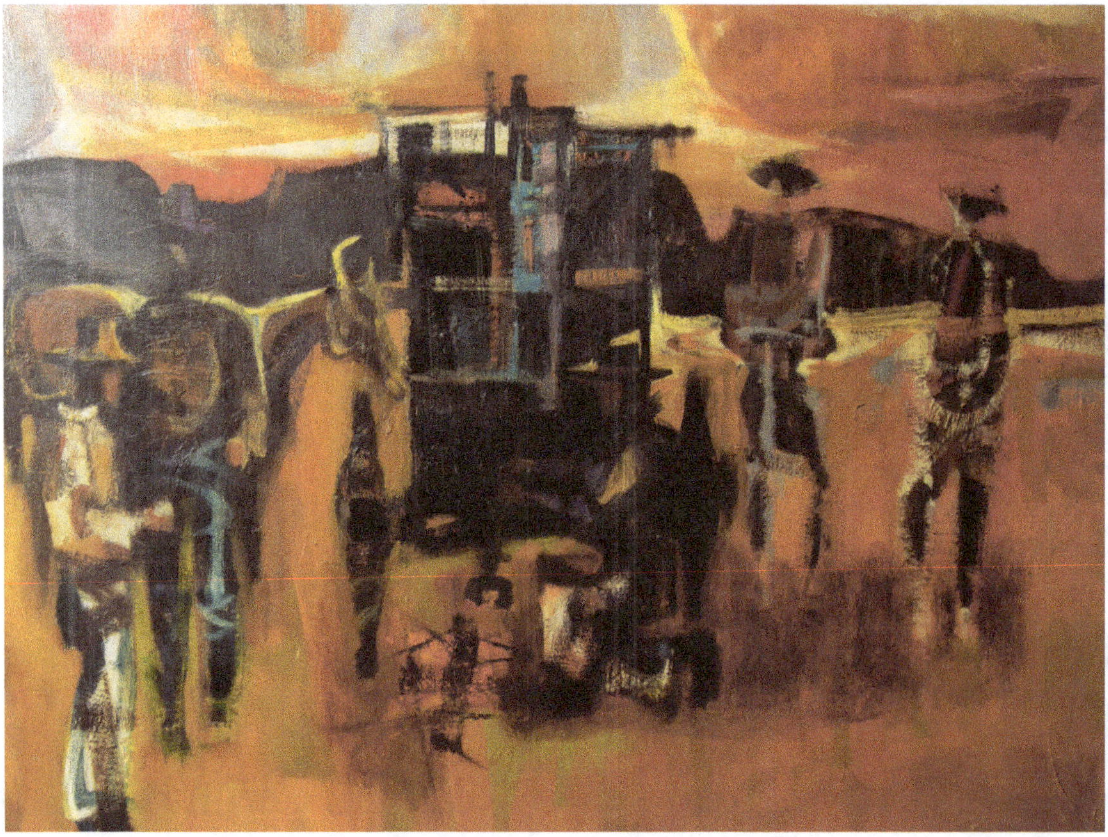

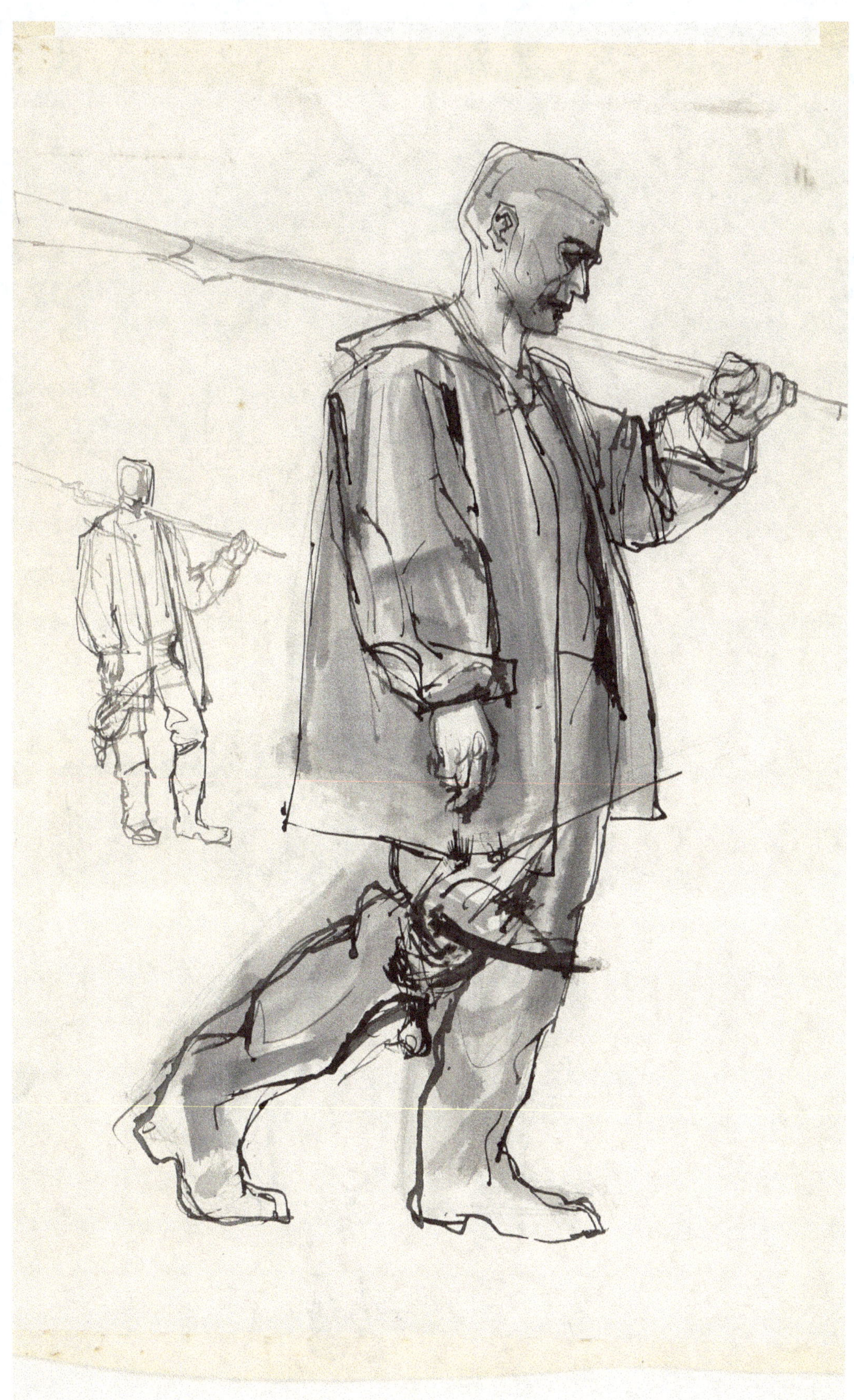

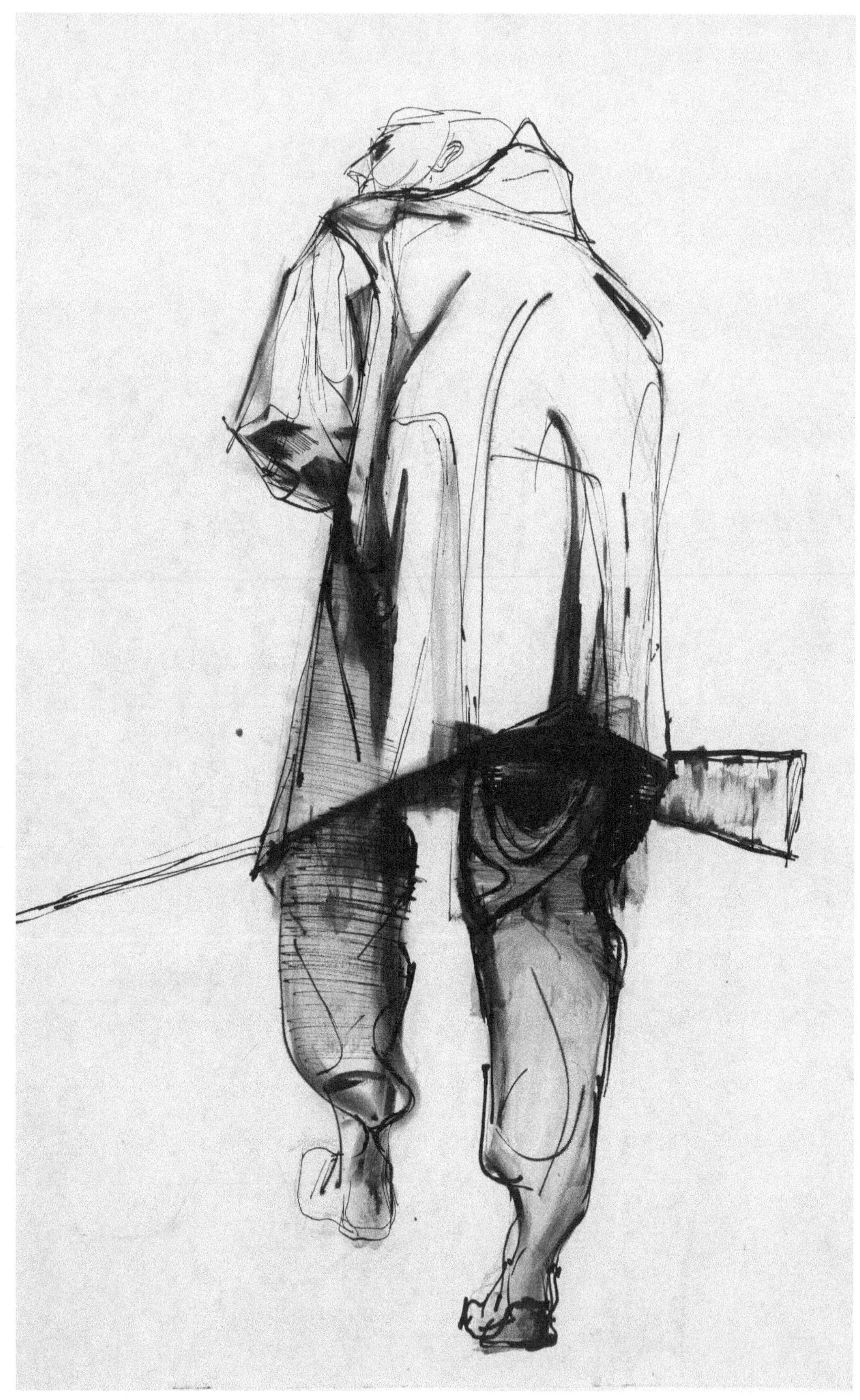

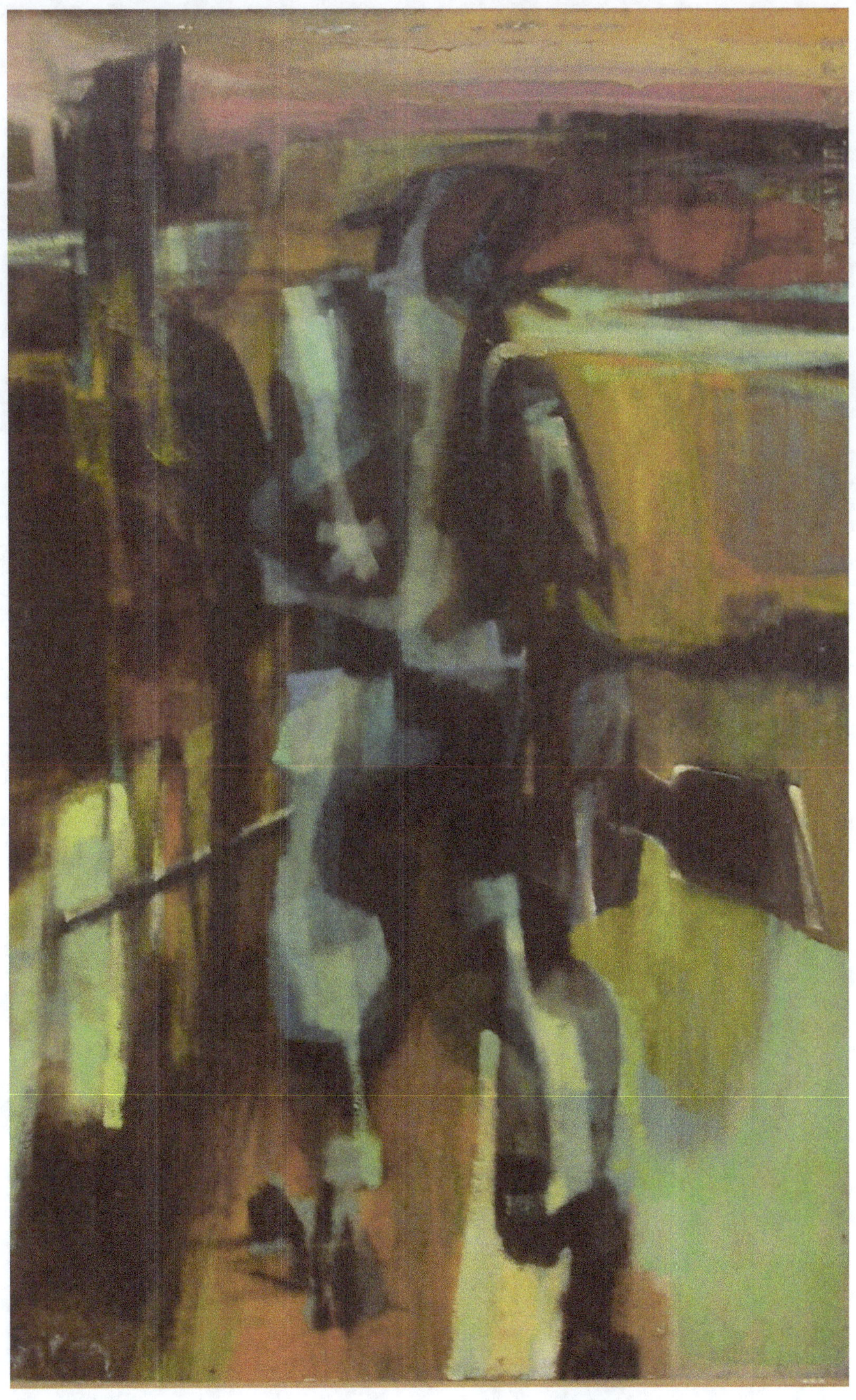

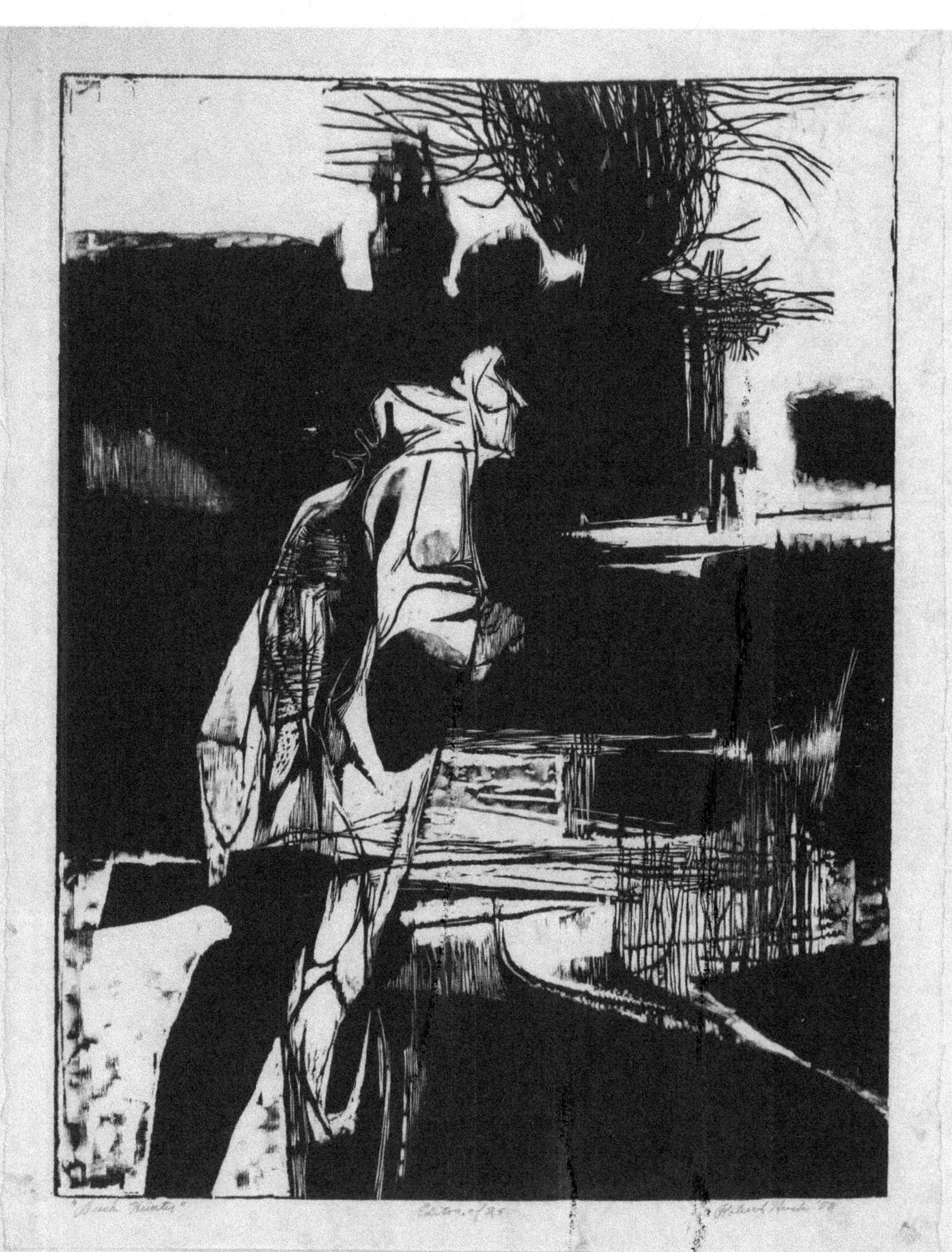

"Duck Hunter" (1958)

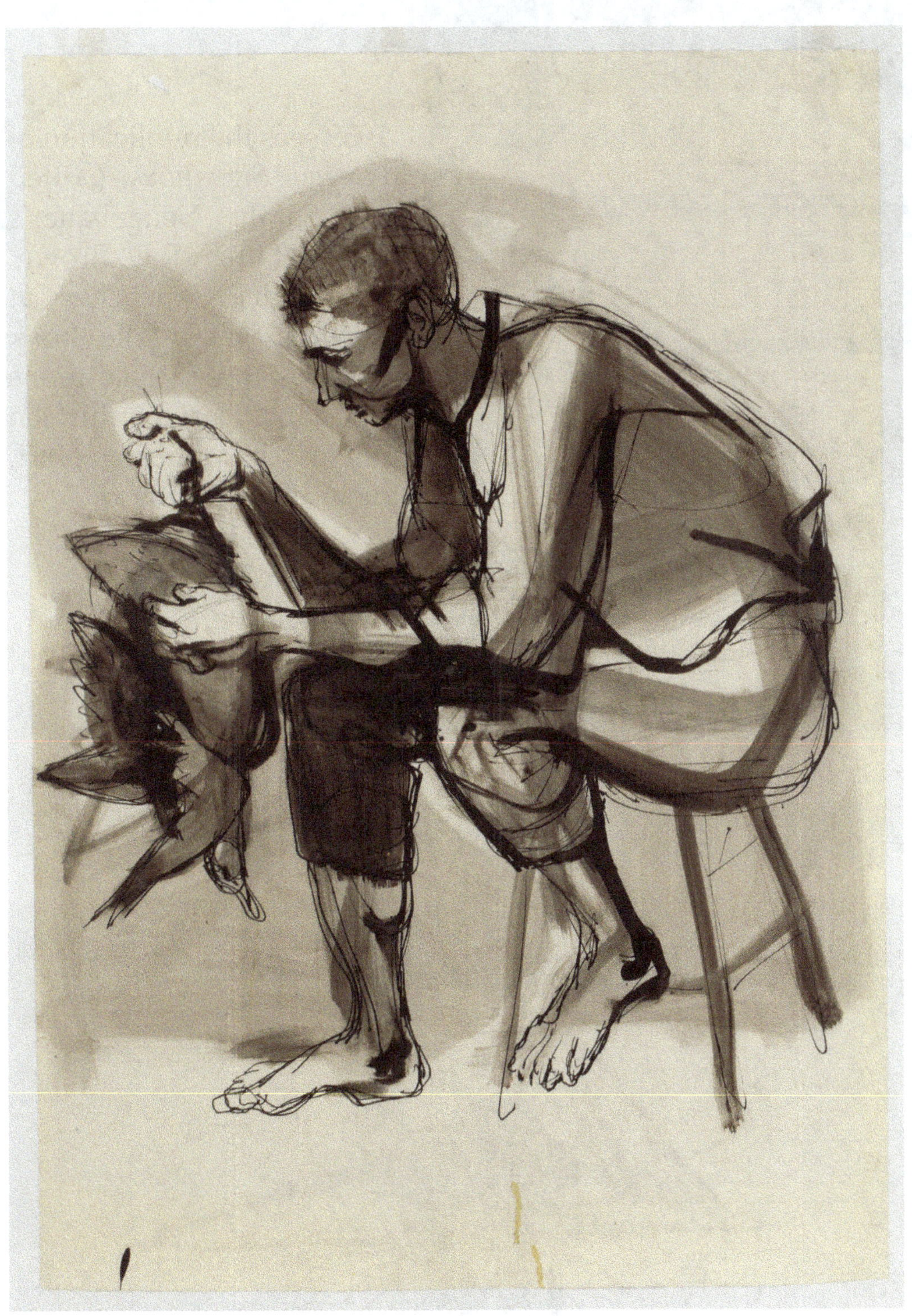

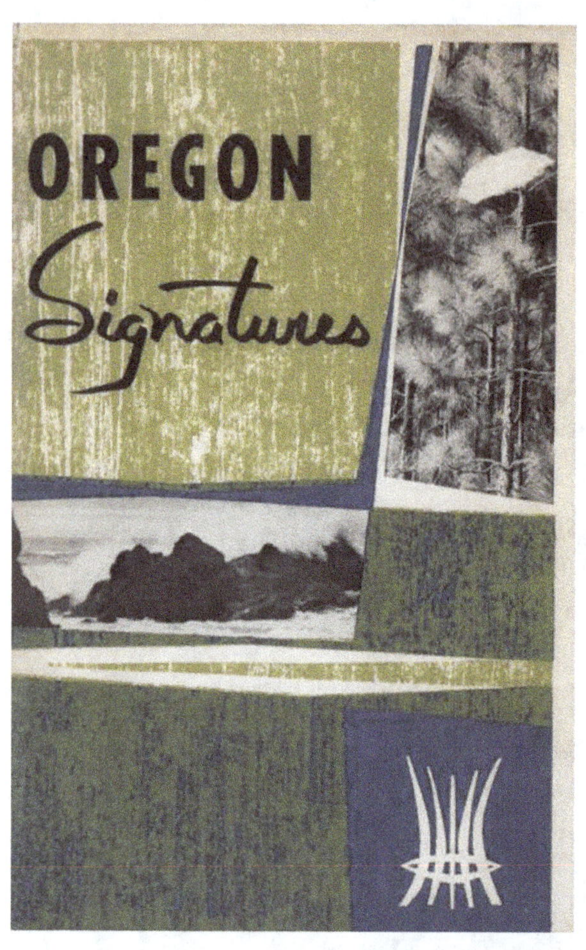

1959 sees the publication of *Oregon Signatures* (edited by Sarah Neugebauer's future father, R.D. Brown, an English teacher at Oregon State). The book features three illustrations by Huck, and thirteen poems by Robert Huff, including "Hunters."

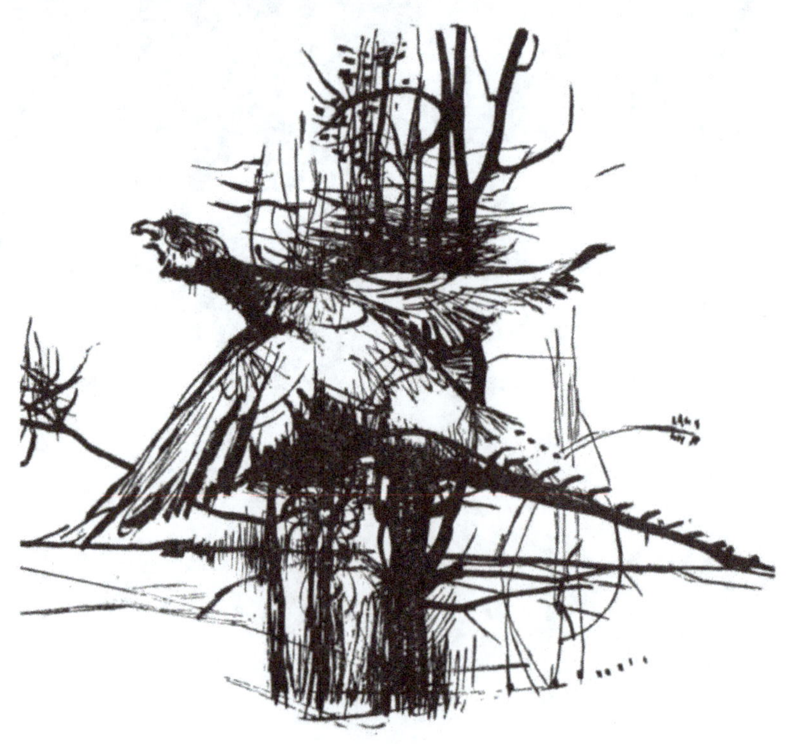

HUNTERS

Especially when it's foggy men are fooled
By birds, beasts, and the skeletal remains
Of stumpy trees; when it's frosty by leaves;
And almost any time at all by sound.
So poetry can happen to the mind
If senses want to make the beautiful.

An old man listening in a blind can feel
That every wildfowl he has killed is still
Alive, because his ears are filled, and think
That fog contains within its wary world
His first love with her pack of flying hounds
And let sounds make a bower of his blind.

Young men who look into the mist at dawn
May see the beast unclearly and declare
The image brings a fever on; that deer
Are seen whose antlers cannot fall, whose heads
Shall grace no trophy walls; and that they are
Afraid before a perfect animal.

And there are men who hunt for ghostly trees.
These sawyers have been known to wince and cry,
Her pain, the old hag's, hear her falling pain.
As if they found old snags unnatural
Or men became their natures' best when fooled,
Their voices made their actions beautiful.

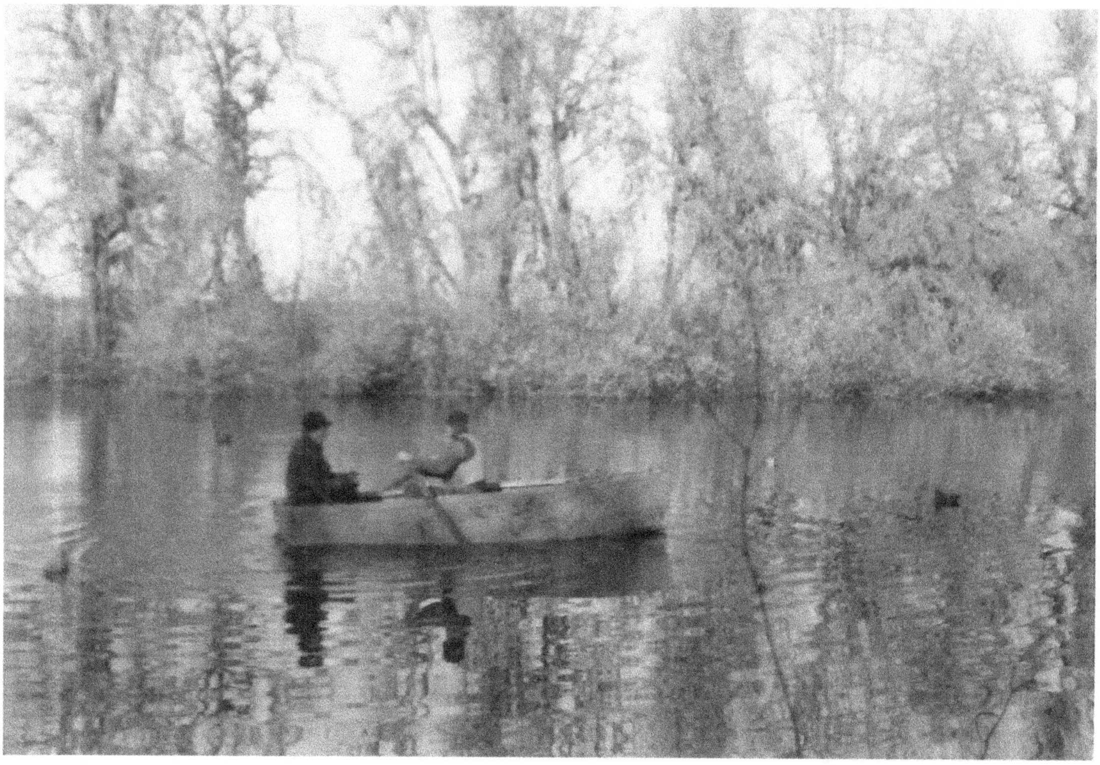

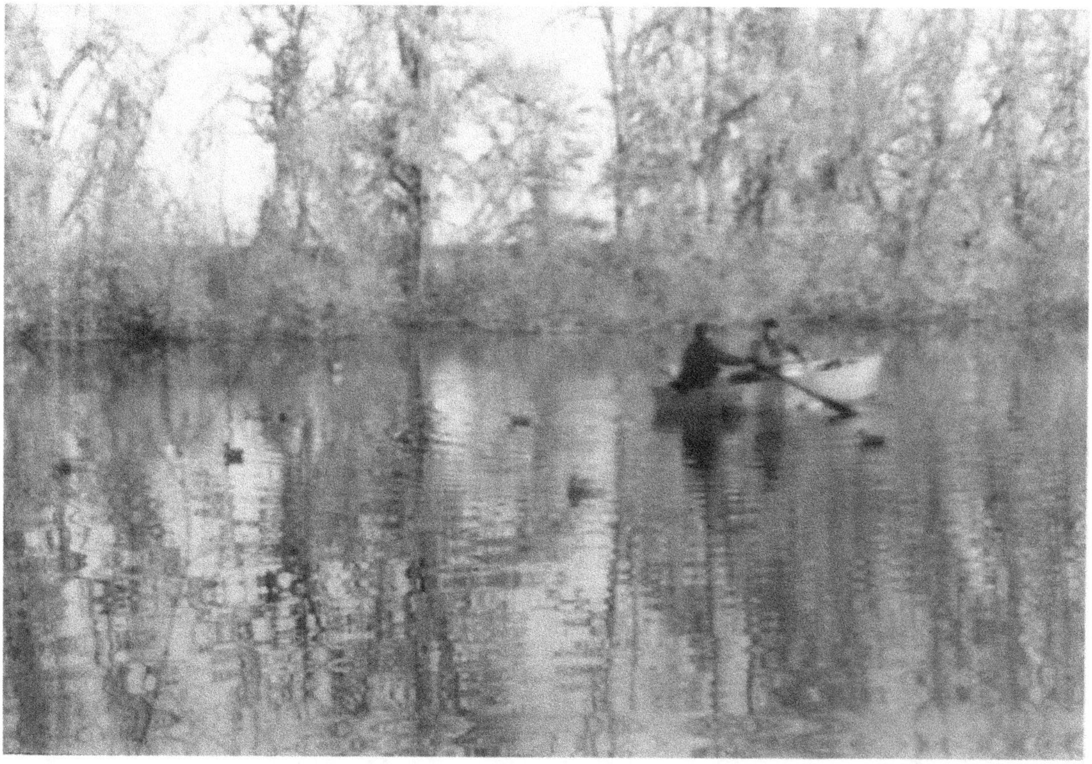

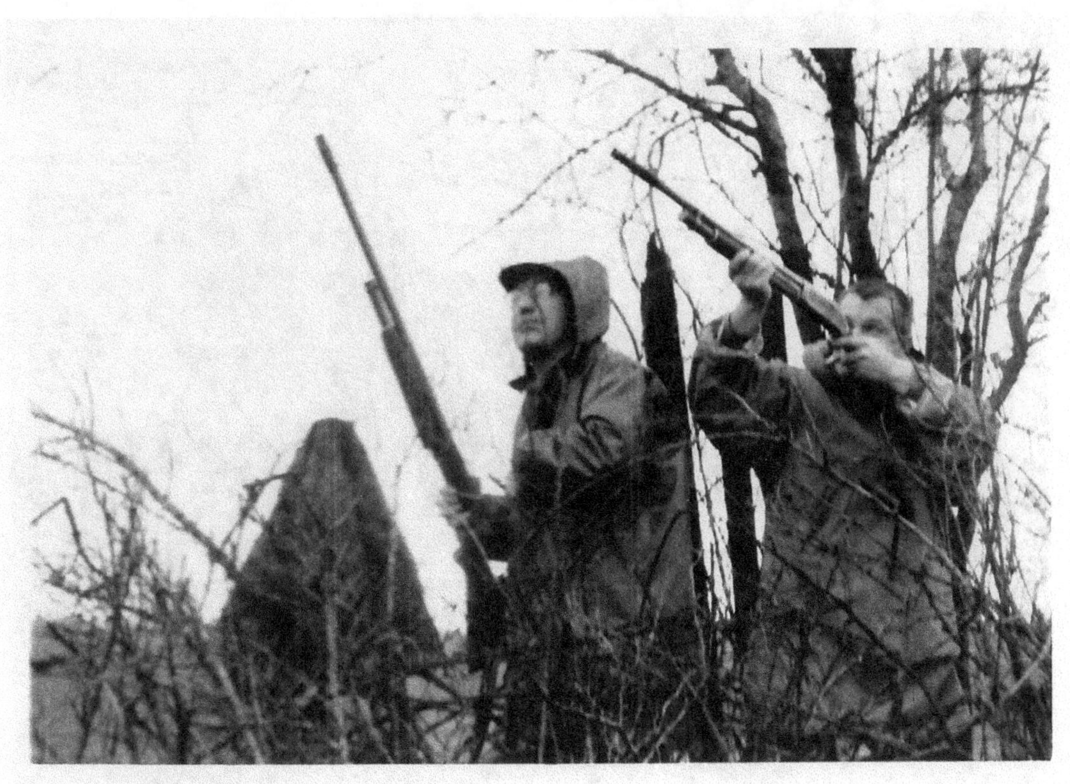

1958 Duck Hunting. Robert Huck and Robert Huff

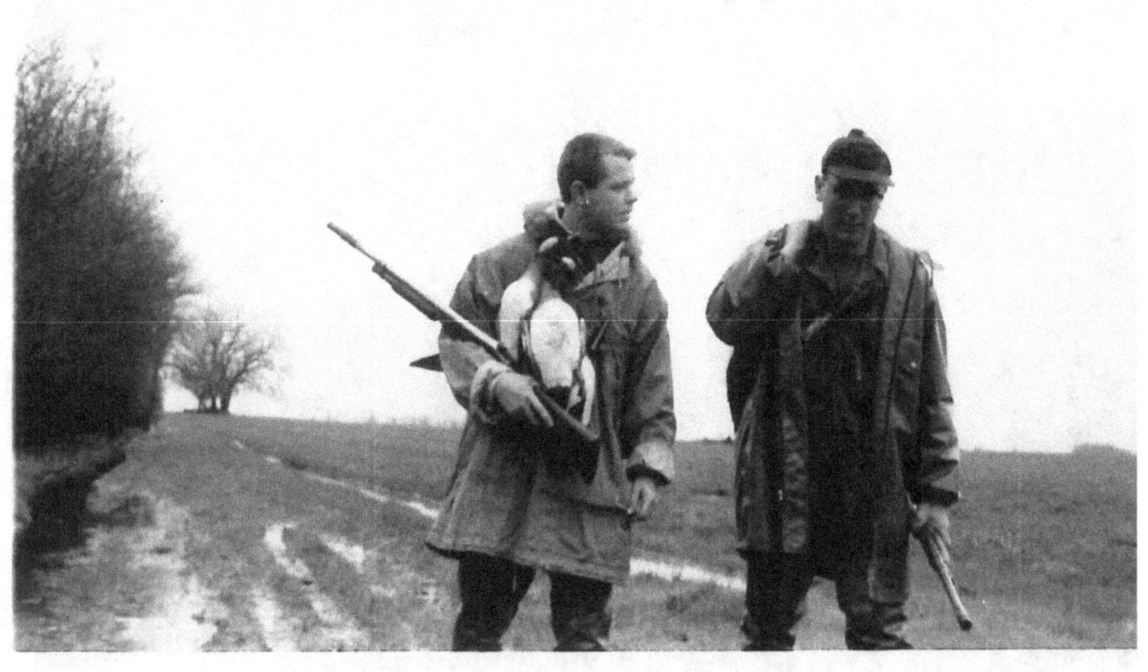

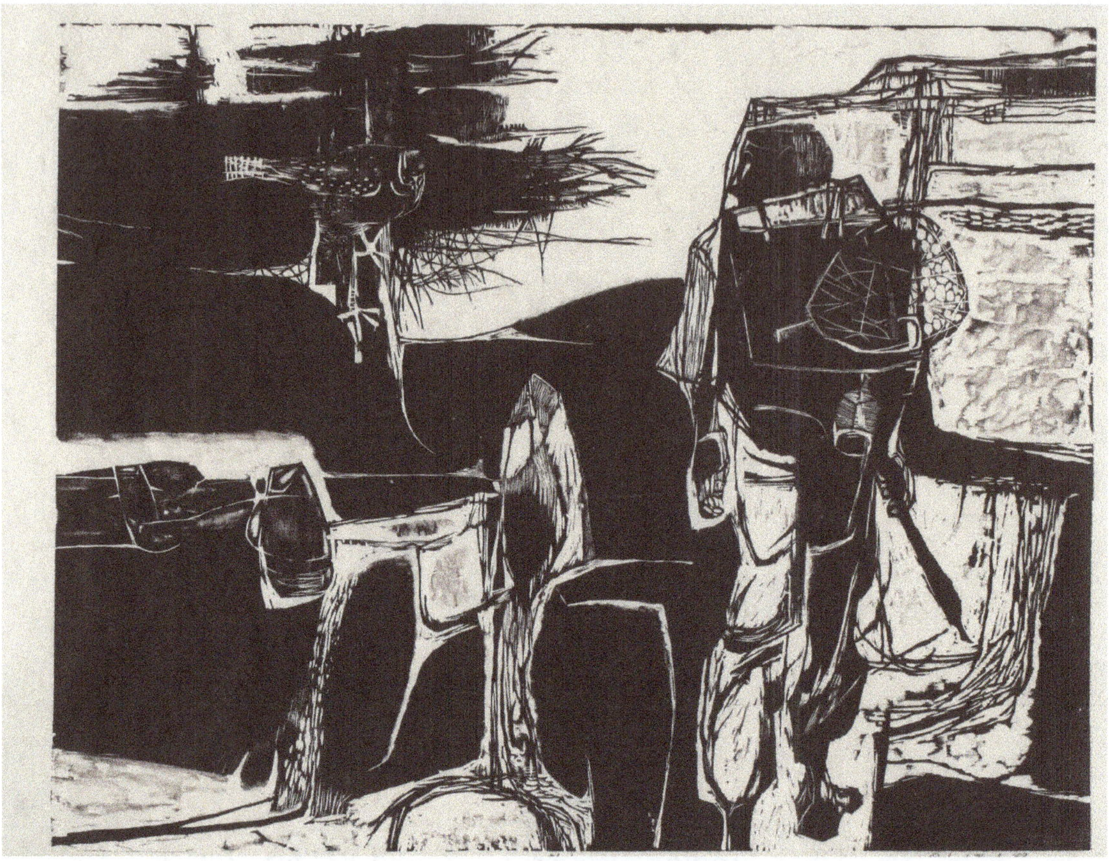

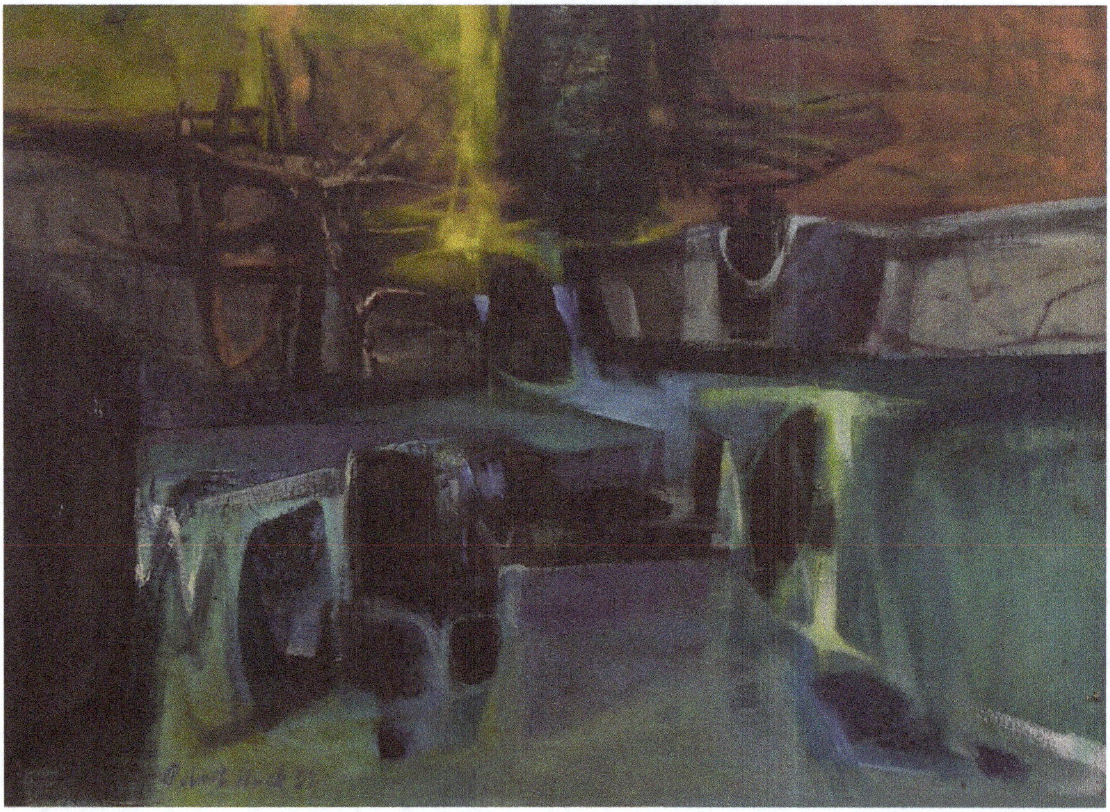

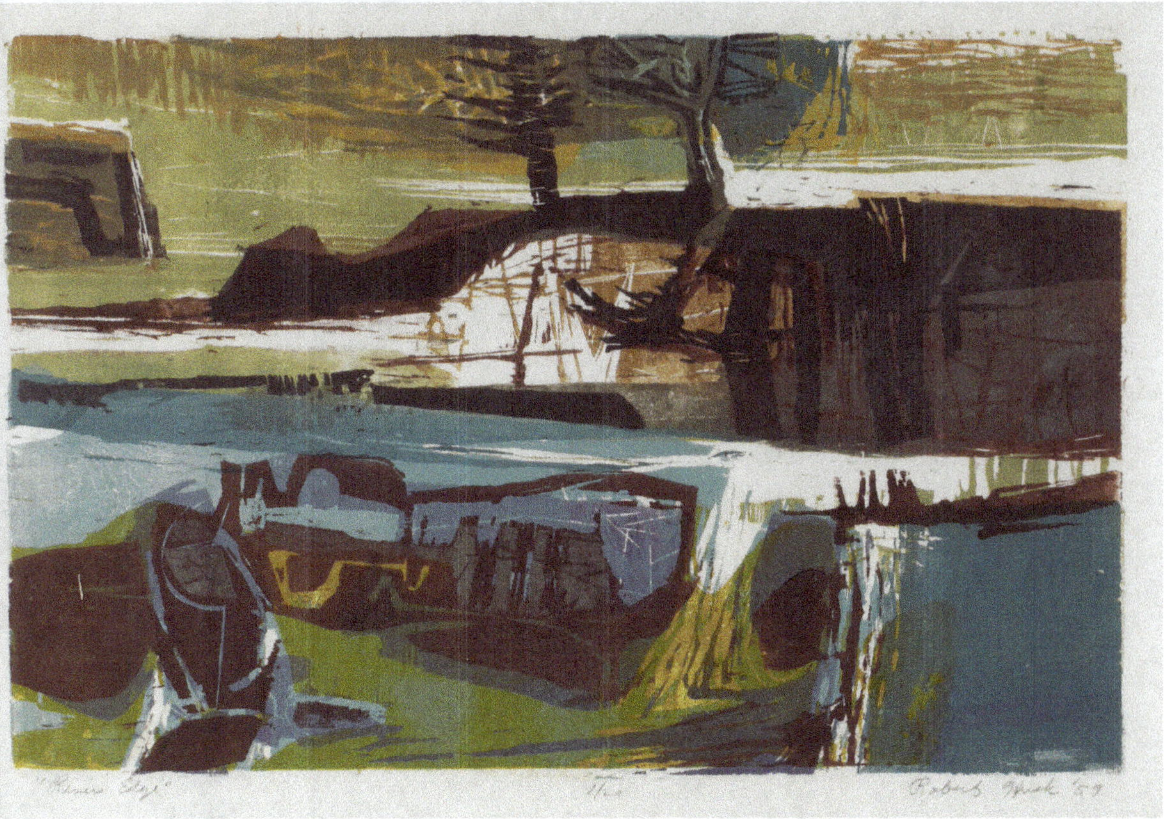

Opposite: "Hiker" and "River Forms" (1959)

"Rivers Edge" and "Tideland" (1959)

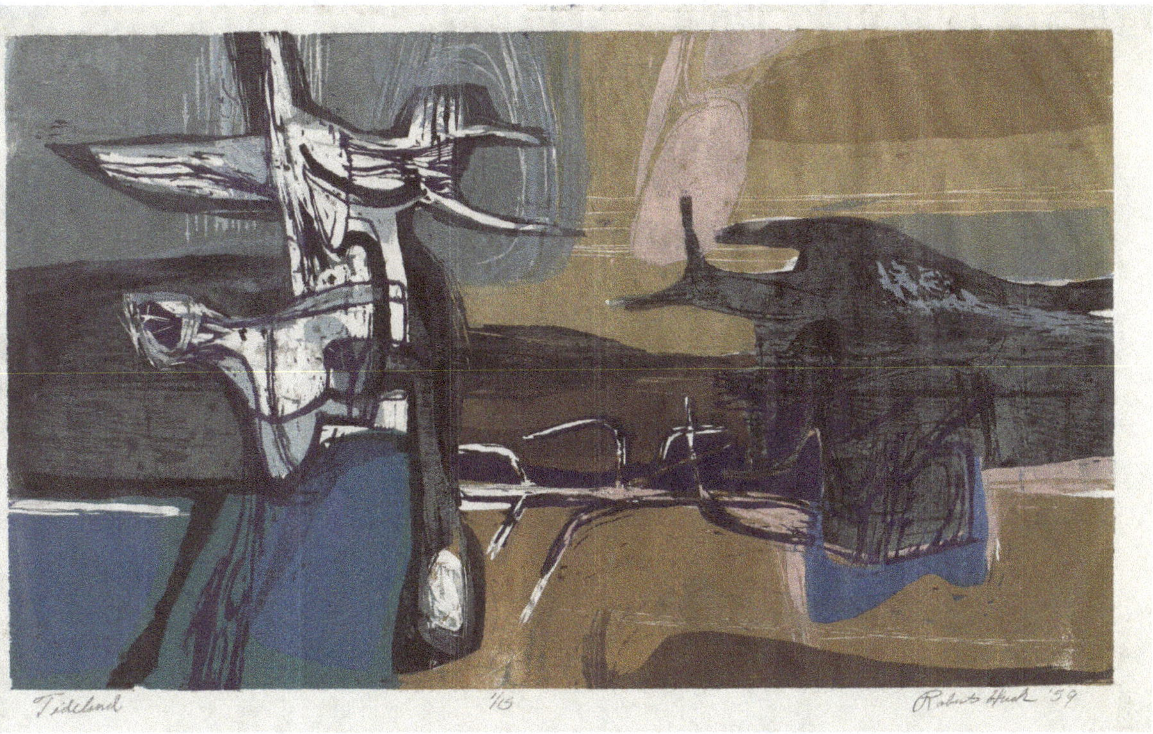

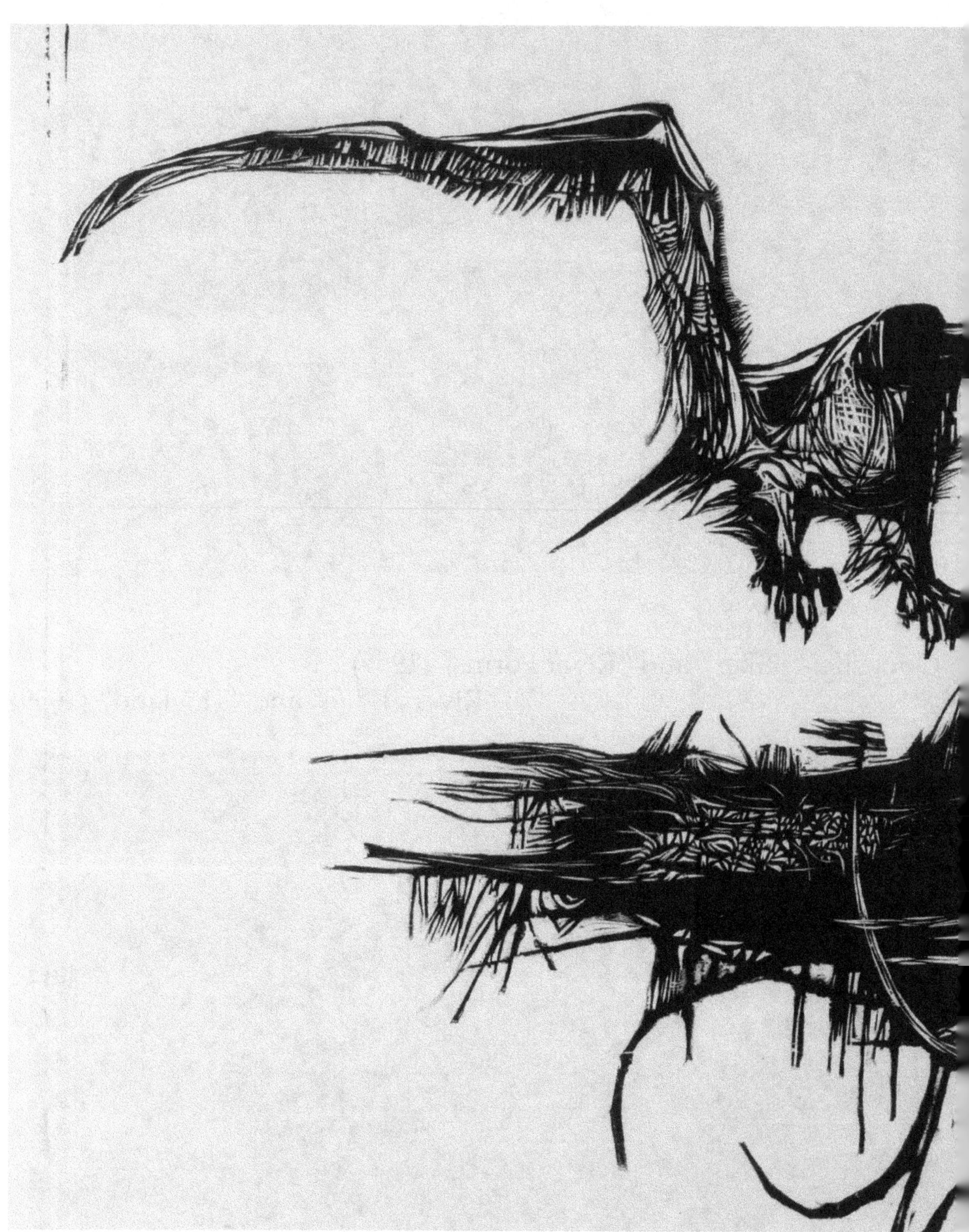

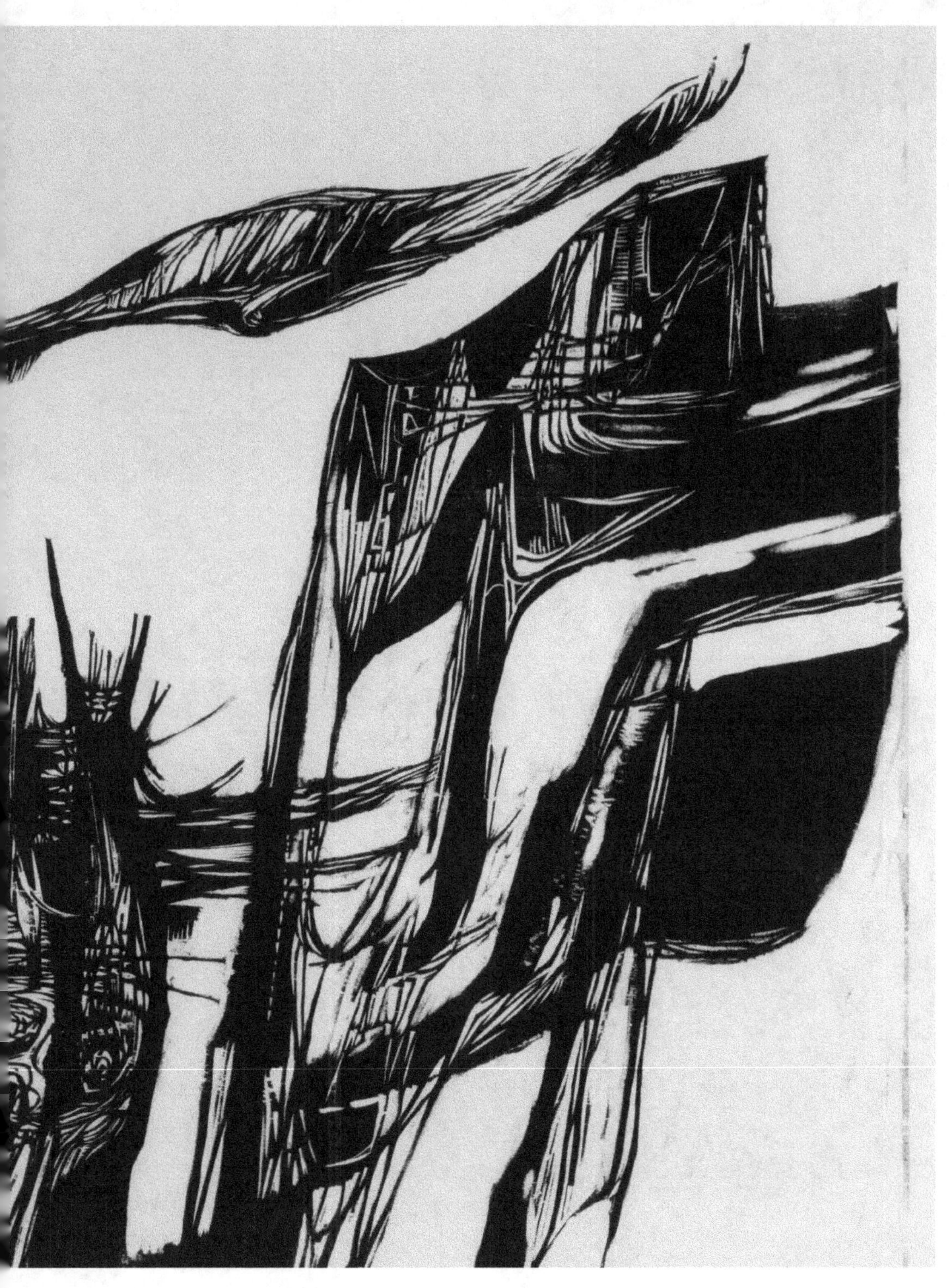

"Eagle" (1959)

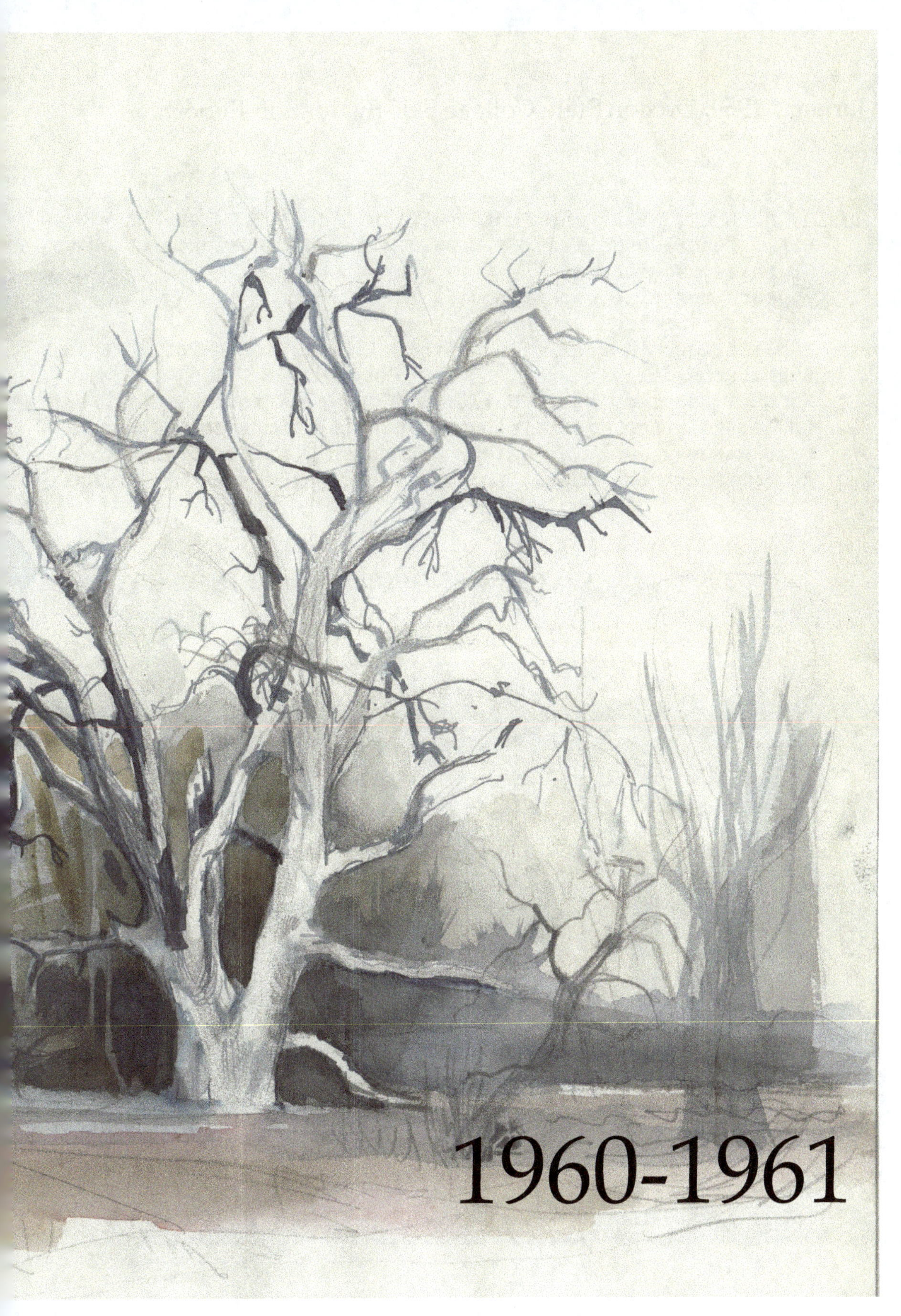
1960-1961

ROBERT E. HUCK, Assistant Professor, full time. Salary $5,950.
B.A., Colorado College; M.F.A., Colorado. Fields: Painting,
Graphics, Sculpture.
7 years teaching experience; 4 at OSC.
Member: Portland Art Association.
Publications in past five years: Illustrations for "Oregon
Signatures."
Honors: Juried, Henry Gallery; Honorable Mention, Northwest
Annual Painting. Participated in exhibitions at Oakland
Printmakers', Gump's, Walker Art Museum, and others. Mural
at new Sheraton Hotel. One-man show, University of Montana.

"Sea Growth" (1960)

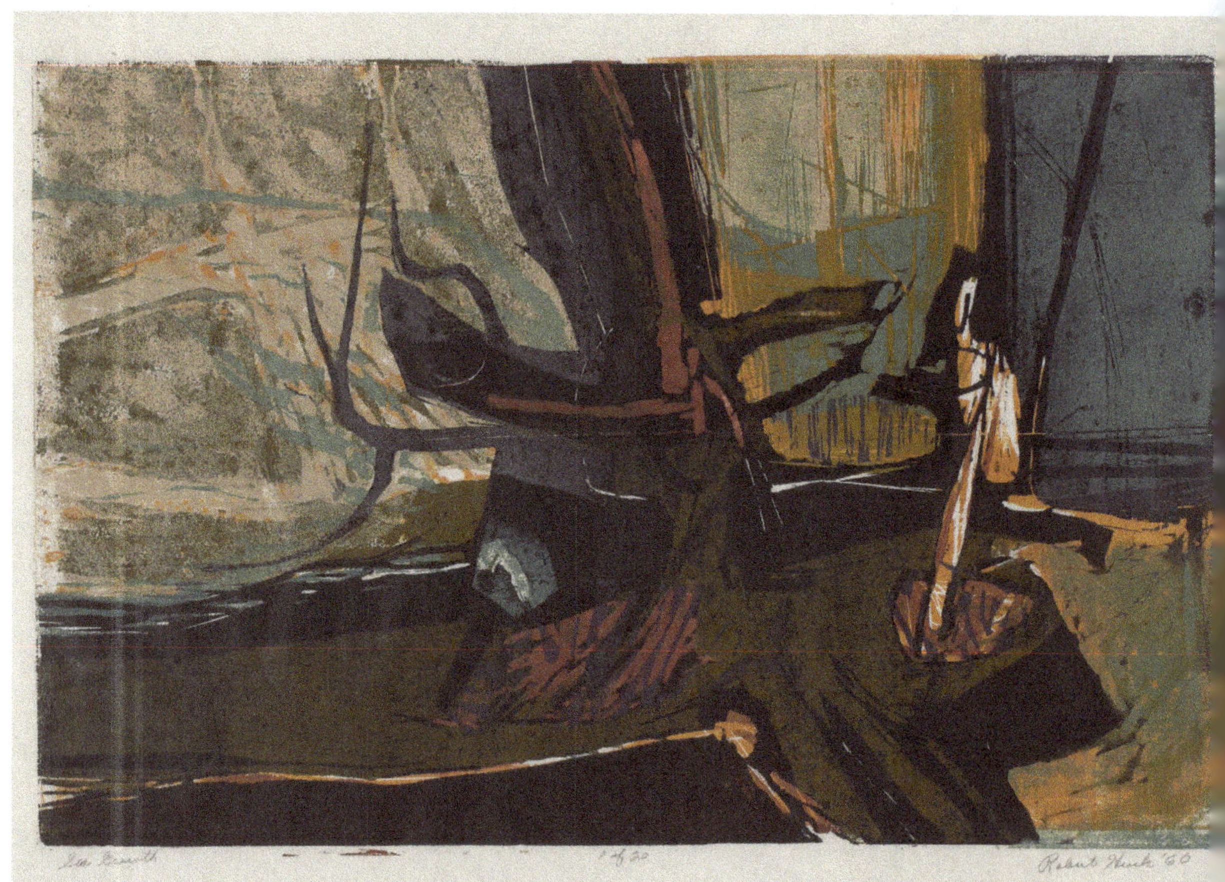

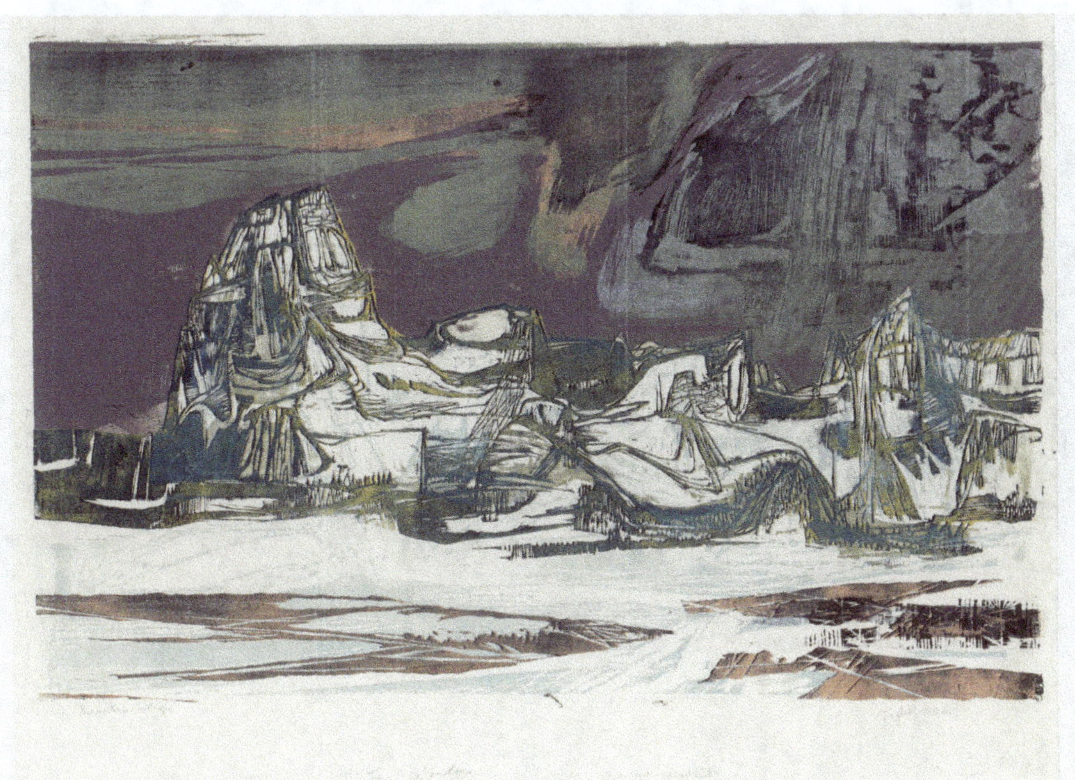

"Mountain Landscape" (1960)

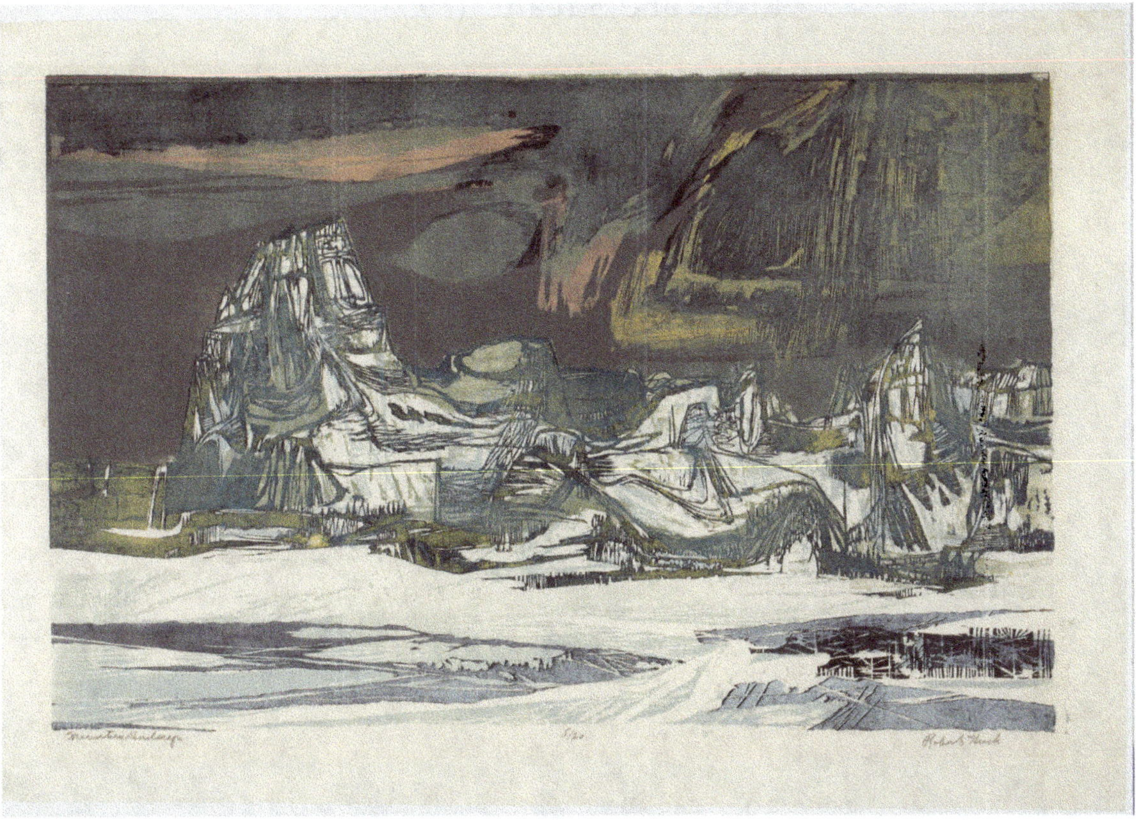

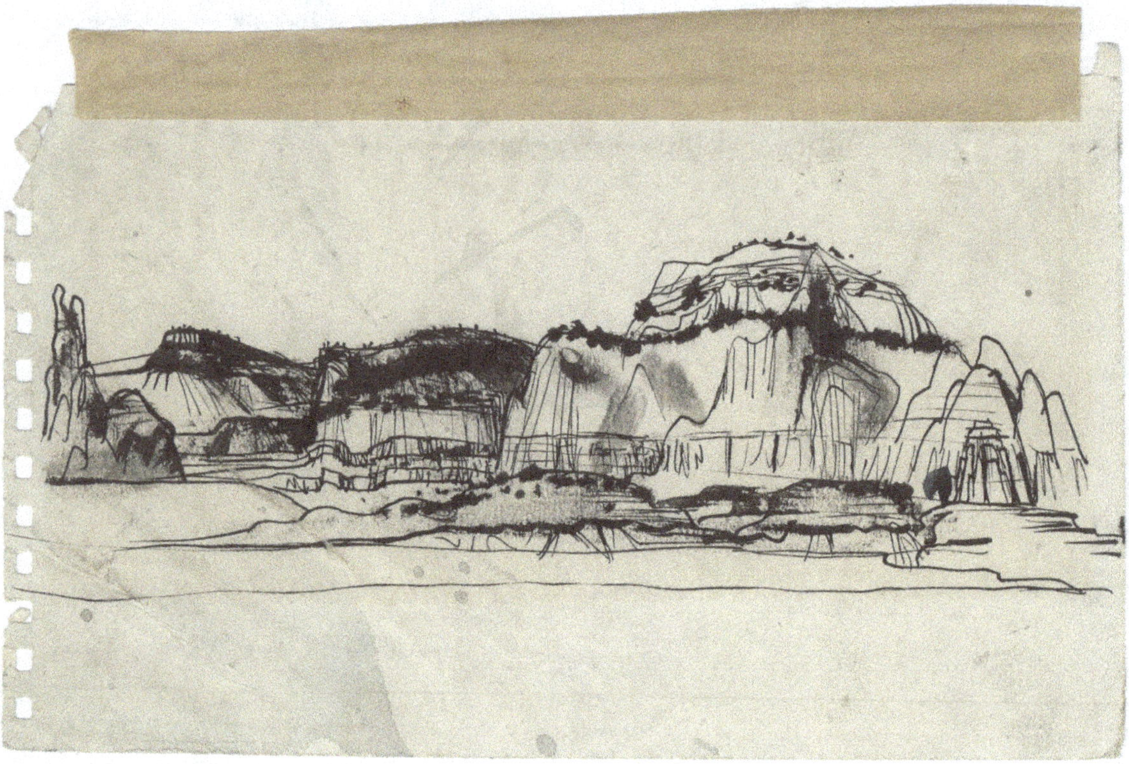

"Rocks and Stream" (1960)

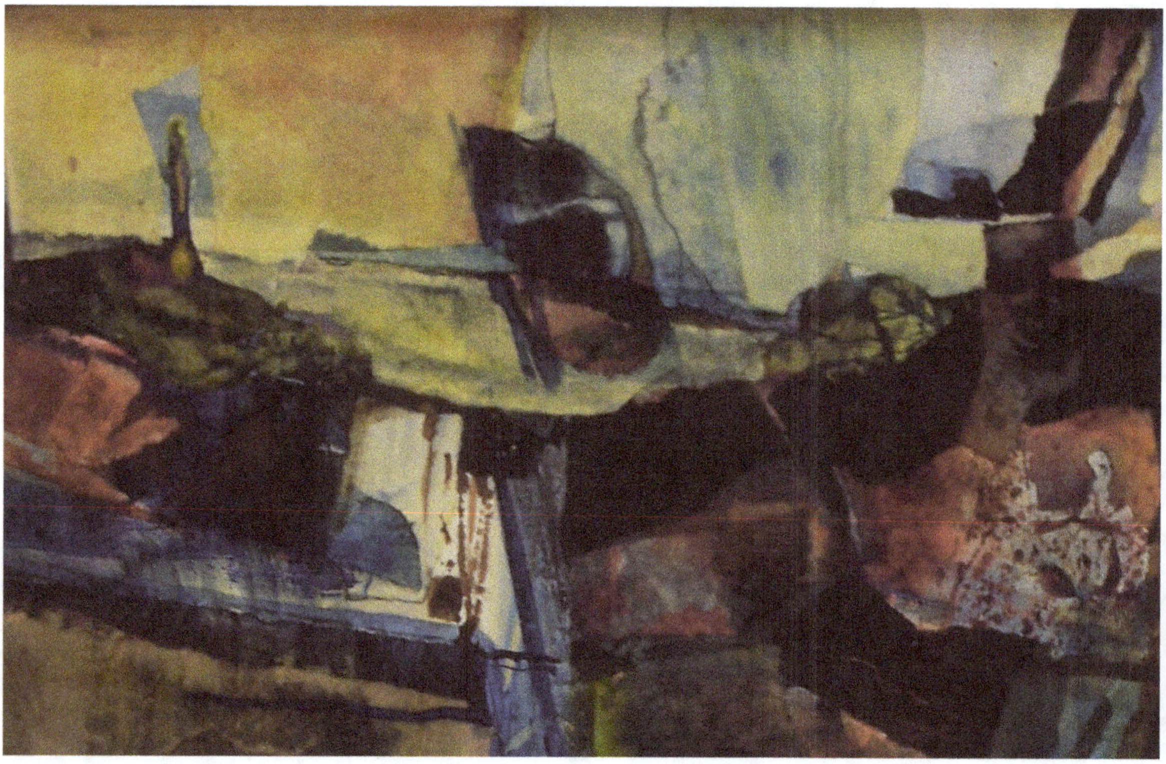

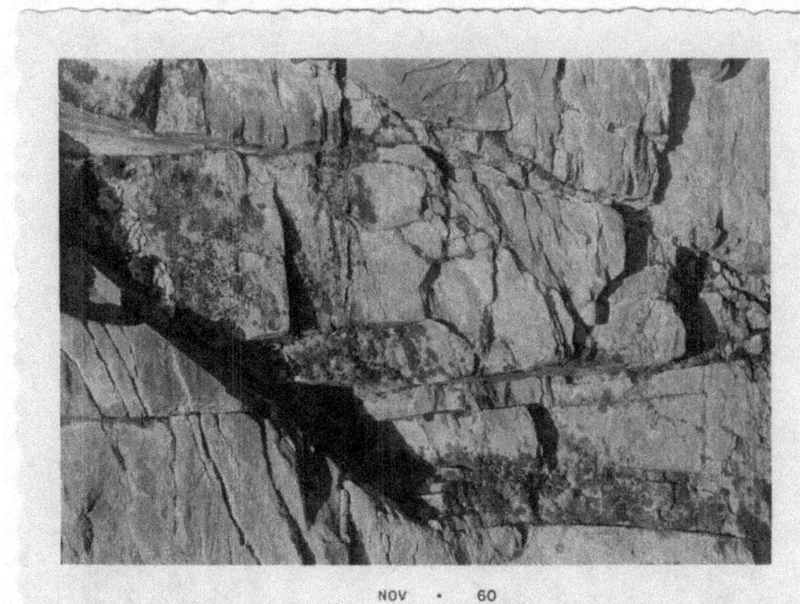

NOV · 60

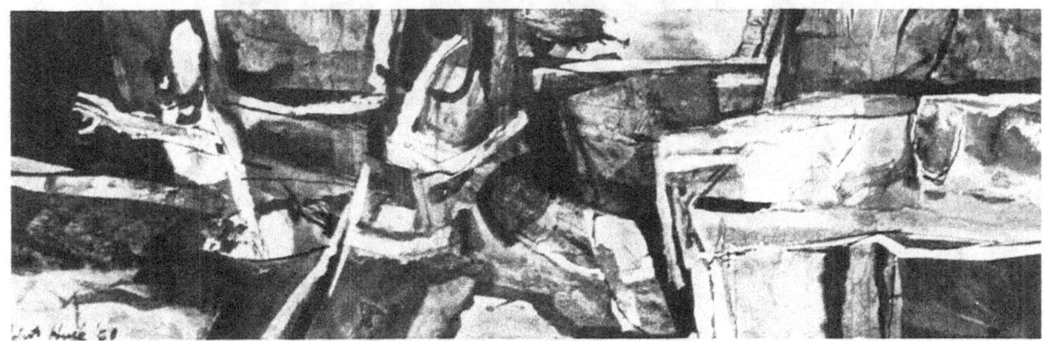

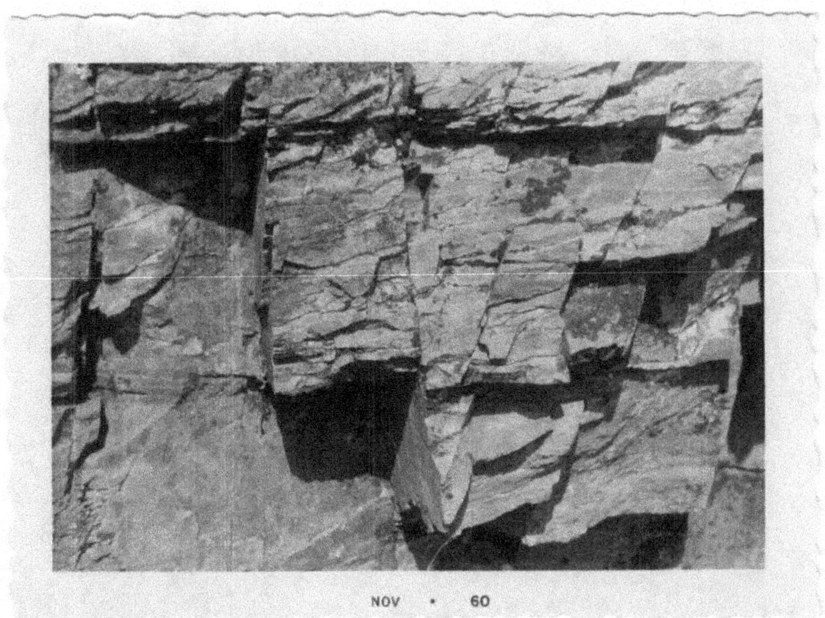

NOV · 60

143

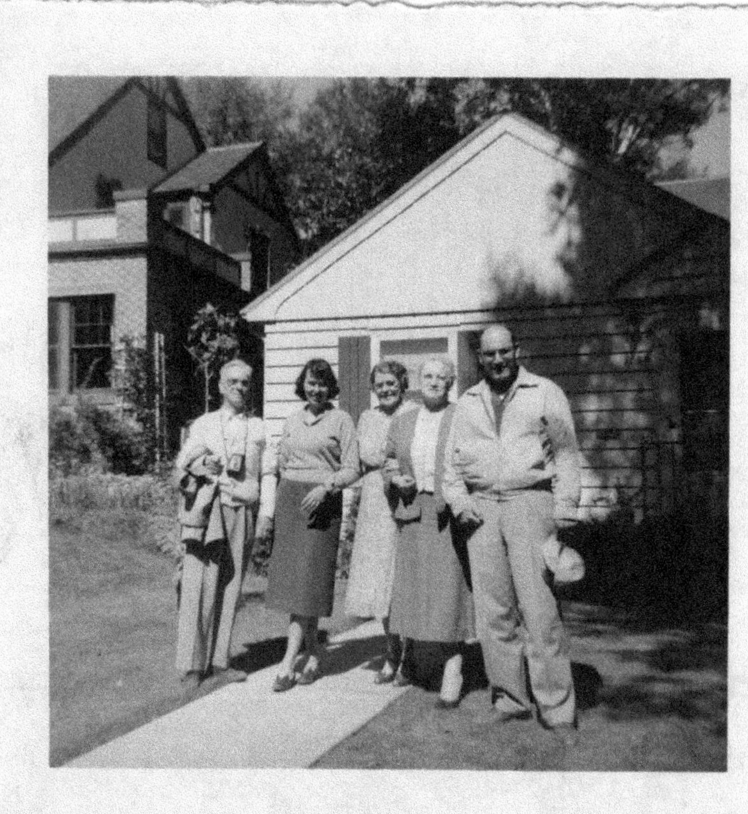

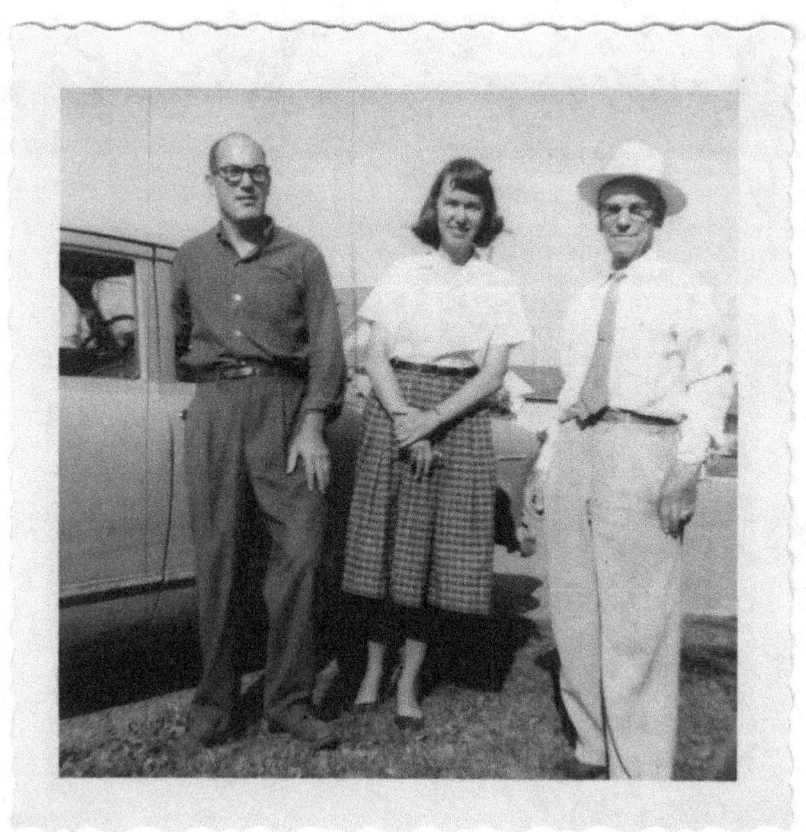

COOP BOOK STORE
Union Building
PHOTO SERVICE

Name _Huck_

_1_ Rolls _135_ _1 8x J_ Develop and Print

____ Reprints ____ Develop Only

Remarks ____________________

_11-25-60_ Date Amount Due ____ _75_

**Quality Service for Forty-four Years
to Oregon State Students**

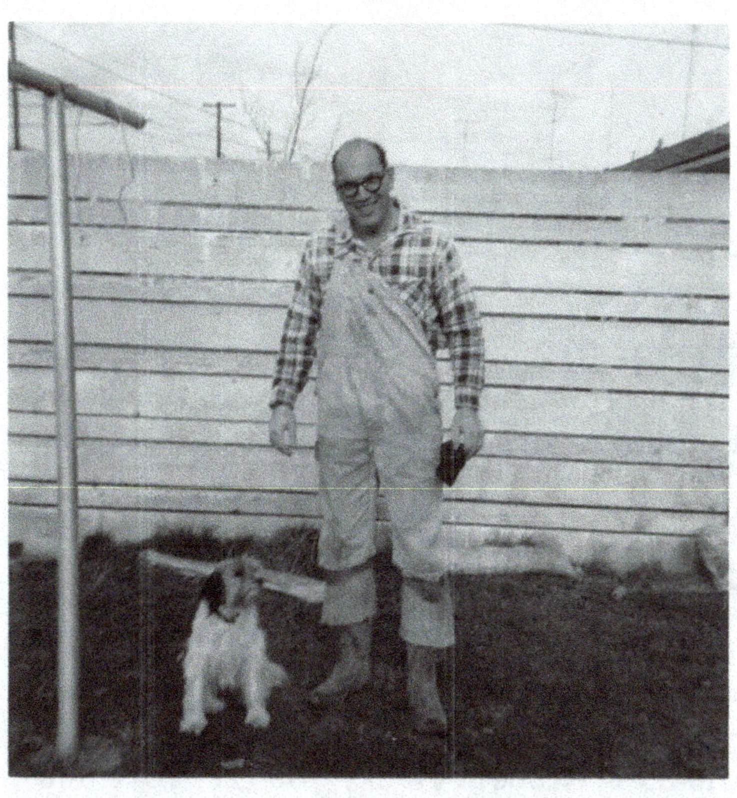

145

Huck Paints Huge Mural for Hotel

Robert E. Huck, member of the art department of Oregon State College, has been visiting his parents. Mr. and Mrs. H. Milton Huck in Kalispell for several days.

He recently completed the painting of one of the largest murals done in oil in the Northwest for the New Sheraton Hotel in Portland. It depicts in a panoramic sweep the course of Oregon rivers from their primitive settings, past cities and farms to the sea.

Huck and his wife, Dorothy, and baby spent several weeks in Duluth where they have been for several weeks at the home of her parents. They expect to spend another week in Kalispell and at the Huck cabin on Red Meadow.

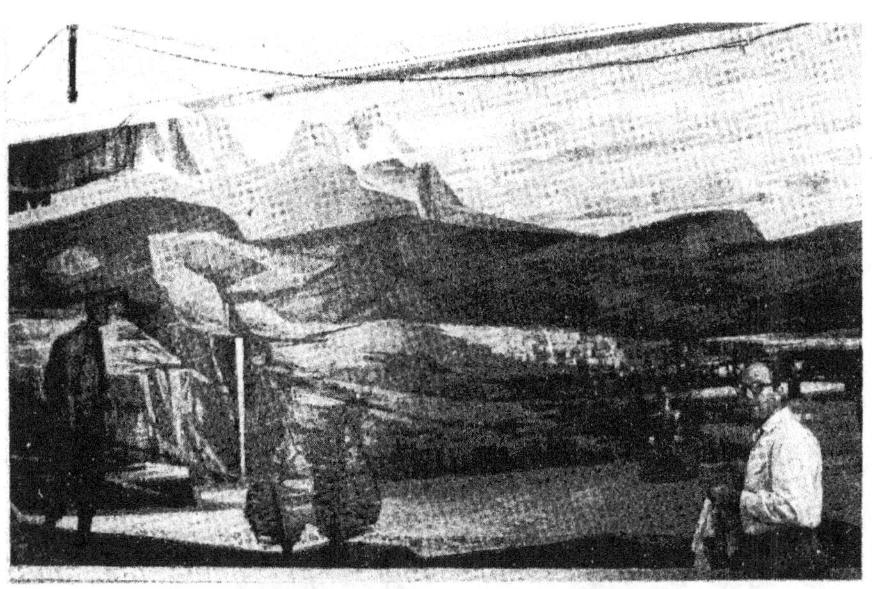

OIL ON LINEN

A portion of the large 48 ft. semi-abstract mural by internationally famous painter and printmaker, Robert Huck, for the Portland Sheraton hotel's Pacific Suite.

146

In **1960** Huck painted two large murals, the first for the Sheraton Hotel in Portland, Oregon. The second mural, commissioned by the First National Bank, brought him back to his birthplace in Kalispell, Montana. 6 feet tall, 32 feet wide, the mural was later relocated to the Flathead Valley Community College where it currently resides.

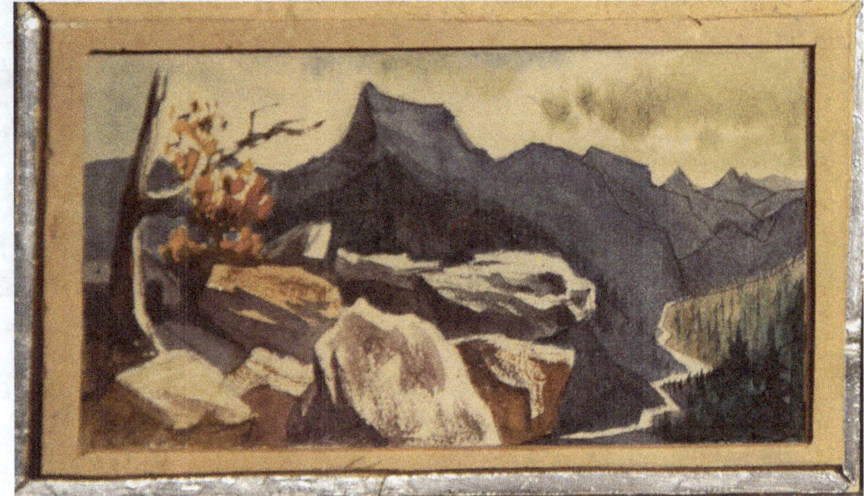

Huck originally proposal three paintings for the bank's wall, shown here, to "suggest the mountains, waterfalls, lakes and rivers" of the region. However, a single mural was decided upon instead. The following three pages show his first verion of the mural, sketch, and final rendition.

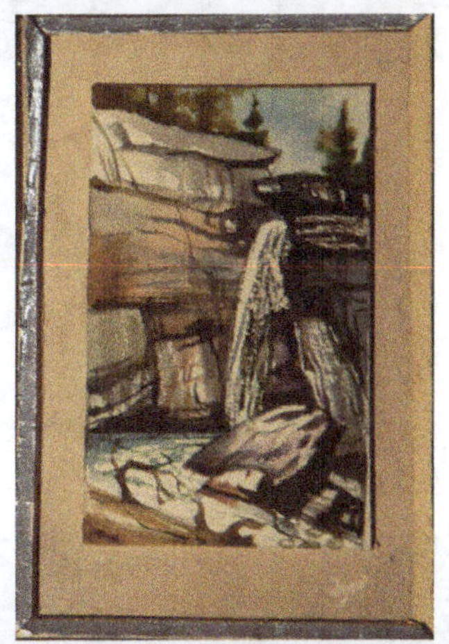

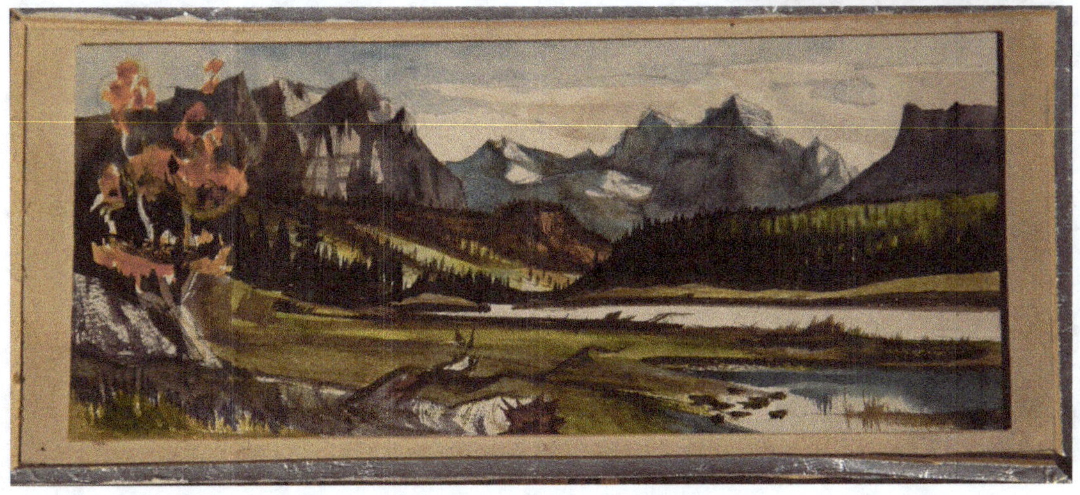

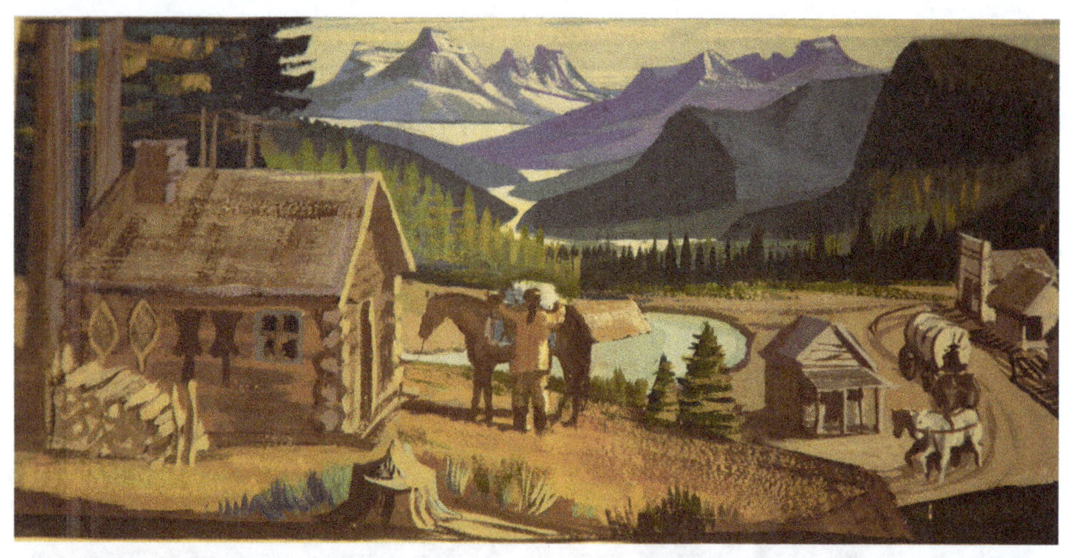

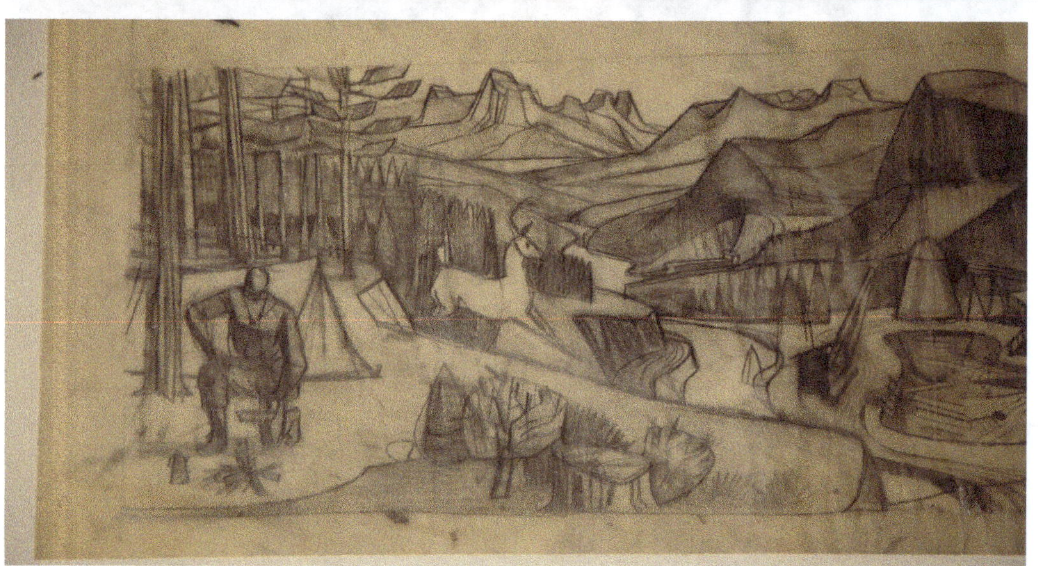

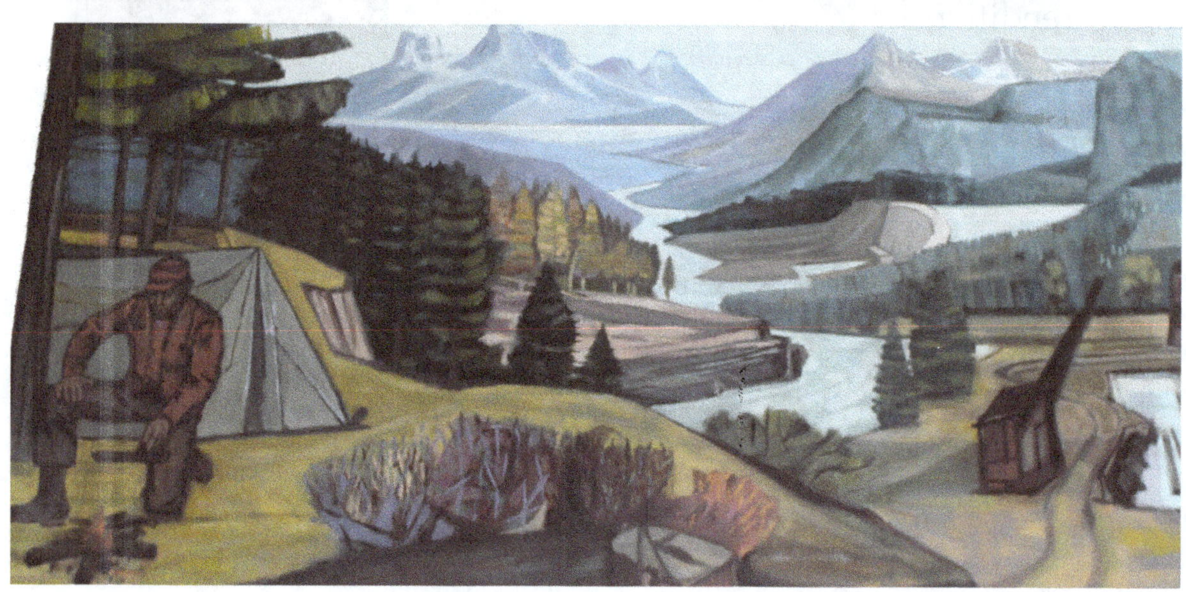

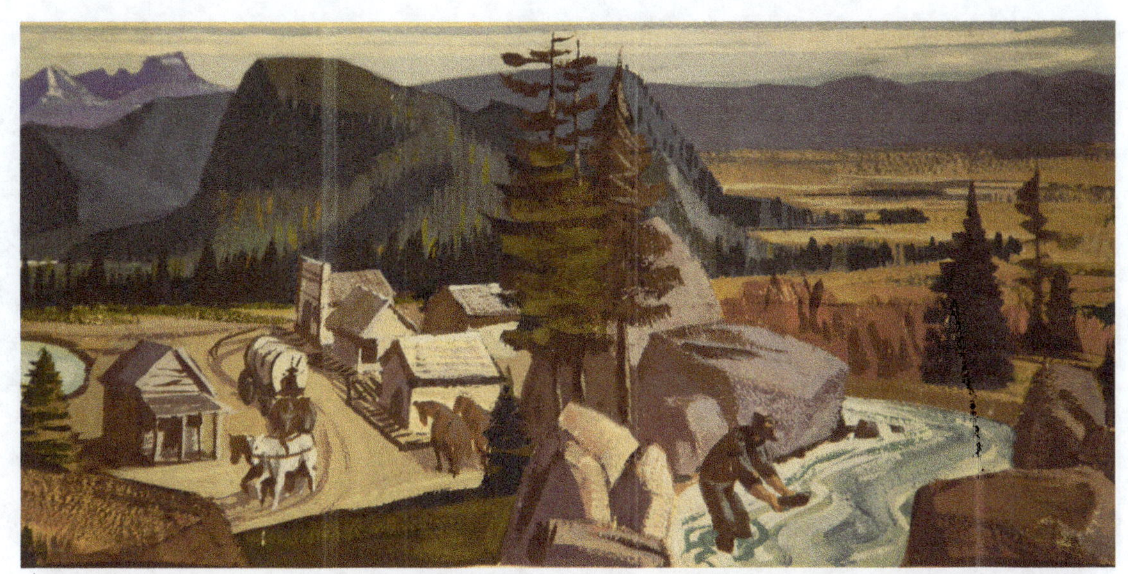

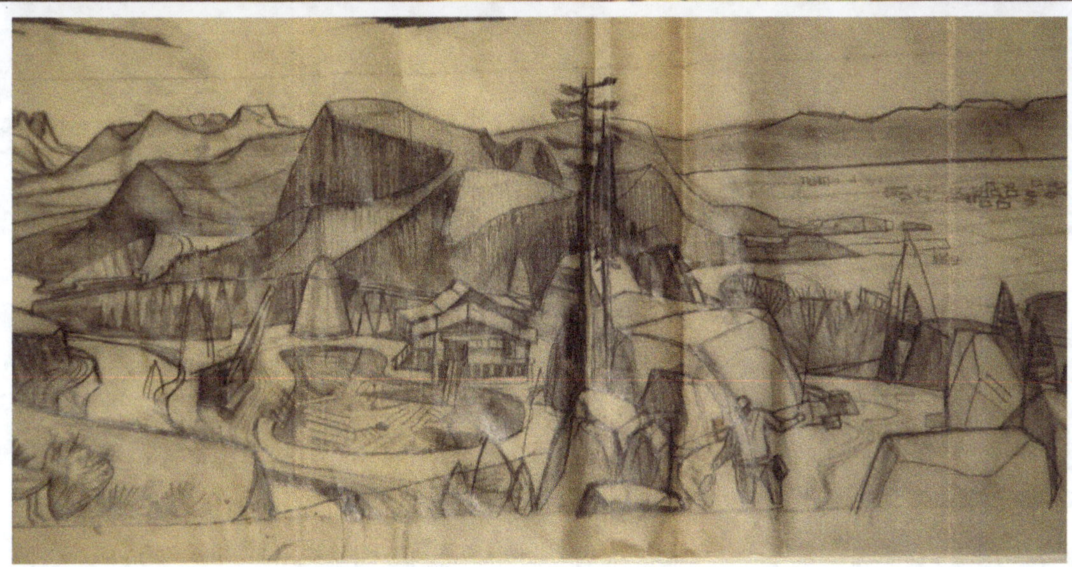

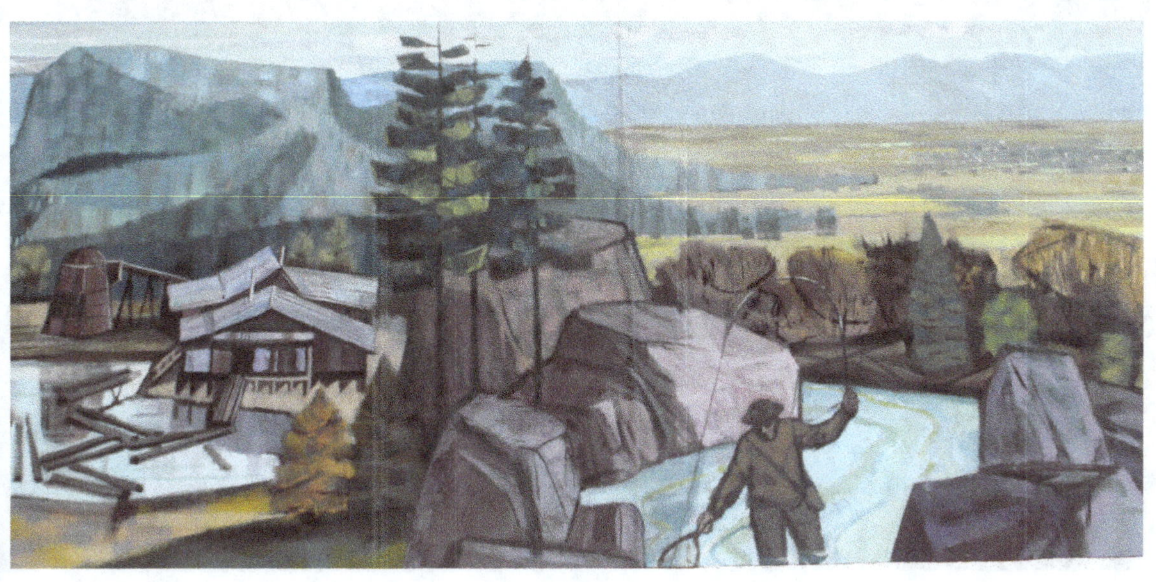

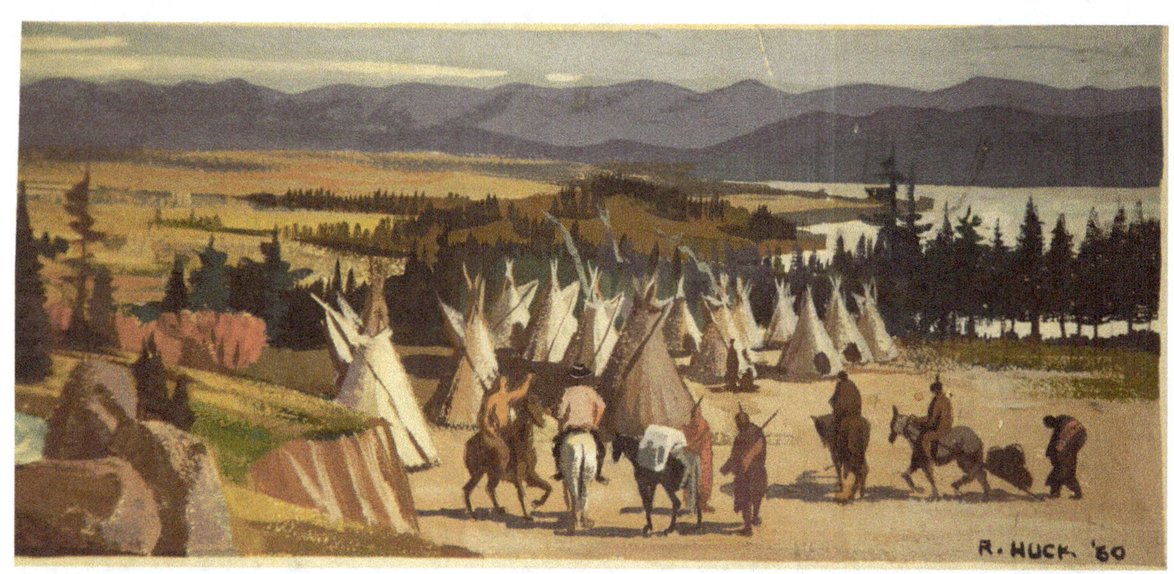

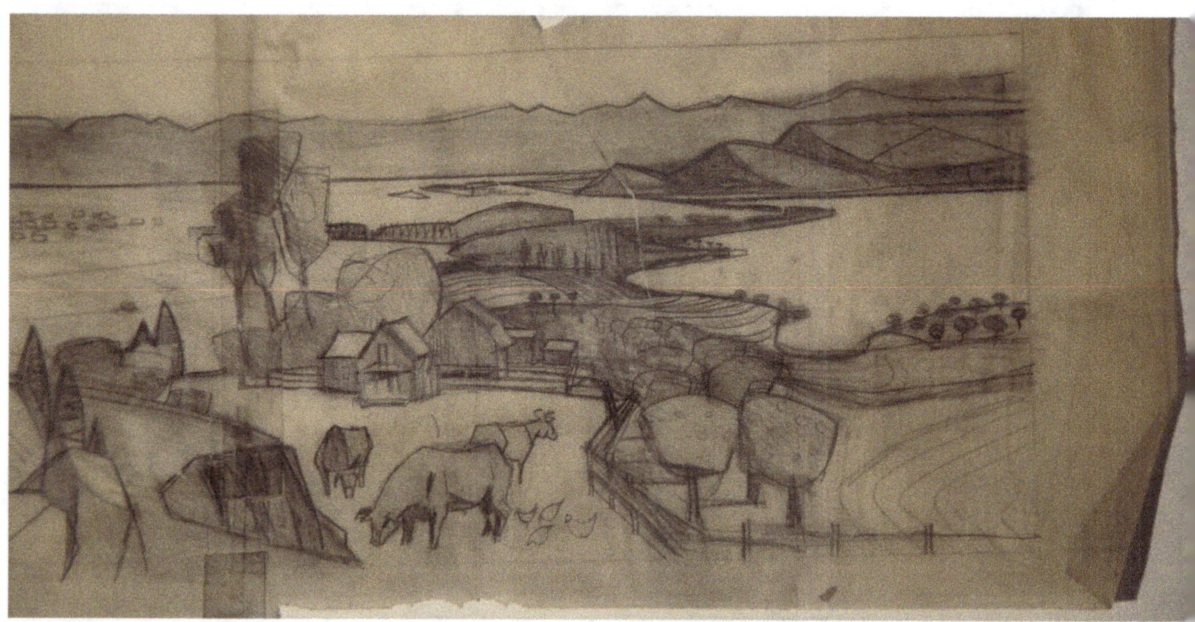

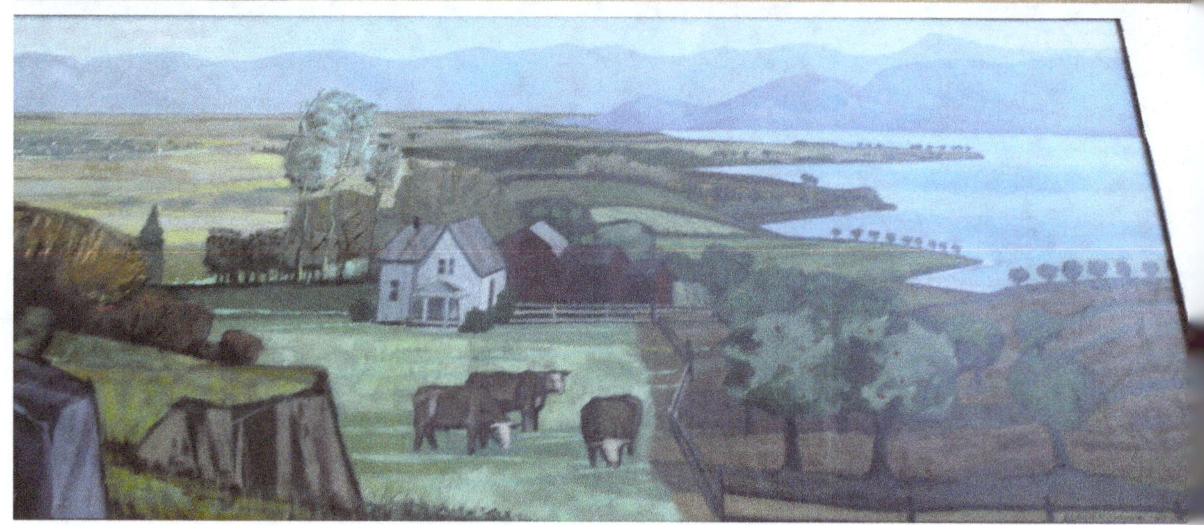

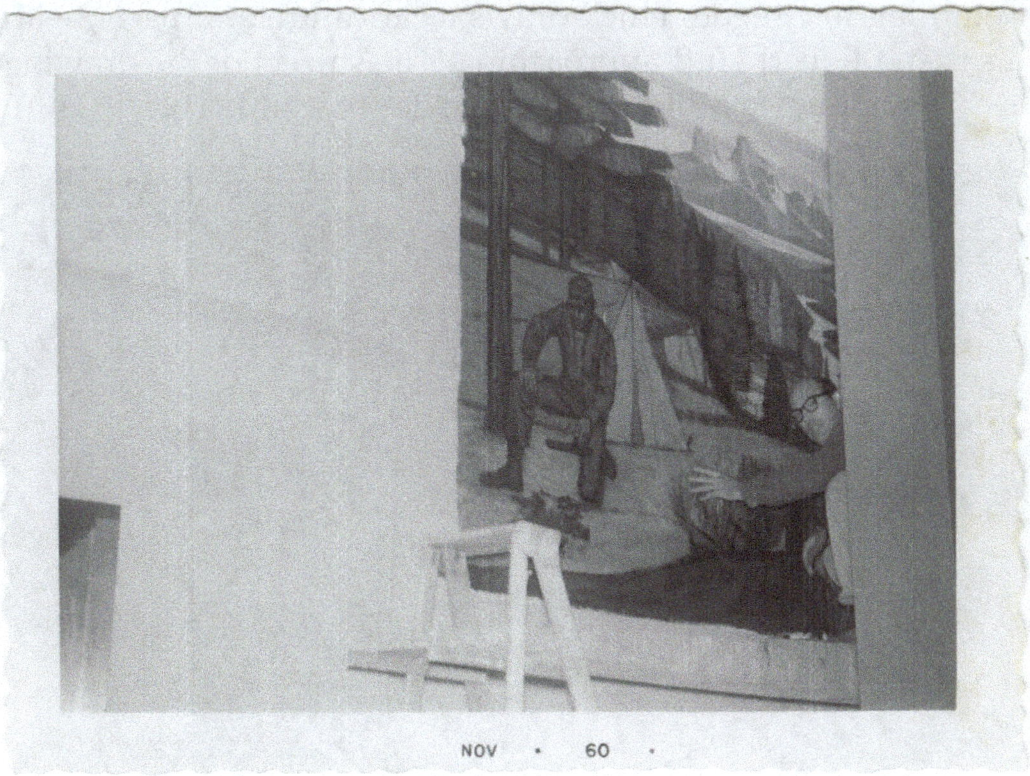

Above: Huck at work on mural   Below: The mural today

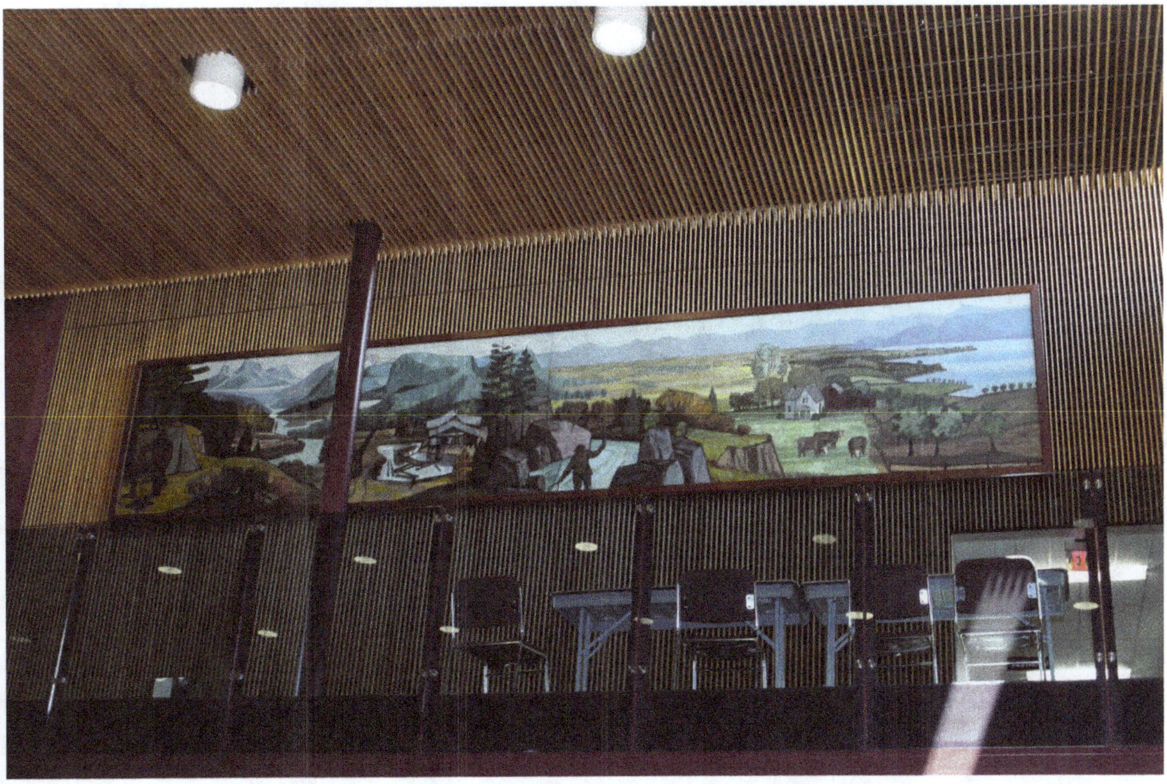

Returning to Oregon, Huck draws a caricature at a party, with his friend Robert Huff approaching. The subject of the drawing is "T. Kranidas," a Milton scholar, no doubt well-known to Huff.

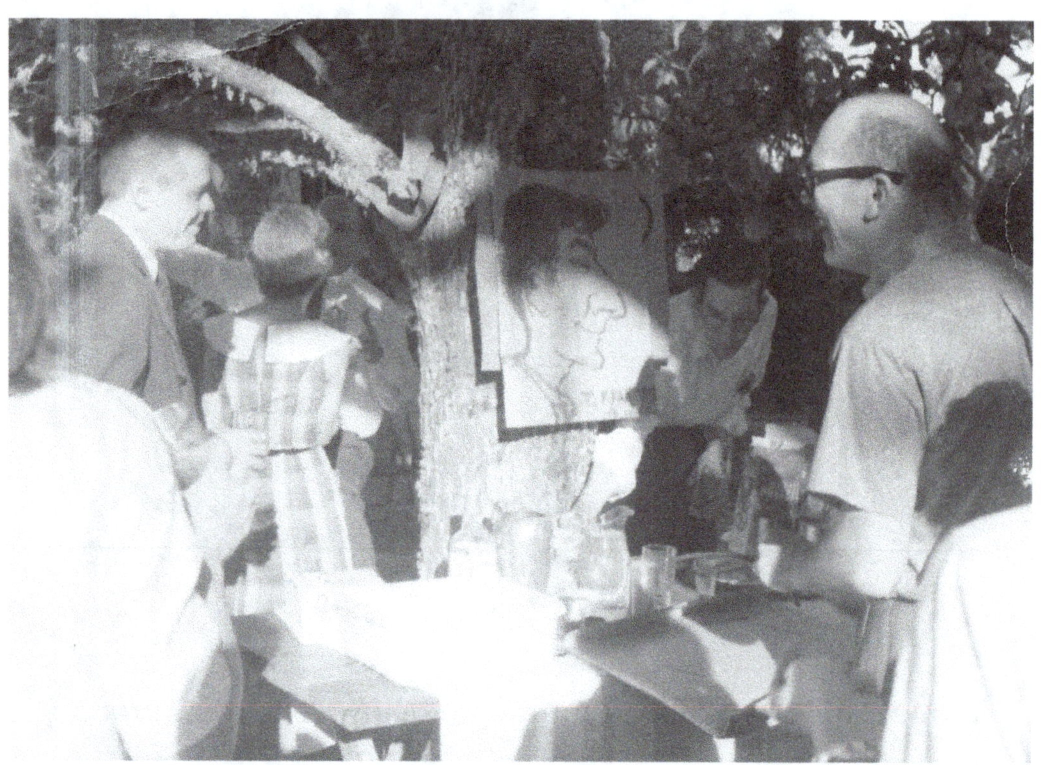

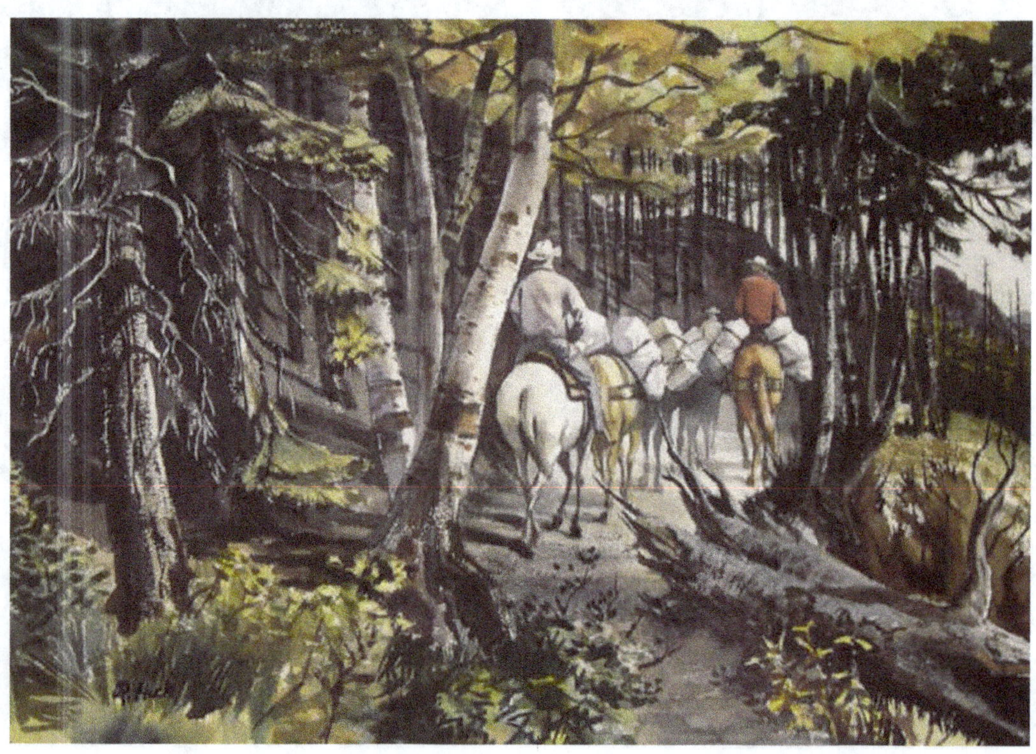

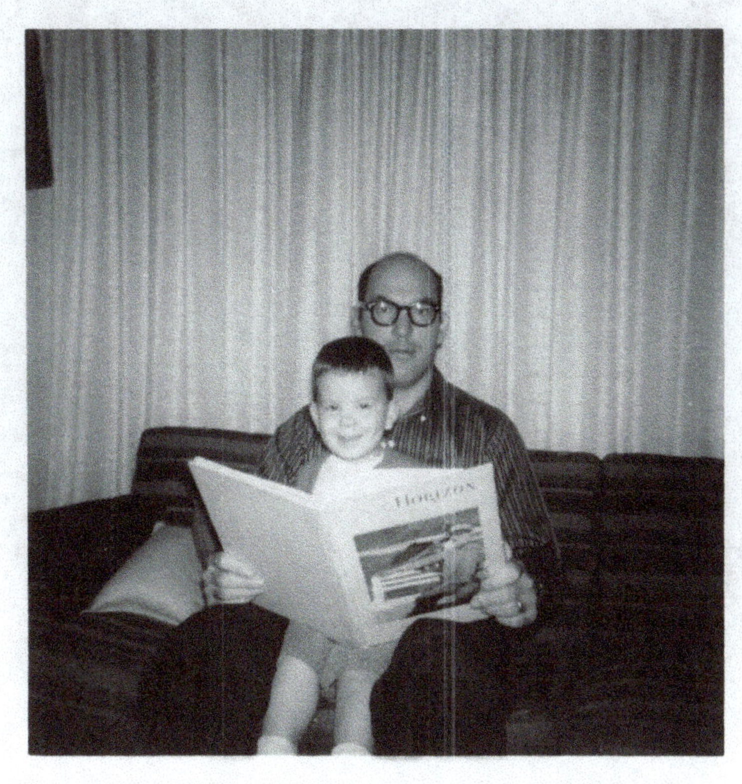

Robert Huck with son Clayton.

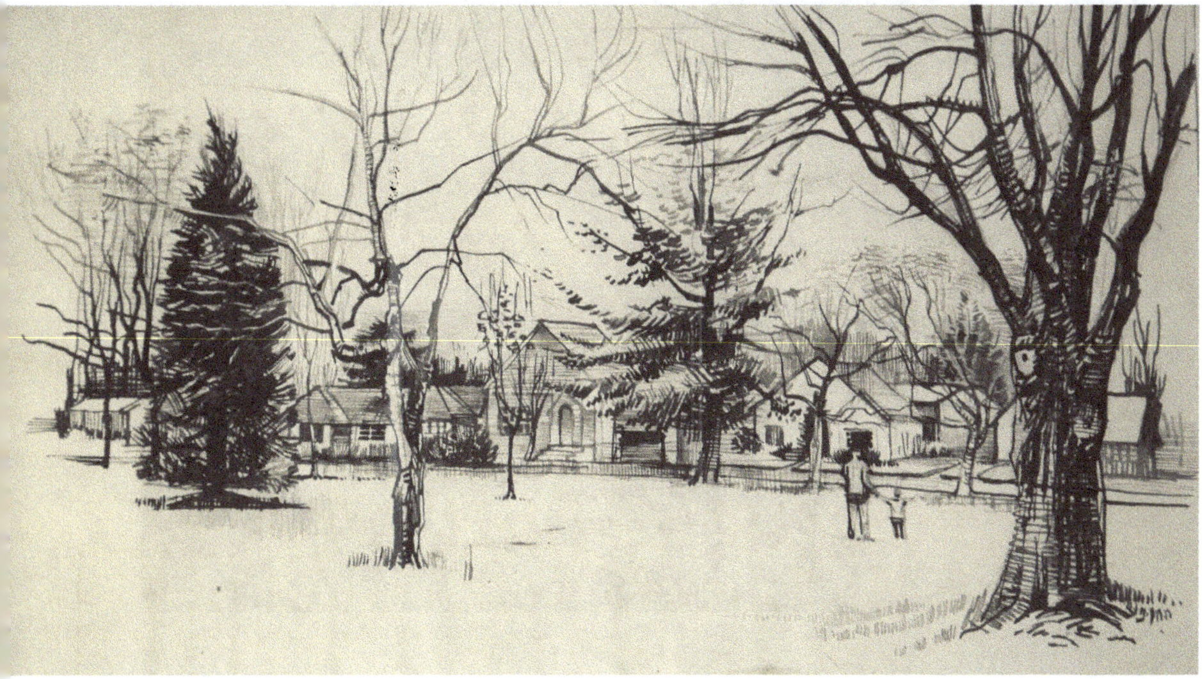

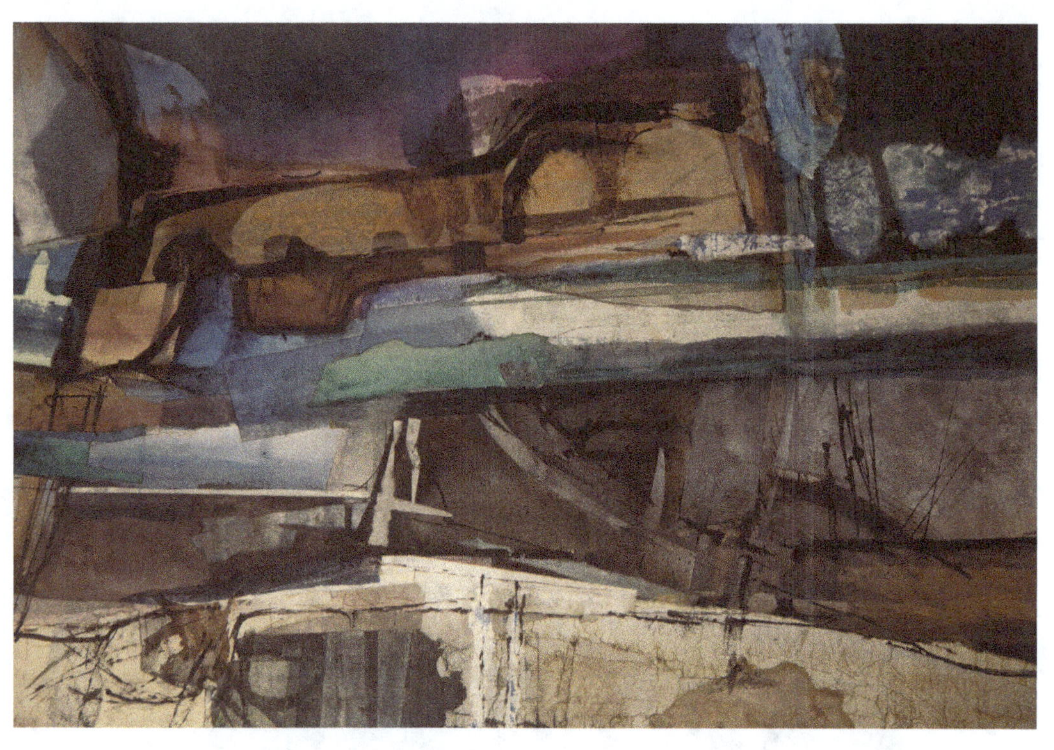

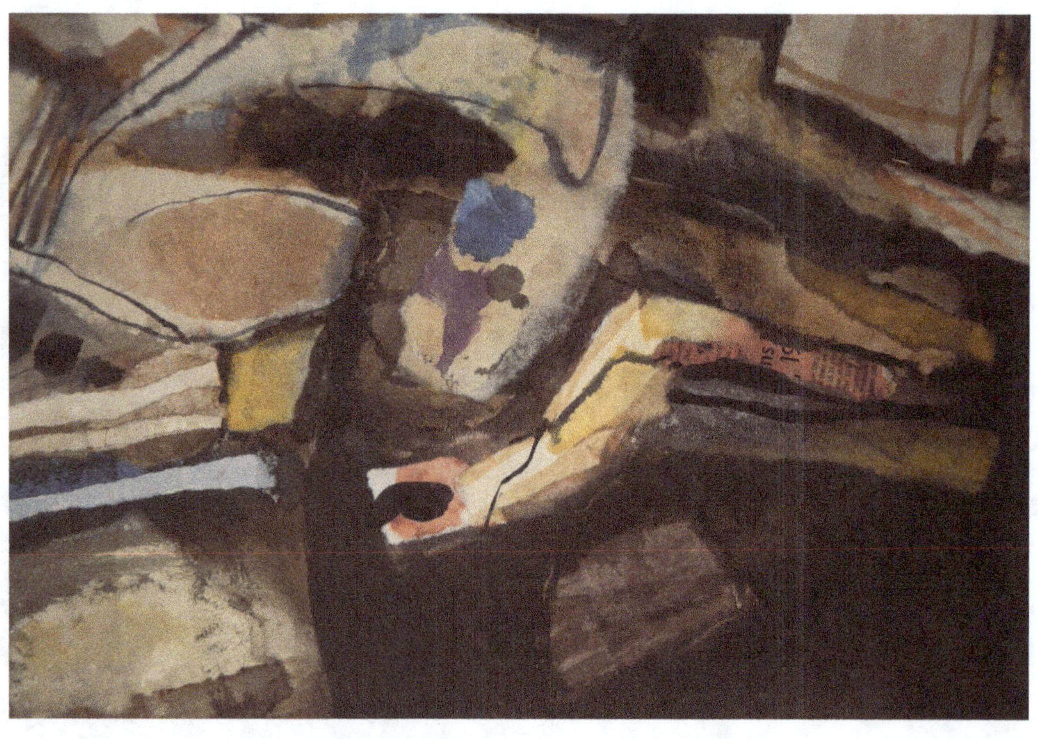

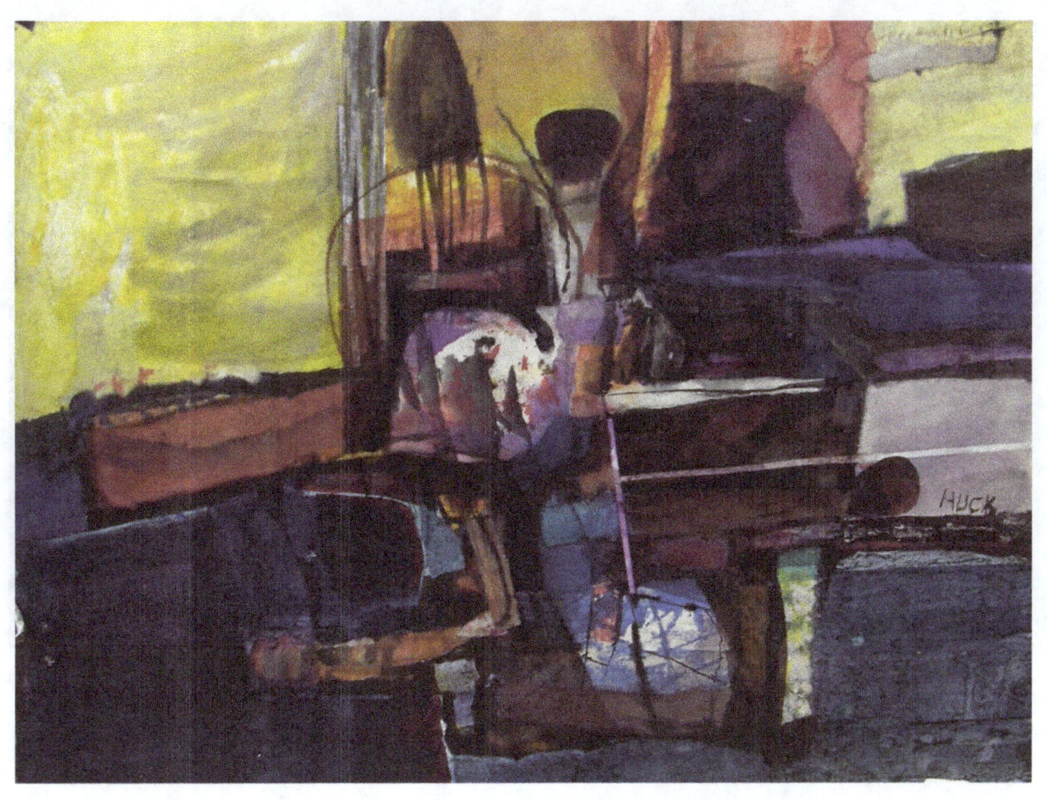

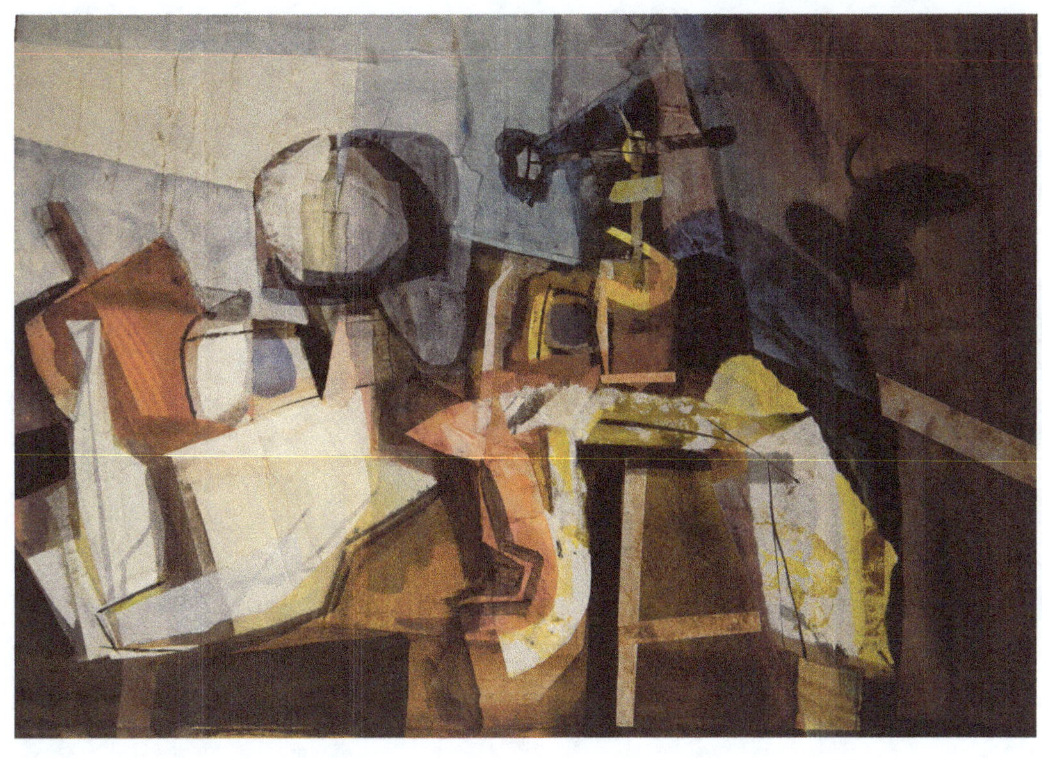

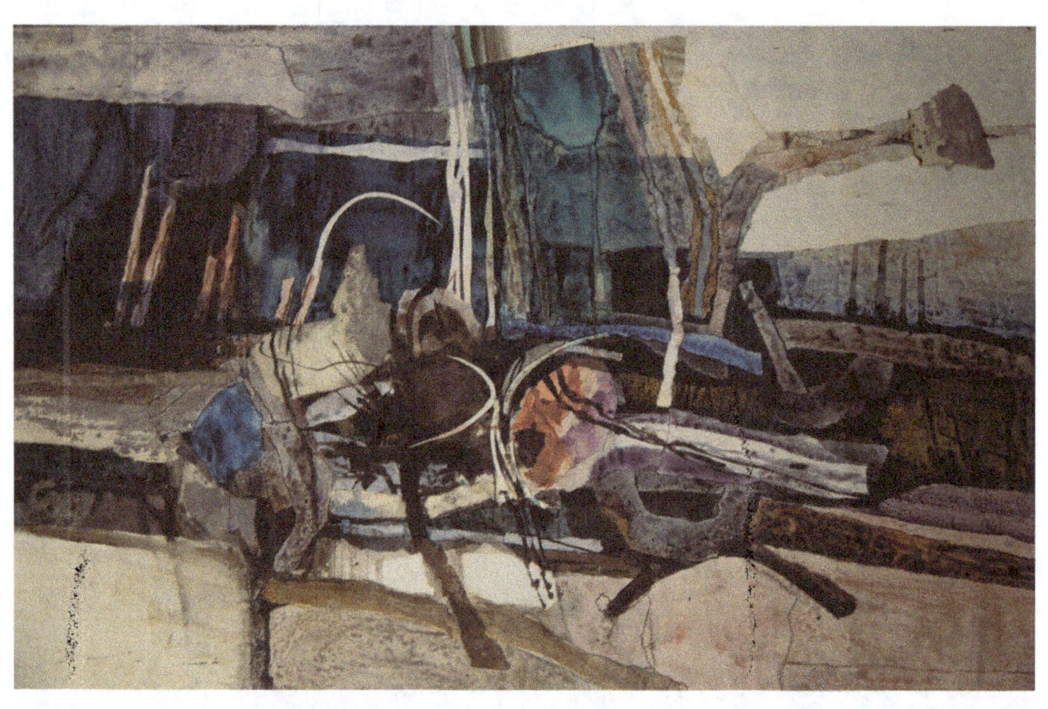

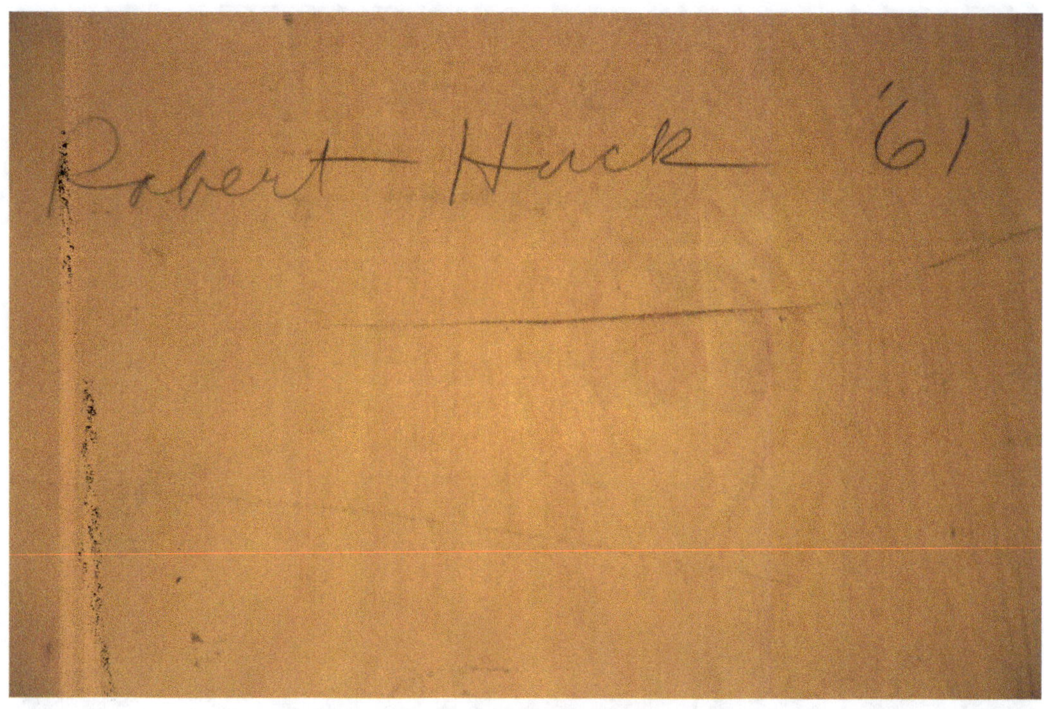

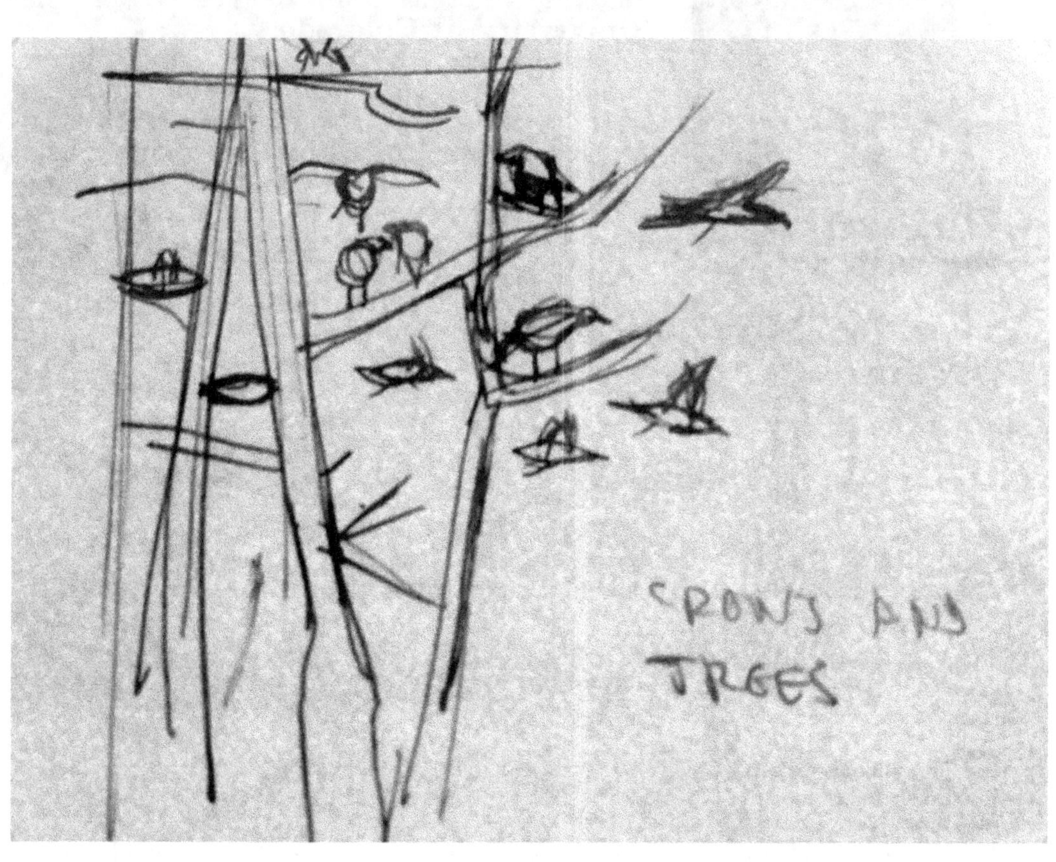
CROWS AND
TREES

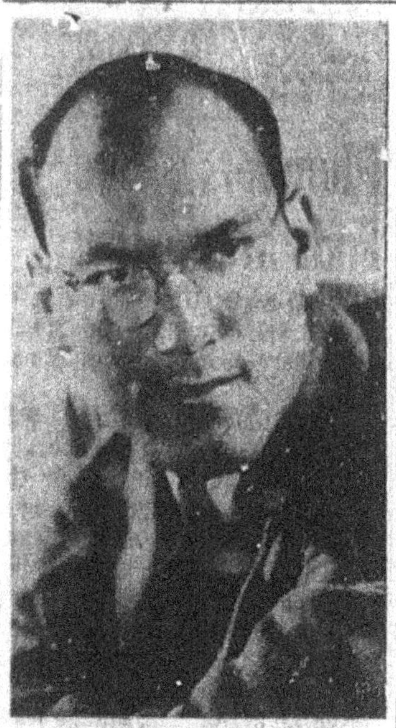

ROBERT E. HUCK

Robert E. Huck Dies In Crash

Robert Emerson Huck, assistant professor of art at OSU, was killed yesterday when his car skidded off wet Highway 99W south of Monmouth. The car struck the railroad trestle pier near Helmick Park.

Professor Huck was a staff member at Oregon State since September, 1955, when he returned to America after a Fulbright scholarship training in Italy. He was born in Kalispell, Mont., February 26, 1923, the son of Mr. and Mrs. H. Milton Huck who still reside in that city. He received the B.A. degree from Colorado College in 1950 and master of fine arts degree from the University of Colorado, in 1952. He served with the U.S. Army in Alaska during World War II.

His work as a painter and print maker won wide recognition both in Europe and America. His art is located in the permanent collections of the Joslyn Museum of

Robert Emerson Huck, assistant professor of art, was killed March 13 when his car skidded off highway 99W near Helmick state park about 12 miles north of Corvallis. Professor Huck had been on the staff since 1955 when he returned to the United States after Fulbright scholarship training in Italy. He was born in 1923 and received a B.A. degree from Colorado College and a master of fine arts degree from the University of Colorado.

His work as a painter and print maker won wide recognition both in Europe and America. His art is located in permanent collections in many parts of the world. Murals completed during the past two years are installed in the Sheraton hotel, Portland, and in a bank in Kalispell, Montana. Professor Huck is survived by his wife, infant son, a brother, and parents.

Art Professor Dies In Crash

Paintings Shown In Student Union

A memorial exhibition of the work of artist Robert Emerson Huck is in the Memorial Union. The exhibition includes 20 paintings and 20 prints.

Huck was a member of the art staff of Oregon State University from Sept. 1955, until his death March 13, 1961. Huck was born Feb. 26, 1923, at Kalispell, Montana.

He received his education at the University of Montana, Colorado College. The Colorado

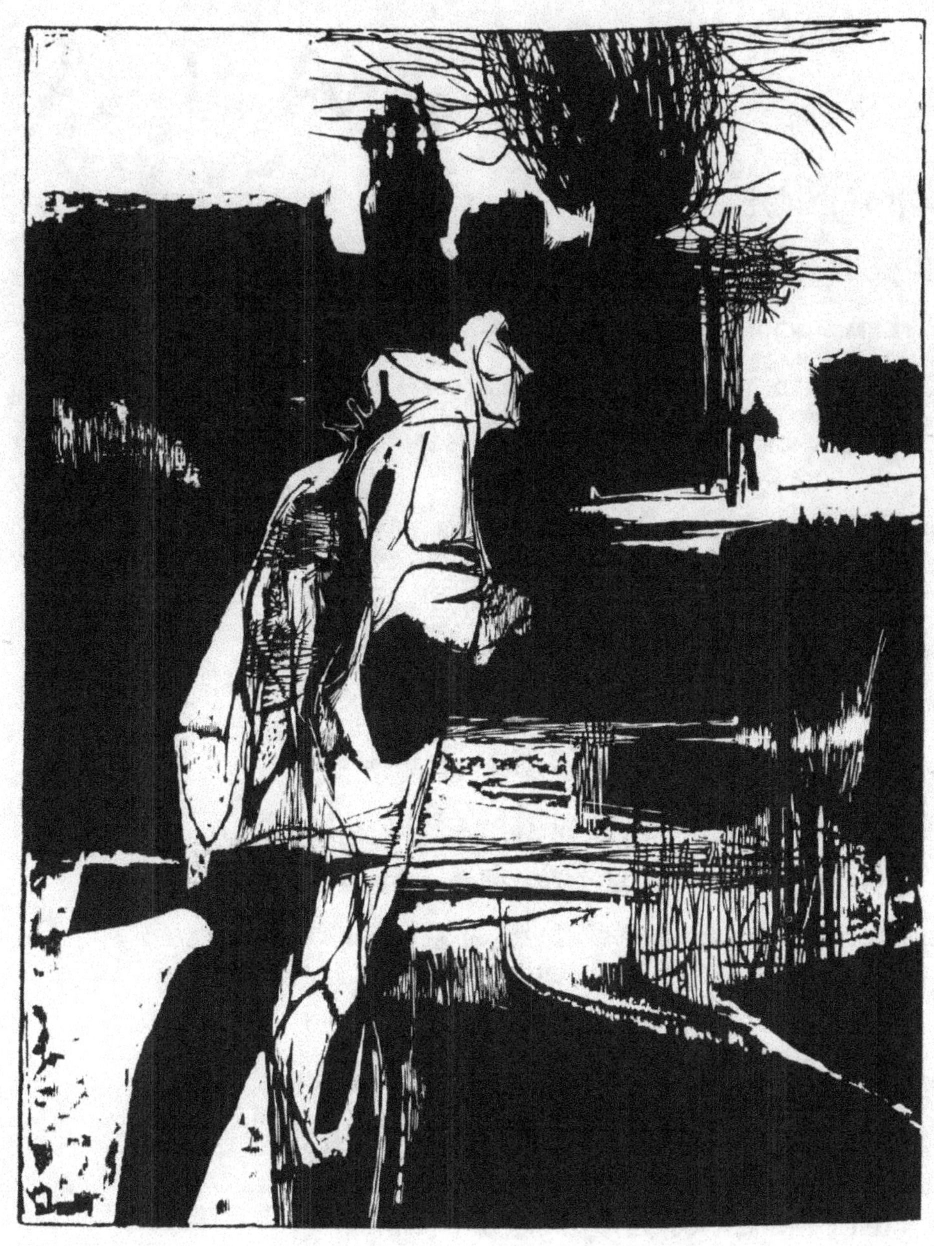

ROBERT E. HUCK

1923 ★ A MEMORIAL EXHIBITION ★ 1961

CATAL

PAINTINGS

1. **LOG JAM**, 1953, 24½ x 34, oil on canvas

2. **FARM MACHINERY**, 1953, 27¾ x 36, oil on canvas

3. **FARM YARD**, 1953, 26 x 32, oil on hardboard

4. **ARMORY OF CASTEL SAN ANGELO**, 1955, 33½ x43, oil on canvas
Collection—Oregon State University

5. **ETRUSCAN EXCAVATION**, 1955, 33 x 43, oil on canvas, NFS

6. **COLOSSEUM**, 1955, 23½ x 35½, oil on canvas, NFS

7. **CATHEDRAL THEME**, 1956, 40 x 28, oil on canvas

8. **RUINS #1**, 1957, 23½ x 40, oil on canvas

9. **FOUNTAIN GROUP**, 1957, 38 x 48, oil on canvas

10. **GONDOLIER**, 1957, 48 x 30, oil on hardboard, NFS

11. **CHUCK WAGON**, 1958, 32 x 47½, oil on hardboard, NFS

12. **HADRIAN'S VILLA**, 1958, 40 x 61½, oil on canvas

13. **HUNTER RESTING**, 1958, 45½ x 58, oil on canvas
Collection—Oregon State University

14. **DUCK HUNTER**, 1958, 47½ x 38½, oil on hardboard

15. **COASTAL FORMS**, 1958, 37¾ x 47¾, oil on canvas
Collection—Oregon State University

16. **ALPINE THEME**, 1958, 26¼ x 39½, oil on canvas

17. **PACIFIC SHORE**, 1959, 36 x 48, oil on canvas

18. **ROCKS AND STREAM**, 1960, 24¾ x 34, collage on plywood

19. **HUNTERS WITH GAME**, 1960, 28 x 36, oil on canvas, NFS

20. **BIRD AND RIVER**, 1960, 35 x 57½, oil on canvas

The paintings and duplicate "Artist Proof" original prints
directed to: THE CLAYTON HUCK SCHOLARSHIP FUND, I

OGUE

PRINTS (WOODCUTS)

21. HUNTER WITH GAME, 1952, 19 x 24, color

22. THE COVE, 1953, 14 x 21¼, color

23. ICE FISHING, 1954, 7½ x 33¼, color

24. ITALIAN CAMERA MAN, 1955, 14¾ x 22¾, color

25. EARTH PEOPLE, 1955, 17¼ x 30¼, black with dark green chiaroscuro block

26. ETRUSCAN STILL LIFE, 1955, 9½ x 23, color

27. BROOM VENDER, 1956, 22 x 28¾, black and white

28. ITALIAN LANDSCAPE, 1957, 20 x 30½, color

29. DUCK HUNTER, 1958, 28¾ x 22, black and white

30. TRAPS, 1958, 22 x 13½, color

31. ROMAN BEGGARS, 1958, 22 x 27¾, black with brown chiaroscuro block

32. COASTAL FORMS, 1958, 20 x 34, color

33. RIVER'S EDGE, 1958, 20¼ x 30¼, color

34. MELANCHOLIA, 1959, 22 x 28¾, black and white

35. HIKER, 1959, 22 x 28½, black and white

36. TIDELAND, 1959, 20 x 35, color

37. EAGLE, 1959, 15¾ x 20, black and white

38. RIVER BEND, 1960, 15½ x 23½, color

39. SEA GROWTH, 1960, 15¼ x 23¾, color

40. MOUNTAIN LANDSCAPE, 1960, 19½ x 31, color

·e available unless otherwise indicated. Inquiries may be
ɔartment of Art, Oregon State University, Corvallis, Oregon

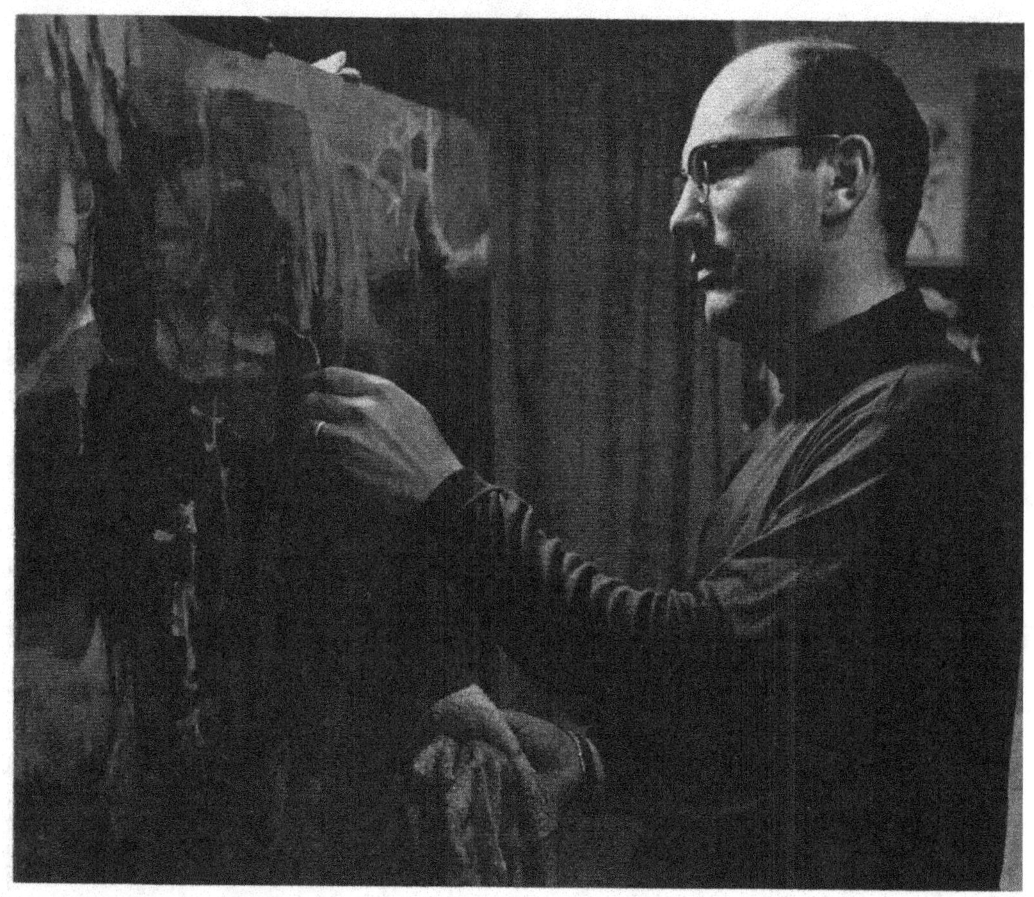

EXHIBITION SCHEDULE

1—29 October 1961 . . . Oregon State University Memorial Union Gallery
Corvallis, Oregon

15 November—15 December 1961 . . . . . . Portland Art Museum
Portland, Oregon

3 January—4 February 1962 . . . . Seattle Art Museum, Volunteer Park
Seattle, Washington

15 February—31 March 1962 . . . . Colorado Springs Fine Arts Center
Colorado Springs, Colorado

11-29 April 1962 . . . Department of Fine Arts, University of Colorado
Boulder, Colorado

7 May—1 September 1962 . . . Art Galleries, Historical Society of Montana
Helena, Montana

18 September—28 October 1962 . . . Museum of Art, University of Oregon
Eugene, Oregon

VITA

ROBERT EMERSON HUCK was born February 26, 1923, at Kalispell, Montana, the son of Mr. and Mrs. H. Milton Huck of that city. After completing high school in Kalispell he served with the Signal Corps, Army of The United States, November 1942 to November 1945. He was married to Dorothy Schroeer of Duluth, Minnesota, June, 1948. Their son, Clayton, was born November 25, 1958. Death came tragically in an automobile accident on March 13, 1961.

EDUCATION: January, 1946—June 1946, The University of Montana, Missoula; September, 1946—June 1950, Colorado College and The Colorado Springs Fine Arts Center, Bachelor of Arts degree, 1950; September, 1950—June, 1952, The University of Colorado, Boulder, Master of Fine Arts degree, 1952 (tuition scholarship student). During the academic years in Colorado, Robert Huck studied with Professors Jean Charlot, Alden F. Megrew, William Johnstone, Peppino Mangravite, John Heliker, Boardman Robinson, Howard Cook, Wendell Black, Edgar Britton, Paul Burlin, Lynn Wolfe, and others. He was a Fulbright Fellow in Italy during the school year of 1954-1955.

ART STAFF MEMBER: September, 1952-June, 1954, Northern State Teachers College, Aberdeen, South Dakota; September, 1955-March 13, 1961, Oregon State University, Corvallis, Oregon.

RECOGNITION AS A PAINTER:

Purchase Awards—Northwest Annual, Spokane, 1948; Joslyn Museum, Omaha, 1950; Canon City Exhibition, Colorado, 1950; Alabama Watercolor Society Medal, 1950; Colorado State Fair, 1950; Taylor Museum, Colorado Springs, 1950; Butler Museum, Youngstown, Ohio, 1953; Portland Art Museum, Oregon, 1955; Seattle Art Museum, 1956.

Exhibitions—Joslyn Six States Show, Omaha, 1950-1952; Artists West of The Mississippi, Denver Art Museum, 1950-1951-1952-1956-1957; Corcoran Biennial, Washington, D. C., 1951; Institute of Contemporary Art, Boston, 1951; Birmingham Museum of Art, 1951; Institute of Art and History, Albany, New York, 1952-1953; Paul Sargent Gallery, Charleston, Illinois, 1952; Brooks Memorial Gallery, 1953; The University of Georgia, 1953; "Great Stories of Man," Denver Art Museum, 1953; Artists of Oregon, Portland Art Museum, 1955-1956—1957-1958-1959-1960; Northwest Annual Exhibition, Seattle Art Museum, 1955-1956-1957-1959; Fulbright Artists Exhibit, Duveen Galleries, New York City, 1957; Oregon Centennial Exhibition, Portland, 1959; Pacific Profile, Pasadena Art Museum, 1961; and elsewhere.

One Man Exhibitions—Chapman House, Colorado Springs, 1950; University of Colorado, 1952; Galleria Il Camino, Rome, Italy, 1955; University of Redlands, California, 1956; Portland Art Museum, Oregon, 1957; Willamette University, Oregon, 1957; Oregon State University, Corvallis, 1955-1956-1957-1959.

Murals—Sheraton Hotel, Portland, Oregon, 1959-1960; First National Bank, Kalispell, Montana, 1960.

RECOGNITION AS A PRINTMAKER:

Purchase Awards—Northwest Printmakers International, Seattle Art Museum, 1953; Bradley University Annual, 1953; University of Southern California, 1953; University of Minnesota, 1953; Library of Congress, 1953-1958; Portland Art Museum, Oregon, 1955; Henry Gallery, University of Washington, Seattle, 1956-1957; Bay Printmakers National, Oakland, 1958; Pasadena Art Museum, 1958; Bibliotheque Nationale, Paris, 1959; Victoria and Albert Museum, London, 1959; Silvermine Guild National, 1959.

Exhibitions—Northwest Printmakers International, Seattle Art Museum, 1950-1951-1952-1956-1957-1958-1959-1960-1961; Colorado Springs Fine Arts Center, 1951; Brooklyn Museum National Print Annual, 1952, 1953, 1960; Carnegie Institute, 1952; J. B. Speed Art Museum, 1952; Cincinnati Art Museum, 1953; City Art Museum of St. Louis, 1953; University of Georgia, 1953; Wichita Print and Drawing Exhibition, 1953; Society of American Graphic Artists, New York City, 1953; Portland Art Museum, 1955, 1956, 1957, 1958, 1959, 1960; Bay Printmakers National, 1955, 1956, 1957, 1958, 1960; Northwest Printmakers Regional Exhibit, Henry Gallery, University of Washington, 1955, 1956, 1957, 1958, 1959; IV Bordighera Biennale, Italy, 1957; Centre Culturel Americain, Paris, 1957; Victoria and Albert Museum, London, 1958; Bath Academy of Art, England, 1958; USIA and Society of American Graphic Artists "American Prints" selected for numerous exhibitions abroad, 1960; Parnassos Hall, Athens, Greece, 1960; and elsewhere.

THANK YOU,

Robert Hucil

ROBERT HUCIL

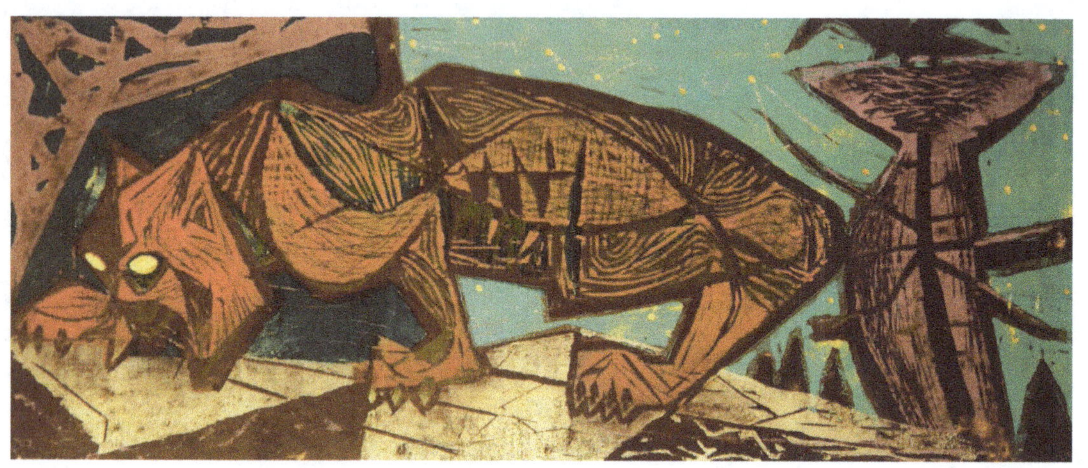

CREDITS

Unless noted otherwise, all artwork and materials are the property of Sarah Neugebauer and Clayton Huck Brown.

Page 13, "A Posthumous Exhibition of the Art of Robert Huck," Robert Huff, *Taking Her Sides on Immortality*, Good Deed Rain, 2019.

p.16, p.18, Flathead High School yearbook, 1941-42, Kalispell, Montana.

p.17, *Mountaineer*, Spring 1944, Montana State University.

p.18 (1)&(2), p.20 (3)&(4), p.32 (5), *The Montana Institute of the Arts Quarterly*, Vol. 7, No. 4, Summer 1955.

p.23, *The Montana Kaimin*, Montana State University, Vol. XLIV, December 8.1944.

p.26-27, *The Sentinel*, A Review of 1946-47 at Montana State University.

p.31, *Colorado Springs Free Press*, August 16, 1949.

p.34, Hindman Auctioneers, 2020, "Antique Store," 1949, Lot 322. Retrieved from: https://www.bidsquare.com/online-auctions/hindman-auctions/robert-huck-american-1923-1961-antique-store-1949-1738543.

p.45, "Fisherman and Catch," 1952, woodcut on paper, image: 11 5/8 in x 19 3/4 in; sheet: 14 7/16 in x 21 in, Gift of the Bill Rhoades Collection in memory of Murna and Vay Rhoades. Portland Art Museum, Portland, Oregon, 2013.92.6.

p.46, "Hunter with Game," 1952, color woodcut on paper, image: 19 1/4 in x 24 1/2 in; sheet: 21 1/16 in x 27 1/8 in, The Vivian and Gordon Gilkey Graphic Arts Collection. Portland Art Museum, Portland, Oregon, 83.57.449

Page 47--53, Colorado University, Robert Huck MFA Thesis, *An Approach to a Painting Problem*, 1952,

p.56, "Entombment," 1952, color woodcut on paper, image: 13 3/4 in x 23 1/2 in; sheet: 21 1/16 in x 27 5/8 in, The Vivian and Gordon Gilkey Graphic Arts Collection. Portland Art Museum, Portland, Oregon, 86.13.48.

p.61, "The Cove," 1953, color woodcut on paper, image: 14 5/16 in x 21 1/2 in; sheet: 17 5/8 in x 22 5/8 in, The Vivian and Gordon Gilkey Graphic Arts Collection. Portland Art Museum, Portland, Oregon, 83.57.323.

p.61, "Sailor's Cottage," 1953, color woodcut on paper, image: 15 in x 21 3/16 in; sheet: 17 in x 23 1/16 in, The Vivian and Gordon Gilkey Graphic Arts Collection. Portland Art Museum, Portland, Oregon, 82.80.510.

p.62, "The Rack," 1953, color woodcut on paper, image: 14 1/4 in x 21 5/16 in; sheet: 17 3/4 in x 22 9/16 in, The Vivian and Gordon Gilkey Graphic Arts Collection. Portland Art Museum, Portland,Oregon, 84.25.253.

p.62, "Equestrian," 1953, color woodcut on paper, image: 27 in x 11 7/8 in; sheet: 28 13/16 in x 13 7/16 in, The Vivian and Gordon Gilkey Graphic Arts Collection. Portland Art Museum, Portland, Oregon, 91.84.634.

p.66, "Old Magician," 1954, woodcut on paper, image: 33 in x 15 1/4 in; sheet: 36 1/16 in x 21 in, The Vivian and Gordon Gilkey Graphic Arts Collection. Portland Art Museum, Portland, Oregon, 84.25.667.

p.67, *Aberdeen (S.D.) American-News*, Sunday, May 2, 1954.

p.74, "Perugia--Italian Scene," Watercolor, 1955, *The Montana Institute of the Arts Quarterly*, Vol.7 no.4, Summer 1955.

p.78, "Venetian Night," 1955, lithograph on paper, image: 11 7/8 in x 15 5/8 in; sheet: 17 3/8 in x 22 1/2 in, The Vivian and Gordon Gilkey Graphic Arts Collection. Portland Art Museum, Portland, Oregon, 83.57.383.

p.79, "Venetian Night," 1955, color lithograph on paper, image: 11 13/16 in x 15 9/16 in; sheet: 17 1/2 in x 17 7/16 in, The Vivian and Gordon Gilkey Graphic Arts Collection. Portland Art Museum, Portland, Oregon, 85.14.175.

p.87, "Some Reactions to Italy," by Robert Huck, Rome, Italy, from *The Montana Institute of the Arts Quarterly*, Vol.7 no.4, Summer 1955.

p.92, "Italian Camera Man," 1955, color woodcut on paper, image: 14 11/16 in x 22 15/16 in; sheet: 18 5/16 in x 24 3/4 in, The Vivian and Gordon Gilkey Graphic Arts Collection. Portland Art Museum, Portland, Oregon, 83.57.322.

p.93, "Sacrifice," 1955, color woodcut on paper, image: 23 in x 9 3/4 in; sheet: 24 3/4 in x 11 3/4 in, The Vivian and Gordon Gilkey Graphic Arts Collection. Portland Art Museum, Portland, Oregon, 82.80.606.

p.94-95, "Sheep and Goat Farm," 1956, woodcut on paper, image: 8 15/16 in x 22 15/16 in; sheet: 10 3/4 in x 24 1/2 in, The Vivian and Gordon Gilkey Graphic Arts Collection. Portland Art Museum, Portland, Oregon, 82.80.509.

p.94-95, "Sheep and Goat Farm," 1956, color woodcut on paper, image: 9 in x 22 7/8 in; sheet: 9 3/4 in x 24 1/8 in, The Vivian and Gordon Gilkey Graphic Arts Collection. Portland Art Museum, Portland, Oregon, 82.80.508.

p.96-97, "Fish Weigher," 1956.

p.99, "Ruins No. I," 1956, color woodcut on paper, image: 14 1/8 in x 21 9/16 in; sheet: 17 1/2 in x 22 7/8 in, The Vivian and Gordon Gilkey Graphic Arts Collection. Portland Art Museum, Portland, Oregon, 83.57.321.

p.99, "Theme on H and G," 1956, color woodcut on paper, image: 16 9/16 in x 23 in; sheet: 19 3/4 in x 24 3/4 in, The Vivian and Gordon Gilkey Graphic Arts Collection. Portland Art Museum, Portland, Oregon, 83.57.468.

p.100, "Italian Landscape," 1956, color woodcut on paper, image: 19 15/16 in x 30 5/8 in; sheet: 24 3/4 in x 34 3/4 in, The Vivian and Gordon Gilkey Graphic Arts Collection. Portland Art Museum, Portland, Oregon, 85.14.395. p.101, "Broom Vendor," 1956, woodcut on paper, image: 22 1/8 in x 28 13/16 in; sheet: 24 7/8 in x 33 1/2 in, The Vivian and Gordon Gilkey Graphic Arts Collection. Portland Art Museum, Portland, Oregon, 91.84.707.

p.103, "Forest and Eagle," 1956, oil on Masonite, 32 1/2 in x 45 3/4 in, Museum Purchase: Caroline Ladd Pratt Fund. Portland Art Museum, Portland, Oregon, 56.10.

p.104, "Gondolier" (1957) and p.104-5 "Nocturne."

p.108-109, "Mountain Fish," 1957, color woodcut on paper, image: 9 in x 23 in; sheet: 13 in x 25 in, The Vivian and Gordon Gilkey Graphic Arts Collection. Portland Art Museum, Portland, Oregon, 82.80.588.

p.111, "Melancholia," 1957, woodcut on paper, image: 22 1/8 in x 28 3/4 in; sheet: 24 5/8 in x 34 1/2 in, The Vivian and Gordon Gilkey Graphic Arts Collection. Portland Art Museum, Portland, Oregon, 85.14.384.

p.115 "Fish Shack," (1957) courtesy of Tazia Wisdom.

p.120, "Coastal Forms," Coastal Forms, (2 versions) 1958, color woodcut on paper, image: 20 1/8 in x 34 3/16 in; sheet: 23 3/8 in x 36 7/8 in, Gift of John Henry Rock. Portland Art Museum, Portland, Oregon, 88.40.4 &

86.13.112.

p.121, "Log Jam," 1958, color lithograph on paper, image: 20 1/8 in x 30 5/16 in; sheet: 24 3/4 in x 34 in, The Vivian and Gordon Gilkey Graphic Arts Collection. Portland Art Museum, Portland, Oregon, 82.80.143.

p.125, Untitled (Hunter with Pheasant), graphite on paper, image: 21 1/4 in x 17 1/4 in; sheet: 26 in x 18 1/4 in, The Vivian and Gordon Gilkey Graphic Arts Collection. Portland Art Museum, Portland, Oregon, 2016.115.164.

p.126, Untitled (hunter), ink wash, image: 30 7/8 in x 20 3/4 in; sheet: 34 7/8 in x 23 11/16 in, The Vivian and Gordon Gilkey Graphic Arts Collection. Portland Art Museum, Portland, Oregon, 2016.115.166a,b.

p.128, "Duck Hunter," 1958, woodcut on paper, image: 28 3/4 in x 22 1/8 in; sheet: 32 in x 24 3/4 in, The Vivian and Gordon Gilkey Graphic Arts Collection. Portland Art Museum, Portland, Oregon, 84.25.680.

p.129, Untitled (Seated Hunter with Ducks), 1950/1961, ink wash on paper, image/sheet: 33 1/2 in x 24 in, The Vivian and Gordon Gilkey Graphic Arts Collection. Portland Art Museum, Portland, Oregon, 1997.228.310.

p.130, "Pheasant," Robert Huck, *Oregon Signatures*, Oregon State College, Corvallis, 1959.

p.131, "Hunters," Robert Huff, *Oregon Signatures*, Oregon State College, Corvallis, 1959.

p.134, "Hiker," 1959, woodcut on paper, image: 22 in x 28 5/8 in; sheet: 24 11/16 in x 34 7/8 in, The Vivian and Gordon Gilkey Graphic Arts Collection. Portland Art Museum, Portland, Oregon, 84.25.681.

p.135, "Rivers Edge," 1959, color woodcut on paper, image: 15 1/4 in x 23 7/8 in; sheet: 19 1/8 in x 28 7/8 in, The Vivian and Gordon Gilkey Graphic Arts Collection. Portland Art Museum, Portland, Oregon, 91.84.692.

p.135, "Tideland," 1959, color woodcut on paper, image: 20 in x 35 in; sheet:

22 7/8 in x 37 in, The Vivian and Gordon Gilkey Graphic Arts Collection. Portland Art Museum, Portland, Oregon, 84.25.666.

p.136-137, "Eagle," 1959, woodcut on paper, image: 14 in x 19 15/16 in; sheet: 18 1/2 in x 22 13/16 in, The Vivian and Gordon Gilkey Graphic Arts Collection. Portland Art Museum, Portland, Oregon, 85.14.176.

p.140, "Sea Growth," 1960, color woodcut on paper, image: 15 3/8 in x 23 7/8 in; sheet: 18 7/8 in x 27 3/4 in, The Vivian and Gordon Gilkey Graphic Arts Collection. Portland Art Museum, Portland, Oregon, 82.80.605.

p.141, "Mountain Landscape," 1960, color woodcut on paper, image: 19 13/16 in x 31 1/8 in; sheet: 24 3/4 in x 32 1/4 in, The Vivian and Gordon Gilkey Graphic Arts Collection. Portland Art Museum, Portland, Oregon, 91.84.710.

p.141, "Mountain Landscape," ca. 1957, color woodcut on paper, image: 19 3/4 in x 31 1/2 in; sheet: 23 1/2 in x 35 1/8 in, Gift of Mr. and Mrs. Andy Rocchia. Portland Art Museum, Portland, Oregon, 73.9.

p.143, Untitled, 1960, paper collage, ink, and watercolor on composition board 14-l/2" x 44- 1/2" *A University Collects: Oregon Pacific Northwest Heritage*, University of Oregon, Eugene, Oregon, 1966.

p.152, "Pack Train" 1960, Luther College Fine Arts Collection, Decorah, Iowa, 2008.08.01.

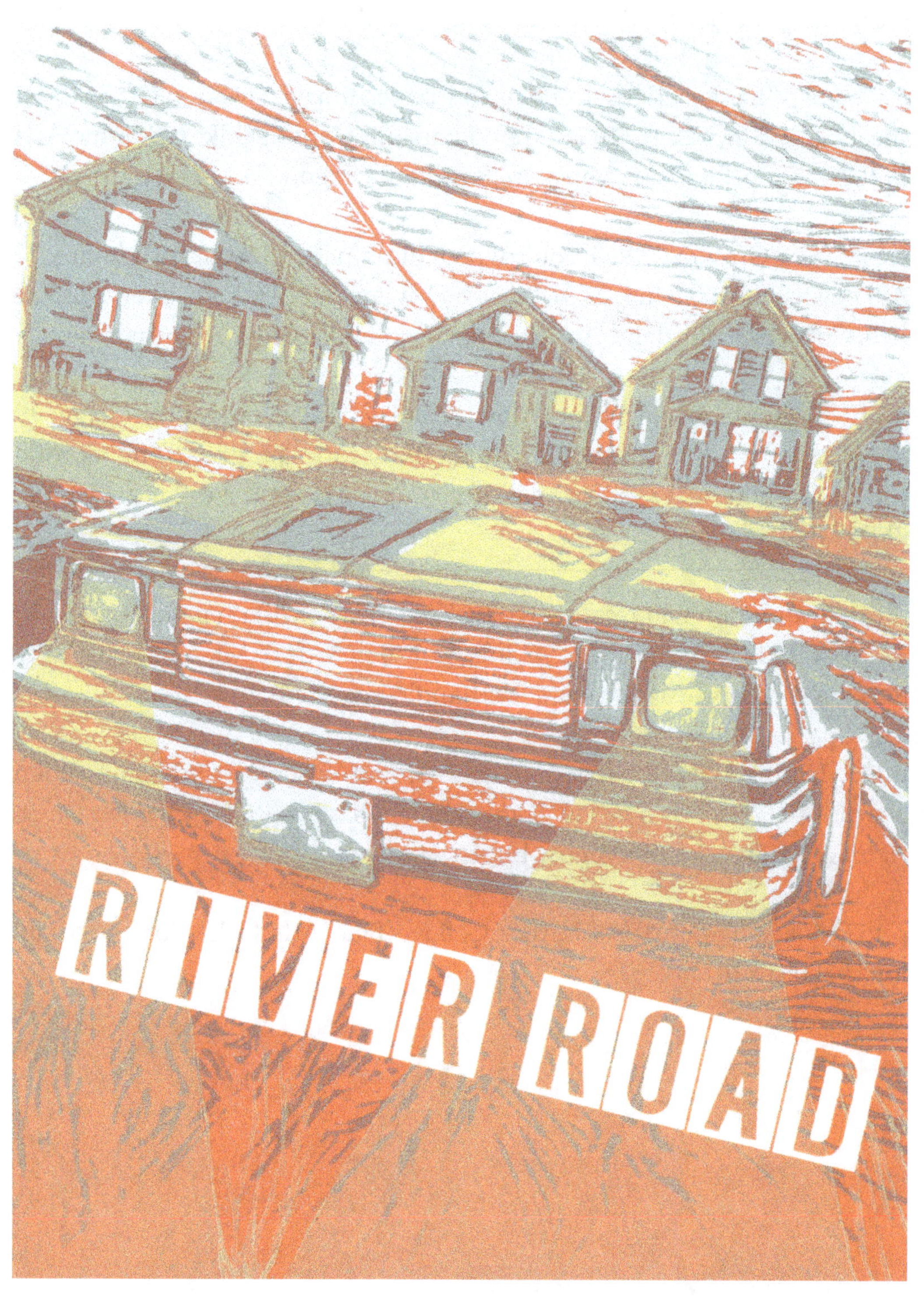

River Road novel, cover illustration by Julia McIntyre (2020).

Other Books by GOOD DEED RAIN

Saint Lemonade, Allen Frost, 2014. Two novels illustrated by the author in the manner of the old Big Little Books.

Playground, Allen Frost, 2014. Poems collected from seven years of chapbooks.

Roosevelt, Allen Frost, 2015. A Pacific Northwest novel set in July, 1942, when a boy and a girl search for a missing elephant. Illustrated throughout by Fred Sodt.

5 Novels, Allen Frost, 2015. Novels written over five years, featuring circus giants, clockwork animals, detectives and time travelers.

The Sylvan Moore Show, Allen Frost, 2015. A short story omnibus of 193 stories written over 30 years.

Town in a Cloud, Allen Frost, 2015. A three part book of poetry, written during the Bellingham rainy seasons of fall, winter, and spring.

A Flutter of Birds Passing Through Heaven: A Tribute to Robert Sund, 2016. Edited by Allen Frost and Paul Piper. The story of a legendary Ish River poet & artist.

At the Edge of America, Allen Frost, 2016. Two novels in one book blend time travel in a mythical poetic America.

Lake Erie Submarine, Allen Frost, 2016. A two week vacation in Ohio inspired these poems, illustrated by the author.

and Light, Paul Piper, 2016. Poetry written over three years. Illustrated with watercolors by Penny Piper.

The Book of Ticks, Allen Frost, 2017. A giant collection of 8 mysterious adventures featuring Phil Ticks. Illustrated throughout by Aaron Gunderson.

I Can Only Imagine, Allen Frost, 2017. Five adventures of love and heartbreak dreamed in an imaginary world. Cover & color illustrations by Annabelle Barrett.

The Orphanage of Abandoned Teenagers, Allen Frost, 2017. A fictional guide for teens and their parents. Illustrated by the author.

In the Valley of Mystic Light: An Oral History of the Skagit Valley Arts Scene, 2017. A comprehensive illustrated tribute. Edited by Claire Swedberg & Rita Hupy.

Different Planet, Allen Frost, 2017. Four science fiction adventures: reincarnation, robots, talking animals, outer space and clones. Cover & illustrations by Laura Vasyutynska.

Go with the Flow: A Tribute to Clyde Sanborn, 2018. Edited by Allen Frost. The life and art of a timeless river poet. In beautiful living color!

Homeless Sutra, Allen Frost, 2018. Four stories: Sylvan Moore, a flying monk, a water salesman, and a guardian rabbit.

The Lake Walker, Allen Frost 2018. A little novel set in black and white like one of those old European movies about death and life.

A Hundred Dreams Ago, Allen Frost, 2018. A winter book of poetry and prose. Illustrated by Aaron Gunderson.

Almost Animals, Allen Frost, 2018. A collection of linked stories, thinking about what makes us animals.

The Robotic Age, Allen Frost, 2018. A vaudeville magician and his faithful robot track down ghosts. Illustrated throughout by Aaron Gunderson.

Kennedy, Allen Frost, 2018. This sequel to *Roosevelt* is a coming-of-age fable set during two weeks in 1962 in a mythical Kennedyland. Illustrated throughout by Fred Sodt.

Fable, Allen Frost, 2018. There's something going on in this country and I can best relate it in fable: the parable of the rabbits, a bedtime story, and the diary of our trip to Ohio.

Elbows & Knees: Essays & Plays, Allen Frost, 2018. A thrilling collection of writing about some of my favorite subjects, from B-movies to Brautigan.

The Last Paper Stars, Allen Frost 2019. A trip back in time to the 20 year old mind of Frankenstein, and two other worlds of the future.

Walt Amherst is Awake, Allen Frost, 2019. The dreamlife of an office worker. Illustrated throughout by Aaron Gunderson.

When You Smile You Let in Light, Allen Frost, 2019. An atomic love story written by a 23 year old.

Pinocchio in America, Allen Frost, 2019. After 82 years buried underground, Pinocchio returns to life behind a car repair shop in America.

Taking Her Sides on Immortality, Robert Huff, 2019. The long awaited poetry collection from a local, nationally renowned master of words.

Florida, Allen Frost, 2019. Three days in Florida turned into a book of sunshine inspired stories.

Blue Anthem Wailing, Allen Frost, 2019. My first novel written in college is an apocalyptic, Old Testament race through American shadows while Amelia Earhart flies overhead.

The Welfare Office, Allen Frost, 2019. The animals go in and out of the office, leaving these stories as footprints.

Island Air, Allen Frost, 2019. A detective novel featuring haiku, a lost library book and streetsongs.

Imaginary Someone, Allen Frost, 2020. A fictional memoir featuring 45 years of inspirations and obstacles in the life of a writer.

Violet of the Silent Movies, Allen Frost, 2020. A collection of starry-eyed short story poems, illustrated by the author.

The Tin Can Telephone, Allen Frost, 2020. A childhood memory novel set in 1975 Seattle, illustrated by author like a coloring book.

Heaven Crayon, Allen Frost, 2020. How the author's first book *Ohio Trio* would look if printed as a Big Little Book. Illustrated by the author.

Old Salt, Allen Frost, 2020. Authors of a fake novel get chased by tigers. Illustrations by the author.

A Field of Cabbages, Allen Frost, 2020. The sequel to *The Robotic Age* finds our heroes in a race against time to save Sunny Jim's ghost. Illustrated by Aaron Gunderson.

River Road, Allen Frost, 2020. A paperboy delivers the news to a ghost town. Illustrated by the author.

The Puttering Marvel, Allen Frost, 2021. Eleven short stories with illustrations by the author.

Something Bright, Allen Frost, 2021. 106 short story poems walking with you from winter into spring. Illustrated by the author.

The Trillium Witch, Allen Frost, 2021. A detective novel about witches in the Pacific Northwest rain. Illustrated by the author.

Cosmonaut, Allen Frost, 2021. Yuri Gagarin stars in this novel that follows his rocket landing in an American town. Midnight jazz, folk music, mystery and sorcery. Illustrated by the author.

Thriftstore Madonna, Allen Frost, 2021. 124 summer story poems. Illustrated by the author.

Half a Giraffe, Allen Frost, 2021. A magical novel about a counterfeiter and his unusual, beloved pet. Illustrated by the author.

Lexington Brown & The Pond Projector, Allen Frost, 2022. An underwater invention takes three friends through time. Illustrated by Aaron Gunderson.

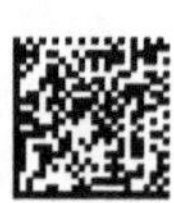
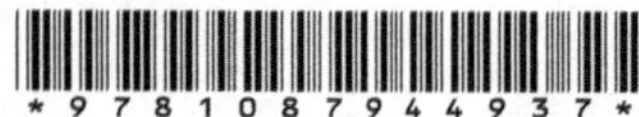

www.ingramcontent.com/pod-product-compliance
Lightning Source LLC
Chambersburg PA
CBHW080327030726
47593CB00010B/2914